Campfires of Freedom

Campfires of Freedom

THE CAMP LIFE OF BLACK SOLDIERS
DURING THE CIVIL WAR

Keith P. Wilson

THE KENT STATE UNIVERSITY PRESS   KENT & LONDON

© 2002 by The Kent State University Press, Kent, Ohio 44242
ALL RIGHTS RESERVED.
Library of Congress Catalog Card Number 00-012802

06 05 04 03 02   5 4 3 2 1

ISBN 0-87338-709-0

Manufactured in the United States of America

Library of Congress Cataloging-in-Publication Data
Wilson, Keith P., 1944–
Campfires of freedom : the camp life of black soldiers during the Civil War / Keith P. Wilson.
    p.   cm.
Includes bibliographical references and index.
    ISBN 0-87338-709-0 (hardcover : alk. paper)∞
    1. United States—History—Civil War, 1861–1865—Participation, African American.
    2. African American soldiers—History—19th century.
    3. African American soldiers—Social conditions—19th century.
    4. United States—History—Civil War, 1861–1865—Social aspects.
    5. United States. Army—Military life—History—19th century.
    I. Title: Campfires of freedom. II. Title.
E540.N3 .W72 2000
973.7'415—dc21   00-012802

British Library Cataloging-in-Publication data are available.

"From East to West, from North to South, the sky is written all over, 'Now or never.' Liberty won by white men would lose half its luster. 'Who would be free themselves must strike the blow.' 'Better even die free, than to live slaves.'"

—Frederick Douglass, March 23, 1863.

Contents

Illustrations

Preface

The Civil War liberated millions of slaves and radically changed the face of U.S. society. Black soldiers were active participants in this process of revolutionary change. Certainly Sgt. Alexander Newton, a former North Carolina slave, was acutely aware of the momentous changes that had been wrought by the triumph of Union arms. As he marched through the streets of New York in a victory parade, he proudly reflected upon the way the black soldiers' military service had helped to turn the tide of public opinion: "And we were inwardly revolving the thought that as Black men we had done our part in bringing about a change of sentiment that would make a new city out of New York and every other city in the Union. And we felt that it was but just that we should receive some of the plaudits of praise and reward. When we passed down Broadway in front of the St. Nicholas Hotel, the flags of the Nation and of the state were suddenly hoisted by a Colored man and we gave three lusty cheers for the flag and country and home."[1]

While Sergeant Newton may have exaggerated the change in racial attitudes brought by black war service, the sincerity of the "three lusty cheers for flag and country and home" could not be denied. It was a vocal affirmation of the soldiers' new status as free men. Black soldiers knew that the Union army had placed them at the vanguard of change, and for this reason the cheering was loud and long.

The Union army was an expression of the society from which it had sprung. The objectives for which it fought, and the way it fought, were determined largely by the North's expectations of war. As a formative institution, it left its mark on all recruits. The newly arrived German migrants from New York, the Ohio farmers, and the Boston Irish all had to adjust to army life. Although these soldiers never lost their ethnicity and antebellum cultural traditions, there was a sense in which military service changed their lives. The Union army was, therefore, an agent for social integration. When blacks entered in the army, they too were subjected to these powerful forces. However, because their cultural traditions were so alien to the society from which the army sprang, and because the legacy of racism was so strong, the process of integration was painfully slow. Herein lay the essential problem of race relations within the Union army. A small, zealous minority of abolitionist officers wanted to speed up the process of integration, but most officers serving in black regiments had, at best, ambivalent attitudes to black soldiers. While they welcomed their military contributions, they did not rejoice at the soldiers' calls for racial justice.[2]

If the black soldier's life was fraught with hardship and difficulty, military service did provide him with an opportunity to make the transition from slavery to freedom and lay claim to the privileges of citizenship. The time-honored goals of military service, for example, parade-ground drill, weapon training, picket and guard duty, changed the soldier's perception of his role in American society. He gained in confidence as he fought against the rebels on the battlefield and against discrimination in camp. Therefore, social reconstruction was occurring in black regiments concurrently with the social reconstruction in the Southern states. Although this intramilitary reconstruction was less violent than its social counterpart, lacked precise political direction, and was enmeshed in regimental orders and regulations rather than in statutes and legislative procedures, it was by no means less meaningful.

In order to describe the change that occurred in the soldiers' lives, I have relied upon the work of a number of social historians, especially John Blassingame, Herbert Gutman, and Charles Joyner, whose work helped me to shape the purpose of my study, and Lawrence Levine. All describe cultural change in the slave quarters as an interaction between the past and the present, tradition and environment. Their analyses place the slaves at the center. They depict slaves not as passive victims but as active agents of change. This process of creative interaction did not end with emancipation. The Freedmen and Southern Society Project reminds us that "in throwing off habitual restraints, freed men and women redesigned their lives in ways that spoke eloquently of their hidden life in bondage, revealing clandestine institutions, long cherished beliefs, and deeply held values." The project's monumental history of the transition from slavery to freedom, *Freedom: A Documentary History of Emancipation, 1861–1867*, especially Series 2: *The Black Military Experience*, has proved a rich mine of information. In common with Ira Berlin and his fellow editors, I have depicted black military service as an essentially liberating and empowering process.[3]

Camp life represents but a small fragment of the black Americans' liberating experience. Much remains to be examined before a more detailed picture can be drawn of the transition from slavery to freedom. Nevertheless, the army camp is a rich site for historical excavation; army life itself was similar enough to the plantation to encourage cultural continuity and transfer, but different enough to stimulate cultural re-creation and change.

The black soldiers had to make a number of important personal adjustments to adapt to the demanding routine of military service. In the process their cultural values were challenged. *"Campfires of Freedom"* examines this reaction and analyzes the process of cultural change by describing life in the black army camps.

The first purpose of this book, then, is to describe the soldiers' lives in their camps. This particular description is not based on analysis of any particular regiment or geographical area. It is a composite, a collage of collected memories gleaned from white officers and black soldiers alike. Encompassing the great variety of human experiences that are described is the institutional framework of the army. Army regulations, customs, and the chain of command gave order and a degree of meaning to a bewildering plethora of experiences; a stamp of commonality was left on all soldiers.

The second purpose of this book is to bring into focus the emotional texture of military life, to describe the dreams, aspirations, ambitions, and desires of the common soldier. Of course, this attempt to explore the collective memories of the black soldiers is a complex task. It is one thing to describe the pattern of human behavior but quite another to understand it and offer a comprehensive, rational explanation. However, an explanation must be attempted if the soldier's life is to be understood.

The third purpose of this book is to analyze the process of cultural change that occurred within the army camps. To limit the book to a mere description of the black soldiers' military routine is to ignore the dynamic forces that were surging in them. Army ways were not plantation ways and herein lay the inherent tension of cultural change. Conflict emerged as the soldiers grappled with their desire to exercise their freedom and confirm their identities. Liberation enhanced the former slaves' scope for cultural autonomy, but their expressions of freedom were constrained by an ideal of citizenship and a determination to be good soldiers. Military service meant obedience to orders and regulations. Such obedience was not given grudgingly, for the soldiers were proud of their blue uniforms—their badges of freedom. However, at times the demands of army life came into conflict with the soldiers' expressions of liberty. Somehow the soldiers had to find a path between a self-indulgent autonomy and a subservient conformity, a path that would enable them to develop their military prowess without sacrificing their cultural integrity.

The flag of the 6th United States Colored Troops. Columbia invites a proud, well-dressed black Union soldier, the antithesis of the cringing slave, to step forward and defend the United States and win "Freedom for All." Citizenship rights are implicit in this defense. The background reveals a scene of family unity. Happy, contented children rejoice at their father's willingness to defend hearth and home. The soldier's devoted wife sits on a bale of cotton, doubtless the product of free, self-reliant labor. MOLLUS Massachusetts Collection, USAMHI.

The cultural life of the slave was never moribund or static. Processes of renewal and enrichment continually had changed the contours of slave life on the plantation; this process of dynamic growth continued with increasing vigor when the freed slaves entered the Union army camps. The soldiers began to think and act less like slaves and more like citizens. Indeed, the process of cultural change validated citizenship status. Those who would be citizens had to demonstrate their physical courage as well as their moral fiber. Both the battlefield and the parade ground were important for the soldier; on one he could prove his manhood, on the other his social responsibility. Of course, this fact was not lost on those primarily responsible for enlisting blacks into the Union army.[4]

Whenever colors were presented to newly formed regiments, almost invariably orators publicized the national significance of military service. Speakers at these very symbolic occasions constantly expounded upon the broader, elevating, and educative aspects of military life.[5] These sentiments echoed those of the witnesses who gave testimony before the American Freedmen's Inquiry Commission. The commissioners themselves believed that "of all present agencies for elevating the character of the colored-race, for cultivating in them self respect and self reliance, military training under judicious officers, . . . is at once the most prompt and the most efficacious." Therefore, military service was "a blessing" to the Negro, one "brought cheaply at any price."[6]

Abolitionist officers were the most ardent advocates of using the army as a school for citizenship education. Strongly influenced by "noblesse oblige" attitudes, young officers like Colonels Robert Shaw and Edward Hallowell, scions of New England's wealthy families, believed they could make the Negro a model soldier, an example for working-class whites. Class attitudes, therefore, reinforced racial beliefs. Yet this commitment to using the army as a medium of cultural change was not ideologically exclusive. Indeed, there was throughout the officer corps a general and all pervasive belief in the benefits of army life. Billy Yank, black or white, had to learn appropriate patterns of behavior; he had to learn the connection among power, authority, and service.[7]

To acknowledge the influence of the military environment on the life of the black soldier is not to adopt the creed of environmental determinism. Each soldier brought with him cultural traditions. The new environment provided him opportunities and incentives to modify preexisting patterns of behavior. In the process of acquiring new identities, the soldiers had to temper old values and adopt new ones. Therefore, a critical tension emerged between traditions and environment. Confronted by new circumstances and new "masters," the raw recruit faced a dilemma. The Union army officer was not a slave owner in a different guise; on the contrary, he was an ally, a comrade in arms. Soldiers could not relate to him simply by reproducing patterns of plantation behavior. Yet empathy could not yield simple conformity; in order to defend and define their newly won rights and freedoms, the soldiers had to maintain their cultural integrity. In short, they had to learn how to accommodate change in a way that did not alienate past heritage or nullify present training. Tradition and environment had to be reconciled.

The medium for this process of reconciliation was the leadership elite. But precisely which elite was to define appropriate patterns of behavior? The white officers assumed that since they were the military leaders of their men, they were their moral guardians as well. Such assumptions were based on a vision of the plantation as a place in which the slave was reduced to depravity. Abolitionist officers felt this sense of moral obligation much more keenly than most. Indeed, it provided them with their basic rationale for service in black regiments. They believed they had the power not only to command but to educate and civilize the degraded black. Yet the work of these moral guardians and cultural commissioners did not go unchallenged. The black soldiers had their own leaders, and these leaders endeavored to shape the nature and direction of the cultural change that was occurring. It was essentially for this reason that Pvt. William Vaughn wrote to the secretary of war, Edwin Stanton, complaining that he had been forced to wait on an officers' table. Clearly, the soldiers believed the burdens of slavery would be buried on the battlefield, and they fought long and hard against any officer who sought to exhume them. A "civil war" raged in camps where the officers exploited their men. On one side in such units stood the white officer corps, cloaked in the powerful mantle of army regulation and military authority. On the other side, the black leaders. Their strength rested in their heritage and the community life that developed within the camps.[8]

In the process of becoming good soldiers, the enlisted men tenaciously held on to those cultural values that gave meaning to life. The camp leaders, principally the noncommissioned officers, were among the most important guardians of this inheritance, and they, more than any other group, acted as the cultural mediators for their comrades.

This focus on the role of the noncommissioned officers gives us a vehicle, or model, for understanding and explaining the process of cultural change in the army camps. Herein lies the distinctive contribution of this study. *"Campfires of Freedom"* examines the soldier's behavior in camp during his off-duty hours. It describes the soldier at prayer, telling stories, singing songs, reading newspapers, and rejoicing at dances and weddings. In short, it describes the cultural texture of his private life.

While writing this book I gained considerable assistance from a number of friends and teachers. For first having stimulated my interest in black American history while a student at Canterbury University, New Zealand, I am indebted to Professor Alan Conway. A number of teachers and former teachers at La Trobe University, Melbourne, Australia, rendered me invaluable assistance. Tom Dunning encouraged me to embark on a dissertation on the role of black troops in the Union army; his friendship and critical supervision gave me invaluable support when my research was in its early stages. I have a special debt of gratitude to the two supervisers of my Ph.D. dissertation, Warren Ellem and Bob Bessant. Over the many years I have been working on my research, Warren Ellem has generously shared his knowledge of the Civil War with me and offered me useful comment and advice. While engaged in my research at La Trobe, I also received considerable assistance from the university library; in her capacity as interloan librarian, Rosemary Griffiths secured a great amount of material for me from institutions throughout the United States. The librarians at Monash University Grippsland Campus have also greatly assisted me with their friendly and efficient service.

It would not have been possible to do the research for this book without visiting the United States for a lengthy period. To a large extent my visit was made possible by the former principal of Scotch College, Melbourne, Philip Roff, who arranged a teaching exchange for me with Mike Miller of Episcopal High School in Alexandria, Virginia. The headmaster of Episcopal, Archibald R. Hoxton Jr., and the assistant headmaster Robert W. L. Bross, both shared their knowledge of the Civil War with me, and staff and students showed interest in my project. A member of the Episcopal School Council, Dr. Gaylord Clark, also generously assisted me with my research.

During my period in the United States, I visited and corresponded with over sixty archives and research institutions. Although the contacts were not always rewarding in terms of the material they yielded, almost invariably the archivists and librarians were most helpful and knowledgeable. In this regard I would particularly like to thank the staff at the institutions that were the main focuses of my research activity. At the National Archives in Washington, D.C., I received much assistance from Mike Musick, Elaine

Everly, Robert Matchett, and Mike Shaughessy. The late Sarah Jackson gave me much advice and provided some insightful direction to my study of black troops. At the U.S. Military History Institute, Carlisle Barracks, Pennsylvania, Richard J. Sommers shared his knowledge of the Civil War and guided my research of the institute's archives. Finally, Robert W. McDonnell gave me considerable assistance at the Commonwealth of Massachusetts State Archives.

During my time in the United States, I was very much indebted to the late Professor Herbert Gutman, who while visiting Australia, encouraged me in my research and suggested that I contact Ira Berlin at the University of Maryland; Ira was at the time the director of the Freedmen and Southern Society Project. He encouraged me in my research and gave me many leads for researching the National Archives. The interest Ira has shown in my research on black soldiers has been most appreciated. I am also indebted to John David Smith, North Carolina State University, for commenting on my research. When I have visited the U.S., John and Karen Wires have opened their home to me. Their generosity has been much appreciated.

I would like to thank Monash University for supporting my work in African American history. The study leave I received in 1994 proved invaluable, for it was during this time I fundamentally revised the structure of my book. Thanks must also go to my colleagues in the School of Humanities, Communications, and Social Sciences, Monash Gippsland Campus, for their interest in and support of my project. Lyle Munroe has given me good advice on undertaking research, and David Schmitt has generously shared his knowledge of military history with me.

The American Civil War Round Table of Australia has been a great source of support. I would like to thank the members for their comments and advice, particularly Margaret Lee, Barry Crompton, and Neil Saul.

I would also like to thank the staff at The Kent State University Press. John Hubbell's support and advice has been invaluable. Erin Holman and Joanna Hildebrand Craig have been most helpful and understanding editors.

Finally, I would like to acknowledge the support of my son, Timothy; daughter, Lydia; and my wife, Anne. For a number of years Anne has traveled with me to the United States in search of the camps of the black soldiers. Thanks to her support I have been able to narrate a small part of their epic struggle for freedom.

Prologue

Q. Solomon, you are in uniform—do you belong to the South Carolina regiment?

A. Yes sir.

Q. Did you volunteer or were you drafted?

A. I volunteered. I heard they wanted men for the third regiment and I had to go. I was chief cook on board the Steamer "Cosmopolitan" and getting good pay, but I could not stay there. In Secesh times I used to pray the Lord for this opportunity to be released from bondage and to fight for my liberty, and I could not feel right as long as I was not in the regiment.

—Testimony of Pvt. Solomon Bradley before the American Freedmen's Inquiry Commission

Pvt. Solomon Bradley's testimony before the American Freedmen's Inquiry Commission revealed the driving force behind black enlistment. The Civil War was a war of liberation. The prologue focuses on this war by discussing four themes: the evolution of government policy of black recruitment, personal motives for enlistment, the types of camps, and esprit de corps among enlisted men. These themes are related, in that the soldiers' initial motivations to enlist sustained them in the service, and influenced their camp activities and combat performance.

Although blacks had a long tradition of military service, Northern racial prejudice had precluded them from joining state militias. The outbreak of war in 1861 encouraged free black communities in the Northern states to defy public prejudice and not only form their own militia units but offer to volunteer for service in the Union army. These efforts to contribute to military preparedness were supported by New England abolitionists and radical Free-Soilers in the Midwest.[1]

The prospect of black enlistment increased significantly in July 1862, when the Second Confiscation Act and the Militia Act gave President Abraham Lincoln the legislative mandate necessary to begin black recruitment.[2]

Manpower shortages, military setbacks in the summer and fall of 1862, and the continuing loyalty of the slave-holding border states, together with a growing personal conviction that blacks could aspire to citizenship, persuaded Lincoln to accept black enlistment as a legitimate war measure. In August 1862, the secretary of war, Edwin Stanton, authorized Brig. Gen. Rufus Saxton to raise five thousand "contraband" troops in the Department of the South, and Maj. Gen. Benjamin F. Butler, commander of the Department of the Gulf, to organize "Native Guard" regiments composed of free New Orleans blacks. Any doubt about the blacks' eligibility for military service disappeared in early 1863, when the Emancipation Proclamation clearly stated that rebels' former slaves could be used as garrison troops. Thanks largely to the efforts of Governor John A. Andrew of Massachusetts, Connecticut, Massachusetts, and Rhode Island were given permission to organize black regiments. Brig. Gen. Daniel Ullmann and Brig. Gen. Edward A. Wild were sent into Louisiana and North Carolina, respectively, to raise regiments of former slaves. In April 1863 the U.S. Army adjutant general, Brig. Gen. Lorenzo Thomas, was dispatched to the upper Mississippi Valley to conduct a contraband resettlement and recruitment campaign. This initiative signified the federal government's determination to develop a systematic, centrally coordinated black enlistment policy. In May 1863 the Bureau of Colored Troops was established. It implemented measures for the selection of a racially segregated, white-only officer corps, and it set up the administrative machinery necessary to organize black regiments on a national basis.[3]

Until mid-1863, officers were appointed to black regiments by military commanders and politicians, who developed ad hoc selection procedures to suit regional conditions. Though there was considerable variation, one overriding conviction dominated the officer-selection process: commissions were given most frequently to those who could demonstrate a strong commitment to the antislavery cause. This pattern was epitomized by the policy of one of the strongest advocates of black troops, Governor Andrew, who declared that he wanted to appoint to the 54th Massachusetts Volunteers young men with "military experience" and "firm anti-slavery principles . . . superior to the vulgar contempt of color, and having faith in the capacity of colored men for military service." However, by mid-1863 the situation had radically changed. Adjutant General Thomas's extensive recruitment campaign in the Mississippi Valley in April 1863 and the creation of the Bureau of Colored Troops in May 1863 had moved black enlistment into the mainstream of the federal government's recruitment policy. As the number of black soldiers grew, opportunities brightened for those who lacked abolitionist credentials.[4]

More and more, the black Union army camp was exposed to the mainstream social values of Northern society. The camps became national metaphors for social change as two distinct racial groups, the white officers and the black soldiers, developed a working relationship in a new age of freedom.

The officers who strode past the guards through the camp entrances came from diverse backgrounds and were drawn from every geographic region in the North. Many were motivated by the same ideals that induced white soldiers to enlist for service; convictions of honor, patriotism, duty, and manhood weighed heavily upon such men. Freeman S. Bowley, a seventeen-year-old student at the Highland Military Academy, at Worcester, Massachusetts, had been filled with "an intense desire" to "serve his country" as an officer in a black regiment when he witnessed Medal of Honor winner Color Sgt. Thomas Plunkett, 21st Massachusetts Volunteers, parade at a civic reception in February 1864. An amputee who had lost both his arms defending the regiment's colors during the battle of Fredericksburg on December 13, 1862, Plunkett epitomized manly courage, sacrifice, and love of duty as he presented his colors by "grasping" them "in such fashion as he could with his helpless stumps."[5]

Some prospective officers were motivated by clearly defined objectives, such as the commitment to the antislavery cause, but most men were not single-minded in their pursuit of commissions. For them, service in a black regiment was full of contradictions. Col. James Montgomery had fought tenaciously for the antislavery cause in Kansas and had joined the Union army to continue the fight, but Colonels Thomas Higginson and Robert Shaw, two fellow abolitionist officers who served with him in the Department of the South, found his type of warfare "uncivilized." Shaw accused him of being a "fanatic" and a "bush whacker." Henry Crydenwise had been strongly motivated by his Christian convictions when he accepted a commission in a black regiment. He believed his regiment was a "great field for Christian and philanthropic labor, a field where great good may be accomplished." Yet in the same letter, he also admitted that the "prospect of a permanent position at $120 or $130 per month" was "no small temptation."[6]

By the spring of 1863, there was a rush of soldiers seeking to gain commissions in black regiments. Most of these new applicants were motivated by ambition; they cared little about the welfare of the blacks. Moreover, their self-interest was tinged with racism. O. W. Barnard wrote to Lincoln asking for a "commission to go South and raise one regiment of blacks to put down this rebellion." He was perturbed by the fact that blacks were "running at large down there."[7]

As the war progressed and the white soldiers' worst racial fears were allayed, some soldiers gradually changed from staunch opponents to becoming empathetic supporters of black troops. On the battlefields of Fort Wagner, Port Hudson, and Milliken's Bend, the black soldiers had proved that they could fight. The fact that black troops performed a disproportionately large share of fatigue duties also made their presence welcome. As the War Department pursued its policy of black recruitment with resolute vigor, and the appearance of black soldiers became more commonplace, some white soldiers abandoned overtly racist stances and accepted black recruitment as a war measure.[8]

The camp officers were, then, a diverse group, propelled into black regiments by a mixture of motives. Overlying this rich diversity were elements of commonality. Most of the officers were young men, in their early to middle twenties. They possessed "common school" educations and had seen service in white regiments as noncommissioned officers. For these young farmers or artisans, imbued with a spirit of adventure, the camp represented a range of contradictions and challenges (see tables 1, 2). The camp surroundings looked familiar, but the inhabitants were of an alien race, Africans in blue uniforms.[9]

The blacks themselves traveled to the Union army along a variety of paths. Some were representatives of the Northern black communities. George O. De Courcy joined the 1st U.S. Colored Infantry (USCI) "to save our country and dear homes from a savage and invading foe." A few men enlisted as the fighting vanguard of the black abolitionist movement: two sons of Frederick Douglass, Charles and Lewis, served with the 54th Massachusetts Volunteers. Others were fugitives from slavery. For some of these men, military service was a rescue mission, an opportunity to liberate loved ones. When Sidney Joyner joined the 2d North Carolina Volunteers, he believed he would march South to free his wife and child from slavery in Louisiana.[10]

Poverty forced some men into camp. The soldiers' pay, bounties, and monetary rewards enticed some blacks to act as substitutes, or to fill state enlistment quotas. Col. Samuel Bowman reinvigorated the enlistment of blacks in Maryland by promising would-be recruits prompt payment of bounties.[11]

Generally the social character of the camp reflected the nature of the enlistment strategies that had been employed. In some areas, former slaves were coerced into joining the army. Gen. David Hunter, for example, compelled South Carolina Sea Island blacks to enlist in the "volunteer" regiments he

Table 1
Occupational Distribution of Officers in U.S. Colored Infantry Regiments:
Based on Analysis of the Student and Graduate Roll

OCCUPATIONAL CATEGORIES	PERCENTAGE
Farmers	26.15
Skilled Laborers and Artisans	30.39
White Collar, Commercial, Students	26.14
Professional	16.26
Miscellaneous, Unknown	1.06

Total Number Examined: 293

Source: Supervisory Committee for Recruiting Colored Troops, *Free Military School for Applicants for Command of Colored Troops* (Philadelphia: 1864), 29–43.

Table 2
Military Experience of Successful Applicants: Maj. Gen. Silas Casey's Examination Board for the Command of Colored Troops

RANK	PERCENTAGE
Officers	9.0
Noncommissioned Officers	41.5
Privates	25.3
Civilians	24.2

Total Number Examined: 1,773

Source: Supervisory Committee for Recruiting Colored Troops, *Free Military School for Applicants for Command of Colored Troops* (Philadelphia: 1864), 27.

was forming at Hilton Head. When opportunities arose, these reluctant conscripts deserted. Other commanders made successful recruiting raids into rebel territory. Col. Thomas Higginson led expeditions that penetrated the rebel interior, traveling up three rivers: the St. Mary's River in Georgia, the St. John's River in Florida, and the South Edisto River in South Carolina. In some cases, recruitment parties enlisted almost the entire adult male population of plantations they visited.[12]

Blacks played a crucial role in the recruiting process. Martin R. Delany, John Jones, and John M. Langston all scoured Northern black communities urging young men to join the Union army and strike a blow for freedom.

Many men were persuaded to enlist just by seeing black troops in their neighborhood. In the South, black noncommissioned officers such as Sgt. Robert Sutton and Sgt. Andrew J. Campbell became important recruiting agents for Colonel Higginson and Col. Thomas Morgan.[13]

Although each camp had its own unique character, a general pattern of orderliness was prescribed by army regulations. The basic camp layout was a grid. Officers' quarters were positioned at the front of company "streets," and the enlisted men's tents were arranged in parallel lines to the rear. The hospital, kitchen, stables, quartermaster's tent, and sutler's tent were each allocated specific locations, generally in front of the officers' quarters. Company kitchens were located between the officers' tents and those of the enlisted men. In most instances, camps were located near streams and rivers in order to ensure adequate water supplies. Picket lines encircled the perimeter.[14]

A great variety of tents were used in the Union army. Many soldiers lived in "wedge" tents, which resembled the letter A without the crossbar. In these canvas homes, which accommodated anything from two to four men, the soldiers kept their equipment. A glimpse inside the tent reveals the trappings of army life. Each soldier possessed a uniform, which generally consisted of a dark blue dress coat, light blue trousers, an overcoat, two blue jackets called blouses, a blue forage cap with black visor, and a pair of "gunboats," or rough, black shoes. In the soldier's haversack were the accoutrements of war: cartridge box, blanket, bayonet, scabbard, mess kit (including canteen, knife, fork, tin cup, and tin plate), and knapsack. Concealed in the knapsack were personal treasures, such as pen, razor, brush, soap, underclothing, and needle and thread, items essential to good personal hygiene. In the corner of the tent rested the soldier's gun, generally an antiquated smooth-bore musket. While racial prejudice ensured that some black regiments received inferior equipment and clothing, elite regiments recruited in the North were generally well equipped.[15]

During the winter months, the soldiers often abandoned their tents and lived in more permanent log dwellings. Frontier-style "Pen" huts were common. These huts were built of logs horizontally laid in the manner of frontier cabins. Stockade-style dwellings, with logs arranged vertically, were also common. Mud was daubed on the walls, and the roofs were of boards or thatch.[16]

Soldiers emerged from their tents or huts to begin the daily camp routine when the bugler sounded reveille at dawn. Approximately twelve "duty calls" punctuated the soldier's day. After morning roll call, breakfast, and sick call, most of the morning was devoted to fatigue duties, such as cleaning the camp, digging latrines, and cutting wood. Lunch was held at noon, and this was followed by afternoon drill. When dress parades were to be held at dusk, the soldiers were given "free time" after their drill sessions to clean uniforms and weapons for inspection. The supper call was sounded after the drummer had beaten retreat. Then followed another period of free time. Finally, the camp day concluded with the sounding of taps.[17]

Black soldiers followed this general camp routine even when they were outside combat zones. However, some camps were primarily considered sources of military laborers and fatigue workers. Here, racism ensured that the daily military routine became one of backbreaking labor. At times, the exploitation of black soldiers became so severe that regimental commanders were moved to protest officially. Lt. Col. Thomas Morgan, 14th USCI, complained that the excessive fatigue duty imposed on his men "savor[ed] too much of the old regime" of slavery "and if persisted in" would "utterly ruin the prospect of the work of making soldiers here of black men." However, the most vehement protests came from the soldiers themselves.[18]

Soldiers in all branches of the Union army jealously guarded their rights and privileges. Ultimately, the strength of their defense depended upon the ties of personal loyalty and their community spirit. During the Civil War, military communities developed within the Union army. These communities were sustained by the soldiers' commitment to their comrades and the contacts they maintained with their homes. Although the camp communities reflected some features of home, they developed in new directions. Each camp community consisted of a network of related primary groups. The soldiers' primary group consisted of those who were close to him, his messmates, his hometown friends, and his kinfolk. These close personal relationships were linked by a range of cultural and recreational activities, all of which helped to sustain social cohesion. The prayer group, the glee club, and the gambling den all promoted camaraderie. Added to these activities was the powerful influence of tradition and heritage.[19]

The esprit de corps that evolved within the U.S. Colored Troops (USCT) camps reflected some of the features of the slave communities that had developed, with varying degrees of strength, on the Southern plantations. Lawrence Levine, Herbert Gutman, and Charles Joyner refer to communities among slaves living in a somewhat limited space and geographical area, sharing a common culture and nurturing personal relationships. This sense of the term "community" can be meaningfully applied to the social fabric of Union army camps inhabited by black soldiers.[20]

Yet the comparison between plantation and camp communities cannot be exaggerated. In a number of important ways, the communities were distinctly different. The camp communities, for example, lasted only for a few years, and they were not site bound. Their development was not dependent upon being in any fixed geographic area. Moreover, the duties and regulations of military service, the attitude of the officer corps, and, above all, the rights and privileges afforded Union army soldiers ensured that the military communities developed their own character.

In the camps of white soldiers and black soldiers, a number of factors helped to sustain social cohesion and a spirit of camaraderie in the ranks. These factors included: the numerical superiority of the soldiers in comparison to officers, the spatial layout of the camps, the operation of military law, army regulations, deployment policies, and recruitment strategies. In addition to these factors, special forces were at work in USCT camps. Racial prejudice and the legacy of slavery meant that the community life of the black soldiers would take on a distinctive character.

The numerical advantage of the enlisted men allowed community life to develop relatively free from constant surveillance or excessive intrusion. At maximum strength, each regiment had 39 officers to 986 enlisted men. Historians of slavery have noted the important role black numerical superiority and plantation size played in community development. In his study of Good Hope plantation, Herbert Gutman found that "the size of the plantations is what matters." On a relatively large plantation, such as Good Hope, social space was created between the owner and his slaves, and in it a community developed. There, "slaves made choices rooted in a cumulative slave experience." A similar situation existed in USCT camps. While the officers were not "masters," they were interested in controlling their men. However, like the whites on the plantations, they were significantly outnumbered. In this situation, the social space that developed between the officers and their men was large enough for a community life to develop in the ranks.[21]

Geographical factors also helped to maintain social cohesion among the enlisted men. In the regimental camp layout, the officers' tents were located some distance from those of the enlisted men. The camp of the 55th Massachusetts Volunteers on Morris Island, South Carolina, in February 1864 was typical of those of most black regiments in the field under canvas (see map). The tents of the enlisted men were located in ten company groups, directly adjacent to the parade ground. Perpendicular to the company streets, arranged in rows, were the tents of the officers' servants and kitchen hands. Directly behind this line, in a parallel formation, were the company officers' tents, and behind them were the tents of the headquarters' officers and their

Map

CAMP LAYOUT - 55TH MASSACHUSETTS VOLUNTEERS (Morris Is. S.C. Feb. 1864)

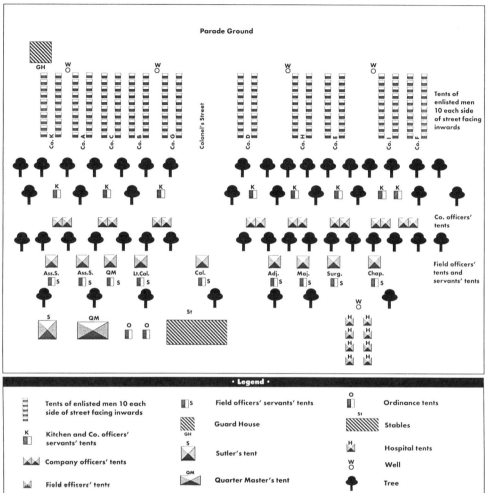

Source: Charles B. Fox, Extracts from Letters Written to Wife, Feb. 23, 1864, Vol. I, p. 174. Massachusetts Historical Society.

servants. At the rear, behind the field officers' tents (a field officer has a rank between a captain and a general) were the sutler's and quartermaster's tents as well as the hospital tents and stable.

Essentially, the camp layout formed a matrix that illustrated the relationship between race and military authority. A soldier traveling from the parade ground to the chaplain's tent would move from one racial community into

Camp of the 10th Regiment, Corps d'Afrique (82d USCI). Andrew Papers, CSMA.

another. In one world, centered upon the company street, the community's strength depended upon cultural cohesion, comradeship, and the leadership of the noncommissioned officers. In the other, authority rested on military regulation and the rule of military law. Yet the two worlds were not entirely separate. The noncommissioned officers acted as intermediaries between the enlisted men and the officers. There were transit zones, such as the officers' servants' tents and the company streets, through which both officers and soldiers could freely move. In these corridors, social communication took place, which helped to maintain regimental unity.

Moreover, it would be incorrect to think of the camp as being divided into two uniform communities. The soldier's social bonds and friendship networks were strongest with the comrades with whom he shared a tent. "Platoon spirit" was also very important. In addition, company loyalty, though less intense, was significant. Similar social patterns also existed among the officers of the 55th Massachusetts Volunteers. Company officers had more in common with each other than with the regimental headquarters officers, partly because they shared common duties. However, the social complexity of the regiment should not blur the deep and fundamental division that existed within it. The demands of military service promoted cooperation, and the work of enlightened noncommissioned officers encouraged understanding; but the Civil War did not, and could not, racially integrate U.S. Colored Troops camps.[22]

The physical separation of the living quarters was enforced for good military reasons. In the interest of discipline and authority, the army emphasized the clear distinction between officers and enlisted men. These distinctions were evident not only in uniform and duties but also in the physical separation in living quarters. They helped to preserve discipline by preventing habits of familiarity from developing between the officers and the men they commanded. Strong army traditions, therefore, helped to promote common attitudes toward army life. These traditions were reinforced by class attitudes. Socially "superior" officers had little desire to socialize with illiterate former slaves. Cultural and class differences also existed between officers and men in white regiments, but in black regiments cultural separation was compounded by racism and the legacy of slavery. On the plantation, slaves wanted their cabins far from the owner's "Big House." They knew that their independence grew as distance from the owner's mansion increased. This desire for privacy did not disappear when freed slaves joined the Union army.[23]

Military regulations protected the rights and responsibilities of black soldiers and placed significant constraints on the power of the officers. For the first time many former slaves were fully free to shape the contours of their private lives. Military service offered the black soldiers a number of roles, some of which challenged the traditional nexus between skin color and authority. Black guards sometimes exercised authority over white officers; black chaplains theoretically ministered to the spiritual needs of all members of the regiment. Service in the Union army provided white soldiers and black soldiers with opportunities to demonstrate their bravery and leadership potential. This was particularly the case in times of stress or crisis. Sgt. Maj. Christian A. Fleetwood, 4th USCI, received the Medal of Honor for saving the regiment's colors at New Market Heights on September 29, 1864. In his report on the battle he stated that when he reached the "line of our reserves" and saw "no commissioned officer being in sight," he "rallied the survivors around the flag, rounding up at first eighty-five men and three non commissioned officers."[24]

Another important factor that indirectly fostered social cohesion was the circumscribed military role imposed on black regiments. Conscious of the intensely racist attitudes that pervaded the Union army and uncertain about the fighting capabilities of the black soldiers, the War Department not only confined black troops to racially segregated regiments but initially restricted them largely to noncombat duties. They served as guards, fatigue workers (that is, laborers), and garrison troops. Moreover, most of the black regiments were located not in vital combat zones but in areas where there were sizeable black populations, for example, in the Mississippi Valley. Sometimes this meant that the soldiers were able to gain sustenance and moral support from their home communities. War Department policy, therefore, actually reduced the amount of contact black troops had with white civilians and white soldiers. This meant that the black soldiers had to make fewer adjustments than would have been necessary had there been an impinging white presence.[25]

The character of the Union army officer corps tended to protect the soldiers from unwelcome intrusion in their activities. As a body, the officers were far more socially and professionally mobile than the enlisted men. This mobility weakened the impact of their intervention in the black soldiers' affairs, because it made the leadership and authority of the officers somewhat inconsistent and unstable. That is, the composition of the USCT officer corps was always changing. Officers moved from one regiment to another to secure promotion, resigned from the service, or sought and were given lengthy periods of leave. Most USCT regiments had an 80 to 100 percent turnover in their officers during their short periods of existence. All this change reduced familiarity with the regiment. Since every regiment had its own unique character, USCT officers were continually learning new routines and continually discovering the peculiarities of the enlisted men they commanded. Of course, change also occurred within the enlisted ranks. However, there the situation was more static, because commissions were denied black soldiers. Moreover, it was much more difficult for enlisted men to secure regimental transfers, long periods of leave, or discharges from military service.[26]

Union army recruitment strategies also had the indirect result of fostering a strong esprit de corps in the ranks. In general, army recruiting was directed at the community rather than at the individual adult male. This community focus reinforced social cohesion by drawing friends and kinfolk into the same units. Black recruitment followed this general principle, and their regiments were largely recruited from particular regions. For example, the 14th USCI was recruited mainly from the Gallatin and Lebanon region in northern Tennessee, and the men of the 20th USCI were drawn mainly from black urban communities of New York and New Jersey. In contrast, the officers, as a group, lacked the degree of social cohesion present in the ranks. This was because the army organized the USCT officer corps on a national basis. The officers of any particular regiment came from diverse vocational backgrounds and a variety of Northern states. Initially, they were more socially isolated than the men they commanded. This situation seldom occurred in the camps of white soldiers, however, because there the officers often had been leaders in the soldiers' home communities.[27]

Recruitment strategies did not stamp USCT camps with social uniformity. Free Northern blacks drilled alongside Southern former slaves; literate, relatively well-educated urban blacks worked tirelessly in their fatigue duties with their illiterate comrades. Even within camps composed entirely of Southern former slaves, there was social diversity. For example, Colonel Higginson's camp contained significant numbers of freedmen from South Carolina, Georgia, and Florida. Within the camps, there was a great range of social values. In some camps, free Northern blacks felt superior to Southern ex-slaves and attempted to "civilize" them. However, they also incorporated slave spirituals into their own musical repertoire. Similarly, soldiers who had been slaves learned hymns sung in Northern black churches. A process of cultural exchange occurred.[28]

Different traditions shaped the soldiers' cultural beliefs, their attitudes toward one another, and their relationships with their officers. Free Northern blacks, for example, shared many of the cultural pursuits of the officers. The newspaper of the 54th Massachusetts Volunteers, the *Swamp Angel,* as well as the Shaw Glee Club and regimental church services reflected many social values in common with Northern white soldiers. In contrast, the stories, songs, spirituals, and religious rituals of liberated Southern black soldiers of the 33d USCI reflected the values of Southern slave communities. The ease with which the soldiers adapted to the routine of army life and obeyed their officers was, therefore, in no small measure related to their degree of exposure to Northern society.[29]

Although each camp had its own unique character and its own cultural mix, there was a sense in which all black soldiers were bound together by their love of freedom and hatred of slavery. "I do not wish to go home till every slave in the South is set free," declared William H. Watson. He had heard firsthand accounts from "old mothers down here" about their ill treatment by their masters. He looked forward to "a day coming where there will be no such thing known as lashing the colored man till the blood runs down his back in streams."[30]

In USCT camps, black soldiers used their leisure activities and cultural pursuits to consolidate their freedom and negotiate significant social changes. Through the mediums of prayer, song, music, storytelling, debating, and newspaper publication, black soldiers were able to build up a positive self-image, an image that was not dependent upon the approval of the white officers. Cultural activities also enabled the soldiers to rationalize their military experiences and place them within their wider belief systems. When the camp newspaper of the 14th Rhode Island Heavy Artillery, the *Black Warrior,* was established, the first edition pledged to "raise the status of colored troops by proving their capability of appreciating and defending the principles of Liberty either by pen or sword."[31]

The cultural life of the army camp was sustained by a strong core of assertive leaders. In white regiments, noncommissioned officers and chaplains often acted as soldiers' representatives in their dealings with the officers. Noncommissioned officers also served this important function in USCT regiments; however, because the cultural texture of USCT camps was so different, their roles were not identical. Themes of freedom and citizenship dominated the ideology of black soldiers and shaped the actions of the leadership elite.

All this is not to suggest that the social cohesion was never disrupted or that all soldiers coped equally well with the stress of military life. Intractable troublemakers, slackers, bullies, drunkards, and thieves were found in all regiments. Sometimes soldiers who had performed military duties well violated community values and succumbed to their passions in stressful situations. For instance, in early April 1865, black soldiers of the 52d USCI, flushed with the hue of victory, made illegal forays into the countryside in the vicinity of Vicksburg "to hunt some rebels" and plunder Mr. J. R. Cook's plantation house. However, although such instances of individual and collective social dislocation were numerous, they were by no means general. Most soldiers displayed considerable resilience and adapted well to the discipline of military service. Moreover, a strong esprit de corps pervaded the majority of camps.[32]

The morale of USCT camps depended upon the strength of the ideological bonds that held the soldiers together. Black soldiers were committed to the ideals that motivated all Union soldiers, such as honor, duty, democracy, and patriotism. However, their attachment to the ideals of freedom, manhood, and citizenship was different from that of white soldiers. The former chattels were devoted to these ideals because they were fighting their own wars of personal liberation. In their group activities, at mess, at the card table, and in prayer meetings, they explored the meaning of these concepts. Army life gave the blacks an opportunity to discover the limits of their freedom and to assert their claims on citizenship. Training and regulations could induce discipline and military bearing, but it required ideological commitment to sustain comradeship. This commitment to a liberation ideology enabled black soldiers to confront racism in the army and to cope with the challenges facing all soldiers, including hardship, injury and wounds, and death. Ultimately, their convictions and their group loyalty gave them the courage necessary to engage the rebels in mortal combat.

CHAPTER ONE

"There Is No Trouble about the Drill"

TRAINING AND DISCIPLINE

To learn drill, one does not want a set of college professors; one wants a squad of eager, active, pliant school-boys; and the more childlike these pupils are the better. There is no trouble about the drill; they will surpass whites in that. As to camplife, they have little to sacrifice; they are better fed, housed, and clothed than ever in their lives before, and they appear to have few inconvenient vices. They are simple, docile, and affectionate almost to the point of absurdity.

—Col. Thomas Wentworth Higginson, *Army Life*

Once a week they read terms to us and tell us that a private dares not do so and so to privates; and parts of the book that would be beneficial to us they omit, for fear we might learn too much.

—"Close Observer," *Christian Recorder,* August 27, 1864

Approximately one week after arriving at Camp Saxton, South Carolina, Col. Thomas Wentworth Higginson was ordered to assign his men to the task of unloading a "steamboat's cargo of boards." The steamboat arrived early in the evening, and the soldiers began their work in the glow of the "bright moonlight." Higginson expected trouble, for he was fearful that after a day's hard labor his men "would grumble at the night-work." Yet to his surprise, his men "went at it." Never had he beheld such a "jolly scene of labor." His men were "running most of the time, chattering all the time, snatching the boards from each other's backs as if they were some coveted treasure, getting up eager rivalries between different companies," and "pouring great choruses of ridicule on the heads of all shirkers." This enthusiasm amazed him. "The impression bequeathed by slavery," that Southern blacks were "sluggish and inefficient in labor" now seemed quite "absurd." The whole scene was so intriguing that he "gladly stayed out in the moonlight for the whole time to watch it." Later, after the task was complete, Higginson noticed one of his men "cooking a surreptitious opossum." When he reproached him for not being asleep "after such a job of work," the soldier replied, "with the broadest grin, O no, Cunnel, da's no work at all, Cunnel; dat only jess enough *for stretch me*."[1]

There was nothing really significant about the events on the night of November 30, 1862. The soldiers of the 1st South Carolina Colored Volunteers were performing a routine military duty. However, Colonel Higginson's reaction to their incessant labor pointed to the way racial beliefs could shape perceptions of military performance.

The relationship that developed in the army camps between the officers and the soldiers was largely influenced by their social backgrounds. Most soldiers had been slaves; all had felt the scourge of racism. This experience set them distinctly apart from their officers. Hence, an enormous social gap existed between even the most empathetic officers and their soldiers. In order to train their men successfully, officers had to learn how to communicate across this gap. The drill manual had to be explained in such a way that even the raw recruit would understand.[2]

Camp discipline may be considered from two broad perspectives: from "above" (the officers' viewpoint) and from "below" (the soldiers' perspective). Both Higginson and the soldiers serving under him took different meaning from shared duty.

Like other abolitionist officers, Higginson endeavored to use military discipline and training to reeducate his men. The nature of the military regime he imposed on his camp was shaped by his idea of education and his perception of the impact of slavery on the soldier's character. At the heart of his beliefs was a conviction that the institution of slavery had corrupted the character of his soldiers. When he punished miscreants he believed he was not only restricting criminal behavior but also teaching valuable lessons in social

Col. Thomas W. Higginson, 33d USCI. MOLLUS Massachusetts Collection, USAMHI.

responsibility, comradeship, patriotism, and respect for private property, the very qualities necessary not only for good soldiering but also for citizenship in American society. Abolitionist officers, who followed Higginson's example and diligently trained and disciplined their men, did so with one eye on martial objectives and the other on the social fabric of American society.[3]

Higginson, a renowned New England scholar and Unitarian minister, had become the commanding officer of the 1st South Carolina Colored Volunteers largely because of his reputation as an abolitionist and a loyal supporter of John Brown, the antislavery agitator killed leading a raid on Harpers Ferry in 1859. Although very conscious of the cruelty of slavery, he believed that "we abolitionists had underrated the suffering produced by slavery among the negroes, but had over-rated the demoralization." It was his belief that the slaves' "religious temperament" had enabled them to check "the demoralization." This religious temperament, "born of sorrow" and suffering, had made the soldiers, he thought, passive, gentle children. The officers' wives could move about the camp, teaching the "big pupils" to read and spell, without fear of "seeing or hearing improprieties not intended for them." The young ladies were sure that "they would not have moved about with anything like the same freedom in any white camp." Higginson explained the good moral conduct of his troops by pointing to their "natural good manners," their "habit of deference" acquired in slavery, their rural upbringing, and, above all, their "strongly religious temperament."[4]

The camp of the 1st South Carolina appears to have been remarkably free from vice or disorderly conduct. Only a few months after arriving in the South Carolina Sea Islands, Colonel Higginson noted in his journal that the guardhouse was almost always empty. The braggart, drunkard, and thief were seldom found in his camp. Even so, the scars of slavery were clearly visible, in the soldiers' apparently promiscuous sexual activity, their "insensibility to giving physical pain," and in their blind obedience to orders.[5] This behavior disturbed him; he believed that habits of servile obedience were a significant obstacle to military training. He made a special point of this when he testified before the American Freedmen's Inquiry Commission. Slaves obeyed "their master . . . not because he was wise and just, but because he was powerful and could enforce obedience."[6] Evidence of the damaging impact of slavery, the colonel felt, was to be found throughout the camp. The "poorest [least skilled] soldiers" were invariably the "most slavish." Years of cruel suffering had made the men insensitive to the pain suffered by others. Ingrained habits of blind obedience meant that "slavish" black soldiers could be induced to commit outrages; if he "ordered them to put to death a dozen prisoners[,] . . . they would do it without remonstrance."[7]

Colonel Higginson was determined to remove all evidence of "slavish," unsoldierly qualities from his troops. In order to achieve this goal, he believed it was vital to impress upon his men a system of sound military training. He reasoned that since "a simple and lovable people" had acquired "vices by training," it would be possible to retrain them in the values essential for military service and national citizenship. He was optimistic about achieving this goal, because he firmly believed that "two thirds of a good soldier consists in good discipline and organization." The remaining third consisted of the "race element," but he did not believe that this presented major difficulties.[8]

The central element in Higginson's system of military discipline was the inculcation of feelings of pride and self-respect. This put his form of military discipline on "a higher grade than plantation discipline." Whereas the plantation owner sought to gain obedience by instilling a sense of fear into his "cowering" slave, Higginson sought to gain compliance by developing in his soldier a feeling of manly pride.[9]

First, Higginson made strenuous efforts to show his men that military law and discipline were based on justice. At first he was fearful that his soldiers would be "so accustomed to plantation discipline that they would deem all discipline to be unjust and irregular." He countered this belief by continually pointing out to his men that he too was subject to the military discipline that governed them; Generals Rufus Saxton and David Hunter were his "masters" in the same way as he was theirs. Second, he vigilantly enforced military decorum. He did this because he wanted to reinforce in his officers and men feelings of mutual respect. The behavioral patterns he tried to develop and encourage were the opposite of those presumably evident on the plantation, for while the black soldier had rights, which had to be acknowledged and respected by his superiors, the slave had none.[10] Even the mundane events of camp life were used to promote training goals. He would "allow no man to stand with his cap off, talking to" him. "Slaves do that," he explained. Instead, soldiers were required to give "a military salute, which the officer is absolutely required to return, as the soldier is to the officer." It was self-evident to him that "the better soldiers they become the more they are spoiled for slaves."[11]

Third, Higginson believed that by proficiently performing their military duties, soldiers would learn the value of military law and discipline. In this respect, the performance of guard duty was vitally important. All soldiers, no matter what rank, were required to obey the guard. The guard could "shoot his own Captain if he interferes with his duty as a guard." Of course, such behavior had been forbidden on the plantation. There, the color of a man's skin rather than the duties he performed shaped the pattern of behavior.[12]

In his effort to retrain the former slaves, Higginson sought to make the camp of the 1st South Carolina the antithesis of the slave plantation. Within its boundaries an experiment in moral rearmament took place. By showing his men their place in the command structure, rigidly enforcing military decorum, and ensuring that all soldiers proficiently performed guard duty, Colonel Higginson sought to prepare his men for their roles as citizens.[13]

Like all well-meaning teachers, Higginson had to contend with recalcitrant pupils. He devised a system of punishment that maintained law and order within the regiment and was consistent with the philosophical framework of his reeducation program. Convinced that "officers who proceeded merely in the slave-driver method were unsuccessful with black soldiers," he employed forms of punishment that were relatively mild and humane. Mutinous language, verbal attacks on sergeants and corporals, appears to have earned offenders a maximum of two weeks' imprisonment with loss of pay. Pvt. Joseph Jennings was given only one month's hard labor and lost only a month's pay for uttering mutinous language and striking an officer in the face. Pvt. Ogaff Williams received the same penalty for disobeying orders and drawing a bayonet on an officer. These relatively light sentences contrasted sharply with the heavy punishments imposed on soldiers who violated the main tenets of Higginson's retraining program. Pvt. Robert Anderson was forced to do a month's hard labor and lost a month's pay for disobeying orders and refusing to do guard duty.[14]

Cruel and unusual punishments were not imposed on soldiers in Higginson's camp; he believed that they would simply reinforce slavish obedience to orders. Some forms of punishment that appeared humane to other regimental commanding officers and that fell well within the compass of army regulations appeared repugnant to him. When Capt. Charles T. Trowbridge imposed a sentence of fourteen days' hard labor with ball and chain and forfeiture of pay and allowances for one month on Pvt. James Dawson for being absent without leave and using insulting language, Colonel Higginson immediately set aside part of the sentence. Private Dawson was not shackled with "ball and chain," because this form of punishment was degrading, besmirched the good name of the regiment, and robbed the soldier of his dignity. Chains were used to control slaves, not Union soldiers.[15]

Desertion was the major crime that plagued the camp. Higginson thought there were two reasons for this problem. First, he considered black soldiers "very home-loving" men. Like white soldiers who lived close to their homes, they believed that it was "perfectly right that they should run home of a night." Second, desertions were attributed to the federal government's inequitable pay policy. Black soldiers were paid only ten dollars a month, compared to the thirteen dollars paid to white troops. For these reasons, deserters in the 1st South Carolina were punished lightly for a crime that statutorily carried a mandatory death sentence. Most deserters merely spent a few months in the guardhouse, with loss of pay. Higginson justified such light sentences by arguing that "these people" were so accustomed "to violent passions on the part of white men," that "the most severe penalties" were "wasted on them. Their child-like minds could not comprehend the enormity of their crimes."[16] Moreover, "very little of severity" went a "great way"; such an approach was not only "utterly new to them" but appealed to their pride as soldiers. His men felt proud to be wearing the Union uniform and ashamed when they besmirched it by foolish actions. Fortunately for Higginson, the level of desertions began to decline significantly in January 1863. However, this decline had little to do with the implementation of his disciplinary strategies; early in January a deserter was shot dead by black soldiers after having escaped from the regimental guardhouse. Describing this incident as "one of the very best things that have happened to us," Higginson noted that every day now he was "recovering the older absentees."[17]

Colonel Higginson had no doubt that his training strategy was very successful. His men appeared to be losing their "plantation ways." The "pride which military life creates" was causing "the plantation trickeries to diminish."[18] He also believed he saw significant progress in the soldiers' developing manhood. This was particularly the case whenever he compared their behavior with that of the white soldiers stationed in the Sea Islands. It was the small details, for example, the way his soldiers wore their uniforms, that were most indicative of their growth in manly stature. On one occasion, late in April 1863, he attended the wedding of one of his soldiers. At this function the appearance and demeanor of his black soldiers, compared with that of the white soldiers present, gave him feelings of satisfaction and accomplishment. At the wedding, he was not surprised to find the "white soldiers with coats unbuttoned & black with them buttoned." For Higginson, maintenance of dress standards was a "cardinal point," a "test of the condition of a regiment" and a marker, if unsatisfactory, of moral decline. He believed that "if a man begins with swearing & stealing, bad practices grow & you always find him at last with coat unbuttoned."[19]

Even in casual camp conversations, Higginson discovered evidence of the soldiers' developing confidence and self-respect. When one of his soldiers was asked if he was a member of Col. James Montgomery's regiment, the 34th U.S. Colored Infantry, he proudly replied, "No! I'se belong to *Colonel Higginson's regulars.*" This answer was a "triumph of self respect with a witness." However, it was the willingness of his soldiers to forsake hearth and home to fight for the Union that pleased him most. He had done much to improve the welfare of his soldiers' families, by settling them in temporary houses on vacant land in the vicinity of Hilton Head. Conscious of his soldiers' strong family ties, he believed that an inevitable consequence of improving family welfare was high military morale. Yet he was also aware that such a policy carried with it certain inherent dangers. By strengthening family ties he ran a risk of indirectly promoting attitudes of self-interest that could negate the ideals of manly self-sacrifice that he was trying to instill. It is not surprising, therefore, that he was overjoyed when his South Carolina men clamored for the regiment to go on an expedition to Florida. This display of martial enthusiasm revealed to him just "how much of the habit of soldiers that they have all acquired."[20]

It is difficult to measure the success of Colonel Higginson's system of military training. No doubt, his paternalistic view of the black race induced him to exaggerate his accomplishments. However, some evidence suggests that his regiment had good morale. Minor frustrations, certainly, were evident in the behavior of his men. For example, the soldiers greatly resented having to receive rebel officers under flags of truce. At least one officer felt that the colonel was too indulgent with his men and too strict with his officers. Nevertheless, although his regiment saw little combat duty, it appears to have borne the hallmarks of a well-disciplined military unit. There was a clear chain of command, with the company commanders, who were captains, exercising what Higginson called "parental" duties. The colonel, for his part, established a unified standard of discipline. The morale of his soldiers was high, partly because he cared for his men and the welfare of their families and also because he did his best to instill in them feelings of pride and self-respect. Of course, the black soldiers were, to a very large extent, masters of their own moral destinies; they were not clay in the potter's hand. They did not have to internalize the values that Colonel Higginson tried to force upon them. He probably overestimated their passivity, but this miscalculation did not prove fatal, for he implemented an approach to discipline and training that was consistent with the soldiers' aspirations for freedom.[21]

In May 1864, Higginson resigned from the army. Ill health due to wounds was given as the official reason for his departure. However, an additional reason may well have been that he felt that few challenges now confronted him. He had entered military service primarily to prove that the slave could become a soldier. As early as July 1863, he had testified before the American

Freedmen's Inquiry Commission that the cringing slave who entered the Union army could "unlearn this servility and develop manhood," so it would seem.[22] When he left the army, he believed he had instilled in his troops the steel of manhood. Yet his 1863 testimony had been seriously flawed. Clouds of paternal racism had blurred his vision and prevented him from seeing what was really happening in his camp. Higginson and his officers did not make their soldiers "men," for slavery had never robbed them of their manhood. However, they did provide an environment in which latent cultural values could be made manifest. Freed from the constraints of the slave plantation and protected by the rule of military law, the soldiers fought for their freedom on the battlefield and asserted their rights in the army. That their victories were incomplete does not mean that their struggle was inconsequential. On the contrary, the military prowess of the soldiers enabled them to make strong claims for citizenship in the still-new republic.

If the training and discipline strategies of Colonel Higginson were humane and fell within the compass of military law, most USCT camps were governed by a volatile combination of legal sanctions and illegal, punitive measures. This situation was common in many Union army camps. Officers who had learned their trade in white regiments applied their well-tried techniques of control on their black troops. In a letter to his parents, Capt. Henry Crydenwise, of the 73d USCI, listed a range of punishments that were common to all branches of the Union army. Camp offenders were commonly imprisoned with "ball and chain" on a diet of "bread and water." However, in addition to these legal punishments, other penalities, sadistic ones, were imposed. Some soldiers were forced to ride the "wooden horse" and in some extreme cases were gagged—the "mouth fastened often with a round stick."[23]

Sometimes dissension occurred in the camps over the demeaning and cruel modes of training and discipline, which angered officers who had faith in the Union army as a vehicle for the elevation of black men. These empathetic officers sought to protect the soldiers by arguing that such repression would undermine military performance and authority. Some chaplains were particularly vocal defenders of black troops. Since they were not part of the camps' command structures, they were not directly involved in implementing training methods. However, they believed they were well placed to nurture "good society" in the camps. They wanted their camps to exhibit Christian morality and the civilizing elements of civilian life. To this end they preached the gospel and did all they could to prevent the soldiers under their pastoral care from becoming brutalized by war and repressive military training regimes. Chaplain Alvah R. Jones, 10th USCI, for example, worked tirelessly to protect

"A method of punishment." *Harper's Weekly*, November 26, 1864.

his men from Col. John A. Nelson's cruel methods of punishment, even though he was subject to a campaign of harassment and ostracism.[24]

The Union army was never totally isolated from civilian influence. The training and discipline practices prevalent in the camps were an amalgam of complex military regulations and traditions and powerful social conventions. Military elements remained dominant, but civilian influence was ever present. Visiting politicians gave camp commanders "helpful guidance"; occasionally, civilians walked the company streets and indirectly impinged on military authority. Wives and loved ones were always ready to give officers advice on how to discipline and train their troops. In some cases, family and friends promoted special forms of discipline for black troops. "Did you see *Harper's Weekly* last week?" wrote Chaplain Thomas Johnson to his "Dear People." In the journal, "there was a [wood] cut, . . . representing a method of punishment said to be common in the Army of [the] James among the Darks." "Mrs. Major Green" sent her husband "a copy of this paper," and her husband duly had a wooden "horse twelve feet high" especially constructed for his recalcitrant troops.[25]

Much of the harsh discipline imposed on black troops was inflicted by officers who were themselves mercenary opportunists and had little sympathy with the antislavery cause. However, this was not always the case. Col. Charles Francis Adams Jr. was a member of a wealthy and politically prestigious Massachusetts family. His father, Charles Francis Adams, was the U.S. ambassador to Great Britain, and both his grandfather, John Quincy Adams, and his great grandfather, John Adams, had been presidents of the United States. One could hardly argue that *he* had been brutalized by poverty or blinded by ignorance. However, his concept of military discipline was influenced by his upper-class view of lower-class behavior. He believed that working-class whites, lacking in self-restraint and the benefits of high culture, were inclined to moral depravity. This view of white working-class behavior reinforced his negative image of the black as well as his perception of slavery.[26] Writing to his father in November 1864, he noted that his observations of his black troops had led him to believe that "two hundred years of slavery" of the "patriarchal type" had so degraded the blacks that they were little more than "greedy animals." This was "the true explanation" of the blacks' "wonderful supiness."[27]

Although Colonel Adams wanted to abolish slavery, because it was "diametrically opposed to the spirit of modern progress and civilization" and corrupted both slave and master, he had no hesitation in threatening to employ forms of punishment that violated the spirit, if not the letter, of army regulations. He deemed such punishments essential because, he believed, his black soldiers' "animal tendencies" were "greater than that of the whites." In this respect, the views of the young Massachusetts officer were similar to those of the former Methodist preacher Col. James Alexander, of the 1st Alabama Infantry, African Descent, who treated his soldiers so cruelly that he was dismissed from the Union army. However, here the similarity ended, for while Colonel Alexander administered his punishments arbitrarily and was indifferent to the fate of his soldiers, Colonel Adams's harsh training and discipline strategies were implemented in order to make his men good soldiers and "useful" members of American society. To this end Adams promoted the Union army as a school that would teach former slaves "every branch of industry" and inculcate in them the habits of self-reliance.[28]

Underlying the controversy over the disciplining of black troops was a much deeper, even nationally significant, debate about the basic social framework of American society. George Fredrickson has argued that the Civil War gave conservative, aristocratic elements in Northern society an opportunity to reassert themselves as leaders of American society. Whether they were successful in their efforts is debatable; however, it does appear that Fredrickson is right in claiming that many young "aristocrats" like Robert Gould Shaw became officers in black regiments not only because of their devotion to the abolition cause but also because of a sense of class pride and noblesse oblige.[29] In particular, Massachusetts black regiments gathered a galaxy of officers who were linked to families that had wealth, high office, or a national reputation in abolitionist circles. Some of these officers were interested in the black soldier as a model of social behavior.

Associated with their antislavery sympathies was an ambivalent attitude toward the structure of American society. On one hand, they hated the cruelty of Southern slavery; but, on the other hand, they despised what they believed was the excessive democracy of Northern society. A number of officers even believed this social sin was the main reason for the North's military defeats. Such men had good reasons for joining black regiments, for they saw them as social incubators that could produce a new breed of men. Their model black soldier was the antithesis of not only the plantation slave but also the white Union soldier. The performance of the ideal black soldier was measured against that of "Sambo" and "Billy Yank," and both of the latter were found wanting. He was more courageous and intelligent than Sambo and much better disciplined and more smartly dressed than Billy Yank. The model black soldier had benefited from his plantation experience. The lessons he had learned were those of strict discipline and obedience. It was these qualities, many officers believed, that were so sorely lacking in white Union regiments. Col. Samuel Quincy believed that Billy Yank needed to be socially reeducated.[30] In *A Manual of Camp and Garrison Duty*, he argued that the "previous social equality between officers and men" had been "urged as an excuse for shameful instances of want of discipline in the volunteer service." This situation violated military etiquette, which forbade "undue familiarity between different grades." Officers commanding black troops did not have to worry about this predicament. Instead, their task was to "create and foster among them a feeling of soldierly pride and self respect." They were to teach their men that "the service required of them" was "no longer cowering submission of the slave to his master, but the manly and respectful obedience of a soldier to his officer."[31]

White soldiers had to learn obedience; black soldiers had to learn manliness. However, Quincy's soldiers, though they had once been slaves, did not have to internalize these manly values; they had acquired them during their struggle against plantation owners. Quincy's effectiveness as an educator depended upon the extent to which he could nurture these basic cultural values and gain the respect of the soldiers in his camp. Yet like many other camp commanders, he was oblivious to these preconditions for success. His training and discipline strategies actually undermined his own authority, to the extent that the camp chaplain, Samuel Gardner, wrote secretly to the brigade commander, Brig. Gen. Daniel Ullmann, that he had witnessed officers inflicting "abusive practices" upon the men, "such as cursing and vilifying, in the most shameful language, striking and kicking—with a manner that indicated it was practised habitually." Such behavior was "evidently against military order and would not be practised upon white soldiers." Chaplain Gardner believed the "discipline of this service" ought to present the soldiers with "a contrast to the irresponsibilities of slave driving, instead of a too faithful reproduction of them."[32]

The training and disciplinary measures implemented in Union army camps generally, and USCT army camps in particular, were never simple expressions of military authority. They were shaped not only by the strictures of the drill book but also the racial beliefs and social conventions of the officers in command. Thomas Higginson, Charles Adams Jr., James Alexander, Samuel Quincy, and Samuel Gardner all had their peculiar visions of American society and their own unique images of the black. These attitudes influenced their perceptions of "sound training" and "efficient discipline." However, training and discipline could never be manufactured by the officer corps alone. In every camp enlisted men played a vital and creative role in the training process.

On January 15, 1865, Pvt. Henry Hoyle wrote to the editor of the *Christian Recorder* to express his hope that the "future conduct of the colored soldiers be such as shall please a most noble and generous public, and wipe out all the prejudices that have been held against our race."[33] Soldiers such as Private Hoyle believed military service gave them a unique opportunity to demonstrate their manhood and vindicate their demands for a fundamental realignment of racial attitudes. They saw their military accomplishments as signposts on the road to racial equality. Imbued with strong senses of racial pride, they boasted of their battlefield triumphs, their mastery of drill maneuvers, and their progress in weapon training. A sergeant known to us only as "H.S.H." proudly claimed that men under his command at Fort Clinch had made splendid progress "studying the new features of heavy artillery." Sgt. William Logan reported that his company was "drilling on large guns." His men had made excellent progress and had done "surprisingly well for so short a space of time." Indeed, they were now "almost the same as veterans." In their keenness to promote their accomplishments, Sergeants H.S.H. and Logan may have exaggerated the progress that was being made. Nevertheless, it does appear that black soldiers trained at least as well as their white comrades.[34]

The reaction of soldiers such as Private Hoyle to military duty was intensely personal. No two soldiers had the same response. However, the soldiers' general perception of military service was strongly influenced by a number of key factors. These included the character of the officers commanding them; the soldiers' intense hatred of slavery; and, finally, the way the soldiers, and particularly the noncommissioned officers, adjusted to the routine of camp life and the changing nature of the war.

Most soldiers openly acknowledged the debt they owed to empathetic and supportive officers. Generally, they looked for three qualities in their officers: "noble" personal attributes, a good practical grasp of military tactics, and, above all, a firm commitment to antislavery principles. Camp nurse Susie K. Taylor noted that when Colonel Higginson announced that he was leaving the regiment on account of his wounds, the men "did not want him to go, they loved him so," because he was "kind and devoted to his men, thoughtful for their comfort." These noble personal attributes had to be matched with a sound military knowledge. Sgt. Maj. Rufus Jones urged the "Washington Authorities" to select officers for black regiments who "feel interested in the welfare of the colored soldier and at the same time demand that respect that is due to an officer." Knowledge of the military regulation and drill had to be complemented by a genuine desire on the part of officers to share all the hardships and deprivations of army life. The officer had to lead by example, and those who did won the plaudits of their men. Sgt. H. D. Dudley, for example, praised Col. James Beecher as a "gentleman and a patriot," largely because "he has ever been with us in the heat of battle" and "shared our privations on the march." As well as sharing the hardships of military life, the officer had to issue his orders fairly, without fear or favor. Soldiers opposed camp commanders who enforced double standards by imposing harsh training and discipline regimes on the men while treating the officers with indulgence.[35]

Of all the qualities that the officers might possess, none was considered as important as commitment to the abolitionist cause. The best officers in black units were reportedly the most ardent abolitionists; the best camps were invariably believed to be those commanded by abolitionists. Certainly this was the view of one soldier who, writing to the editor of the *Weekly*

Anglo-African, commented very favorably on the leadership qualities shown at the battle of Guntown by Lt. Eli Babb, a fervent abolitionist who had "served under John Brown," and by Lt. Col. Arthur Tappan Revee, an "abolitionist of the [William Lloyd] Garrison school." He concluded his remarks with a rhetorical question: "With such officers, how could the regiment be otherwise than an efficient one?"

When Col. Samuel A. Duncan called his regiment together to inform them of General Ulysses S. Grant's victories, he asked for three cheers for the complete emancipation of the African race. The response was instantaneous; however, the jubilation did not end there. The soldiers appeared to welcome Colonel Duncan's antislavery declaration with even more enthusiasm than they did news of the Union victories. Some time later, Sgt. Maj. Christian Fleetwood and other noncommissioned officers assembled the regiment together to thank Colonel Duncan for his open declaration of sympathy for the black cause. The regiment's black chaplain, speaking for the men, assured Colonel Duncan that he had "the men's fullest confidence" and that they would "with willing hearts and strong hands . . . ever battle for and defend the flag of this glorious country."[36]

A mutual commitment to the abolitionist cause was the ideological cement that bound the black soldier and white officer in strong bonds of military service. This common cause helped both groups to deflect the barbs of discrimination thrown at them by officers and white soldiers who were not sympathetic to their cause.[37]

Black soldiers and the abolitionist officers shared similar objectives; both wanted to use the Union army as a vehicle for the social elevation of the black race. Differences arose primarily over the nature of the elevating process; the soldiers and officers traveled to the same destination, but they did so on different paths. If the Union army was a school for the black soldier, it was a school with many reluctant students. Nevertheless, although conflict did arise between the soldiers and their abolitionist allies, this conflict was not nearly as great as that which occurred with careerist officers who were hostile to the abolitionist cause. These officers sought to use the soldiers as stepping stones on the road to prominent military careers.

The second factor that influenced the soldiers' reaction to their military duties was their hostility to servile labor and their determination to safeguard jealously their rights as free men. The most common accusation leveled by soldiers against their officers was that they were treating them like slaves. "If there are any slaves," wrote a soldier who signed himself "H.I.W.," "the men of the 54th are as much slaves as any." Such sweeping generalizations often resulted from the imposition of inhumane forms of punishment. These disciplinary measures included pistol whipping, striking with the flat of the sword, and hanging soldiers up by their thumbs. Such cruel and arbitrary forms of punishment evoked memories of service on the plantation. Joseph Holloway, a Mississippi slave and former body servant of Confederate general James Pettigrew, complained to his "Dear Friend," Governor John A. Andrew of Massachusetts, that in his camp a "parcel of coper head orfices [Copperhead, i.e., Confederate-sympathizing officers]. . . . drive us worse than ever the secash did." He expressed the desire to be "back home with my boss than to be in any such a mess as this."[38]

Soldiers fiercely opposed attempts to make them conform to racist stereotypes. For example, they resented being used as waiters and body servants. "I don't want to be a slave for commission officers," protested William Vaughn in a letter to Secretary of War Edwin Stanton. William Vaughn penned this complaint immediately on hearing news that he had been ordered to "wait on them."[39]

The rights to own property and to receive regular pay were jealously defended by many soldiers. For example, John B. Bowie and Henry W. Butler wrote letters to their commanding officer and the U.S. adjutant general complaining that Lt. O. A. Carpenter had left the service without returning hundreds of dollars entrusted to him by the men in his company. Officers who plundered their men were despised also because they reduced the soldiers' families to poverty. The struggle to protect the integrity of the family relationship may have begun on the slave plantation, but it continued in the Union army camp. Similarly, the struggles for adequate rations, clothing, and medical treatment may be seen as continuations of this antebellum struggle for basic human rights. Circumstances had changed; now, the immediate protagonists were racist Union army officers, not plantation owners. New methods of resistance appeared. Literate ex-slaves wrote letters of complaint to newspaper editors, whereas formerly they might have forged plantation passes. However, basic elements of the conflict remained the same. Black men struggled to *acquire* human rights being denied them by white men who had power and authority over them.[40]

All the soldiers knew that service in the Union army afforded them certain legal rights that no slave could possess. Therefore, they were quick to defend these rights when they were attacked. A "Close Observer" from the 32d USCI wrote to the editor of the *Christian Recorder* on behalf of "men who had charged the very mouth of canon," asking whether "such men as these be beaten to the ground with swords in the hands of foul-hearted, craven, red-taped humbugs?" It was his considered opinion that "they deserve not the name [of] officers."[41] "Close Observer" accused officers in his camp of deliberately failing to inform the soldiers of their legal rights. The officers "once a week" read "the regular terms" to the men, informing them "that a private dares not do so and so to privates." However, the "parts of the book that would be beneficial" to the soldiers "they omit, for fear we might learn too much."[42] Accusations of hypocrisy and double standards were common. Soldiers were particularly sensitive to training regimes that made them appear inferior to white soldiers. Even alleged inconsistencies in the officers' moral standards were noted: "They curse us after telling us not to curse," complained "Close Observer."[43]

Although much discrimination imposed on soldiers was deliberate, it would be a mistake to categorize all prejudicial action in this way. Some officers, though not blindly racist, intent on subjugating the black soldiers under them, simply failed to see the practical implications inherent in the black soldiers' new status. Some were racists, but many more were far more interested in military excellence than the racial component of military service. These officers wanted their men to be well-trained, proficient soldiers, nothing more. They did not see them as model students, attending a school in citizenship education, nor did they see them as unthinking brutes fit only for menial military labor. Yet this did not mean that the majority of officers possessed static, rigid racial attitudes. Military service was a novel learning experience for officers and soldiers alike. At critical times, when under pressure, even the most professional officer reverted to behavioral patterns that were deemed more appropriate to civilian life. When this occurred, the soldiers were treated in a discriminatory manner, a manner that was consistent with antebellum stereotypes.[44]

Often racial conflict occurred when officers became frustrated by the soldiers' apparent inability to learn military duties. "Close Observer" reported that some of the officers in his camp were so disturbed by the soldiers' lack of military demeanor that they would "punch them in the sides with swords, to show how to drill."[45]

A well-drilled company was a credit to both the soldiers and officers involved. On public occasions such as dress parades and review parades, the reputations of both the soldiers and officers were subjected to critical observation. Some officers intent on making a favorable impression treated harshly soldiers who disgraced their companies by indifferent drill. Private Burke was "struck senseless" by his commanding officer for such an indiscretion. Ironically, he had been marching in the procession at Lincoln's funeral.[46]

Officers were particularly sensitive to criticism of their military competence, especially when it emanated from the ranks. One soldier in the 15th USCI noted that it was generally the most incompetent officers who resorted to physical violence to enforce their orders. Nothing incensed incompetent officers more than having their deficiencies brought to account by noncommissioned officers serving under them. When the camp headquarters clerk, Sgt. Theodore Sydel, told Capt. Charles H. Cole that his morning report book was incorrect and incomplete, he suffered considerable verbal abuse. Sgt. Henry Washington denounced the captain commanding Company D, 73d USCI, as "the nearest [meanest] man" who "did alwas punist soldiers for noting." When this "tyrant" took leave to visit a neighboring city, the company was commanded by the first sergeant. This noncommissioned officer "never had a man punish." Assertive behavior by noncommissioned officers such as Sergeants Sydel and Washington challenged traditional power structures that linked authority almost exclusively to race.[47]

The third set of factors that influenced the soldiers' attitude to military service derived from their ignorance of the military routine and the changing nature of the war. Noncommissioned officers, acting as the "natural" leaders, played a vital role in helping their men to overcome this ignorance and to adjust to the changing demands of military life.

Although many of the black soldiers' grievances were undoubtedly rooted in inequitable, discriminatory treatment by their officers, it would be incorrect to accept all protestation as valid criticism of training and disciplinary procedures. Much of it was, but much of it was the result of unrealistic expectations held by the soldiers. At enlistment, the aspirations of many were falsely raised by unscrupulous recruiters who made wild promises of high wages, bounties, and clothing allowances. Many soldiers who had firsthand experience of the brutality of slavery but little knowledge of rigors of military service expected the rights and privileges of civilians when they donned their blue uniforms. Hence, some soldiers who were particularly fearful about the reimposition of slavery protested loudly when their officers employed harsh disciplinary measures that were commonplace in white regiments. Sometimes, officers intent on humiliating the black race imposed ritualized exaggerations of military duties, such as marching with loaded knapsacks for hours. However, on many occasions officers who employed such forms of discipline were simply using *methods* they had learned in white regiments.

Some soldiers made little allowance for the organizational and administrative difficulties associated with maintaining a large army in the field.

Most Union army camps suffered from manpower shortfalls, shortages of rations, clothing, equipment, and regular pay. However, some soldiers exaggerated their suffering and attributed their discomfort solely to the racial prejudice of their officers. For example, an anonymous soldier in the 5th Massachusetts Cavalry complained that the men of his camp were being forced to dismount and serve as infantrymen. They thus allegedly became "sheep for the slaughter—to be treated as dogs." Another anonymous complainant argued that the men of his regiment were "treated more like dogs than men," in that drummers and pipers were forced to do guard duty.[48]

Soldiers who had expected to fight for their freedom on Southern battlefields often became disillusioned when they discovered that their military duties consisted primarily of fatigue work. "Wolverine" complained that such inequitable treatment reduced black soldiers to "squirming worms" and "military laborers." "Did we leave our homes with an idea of being put on that list?" he asked.[49]

"Wolverine's" criticism of the Union army was not entirely justified. True, racial prejudice did result in black regiments doing an inequitable amount of fatigue duty. However, as the nature of the war changed and siege warfare became more prevalent, the burden of fatigue duty increased for all soldiers.[50]

A few soldiers deliberately used accusations of discrimination as subterfuges for personal advancement. For example, one anonymous soldier from the 33d USCI wrote to Maj. Gen. Quincy A. Gillmore in August 1865 claiming that the officers of the regiment were robbing the men of their money, when it should be sent to the men's families. After a painstaking investigation, Lt. Col. Charles T. Trowbridge, an abolitionist who was devoted to the welfare of his men, discovered that the anonymous writer was a "real trouble maker" who had a reputation for making "groundless complaints."[51]

Regardless of whether accusations of racial discrimination were rooted in reality or not, there is no doubt they caused considerable disunity. Soldiers who became depressed and disillusioned by military service sometimes portrayed all white officers as antagonists. J. J. Holloway, of the 54th Massachusetts Volunteers, accused the officers in his camp of being "mule drivers." "H.I.W.," from the same regiment, bemoaned the inequitable rate of pay received by black soldiers and declared that the soldiers of his regiment were "as much slaves as any." Yet these criticisms fell unjustly upon a body of officers who were largely committed to the abolitionist cause. Abolitionist politicians also became the targets for racial hostility. "You will hear from us if we stay here five days after our time is up, we will not be treated like dogs," an anonymous soldier warned Governor Andrew of Massachusetts.[52]

While some soldiers reacted to racial discrimination by condemning all officers, regardless of their ideological positions, others sought to appeal to civilian abolitionists as their protectors.[53] "We suffer in every respects like we was Dogs or cattle," remarked one soldier in a letter to Governor Andrew. The soldier urged him to replace his camp commander, Col. Milton Littlefield, with a more humane officer.[54]

Camp leaders at the forefront of the struggle for equal rights constantly reassured influential politicians and abolitionist officers alike that the black soldiers did, indeed, support their campaign for equality. Embittered soldiers who accused their white "allies" of treachery and hypocritical paternalism were openly ridiculed. Lt. James Trotter accused a soldier in the 55th Massachusetts of being "either an ignoramus or scoundrel" for falsely blaming Governor Andrew for delays in pay.[55] By denouncing outbursts of indiscriminate racial hostility from the ranks, black leaders such as Sergeant Trotter were able to build bridges of confidence between the soldiers and their white allies.

Noncommissioned officers were vital links in the chain of command. Indeed, they were largely responsible for the execution of the officers' orders. The manner in which they carried out their duties could induce the men under them to accept even harsh disciplinary measures. A black chaplain, B. F. Randolph, was a constant advocate of strict discipline, including harsh physical punishment, because he believed that such action would significantly improve the moral condition of the men. Sgt. Alexander Newton favored the imposition of strict disciplinary measures by officers because he feared that without such measures gang warfare would occur within the regiment. Certainly, his experience of discipline problems on the troopship *Demolay* on the journey to Texas led him to this conclusion. Yet the black noncommissioned officers' role as mediators placed them in a very vulnerable position. On one hand, if they were seen as compliant instruments in the hands of the white officers, they would lose credibility in the sight of the men. On the other hand, if they identified too closely with the interests of the enlisted men, they would lose influence with the officers.[56]

Sometimes the soldiers' criticism of their noncommissioned officers appeared justified. "Close Observer" complained that at his camp on Morris Island, South Carolina, fatigue duty was very onerous. Indeed, "at times" he believed that he and his comrades had "exchanged places with slaves." Both the officers and the noncommissioned officers were blamed for the soldiers' plight, for while the officers relaxed in the fort, drunken noncommissioned officers kept the soldiers working. On other occasions, noncommissioned officers were accused of being in league with officers when they were, in fact, quite innocent of the charge. For example, rumors spread that officers of the 29th Connecticut Volunteers had "covenanted together" to take soldiers on board ship in order to sell them as slaves in Cuba; certain noncommissioned officers were accused of being involved in the plot and were ostracized by the men. However, Sgt. Alexander Newton had the "good fortune to escape any insults or indignities."[57] For their part, officers often put considerable pressure on their noncommissioned officers. While gravely ill, on his sickbed, Maj. Joseph J. Comstock urged his noncommissioned officers to make loyalty to the officer corps their first priority.[58]

The extent to which effective communication was maintained between the officers and enlisted men was not entirely dependent upon the resources and ability of the sergeants and corporals. Sometimes, forces over which the camp leaders had no control shaped the development of race relations in the camps. Indeed, to a large extent the noncommissioned officers found themselves reacting to situations that developed as the nature of military service changed. In some cases the change was not for the better. For one thing, the military experience of a minority of officers actually strengthened their racist preconceptions of the black race. Other officers, who had embarked on their military service as ideological enthusiasts, keen to explore new fields of racial understanding, ended their careers somewhat disillusioned. The rigors and frustrations of army life induced some of these officers to revert to traditional behavioral patterns based on white dominance and black subordination. Sgt. John Cajay noted such a deterioration in race relations in his regiment. Before his regiment left "from Rhode Island it was, 'boys,' 'men,' 'lads' etc.; now when they speak to you it is 'come here, d——d nigger,' or something worse, and they will strike you without cause or provocation whatever."[59]

Invariably, as race relations deteriorated, morale declined. The soldiers themselves became disillusioned with military service. Army life appeared to be just another form of bondage. "Rhode Island gets the credit; we do the work, and get nothing but abuse," complained Sergeant Cajay. He added that "the patriotism that was in the men when I first enlisted has disappeared." Yet although Cajay's experience was common, it was by no means universal. Often, the military service of black soldiers transformed the racial perceptions of the white officers who commanded them.[60]

In part, this reevaluation of racial attitudes occurred because racially prejudiced officers had had very low estimations of the ability of black soldiers to cope with military training. Admiration gradually replaced disdain as the soldiers' military performance progressed. One soldier welcomed this change in racial attitudes; Richard H. Black found it "truly astonishing to see the change in the white regiments, both in officers and men" while stationed on Morris Island.[61]

Although the soldiers' military performance did not totally alter the officers' racial ideology, it did confirm the latter's faith in the Union army as a vehicle for the "elevation" of the black race. Blacks made good soldiers because they loved freedom and hated slavery.

"You should see the slaves of Maryland standing in the line of battle at dress parade . . . in the dignity of freemen," wrote Col. Samuel C. Armstrong to his brother Richard. Colonel Armstrong was proud of his men; they were "improving rapidly and give entire satisfaction." On the parade ground, they presented an "imposing array." "Every hand is covered with a white glove, every head is steady to the front, every form is motionless as marble." "The sunlight" that played "upon the forest of bayonets" heralded a new dawn of liberty for the black soldiers.[62]

CHAPTER TWO

"A Matter of Principle"

DISSENT IN THE CAMP

We are not fit for anything but to do all the picket duty and drudgery work on the island; and we don't get our rations as we ought to. All the rations that are condemned by the white troops are sent to our regiment.

—"B.W."

Major Sturgis spoke to the Regt. concerning their pay, last night, and ended after hearing their reasons and decisions by telling them he thought they did right not to take it. It is a matter of principle with most of the men, the best of them certainly and I hope their families will not be allowed to suffer. They brought up the Glee Club or the portion of it not at Botany Bay, to serenade Maj. S. after his remarks.

—Lt. Col. Charles Fox

Excessive fatigue duty and unequal pay became two of the most controversial issues in the black regiments. These issues evoked a response from soldiers and officers alike; no one could adopt a neutral position. These issues also highlight very clearly the developing identity and growing stature of the black soldier and contributed significantly to the development of black leadership.

Most Union officers saw black enlistment as a necessary war measure and attempted to incorporate blacks into the military service in a way that was consistent with their antebellum racial beliefs. Such beliefs restricted the black soldiers' military role. For example, Generals Nathaniel P. Banks and Edward R. S. Canby used black troops extensively as auxiliary forces to carry out fatigue and garrison duty in the Department of the Gulf. The employment of black soldiers as fatigue workers was also consistent with the widely held belief that they were peculiarly suited to labor in the tropical regions of the South.[1]

Nowhere did the burden of fatigue duty weigh more heavily than in the Mississippi Valley and the Department of the Gulf. In part, this situation reflected the military strategy of U.S. adjutant general Brig. Gen. Lorenzo Thomas. A military pragmatist rather than an abolitionist, Thomas wanted to make the Mississippi Valley a Union stronghold by enlisting black troops to guard contraband camps, railroads, and garrison forts. This had the advantage of releasing thousands of white troops for combat. Although he did not preclude a combat role for black troops, the main thrust of his policy limited combat opportunities available to them.[2]

The unremitting labor imposed on black troops in the Mississippi Valley provoked protests from some officers serving in black regiments. In December 1864, Major Daniel Densmore wrote to his brother Benjamin, bitterly complaining that he had joined the army to fight for the Union, yet for days his regiment had been forced to do arduous fatigue duty near Vicksburg. The labor had been so intense and unremitting that he and his fellow officers appeared to be enacting the role of slaveholders. The colonel was "Ole Massa" and the other officers "'bosses', number 1, 2, 3." Squads were "gangs" and court martial sentences "lashes." Such "organization and terminology" appeared to describe accurately the officers' role as "nigger drivers." This was a role that Densmore and Col. J. Blackburn Jones clearly despised. Densmore's disillusionment grew even deeper when he and other officers in his regiment were severely reprimanded for neglecting the health of their men and failing to maintain drill standards. This criticism caused a "deep seated feeling of good natured nausea" among the officers who were compelled to operate as "overseers."[3]

In April 1863, Col. William Wood complained to Brig. Gen. Willis Gorman, commanding U.S. military forces at Helena, Arkansas, that heavy fatigue details had resulted in a high rate of desertion from his regiment. Frustrated by the persistence of discriminatory policies in the Mississippi Valley, Lt. Col. Julian Bryant took his grievances directly to his uncle, William Cullen Bryant, editor of the New York Evening Post. Colonel Bryant complained that black regiments had been most unfairly treated at Vicksburg. There, the duties his men performed actually reinforced the antebellum image of blacks as an inferior, subservient, laboring caste. While his men were kept "constantly at work," white soldiers were "lying about camp, or occupied only in soldierly duties." In response to his nephew's plea for help, William Bryant published editorials condemning the excessive amount of fatigue duty imposed on black troops.[4]

Brig. Gen. Daniel Ullmann was another officer who went outside normal military channels to protest against excessive fatigue duty. He appealed directly to Massachusetts senator Henry Wilson, chairman of the Senate Military Affairs Committee, for assistance in lightening the excessive fatigue duties imposed on black troops in the Department of the Gulf but was unable to effect a substantial improvement in their condition. Upon being appointed post commander at Morganzia in summer 1864, he did what he could to ease the burden of the fatigue duty and to check the post's soaring death rate. However, the poor health of his command and a shortage of civilian labor forced him to impose on his able-bodied men a much heavier workload than he believed any soldier should carry. Drill and weapon training were held in abeyance while his soldiers labored with the spade.[5]

Army inspection officers did not always take fatigue duty into account when assessing the military efficiency of regiments. They measured a regiment's military efficiency by examining standards of dress, performance at drill, weapon training, and camp sanitation. Defects were often attributed to the personal deficiencies of the officers and supposed inherent inadequacies of the black troops. Officers resented such criticism, for they knew that if they continued to function as "slave drivers" they could not train their troops to be effective soldiers. Realizing that their military reputations were intertwined with those of their soldiers, they protested against the excessive amount of fatigue duty allocated to their regiments.[6]

No group of officers campaigned more rigorously against the use of their soldiers as military laborers than the abolitionists. Intent on making the army a school for the elevation of the black, the abolitionist officers were keen to establish a link between free, self-reliant labor and citizenship. Lt. Col. Thomas Morgan believed that the unremitting work imposed on his regiment not only impaired health and morale but also seriously threatened to undermine the whole policy of enlisting blacks. He argued that success depended upon "a favorable decision from the great tribunal public opinion." However, this could not be done "by making laborers of these troops." What incensed him was not the fatigue duties as such, for his soldiers "cheerfully performed any labor incident to camp life." Rather, it was the inequitable distribution of fatigue duties. Such discrimination had a demoralizing influence both on his troops, who labored while white troops stood "idly by," and on his officers, who were expected to act as overseers. Morgan believed that "efficient officers" would "not for any consideration consent to become overseers for black laborers." Instead, they would rather "carry their rifles in the ranks of fighting men."[7]

Col. James Beecher joined the 1st North Carolina Colored Volunteers hoping to demonstrate the black soldier's manhood on the battlefield. However, his idealism received a severe blow when his regiment was assigned to Brig. Gen. Edward Wild's African Brigade and sent to Folly Island, South Carolina, to dig ditches. Although amazed at the physical prowess of his men, he felt that they were being discriminated against in two ways. First, he accused the department headquarters of "petting" rebel prisoners who were sent to comfortable quarters in Hilton Head, while his men had to labor incessantly. Second, he was much disturbed by the fact that his regiment had been assigned the duties of "laying out and policing the camps of white soldiers."[8] In a letter to his brigade commander, Colonel Beecher complained that this discriminatory policy was injuring the health of his men and reinforcing a stereotype that portrayed blacks as inferior laboring "slaves." This was occurring when the former slaves were "just learning to be men." To be called "'d——d Niggers' by so-called 'gentlemen' in uniform of U.S. Officers" was a "draw-back." When they were sent to do menial work for white regiments, they were thrown "back where they were before" and reduced "to the position of slaves again."[9]

Colonel Beecher's protest was forwarded with favorable endorsement through normal military channels to the commander of the Department of the South, Maj. Gen. Quincy Gillmore, who accepted the validity of the complaint and issued orders outlawing discriminatory fatigue duty. Yet General Gillmore's actions did not completely resolve conflict over the allocation of fatigue duty to black troops in the Department of the South. Approximately one year later, prominent abolitionist Col. Edward N. Hallowell, 54th Massachusetts Volunteers, complained that the ordinance department was unfairly appropriating the services of black soldiers from his regiment. In September 1863 his brother, Norwood, colonel of the 55th Massachusetts Volunteers, was officially reprimanded for withholding his regiment from fatigue duties.[10]

In response to the feeling of discontent emanating from black regiments, the adjutant general of the U.S. Army took measures to protect the welfare of black soldiers. In June 1864 he issued general orders that stated that black soldiers would "only be required to take their fair share of fatigue duty with white troops." He adopted this policy because he believed it was "necessary to prepare them for the higher duties of conflict with the enemy." By summer 1864, then, black soldiers enjoyed theoretical protection from exploitation; in practice, however, as the plight of troops in Vicksburg, Port Hudson, and Morganzia reveals, many officers disregarded the spirit and letter of army orders. No one was more aware of this continued exploitation than the soldiers themselves.[11]

Black soldiers made numerous protests against the arduous fatigue duties imposed on them. Excessive and discriminatory fatigue duty was both physically exhausting and psychologically harrowing. One anonymous soldier complained to Secretary Stanton that military service had brought him only dubious benefits. His regiment had been placed under the command of "citizens," and these civilian "slave-drivers" had set the black soldiers to work "cleaning up farms and cutting up stumps." "D.I.I." accused his officers of working the black soldiers on Morris Island "like horses or mules." They made them "haul big guns for a distance of four or five miles, through the hot sun." The soldiers were well aware that excessive fatigue duty not only ruined health but also made nonsense of their meager clothing allowance.[12]

Opposition to excessive fatigue duty from soldiers in regiments recruited from the Northern free black communities was, at times, mixed with attitudes of cultural superiority. Many of these soldiers saw themselves as enlightened liberators, freeing their ignorant Southern brethren from the degrading influence of slavery. "We of this Regt. were not enlisted under any 'contraband act,'" stated Cpl. James Gooding in a letter to President Lincoln. Drawing attention to the inequitable rate of pay, he asked, "Are we *Soldiers*, or are we LABOURERS?" He already knew the answer to this question, but he was keen to get a positive response from the commander in chief. If discrimination was to end, those in the highest positions of power had to act.[13]

The soldiers realized that without adequate preparation for battle, these "auxiliary troops" or "military laborers" were effectively prevented from being their own liberators. "We are not fit for anything but to do all the picket duty and drudgery work," wrote "B.W." to the editor of the *Christian Recorder*. The discriminatory way fatigue duty was allocated also incensed the soldiers; invariably, white troops appeared to get preferential treatment in almost all areas of military life. Protests against inequitable fatigue duty were linked to other injustices as well. "We don't get our rations as we ought to," complained "B.W." "All the rations that are condemned by the white troops are sent to our regiment." The imposition of excessive fatigue duty was, then, a most blatant expression of a whole pattern of discriminatory practices, including the allocation of clothing, weapons, shelter, and general equipment.[14]

Sometimes, the soldiers' protests resulted in official investigations of their grievances. This was particularly the case when the complaints gained the support of sympathetic officers. When "S.T.D." wrote to Maj. Gen. Silas Casey, complaining about the excessive amount of labor being performed by black soldiers at Fort Taylor, near Key West, Florida, Lt. Col. John Wilder was appointed to investigate. Wilder discovered that the complaints were substantially accurate. Soldiers had labored at "coaling steamers, unloading and loading ships, [and] moving stores" under the supervision of "employers and overseers" who had not yet "outgrown the education and brutal manner of slavery." Apparently, little action had been taken against those in charge, for, as Colonel Wilder noted, since the death of the soldiers' commander, Col. Stark Fellows, conditions had improved considerably.[15]

An examination of army inspection reports issued in the Department of the Gulf appears to validate many of the soldiers' grievances. These reports speak of troops working excessively long hours and being deprived of adequate clothing and equipment. Nevertheless, only a few inspecting officers were bold enough to attribute the black soldiers' lack of military bearing to the prejudice of the officers or to the exigency of the war situation. An inspection report by Maj. Lewis Mudgett was a notable exception. When Major Mudgett inspected Brig. Gen. Cyrus Hamlin's Third Division, stationed at New Orleans, he discovered that the black regiments were "poorly dressed." Many men in the 97th USCI had "very long hair, in several cases reaching to the shoulders." Mudgett noted "this regiment has been constantly employed on fortifications and is very deficient in drill and discipline," the latter owing to "intention rather than inefficiency of commanding officers."[16]

Perhaps the heaviest burden of fatigue duty was carried by troops stationed at Morganzia, Louisiana. In July 1864, Lt. George C. Hagerthy noted in his inspection report that General Lorenzo Thomas's General Orders no. 21 outlawing discriminatory fatigue duty was not enforced. "Several Regiments of white Infantry" had "not been required to work a day since receipt of this order, while colored troops had been required to work 8 hours a day hardly allowing them time to police their ground or prepare for Inspection." Three months later, the situation had not improved. Maj. George Baldey noted in his inspection report that the black soldiers were demoralized because time which should have been devoted to "drill and instruction" was "entirely taken up in performing not a share but the whole fatigue duty of white troops."[17]

As the number of black soldiers entering the Union army increased, and as the war dragged on and became in some theaters more and more like a

siege operation, military strategy muted many of the personal and ideological objections to using black troops as laborers. Even abolitionists such
as General Wild were prepared to be flexible in their use of black troops. In
October 1864 he wrote to Col. William Birney, son of antislavery politician
James G. Birney, to inform him that he was returning one of Birney's companies that had been attached to his brigade. In his letter he apologized for
the fact that in the performance of drill and discipline they returned as
"one organized gang of laborers rather than a company of soldiers."[18]

The black soldiers themselves were prepared to accept a certain amount
of fatigue work as part of their normal military duty. Some, such as Henry
Harmon, recognized that trench digging played a vital role in siege operations. Indeed, he wrote to the editor of the *Christian Recorder* that black
soldiers fighting with spades and shovels had been at the forefront of the
attack on Forts Gregg, Wagner, and Johnson in South Carolina. There, in
the trenches, soldiers had "distinguished themselves for bravery and cool-
ness which required more nerve than the exciting bayonet charge."[19]

While most black troops willingly performed fatigue duty under military necessity, few accepted an arbitrary allocation of duties that reinforced
servile work patterns. In spite of intense opposition, patterns of discrimination persisted, albeit in a modified form, in many army camps. Traditional stereotypes were not easily changed, and when change did come, it
came grudgingly and slowly. Johnny Reb remained the enemy, but for many
black soldiers the field of conflict was the trench and the weapon of war,
the humble spade.

In addition to protesting against excessive fatigue duty, soldiers vehemently
opposed their inequitable rate of pay. At first the War Department paid
black soldiers the standard soldiers' pay of $13 a month, plus a $3.50 clothing allowance. Rates of pay for black noncommissioned officers were even
higher. These pay scales operated until June 1863, when Solicitor William
Whiting reviewed the Militia Act of July 17, 1862, that approved black enlistment and argued that the War Department should conform to the provisions of the act and pay black soldiers at the same rate as black government laborers. The War Department adopted this opinion and announced
on June 4, 1863, that the black soldiers' wage would be reduced to $10 a
month, from which $3 would be deducted as a clothing allowance. This
unexpected reduction in pay created waves of protest in USCT camps.[20]

Many officers commanding black troops protested against the inequitable rates of pay. Their opposition was motivated by three considerations.

Some had genuine sympathy for the plight of the black troops. Broken government contracts compounded the suffering of the soldiers and their families. Second, they were also worried about the impact the discriminatory pay rate was having on training, discipline, and morale. Finally, a minority of officers, sympathetic to the abolitionist cause, actively opposed inequitable pay because it undermined their attempts to use the army as a school to elevate the black man.

Officers commanding black troops were acutely aware of the discipline problems caused by the government's inequitable pay policy. The paymaster's visit could provoke ill feeling and discontent, even in camps commanded by empathetic abolitionists. Indeed, Col. Thomas Higginson observed that when his men had their pay reduced, the desertion rate increased dramatically. The men argued that "they had not been treated fairly nor paid what was promised." On the same day his regiment received its first pay, Maj. John Chadwick wrote to his superior officers complaining about the soldiers' meager pay. He hoped the situation would be "speedily rectified" before the "seeds of discord and discontent" could take root. Significant discipline problems did occur in the camp of the 14th Rhode Island Colored Heavy Artillery when Lt. Col. Nelson Viall and Maj. Joseph Comstock attempted to eliminate dissent by imprisoning a number of "ring leaders." On one occasion, during a melee over the pay issue, 2d Lt. Joseph Potter "was obliged to shoot one of the men." Major Comstock, camp commander at the time, noted cryptically in his report on the incident that "the men needed a lesson and received one."[21]

Officers who were intent on raising their regiments to a high point of military efficiency recognized that the inequitable pay rate was particularly galling to the noncommissioned officers. These soldiers did not receive any pay increments to recognize their leadership responsibilities. Col. William Pile believed that this ceiling on wages created administrative chaos in the camps, because it took away incentives to accept leadership responsibilities. Promotion brought no reward.[22]

Abolitionist officers saw the pay dispute as impinging on racial equality as well as military performance. Their commitment to the Union army as a vehicle for the elevation and liberation of the black race induced them to intervene in the pay controversy in a way that other officers were either unwilling or unable to do.

The inequitable pay scale actually reinforced the very attitudes the abolitionists were seeking to destroy. When the humblest white private received more pay than a battle-hardened black sergeant, it would be exceedingly difficult to develop in the black troops a sense of racial pride, self-reliance, and individual initiative. Trust was a vital element in military performance; officers and soldiers had to have confidence in each other, but the pay issue undermined this trust. Even officers with strong empathy for their troops and impeccable abolitionist credentials discovered that the pay inequity lowered morale in their camps. So much suspicion existed in Colonel Higginson's camp that he had great difficulty persuading his men to deposit their savings with the adjutant.[23]

Col. James Beecher argued that the discriminatory pay rate sapped the confidence of his troops because "it becomes a constant reminder to the men that they are held to be inferior." They are "ground between the upper and nether millstones," commented Capt. Joseph Scroggs, as he contemplated resigning over the wage issue. The blatant injustice of the War Department's pay policy appeared to "validate" rebel mistreatment of black soldiers. After all, argued Captain Scroggs, how could the rebel authorities be expected to extend to black soldiers the privileges of prisoners of war when the Union government failed to recognize them as soldiers and pay them accordingly. Lt. Oliver Norton felt somewhat embarrassed when he received two months' pay totaling $213.49, while the paymaster gave only "seven a month for the heroes of Olustee."[24]

Some abolitionist officers encouraged their troops to reject their pay. When Governor Andrew offered to make up the pay differential between black and white soldiers, the men of the 54th Massachusetts Volunteers refused. Col. Edward Hallowell explained, "They were enlisted because men were called for," he asserted, "and because the government signified its willingness to accept them as such not because of the money offered." Money per se was not the issue, but the principle of racial equality. Indeed, Colonel Hallowell claimed that his soldiers would rather fight without pay than, by accepting a lower rate of pay, "acknowledge that because they have African blood in their veins they are less men, than those who have Saxon."[25]

Influential politicians and public figures took up the cause of the black soldiers. Thomas Webster, the chairman of the Philadelphia Supervisory Committee for Enlistment of Black Troops, lobbied the secretary of war for a reversal of the pay policy. However, no abolitionist was more constant and vehement in his criticism of the War Department pay policy than Governor Andrew. In a letter to a political ally, Senator Charles Sumner of Massachusetts, he argued that the policy was stultifying the beneficial impact military service was having on the black soldier. "The government means to disgrace and degrade him," he asserted, "so that he may always be in his own eyes, and the eyes of all men 'only a nigger.'" If the campaign for wage justice was lost, the struggle for black citizenship would fail.[26]

The imposition of inequitable rates of pay provoked considerable opposition among the soldiers. Dissent was greatest in regiments that had been previously paid at the same rate given to white soldiers. A central consideration in the minds of these men was the plight of their loved ones at home. Recently emancipated slaves were in a particularly vulnerable position, for their financial base was narrower than that of the free Northern black. A constant stream of letters from home reminded the soldiers of the effects of government injustice. "We have the same feelings for our wives and children at home and we study the welfare of them as much as do the white soldiers," wrote Sgt. John Morgan to President Lincoln.[27]

For soldiers who had experienced combat, the inequitable rate of pay was particularly repugnant. "They cannot say that they are not good fighting soldiers in the field," proclaimed one anonymous soldier in the 54th Massachusetts. Pay discrimination was based on "color and quality and citizenship of the United States." It was for this reason that "they want us to take ten dollars per month, and three deducted for clothing." Black veterans were further humiliated by the high wages paid to black civilians working for the camp quartermasters.[28]

The soldiers themselves recognized that the pay controversy would undermine discipline in their camps. "We have the promise of seven dollars per month," commented John Tunion, but this rate of pay would "cause insubordination among them." Mutinies occurred in the camps of the 3d South Carolina Volunteers and the 14th Rhode Island Heavy Artillery. In February 1864, Sgt. William Walker, 21st USCI, was executed for persuading his men to stack their arms in protest at the low rate of pay, and in March 1864, twenty-four Rhode Island soldiers were sentenced to hard labor at Fort Jefferson, Florida, for refusing to accept their pay. However, in most camps, instead of mutinies, climates of frustration and anger prevailed.[29]

Given the soldiers' intense hostility to the government's pay policy, it is not surprising to find that they mounted aggressive campaigns to defend their demand for equality. Their enthusiasm owed little to the white officers' leadership, but much to the dynamic leaders who rose from their ranks.

Free blacks from the Northern states defended their stand against the inequitable rate of pay in a number of ways. One of the common forms of dissent was the writing of protest letters. Sometimes these letters went through normal military channels. For example, Sgt. Stephen Swails, a hero of the battle of Olustee, wrote to the War Department, requesting a discharge on

Lt. Stephen A. Swails, 54th Massachusetts Infantry. Swails was appointed first lieutenant in the 54th Massachusetts Infantry in April 1865. MOLLUS Massachusetts Collection, USAMHI.

the grounds that the federal government had by its pay policy broken its contract with him. In order to give more weight to their grievances, soldiers occasionally organized petitions and sent them to influential politicians. In July 1864, seventy-four soldiers from the 55th Massachusetts petitioned Lincoln for redress of their pay grievances.[30]

In a few cases, soldiers actually had the ear of renowned abolitionists. Lt. James M. Trotter wrote to Francis Jackson Garrison, son of William Lloyd

Lt. James M. Trotter, 55th Massachusetts Infantry. Wilson, *The Black Phalanx.*

Garrison, and to Edward W. Kinsley, a prominent Boston merchant who was instrumental in the formation of Massachusetts black regiments. Other soldiers, lacking prestigious friends, wrote numerous protest letters to editors of black newspapers. [31]

Of course, the most obvious and immediate form of protest available to the soldiers was not letter writing but taking their grievances directly to their

Edward W. Kinsley. Andrew Papers, Massachusetts State Archives.

commanding officers. In some cases the men formed committees to press their case. In May 1864 a "Regimental Committee" was formed in the 55th Massachusetts Volunteers to lobby for pay justice. Pvt. Charles Parks put the committee's grievances in writing and placed them before Col. Alfred S. Hartwell. However, in most camps resistance to the inequitable pay rate was rather transitory. It coalesced at critical periods, for example, on payday and diminished after the critical period had passed. Certainly, this was the case in the 32d USCI, where loose factions formed on payday in July and August 1864 to persuade men not to accept the inequitable pay.[32]

Legally, soldiers who refused to accept their pay could be prosecuted for inciting mutiny. Nevertheless, in a few regiments abolitionist officers tolerated this form of protest. This was the case in the 54th and 55th Massachusetts and in the 1st South Carolina Colored Volunteers.[33] In some camps opposition to the inequitable pay was personal as individual soldiers were moved to act on their anger. In contrast, in other camps well-organized resistance campaigns developed. This was particularly the case where substantial numbers of troops refused to accept inferior wages. In these camps, it was the influential noncommissioned officers who organized the resistance. This task required them to develop legitimate and effective protest movements that steered between mutiny and factionalism within the ranks.

Noncommissioned officers employed a variety of strategies against inequitable pay. Foremost was the maintenance of peer-group unity. A "Close Observer" from the 32d USCI proudly proclaimed in August 1864 that "there were but few to pay [i.e., to be paid] the pay rolls and those who did a great many of us tried to influence to the contrary." Such was the strength of peer-group pressure in this camp that soldiers who wanted to accept their pay "sneaked up at night and signed the pay roll." Some pay recipients endeavored to counter social ostracism by appealing to their officers for special protection.[34] Generally, group unity was maintained by holding "resistance strategy meetings." When the men of the 1st District of Columbia Colored Volunteers received news of the inequitable rate of pay they were "very angry about it." At a meeting called to plan a campaign of resistance the fifty-two noncommissioned officers who attended pledged to do all in their power to gain pay justice. [35]

The strategies employed to fight for equal pay were consistent with the cultural background and educational standing of the soldiers. In some regiments of largely free Northern black soldiers, the literacy levels were relatively high. There leaders adapted strategies employed in antebellum campaigns against Northern racial prejudice. They corresponded with old "allies," prominent abolitionists and newspaper editors, in order to seek redress of their grievances. In the ex-slave regiments, in contrast, noncommissioned officers wanted the techniques of resistance developed on the plantation and used them to maintain peer-group loyalty. Although Colonel Higginson and his officers implored their South Carolina soldiers to accept the lower rate of pay, only about one-third did so. The men felt that it was an insult to their manhood. Indeed, one soldier informed Colonel Higginson, "We's willing to serve for not'in, but the Guvment ought not for insult we too, by offering seven dollar." Group loyalty was maintained in Higginson's regiment by putting grievances into song. The ex-slave soldiers also called upon God to give them justice.[36]

The noncommissioned officers who led the opposition took deliberate steps to prevent their protests from degenerating into mutiny or internal factional fights. First, they endeavored to confine their protests to patterns of behavior that the officers found acceptable. This was particularly the case where the officers had clearly demonstrated empathy with the soldiers. In some camps this meant that the leaders actually encouraged dissident soldiers to accept the discriminatory rate of pay. For example, Sgt. Alexander Newton, an influential leader of the 29th Connecticut Volunteers, was disgusted with "this failure on the part of the Government to give us a decent compensate for our work as soldiers." However, when the officers advised the men to accept their pay, Newton admitted, "We decided to follow their advice. We quietened our passions and went to work like good soldiers." Second, the noncommissioned officers reduced the level of dissent in their camps by emphasizing the supreme patriotism of the black soldier. They urged their soldiers to demonstrate their manhood on the parade ground and battlefield. By doing so, they could prove to their officers and the War Department that they were struggling for the principle of justice and equality, not monetary reward. Lt. Col. Charles Fox reported to his wife that the 54th Massachusetts Volunteers went into the battle of Olustee with the battle cry "seven dollars a month" on their lips.[37]

Finally, the maintenance of effective channels of communication between officers and soldiers was a crucial factor in preventing the protest movement from degenerating into open rebellion. Few black regiments were more incensed by the low pay than those from Massachusetts, but the noncommissioned officers who led the protests carefully maintained close communication with their officers. More important still, they made strenuous efforts to convince the men that the officers were their allies.[38]

The same degree of unity did not exist throughout the colored troops. Paradoxically, the pay issue became a source of both racial unity and disunity. Soldiers could agree on the common goal of equal pay but not on the strategies to be employed to achieve this goal. The resistance strategies employed in some regiments, particularly the Massachusetts regiments, actually exacerbated cultural differences among the soldiers. Southern ex-slave soldiers accused Northern comrades of tarnishing the black soldiers' military reputation by aggressively opposing the government's pay policy. Intransigent Northern soldiers were accused of lowering morale, inciting to mutiny, and cultivating attitudes of moral superiority. Northern dissenters vehemently denied these accusations. "You talkin slurs. You bring slurs upon yourselves when you talk about others the way you do," commented Sgt. Ferdinand H. Hughes, 25th USCI, when he accused two sergeants of the 78th USCI of using the *Christian Recorder* to attack the stand taken by Northern regiments against the inequitable rate of pay. "If you southern regiments think that we are fighting for money, you are mistaken. We are not," he boldly asserted. Some soldiers answered their accusers by arguing that they had a moral duty to take action that would publicize the government's injustice. Like their abolitionist officer allies, many Northern black leaders saw service in the Union army as an excellent vehicle for the social advancement of the race. Protestations of "ignorant" Southern former slaves could safely be ignored. In addition, the soldiers claimed that they were simply trying to make the government fulfill enlistment promises of equal pay. Mercenary motives were vehemently disclaimed. It was not really a question of money but of liberty, family security, and commitment to racial equality.[39]

Yet the conflict over resistance strategies cannot be seen exclusively in terms *of cultural* differences. These variables were important, but sometimes other factors were more significant. For example, soldiers who shared common resistance strategies forged bonds of unity that transcended their cultural backgrounds. Hence, literate Northern free black soldiers wrote to the editor of the *Christian Recorder* not only praising South Carolina troops for refusing to accept the inequitable pay but also defending their moral stand against censure from other Southern black soldiers.[40]

The pay controversy also divided Northern regiments. Some Northern soldiers accused the leaders within the ranks of the Massachusetts regiments of being a disruptive force and flaunting the banner of elitism. Such accusations brought a spirited defense. Mr. Corporal of the 54th Massachusetts Volunteers accused "G. C. D. Sergt in Co. F, 1st U. S. C. infantry" of "eulogizing the regiment" he was a member of, while at the same time pleading with "those who are misused to keep silent." "This idea of keeping silent is out of reason," asserted Mr. Corporal. "By keeping silent everyone would suppose that all was right, and that every colored soldier was satisfied." Yet accusations of Massachusetts elitism were not without some substance, for some Massachusetts soldiers did adopt a position of moral superiority. They believed they were guardians of black abolitionism and they acted accordingly.[41]

In the early stages of the protest against the government's pay policy, the officers of Massachusetts regiments managed to control the level of dissent within their regiments. Their success owed much to the influence of non-commissioned officers such as Sgt. Frederic Johnson, 54th Massachusetts Volunteers. In August 1863 he wrote to Governor Andrew to inform him that he and other noncommissioned officers were making strenuous efforts to prevent a mutiny. Although the men felt "duped," he thanked "God there are some of us who know better." Because "a few of us" had used "our influence with the men," they were "now working as though nothing had happened." In October 1863, Colonel Hallowell of the 54th Massachusetts assured Governor Andrew that the sanitary condition of the regiment was "very good" and that the men were in "good spirits, notwithstanding they are worked hard both night and day." The only cause of complaint was that they were "still unpaid." By December 1863, however, a critical situation developed. Early in the month, Maj. James Sturgis, the Massachusetts paymaster, had visited the camps and spoken to the men regarding their pay. He brought with him the good news that the state was prepared to subsidize their pay to match the amount given to white soldiers. This generous offer from Governor Andrew placed the leaders of the protest campaign in a serious predicament. On one hand, if they urged their men to accept the governor's offer, they ran the risk of breaking group unity and exposing themselves to accusations of being more interested in monetary rewards than moral principles. On the other hand, if they refused the offer, they ran the risk of alienating Massachusetts officers and politicians who supported their demands for equitable pay. Thanks largely to the diplomatic skill displayed by the black leaders, a breakdown in communication between the officers and the men was averted. Lieutenant Colonel Fox reported that in his regiment "several noncommissioned officers and privates expressed their views and those of their comrades, in a quiet and proper manner, the remarks of Sergeant Major Trotter being especially good." These noncommissioned officers acknowledged their "gratitude to Gov. Andrew, and to Massachusetts," but they declined to accept the subsidy, arguing instead that "they would wait justice from the proper source." The soldiers of the 54th Massachusetts Volunteers adopted a stand similar to that of their brothers in the 55th. Major Sturgis and the officers from both regiments were so moved by the soldiers' arguments that they reversed their position and urged the men to reject the subsidy. This reversal had the effect of cementing strong bonds of loyalty between the officers and the men. Much praise and gratitude was heaped on Major Sturgis. The soldiers even "brought up the Glee Club or the portion of it not at Botany Bay, to serenade Maj. S. after his remarks."[42]

Col. Alfred S. Hartwell, 55th Massachusetts Infantry. USAMHI.

By spring 1864, however, tension in the Massachusetts camps had increased. Discipline problems arising from the government's pay policy were alarming. Cries such as "money or blood" and "muster us out or pay us" continually arose from the ranks. As the incidents of insubordination increased, the officers took strict disciplinary action to counter the activities of a "few malcontents." By April it appeared evident that the policy of

GENERAL ORDERS, }
    No. 120.   }

The following circular is hereby re-published for the information of all concerned :

CIRCULAR. }   WAR DEPARTMENT,
              ADJUTANT GENERAL'S OFFICE,
No. 60.   }   *Washington, August* 1, 1864.

In pursuance of Section 4, of the Act of Congress making appropriations for the support of the Army for the year ending thirtieth of June, eighteen hundred and sixty-five, and for other purposes, approved July 4th, 1864, all officers commanding regiments, batteries and independent companies of colored troops, will immediately make a thorough investigation and individual examination of the men belonging to their commands, who were enlisted prior to January 1st, 1864, with a view to ascertaining who of them were free men on or before April 19th, 1861. The fact of freedom to be determined in each case on the statement of the soldier, under oath, taken in connection with the most reliable information that can be obtained from other sources. And when, in view of all the facts in each case, commanding officers are of the opinion that any enlisted men of their commands were free on the date aforesaid, they will, upon the next muster rolls, enter the following remark opposite the names of such soldiers, viz : " Free, on or before April 19th, 1861 ;" and such soldiers shall be mustered for pay accordingly. Such muster shall be authority for the Pay Department to pay said soldiers, from the time of their entry into service to the 1st day of January, 1864, the difference between the pay received by them as soldiers under their present enlistments, and the full pay allowed by law at the same period to white soldiers.

By order of the Secretary of War :

E. D. TOWNSEND,
Assistant Adjutant General.

BY COMMAND OF MAJOR-GENERAL J. G. FOSTER,

W. L. M. BURGER,
Assistant Adjutant General.

OFFICIAL :

inflicting reprisals on selected troublemakers was not working. Under this extreme pressure, Colonels Hallowell and Hartwell did their best to placate their men with reassurances about the rapid passage through Congress of equal-pay legislation. Unfortunately, sometimes these assurances were based on rumors, inaccurate newspaper reports, and false assessments of the government legislative process. As a result, the expectations of the soldiers were falsely raised. When the inaccuracy of these reports became apparent, the channels of communication between the officers and the protest campaign leaders became clogged with recrimination and suspicion. Now, any illusions that the officers could control or even monitor the level of dissent in their camps rapidly disappeared. Dissent simmered, and mutiny appeared a real possibility. In July noncommissioned officers in the 55th Massachusetts even went so far as to form their regiment in ranks before reveille to protest continual delays in wage justice. Tension eased considerably in August, when the War Department finally began to implement equal-pay provisions contained in the military appropriations bill passed by Congress in June 1864. By the time November arrived, a new spirit of celebration pervaded the camps on payday.[43]

Festivities held by the 55th Massachusetts Volunteers in November 1864 to celebrate equal pay encapsulated the quintessential nature of the soldiers' protest movement. These celebrations were conceived and organized exclusively by the regiment's noncommissioned officers. There was nothing fortuitous about this; after all, they had organized the protest movements. The celebrations heralded two important victories on this "second front." First, the provision of equal pay was an official admission by the federal government that the blacks could not be treated as second-rate soldiers. Implicit in this admission was the possibility of citizenship. Second, the victory was a triumph for the black leadership, which had organized the campaign for equal pay. During this campaign, abolitionist officers and politicians had become valuable allies. Favorable legal opinions, most notably those given by the attorney general of the United States, Edward Bates, were also very significant. Ultimately, Congress had bent to this political pressure, a pressure sustained only because of the noncommissioned officers' leadership. These leaders alone provided the dynamism and direction necessary to sustain resistance campaigns that promoted the soldiers' grievances without undermining their military reputations.[44]

At left: Circular No. 60. 54th Massachusetts Infantry Regiment Papers. Massachusetts Historical Society.

Black soldiers linked their struggle against the government's inequitable pay policy with their fight against slavery. Most soldiers believed that a triumph in one area would inevitably lead to progress in the other. However, they never considered the two conflicts synonymous. Because pay discrimination did not evoke the same hatred as slavery, the men did not challenge it with the same vigor. No soldier would accept a reintroduction of slavery, but many were prepared to accept, if somewhat grudgingly, a lower rate of pay. Compromise and accommodation were possible because different groups of soldiers pursued very different resistance strategies. Clearly, the pay controversy was an intricate struggle that cannot be explained simply by black solidarity and white intransigence.

Above all else, the pay dispute may be seen as an anvil upon which the black military community forged its leadership. The leaders of the Southern slave communities and the Northern black urban communities provided the essential raw material that had to be shaped to meet the demands of new situations. Modes of resistance that had been appropriate against the antebellum slave master and the Yankee racist were not appropriate against Union army officers and a federal government that was waging a war against the Confederacy.

New patterns of resistance developed as indigenous leaders emerged in the camps. These leaders reshaped the traditional resistance strategies to meet the challenge of new forms of racism. For men such as Sgt. Maj. James Trotter, the struggle for equal pay was part of a much wider struggle to acquire a new identity that underscored the black's basic humanity. Trotter asserted this view in a letter to his friend Edward Kinsley shortly after Congress had granted black soldiers equal pay in June 1864: "The passage of the bill equalizing the pay of soldiers is a 'big thing' not because it is more than our rights, but because it belongs to a great principle, that for the attainment of which we gladly peril our lives—Manhood and Equality."[45]

CHAPTER THREE

"This Is Their University"

PASTIMES

This is their university; every young Sambo before me, as he turned over the sweet potatoes and peanuts which were roasting in the ashes, listened with reverence to the wiles of the ancient Ulysses, and meditated the same.
—Col. Thomas Higginson, 33d USCI

When Capt. R. J. Hinton appeared before the American Freedmen's Inquiry Commission, he was asked to compare the leisure activities of black soldiers to those of whites. "They seem to spend more time playing like children," he replied. In contrast, the white soldiers were more likely to be dissolute and self-indulgent, gamblers who would risk their wages with one throw of the dice.[1]

Although Captain Hinton was more openly critical of white soldiers than of black soldiers, his testimony was laced with paternal racism. Like many officers serving in the Union army, he believed that an essentially idle and dissolute planter class had corrupted the *ex-slave's* character. "Slavery makes brutes of men," commented Col. Samuel C. Armstrong, 8th USCI, to his brother, Richard, "and then refuses to give them freedom because they are so brutish." After seeing a classroom of recently freed slaves, Lt. Col. Giles Shurtleff, 5th USCI, wrote to his wife commenting that he detected "a peculiar sadness" expressed in their "countenance," "tone of voice," and "gestures." Their dejected state convinced him that slavery "must be destroyed," and "ruthlessly rooted up."[2]

Union army officers had an obligation to act as role models and mentors to their men. Because military service was seen essentially as a journey into manhood, the officers believed they had a duty to make their soldiers "men" by sharpening their courage and instilling in them the habits of self-discipline and the virtues of civilized morality. This was no easy task, for vice flourished in the masculine world of the army camp. USCT officers felt this duty more heavily than most because they believed that slavery had robbed their men of their manhood. "The spirit of the officer in command works down through his men," commented Colonel Armstrong, "and if he is what he should be, his own manhood impresses on those under him." Part of the mentoring process involved teaching the soldiers how to gainfully use their leisure time. "Free time" presented a problem for USCT officers because they believed their black soldiers had little idea on how to husband time. Camp discipline demanded that officers educate their men in the use of leisure time. Therefore, they condemned "sinful recreations" that would lead to idleness and dissipation and encouraged "useful pleasures," which they believed would make the soldiers amenable to discipline, economically self-reliant, and morally respectable.[3]

Few officers appreciated the true significance of the soldiers' recreational activities. What the soldiers did in their off-duty hours, around the campfire or in the privacy of their tents, shaped their military experience just as much as drill and combat duty; for here, the soldiers had an opportunity to create their own world, a world that was not dominated by white officers and that was sustained by the soldiers' values. The sheer enjoyment of these recreational activities enabled the soldiers to unravel the routine of camp life and cross social boundaries. Pastimes were both reflective and creative. They helped the soldiers to maintain vital links with their cultural heritage, and they enabled them to creatively interact with their new environment. Around the campfire at night, the storyteller continued to weave his enchanting tales. The grammar of expression remained basically the same, but new tales were created and old stories refashioned to meet the challenge of the military environment.[4]

Life in the Union army consisted of short periods of intense military operations followed by long periods of relative peace. This quiet time was a time of recuperation, reorganization, and training. However, the daily routine of camp life generally allowed the soldiers leisure time in the late afternoon and during much of the evening. Sunday afternoon was another important recreational period. During the long hours spent in camp, the soldiers devised a great range of recreational activities, including mending uniforms, gambling, drinking, entertaining camp visitors, storytelling, letter writing, holding literary discussions, publishing newspapers, performing religious rituals, singing, dancing, and learning to read and write. These activities occurred largely away from the direct gaze of the officers, but the officers were not oblivious to them. Within the army camp a fragile frontier existed between "army time" and "free time." Soldiers and officers traversed this temporal boundary, and subtle conflicts developed. Soldiers used their leisure time to relax, express their personalities, and develop their culture. However, in the process of creating their own worlds, of forging a link between identity and freedom, they challenged some of the basic principles of army life.[5]

Much of the Union soldiers' leisure time was spent on army-related activity—for example, cleaning and maintaining weapons and uniforms. Such "useful pleasures" were strongly encouraged by the officers because they played a vital role in making civilians soldiers. A well-turned-out soldier was a creditable endorsement of the officers' leadership and an affirmation that army life was having an edifying impact on enlisted men. Yet military bearing and appearance were not simply imposed from above, for most soldiers took a personal pride in their military performance and appearance. This was particularly the case in USCT regiments. Col. Thomas Morgan knew this. His ex-slave soldiers from Tennessee exhibited "great pride in appearance on parade with arms burnished, belts polished, shoes blacked, clothes brushed, in full regulation uniform, including white gloves." In order to encourage the soldiers to spend their "free time" in a "productive" manner, some officers gave their troops special incentives. Col. Herman Lieb, for example, gave extra passes to soldiers who were well turned out. Some perceptive officers believed that they could see the process of moral elevation beginning from the very moment their black troops shed their ragged clothing and changed into their uniforms. Col. Robert Shaw reported that once recruits to the 54th Massachusetts Volunteers had washed and donned their uniforms, "they feel as big as all creation."[6]

Black soldiers were proud to wear the army uniform because it dramatically symbolized their change of status. However, it did not indicate a moral revolution. The officers did not have to teach the soldiers personal pride, for blacks were not slovenly in their dress. Slaves wore ill-fitting, shabby clothing primarily because their masters kept them in poverty and supplied them with inadequate clothing allowances. Their untidy appearance did not signify a lack of self-respect or personal hygiene. On Sundays, clean "Sunday clothes" were worn with pride. Similarly, the poor dress of the Northern free black reflected their low socioeconomic position.[7]

Not all black regiments were well dressed. Regiments recruited in the Mississippi Valley generally had lower dress standards than those raised in the North. Lt. V. Bergen, inspector of U.S. forces at La Fourche District in Louisiana, reported in April 1864 that the 91st USCI was very badly dressed. Some of the soldiers "appear[ed] on inspection in short sleeves, others barefooted while nearly all were ragged and dirty." Excessive fatigue and guard duty often robbed many Southern black soldiers of the leisure time they needed to maintain their uniforms. Moreover, black soldiers were generally issued with inferior uniforms and equipment. The soldiers protested loudly against these forms of discrimination, for they believed their ragged appearance made a mockery of their new status. Regardless of the state of their dress, black soldiers used their mode of dress in a traditional manner to express their sense of identity. Of course, there were limits to this form of self-expression. The Union army provided the clothing, supposedly uniforms of a regulation issue, in order to indicate status and facilitate control. Even so, the soldiers were able to give a personal dimension to their dress by the way they wore it. Occasionally this exercise of personal preference brought soldiers into conflict with their officers. For example, Maj. William Hart discovered that his North Carolina ex-slave soldiers created problems by disregarding dress regulations and rearranging uniform insignia according to their personal preferences.[8]

Racial prejudice had a significant impact on the provision of armaments for black troops. It was argued that the best troops should have the best arms, and, since white soldiers were considered superior to black soldiers, the blacks were generally given inferior weaponry. Maj. Edward Cameron expressed this view succinctly in an inspection report of August 1863. Commenting on Gen. Edward Wild's "African Brigade," Major Cameron declared, "Colored troops as far as I have seen are not equal to white ones. . . . [I]t is not intended I presume to put first class arms into their hands but I would recommend that some of the Austrian rifles now at the depot on Morris Island also be substituted for the unserviceable ones which they have now." Linked with this deficiency in arms and equipment was the former slave's relative ignorance of the operation of weapons. Fearing revolts, slaveholders had kept firearms out of the reach of most slaves. Some commanding officers, such as Gen. Christopher Andrews, were acutely aware of this deficiency and did all they could to improve the situation. In a letter to Col. John Eaton Jr., superintendent of freedmen in the Mississippi Valley, he explained that "few colored men have had use of arms previous to entering the service. To make a first rate soldier whether white or black he should feel that his musket is his friend. It requires drill and target practice to accomplish this." Not all officers shared General Andrews's intense interest in weapon training. Lt. Oliver Norton, 8th USCI, attributed panic in his regiment at the battle of Olustee partly to Col. Charles W. Fribley's failure to give his men adequate weapon training. Inferior armaments also hindered battlefield performance. Col. James Beecher also believed the combat performance of his men was seriously hindered by poor weapons, and Col. Herman Lieb noted in his report on the Battle of Milliken Bend that many of his men fought with "Austrian rifles" that "failed to fire."[9]

Abolitionist officers strongly defended the black soldiers' right to be well armed. One of the most fervent defenders was Brig. Gen. William Birney, who believed that poor armaments undermined combat performance and tarnished the soldiers' reputations. He wrote to Maj. C. W. Foster, bureau of colored troops, accusing the government of instigating "the tomfoolery of war." "All this is very stupid. Is the Government to keep whole regiments under pay with arms that won't go off?" Birney asked. He warned Foster, that the "design of Government" to arm black soldiers was "defeated by the underhand opportunities of subordinates whose prejudices [were] stronger than their patriotism." Finally, he reminded Major Foster that "to put men into the field with poor weapons when it is known they will be massacred if they are whipped is little short of murder."[10]

Even though many black soldiers carried inferior weapons, they remained intensely proud of their arms. The rifle indeed became their "friend," not only because it was essential for their survival on the battlefield but also because it was a powerful symbol of their changed status. During their leisure hours, the soldiers cleaned their weapons with devotion and pride, for these armaments gave meaning to their claim to equality.

Often the tedium of camp life was broken by "sinful recreations." In the privacy of their tents, soldiers spent their time eating and drinking. Cards were produced and wages gambled. Occasionally kinfolk wandered along the company streets, and "ladies of the night" were privately entertained. During the off-duty hours, the tight grip of military discipline was relaxed, and the soldiers were left largely to their own devices.

Many soldiers bought tasty morsels from sutlers (who were civilian provisioners on contract to the army) on payday. Lt. John Meteer noticed that when his soldiers were paid, they spent "two or more days . . . feasting on fresh peaches, strawberries, fruits etc." The simple joy of buying extra provisions enriched the soldier's life by improving his diet and strengthening social bonding. The tasty morsels bought from the camp sutler were shared among comrades in a way that affirmed friendships and enhanced status.[11]

Drinking was a favorite pastime of Union soldiers and drunkenness was a serious problem in many camps. White men drank because they were lonely, for reasons of camaraderie, and to ease stress and anxiety. Black soldiers also drank for these reasons. In some USCT camps, liquor flowed so freely that drunkenness became a problem. Yet the extent to which drunkenness was considered a major disciplinary issue depended very much on the officers' perception of it as a moral crime. Officers who believed that their black troops were particularly susceptible to "demon drink" argued that excessive drinking stripped the layer of civilization from their men, that it robbed them of their self-control and fed their physical appetites. All the lessons of manly discipline and self-respect, in this view, were lost and the "brute" passions of the plantation released. Capt. Joshua M. Addeman, 11th U.S. Cold H Artillery, "never knew any stimulant more demoralizing" than Louisiana rum. "This fiery fluid would rouse all the furies in a man when it had him under its control." Some camp commanders attempted to control excessive drinking by simply enforcing abstinence. On July 16, 1864, Col. Ernest Holmsted curbed the drinking in his camp by confiscating three hundred dollars' worth of liquor from the camp sutler. He turned some of it over to the hospital and poured the rest out on the sand. In his diary, 2d Lt. Rufus Kinsley tersely commented that it was "no wonder the officers don't like the new colonel." Col. James Beecher restricted the sale of liquor in his camp, because he believed drunkenness would blur his soldiers' judgment and contribute to depravity.[12]

Drunkenness allegedly posed a serious problem for even the "elite" black regiments organized in the North. Lt. Col. Charles Fox, of the 55th Massachusetts Volunteers, believed that his black troops were so tainted by the evils of Northern society that they were constantly drunk. He was convinced that two-thirds of the regiment's problems appeared to arise from excessive drinking. Col. Robert Shaw also had serious doubts about the ability of his soldiers to handle alcohol. Fearful that drunken soldiers would mar the fine image of his regiment, he wrote to Governor Andrew pleading for the swift departure of his regiment to South Carolina on the day it paraded through Boston. He argued that if the regiment were forced to return to its training camp in Readville, desertions would occur and drunkenness would

Col. Robert G. Shaw, 54th Massachusetts Infantry. MOLLUS Massachusetts Collection, USAMHI.

become commonplace. Colonel Shaw's fears had some foundation. Two weeks after he wrote to Governor Andrew, drunken soldiers rioted on board the steamer *De Molay*, and the officers were forced "to do some fighting" in order to enforce discipline.[13]

There was nothing really unusual about the opposition of Colonel Shaw and other officers commanding black troops to end excessive drinking.

Negative attitudes toward alcohol consumption were commonplace in many Union regiments. In some regiments, the soldiers took pledges of abstinence and formed temperance organizations. Influenced by the operation of the "Maine Law," the officers and soldiers of the 5th Maine established a temperance movement that spread to other regiments in the Army of the Potamac. Like their counterparts in USCT regiments, Protestant officers who considered themselves enlightened "reformers" also sought to curb drinking habits of certain supposedly dissolute ethnic groups, particularly Irish and German soldiers. In USCT regiments the moralists' concern over excessive drinking was related to their view of the slave plantation. Some abolitionist officers who saw drunkenness as clear evidence of a lack of self-control in Northern white working-class society argued that pliable slaves were also victims of this vice. They believed that planters gave their slaves liquor to minimize resistance. Yet there is no clear evidence that liquor was used in this way.[14]

Almost every camp had its quota of inebriated officers. They drank to escape boredom, relieve combat stress, and, above all, to carouse with their comrades. Although intoxication was not a military crime, drunks who otherwise violated military discipline were dealt with by court-martial. Colonels James Alexander and John Nelson were two commanding officers whose drinking problems marred the administrations of their camps and goaded their soldiers into rebellion. Eventually camp discipline deteriorated so much that both commanders were dismissed from the service. Such displays of drunken incompetence were relatively rare. Most officers enjoyed an occasional drink, but they were not habitually drunk. Alcoholism was a problem in the Union army, and the USCT officer corps suffered its share from this social vice. Evidence suggests that proportionally the officers consumed more liquor than the enlisted men. However, this may have been the case simply because they had more opportunities to imbibe.[15]

Many officers believed that drinking was a normal pastime. Sometimes this tolerant attitude was reinforced by a belief that slaves had not succumbed to this moral vice. Col. Thomas Higginson believed that his ex-slave soldiers were remarkably sober; he indirectly attributed this to the black's "peculiar" racial traits. Certainly two "moral guardians," Chaplains John Mars and George Rockwood, believed that unlike the situation with white troops, drunkenness was one of the few vices that was conspicuously absent from the black soldiers' camps.[16]

Gambling was another activity against which some officers waged a constant war. Yet in spite of attempts to stamp out this evil, gambling continued even in camps under the command of the most devout officers. In

Col. James M. Williams, 79th (new) USCI. MOLLUS Massachusetts Collection, USAHMI.

an inspection report, Lt. C. Blake reported to his brigade commander, Col. James Montgomery, that the good standing of the brigade was marred by "the use of cards and profanity" observed "to some extent in all camps." A God-fearing, Bible-carrying abolitionist, James Montgomery was deeply disturbed by this sinful behavior.[17]

Officers like Colonel Montgomery opposed gambling partly because they saw it as a stimulant to brawling and disorderly conduct. This was precisely the reason Edward Hallowell gave for banning card playing in the camp of

Col. James C. Beecher, 35th USCI. MOLLUS Massachusetts Collection, USAMHI.

the 54th Massachusetts. This motive was common to officers in white regiments but some officers in black army camps, most notably the abolitionists, enforced antigambling regulations more strictly because they believed that gambling easily damaged morality. Black gamblers appeared to be the inevitable victims of avarice and financial profligacy. Since slavery ostensibly had not taught them to value money or act responsibly, the officers feared they would be easily duped. The activity of the professional gambler was particularly worrisome. Charles Fox banned gambling in his camp, because he believed his men would be easy prey for the card sharp. Describing the professional gambler as "the meanest and most cowardly of men, a robber in all but name," Colonel Fox warned his soldiers that stakes would be seized and paid into the hospital fund. Lt. Col. John Rice was particularly incensed at an outbreak of gambling in his camp. What really disturbed him was less gambling per se than the fact that his men had allowed themselves to be duped by a white soldier, from the 87th Illinois Volunteers. With one throw of the dice, this man appeared to have seriously undermined Colonel Rice's attempts to teach lessons in thrift and economic self-reliance.[18]

Officers like Colonel Rice were generally assisted in their efforts to make the Union army a school for blacks by the work of camp chaplains. Although lacking the power to discipline the troops, the chaplains played an important role in the discipline process. They acted as psychological persuaders, endeavouring to win the confidence of their men by continually reminding them of the religious and moral dangers of vices like gambling and drinking. In this way the chaplains gave significant support to the measures commanders took to discipline their troops. Chaplain George Rockwood waged a moral crusade against gambling and drinking in his regiment. Yet his efforts to root out these activities simply forced the soldiers to behave in a "clandestine manner." Like many chaplains he discovered his powers of surveillance were limited and it was "almost impossible to stop" them from gambling and drinking. Chaplain Chauncey Bristol proudly noted in his chaplaincy report that "card playing is unpopular and if it is done at all it is secretly." For Chauncey Bristol and many other chaplains, there seemed to be an indivisible and mutually dependent relationship between military discipline and moral elevation. Therefore, what the soldiers did in their leisure time was to them a matter of grave concern.[19]

The presence of kinfolk and women in camp was almost universally recognized as a source of disorderly behavior. Some women, such as nurses, teachers, and laundresses, had very valuable supporting roles. However, unauthorized intruders, especially "lewd women," were not welcome. Keen to eradicate all plantation influences, commanders endeavored to keep tight control over the entry of civilians. Conscious of the alleged sexual prowess of black males and immorality of the slave plantation, Col. James Williams, 79th (new) USCI, believed that if he failed to take decisive action against sexual immorality in his camp, discipline would be destroyed and his efforts at moral reform subverted. In May 1864 he issued General Orders No. 2, which strictly forbade any soldier in his regiment from harboring women. First offenders had their pay stopped for a month. The money saved was given to support colored schools in the vicinity of the camp. Those female intruders who were apprehended were dispatched to the "Freedmen's House." Soldiers who offended a second time were sentenced to one month's hard labor without pay. In General Orders No. 9, entitled "Scandal to the Regiment," issued in May 1865, Col. James Beecher forbade women from entering the enlisted men's quarters in the Charleston Citadel. No women were allowed in the Citadel environs after tattoo.[20] Col. Henry W. Fuller regulated the presence of women in his camp by issuing to laundresses who came to his regiment a "certificate of employment." Any woman who failed to produce the certificate on demand was promptly arrested.[21]

Common pastimes, such as eating, drinking, gambling, and entertaining, all involved expenditure of money. The soldiers' leisure pursuits were indicative not only of their social priorities but of their increased purchasing power. The way the soldiers spent their money became an expression of their personalities and a measure of their newly acquired freedom. Not surprisingly therefore, they protested loudly against the inequitable rate of pay. In the interest of discipline and training, many officers were keen to curtail reckless expenditure and to inculcate in their troops habits of thrift and sobriety.[22]

Persuasion was employed to regulate the money supply and indirectly shape the soldiers' leisure activities and control their moral development. For example, Chaplain James Schneider was so horrified by the wasteful habits in his camp that he made a special point of preaching to his Virginia soldiers, former slaves, on the subject of "economy." However, when persuasive strategies failed, some officers resorted to more direct and pragmatic action. George Rockwood was convinced that gambling and drunkenness were the main symptoms of the black soldiers' financial recklessness; in his war against vice, he employed the dicta of Holy Scripture and military orders that forbade card playing. In this way, he hoped that "protection" would be "afforded to the weak against the strong." Brig. Gen. Edward Wild strongly supported the action of Lt. Col. Abiel Chamberlain, who forbade the appointment of a sutler to his camp of North Carolina former slaves. Conscious of the habits of "improvidence in which these people have been brought up," he felt certain that the appointment of a sutler would merely give the soldiers "a way of disposing of what little remains of their pay."[23]

In order to link financial responsibility with sober, worthwhile leisure activities, officers stressed the numerous benefits to be gained from saving. The free man was portrayed as a frugal man, the slave as an irresponsible profligate. Col. James Williams advised his recently enlisted soldiers to look to the future and "carefully save the money which is about to be paid you, for the support of your families; and as a foundation upon which to build a home for your wives and children." The themes of family, land ownership, and prosperity were all linked to the careful use of money. Invariably, it was the loving father, husband, and future farmer who would prosper, not the glutton, drunkard, gambler, or lecher. Money, then, was the oil that "lubricated" the operation of pastime activities. By regulating the money supply, the officers sought to modify social behavior.[24]

One broadly acceptable pastime was letter writing, which was the most important recreational activity in Union army camps. Billy Yank wrote letters to ease the pangs of homesickness, narrate his experiences in an alien land, gain material assistance, and seek redress for grievances. Mail call was the highlight of the camp's daily routine. Black soldiers were also enthusiastic letter writers. Those who could wrote for the same reasons as their white comrades. However, because Southern laws had kept slaves illiterate, letter writing took on a special meaning for black soldiers. This engaging pastime became a visible symbol of the soldiers' new liberated status. Letter writing became part of the ritual of defining personal identity. The letter itself was a document of entitlement: it was sent privately by mail, there was a conventional form of address and reply, and elements of reciprocity existed. In the letter, the soldier revealed his military rank and placed himself in time and geographic space. Even the signature scrawled on the last page underlined his freedom.[25]

In some camps a small band of officers and literate soldiers acted as scribes for illiterate ex-slave soldiers. As the soldiers became better educated, letter writing became more common and more personal. Even so, by the end of the war most soldiers remained functionally illiterate.[26]

The ability to communicate with loved ones at home was a powerful incentive for learning to read and write. Sergeant "H.S.H." claimed with considerable pride that while many of his comrades had entered military service illiterate, they "were now writing their own letters to their families." The steady ebb and flow of letters to and from home sustained the morale of many soldiers. A black chaplain, Henry Turner, noted during the Petersburg campaign that soldiers who received their mail "after a long suspense" appeared to be "illuminated in their very souls with joy," while those who failed to receive letters looked "down hearted."[27]

The poverty and general hardship facing soldiers' families were important sources of heartrending correspondence. Soldiers who had been slaves wrote letters appealing to their officers and military authorities to help them rescue their loved ones from the cruel lash of the master. Sidney Joyner informed General Wild that he had enlisted because the army had promised to rescue his family. "They had promised" him that he could "go on the first expedition so that I could get my wife and children." Northern soldiers also sent a steady stream of letters to military authorities and politicians seeking to redress the plight of their families.

Officers commanding black troops were encouraged by all this familial correspondence. As far as they were concerned, this leisure-time activity simply strengthened morale. They looked upon the growing stream of letters emanating from their camps as evidence of the soldiers' developing sense of moral responsibility. Men who took their duties as fathers and husbands seriously were bound to be good soldiers.[28]

It is perhaps ironic, then, that during their off-duty hours soldiers wrote thousands of protest letters about the behavior of line officers commanding them. While many of these letters were dismissed, some were seriously considered. Letter writing thus became a powerful avenue of redress, an empowering pastime. Perhaps few soldiers realized this more clearly than those who campaigned against excessive fatigue duty and an inequitable rate of pay. Many of these soldiers publicized their grievances by writing letters to the editors of newspapers. "We have been worked almost to death since we came here" protested "R.W.W." to the editor of the *Christian Recorder*. In some cases the soldiers wrote to influential politicians. On July 22, 1865, an anonymous soldier in the camp of the 5th Massachusetts Cavalry wrote to Governor Andrew earnestly complaining that the men "are treated worse than dogs and slaves." They were "noced [noosed] and draged [dragged] about and dying like sheep. . . . For god's sake and ours do something for us," pleaded the soldier.[29]

Another leisure activity in camp was listening to the tales of storytellers. Each black regiment had a number of such men. These men, who had enriched the cultural life of the slave communities, continued to spin their tales in the army. The environment had changed, but storytellers served the same basic social function of giving meaning and emotional unity to the diverse range of experiences. Col. Thomas Higginson observed one storyteller, known as Uncle Cato, fulfilling this social role in his camp by narrating the personal epic of his escape from slavery. Higginson noted that "every young Sambo before me, as he turned over the sweet potatoes and peanuts which were roasting in the ashes, listened with reverence to the wiles of the ancient Ulysses, and meditated the same."[30]

Storytellers served an important educational function, for they taught their listeners the mode of behavior appropriate to the new environment. Moreover, since storytelling was a communal activity, involving the active participation of both the storyteller and the audience, it created a strong sense of social solidarity. This social cohesiveness transcended the limits of regimental loyalty. Capt. John McMurray reported that when "Big Sam" Johnson began to spin his "yarns," soldiers gathered around him from a number of regiments.[31]

The social function of the storytellers extended far beyond mere entertainment. They were able to act as cultural mediators; that is, they were able to take the collective folk wisdom of the slave community and share it with both black soldiers and white officers. On the plantation the storytellers had hidden some of their folk wisdom from their masters, because this valuable resource helped to protect them from exploitation. However, in the Union army there was less need for secrecy. The white officers and the black soldiers were allies in the fight against slavery, and this alliance enabled the soldiers to share their folk wisdom more freely. Occasionally, when the officers became part of the storyteller's audience, new bonds of unity were forged in the regiments. This appears to have been the case in the 6th USCI. Capt. John McMurray reported that "often when trudging through the Virginia mud, or feeling tired near the end of a long march," he "would drop back to hear what 'Big Sam' had to say." After "hearing his pleasant stories," Captain McMurray "would go forward with renewed energy." A strong bond of friendship developed between "Big Sam" and Captain McMurray, a bond not broken until "Big Sam" fell on the battlefield near Fort Harrison in September 1864; hearing of his death, Captain McMurray shed tears.[32]

However, McMurray's interest in storytelling was exceptional. Most officers dismissed storytellers simply as primitive entertainers intent on preserving the relics of slave folklore. They failed to see them as agents of social change who were meeting the challenges of freedom by reinvigorating black culture.

Yet another off-duty possibility, at least in camps composed mainly of Northern black soldiers, were debating and literary societies. Often these cultural activities were in scope and purpose similar to those in which the officers engaged. They were not, however, modeled on those of the officers; on the contrary, they had their origin in the political activities of Northern black communities in the decades immediately preceding the war.[33]

The formation of literary and debating societies among enlisted men was generally promoted by politically active, well-educated, noncommissioned officers. One such soldier was Sgt. Alexander Newton, 29th Connecticut

Volunteers.[34] Sergeant Newton's bitter experience of slavery and the New York draft riots, together with his practical association with black abolitionists such as his father-in-law, Robert Hamilton, editor of a black newspaper, the *Weekly Anglo-African,* gave him excellent qualifications to act as the voice of his regiment. His literary and debating talents enabled him to give voice to the inner feelings of his less-articulate comrades. In December 1864 he played a vital role in the formation of The Douglass and Garnet Young Men's Literary Association. With an ardent desire "to promote the cause of justice and universal liberty," a group of young men held the first meeting of the association on December 19, 1864, in Sergeant Newton's tent. As a result of this meeting, a constitution was drawn up that clearly outlined the soldiers' commitment to black abolitionist ideology.[35] The objective of the association was "the elevation and promotion of the members of the regiment and the race, in general." It also aimed at creating "a fraternal feeling throughout the regiment and well wishes of the same."[36] Formed under the banner of two renowned black abolitionists, Frederick Douglass and Henry Highland Garnet, the literary association of the 29th Connecticut encouraged racial unity through the promotion of educational and literary pursuits. At the same time, it continued the tradition of black antebellum abolitionist societies and endeavored to maintain links with empathetic officers and white Northern abolitionists, those allies and "friends in the North," who were actively fighting on the home front.

Sometimes the literary and debating societies expressed the collective voice of the enlisted men, by arranging special religious services and political gatherings. For example, the Soldiers Literary and Debating Association of the 22d United States Colored Infantry had a special service held in the camp chapel to honor of the fall of Charleston and the passing of the Thirteenth Amendment, abolishing slavery.[37]

The reading of newspapers also occupied much of the leisure time of Northern soldiers. Black newspapers circulated widely in some camps. In April 1864, Andrew Rusk wrote to the editor of the *Christian Recorder* congratulating him on the standard of his newspaper, commenting on its popularity in the regiment and forecasting greatly increased sales. These sentiments were echoed by Sergeant James Payne, who labeled the paper "a symbolic star of a fast aspiring race from the deep ditch of degradation and bondage." Payne submitted plans for increased circulation of this "production of the colored man's genius."[38] Officers generally encouraged newspaper reading in their camps, because they saw it as the habit of a civilized man, a man who took an intelligent interest in national and world affairs. There is little doubt that the circulation of newspapers in camps improved the soldiers' educational standards, raised morale, and stimulated letter writing.

Black soldiers sent a steady stream of letters to newspaper editors. At times truth became the victim in these letters of regimental pride and a desire for personal aggrandizement. This was particularly the case when the soldiers wrote battle reports. For example, black chaplain William Hunter accused "Africano" of writing a grossly exaggerated account of a 5th Massachusetts Cavalry engagement before Petersburg.[39]

News from home was welcomed by officers and soldiers alike. However, while not directly challenging military discipline, newspaper circulation subtly undermined the officers' authority in a number of ways.

The circulation of black newspapers actually weakened the officers' hold over the flow of information entering the camp. Newspapers fulfilled a valuable social-bonding role, for they strengthened the lines of communication between the black soldiers and the free black community in the North. The soldiers were thus exposed to a range of social attitudes that were distinctly different from those of the white officers. The influence of black newspapers, such as the *Weekly Anglo-African* and the *Christian Recorder*, was particularly potent, because the Northern black communities used these newspapers as notice boards on which to post morale-boosting messages of devotion, commitment, and indebtedness to their sons fighting in the South. The soldiers, for their part, used the newspapers to report the valor of black heroes and complain about the tyranny of their officers and of the hardships of army life.

Similar but far less developed channels of communication also existed in the Northern white abolitionists' newspapers, such as the *National Anti-Slavery Standard* and the *Liberator*. These also printed correspondence from black soldiers and articles addressed specifically to men in the black regiments.

The black newspapers also promoted communication among regiments. This form of intercamp communication enabled soldiers to view the war from new perspectives. It also helped to nourish strong feelings of racial unity that transcended regional differences. For example, personal tragedies were explained in a way both Northern and Southern black soldiers could understand. In April 1864, the *Union*, a black New Orleans newspaper, reprinted a letter from an anonymous soldier in the 54th Massachusetts Volunteers that had first appeared in the *Weekly Anglo-African*. This letter protested about the execution of ex-slave Sgt. William Walker, 3d South Carolina Colored Volunteers, for leading a mutiny against pay injustice, and the summary execution of three soldiers from the 55th Massachusetts for rape. Thanks to the

THE SWAMP ANGEL.

Vol. 1   Morris Island, S. C., May 26, 1864.   No. 2

THE SWAMP ANGEL.

The salutatory below was prepared for our first issue, but was crowded out by the glorious news from Virginia.

About mid-way between our office and Charleston, may be seen a small bank-like mound, breaking the otherwise dead level of the far surrounding marsh. That little pile is made of sods and bags of sand. Its merits have been discussed by the London Times, the Moniteur, and other Continental journals. The nation and the world was startled by its sudden appearance.

When an Engineer officer made requisition for a detail of men, fifteen feet tall, to operate in the marsh, Gen. Gillmore was not able to fill the requisition, and some of the men who aided in performing the service are now on Morris Island. The incessant shelling received at the time, from the rebel "Bull of the Woods, are to them, among the reminiscences of the past. Nor will Beauregard ever forget his night-mare vision of the last Judgement, and utter bewilderment and terror when he imagined that the loud Trumpeter was an Angel, not "flying through the midst of the heavens," but crouched low in the salt marsh one mile and a quarter miles from his doomed city.

This was the "Swamp Angel" Some had supposed its day was past. Not so, gentle reader. We propose to catch its falling mantle and preserve a measure of its spirit. As that name will long live in history, so its power and daring must burn in the breast of the army and animate the whole Republic. We intend to make it still speak, though in a softer tone, through these columns.

The project of issuing this humble sheet was a happy conception. We only regret that Col. Davis, with whom it originated, is not present to give it his personal attention.

No pains will be spared to make it worthy of general patronage. We leave our readers to form, from personal inspection, their opinion of its character.

SAD CATASTROPHE AT A FUNERAL —At Fort Allegany, Pa., a few weeks ago, a funeral procession was passing over a bridge to bury a child of Mr. George Moore, when the bridge gave way, and precipitating the mourners into the water, another child belonging to Mr Moore was drowned, together with three of his brothers children, and one or two other lives were lost.

What is the merriest Sunday in the year — Whitsunday.

SOUTHERN NEWS.

FEMALE CLERKS IN THE TREASURY DEPARTMENT. —A recent number of the Petersburg & press says, one hundred and thirty ladies, employed as note-signing clerks in the Treasury Department, passed through this city yesterday morning on route for Columbus, S. C., where they are hereafter to conduct their peculiar branch of the business. It has been ascertained that living is cheaper in Columbia —how much we do not know — than it is in Richmond, and the policy of the Government, which is an economical one, is to remove their field of operations thither. The ladies filled three coaches, and were conveyed from the depot in Pocahontas to the Southern depot, where they attracted much attention until the train left for the South. A good many of them found friends and acquaintances waiting for them, who entertained them during the several hours of their stay, in front of Jarratt's Hotel.

It is an unfortunate necessity that compels the removal of these ladies so far away from their homes and friends, and the sympathy of the public is very naturally extended to them. Many of them are young, handsome and intelligent, but by the force of circumstances are forced to labor for their living, and as matters now turn out, not at home where the company of family and friends is enjoyed, but hundreds of miles distant, where everything is strange and every-body a stranger.

A MODEL LOVE LETTER —The following is a copy of a letter appended to an application for a furlough, forwarded a few weeks since to Joe Johnson's head-quarters. This application for indulgence was made for the purpose of getting leave to go to Georgia to carry out a matrimonial engagement, and was approved by the Rebel General for fifteen days. The writer's orthography is retained :

"FEBRUARY, 13th, 1864.

My Most Esteemed Friend: I am awair that you will be surprised to hear that father and mother have consented for myself and you to get married which affords me great pleasure ; for I don't feel as though I could ever give my consent to marry any other gentleman, for you know yourself that I always esteemed you higher than any one else.

Mr —— bear in mind- you know you once said that you could never live and se me in the arms of Another man. Know is the time to prove it. You will haf to come home immediately . I am shore that the commanding officers will not object to your having a furlow to come home on such important business as that

Ms and as have give that re ment, thinking that you would hardly get a furlow, and then they could say it was not thair fault ; but I want to take them on a surprise. I know if you love me as you say you do, you will not fail to come. Give my kindest regards to General Johnson and tell him to be a friend to in it I may this time k r my sake.

Nothing more till I hear from you ; an be assured that I sha'l await your arrival with the greatest anxiety.

Yours, as ever, Tou Ann.   H T W

☞ The printers of Atlanta, Georgia, having "struck" for $1 67 per thousand ems, find four journals published at that place have been compelled to temporarily suspend the publication of their papers. As soon as the printers quitted work, the c m r of officers siezed and marched them off to camp, the "typos" thus getting "from the frying pan into the fire."

☞ An alarming riot of females — demanding "bread or blood"—took place in Savannah on the 17th ult. The amazonian band appeared armed in the streets seizing all the food they could find. The military were called out and suppressed the tumult. The ringleaders were consigned to prison.

SUPERSEDURE OF GENERAL BANKS —General Canby has been promoted to be Major General of Volunteers, and ordered to the command of all the troops west of the Mississippi, thus superseding General Banks. He leaves at once to assume the command.

The navy are now in receipt of large numbers of recruits daily, under the law recently passed authorising transfers from the army to the navy, and in a short time all the vessels will be put in commission.

A Prussian letter from Mexico, published in Berlin, expresses the highest hopes of the prospects of the new empire, and says that if the North Americans oppose it, the republic will be surrounded " on all sides " by monarchial institutions.

☞ The number of printing presses now in operation or ready for use in the Treasury building in Washington, is so large that if placed in a line, they would extend a quarter of a mile.

☞ A dealer is ready made linen advertises his shirts and chemisettes under the mellifluous appellation of " male and female envelopes.

Major Generals French and Keyes have been mustered out of the volunteer service by order of the President.

medium of the newspaper, these condemned men appeared not as infamous criminals but as "martyrs."[40]

However, black newspapers did more than publicize injustices and sustain a spirit of racial unity; they also became vehicles for political education. Lessons in agitation and protest were indirectly imparted to literate Southern former slaves and free Northern blacks alike.[41]

A few Northern black regiments actually produced their own newspapers. For example, the 14th Rhode Island Heavy Artillery produced a paper entitled *The Black Warrior,* which was edited by QM Sgt. George W. Hamblin. Displaying under the banner "FREEDOM TO ALL, DEATH TO COPPERHEADS AND TRAITORS," the first edition was published at Camp Parapet, Louisiana, on May 17, 1864. The prime objectives of this newspaper were to make the former slave a patriotic soldier, to promote "discipline and good order in the camps," and "to incite the soldier" to "efficiency" by cultivating a "thorough knowledge of his duty." The government was to be sustained by "morals as well as physical force," and a fierce war was to be waged "against Copperheads and Traitors."

Few officers could have objected to these aims, for they promoted the ideal military virtues of discipline, patriotism, diligence, and love of liberty. Still, the fact that the interests of the black soldiers and white officers coincided did not mean that their objectives were identical. Quartermaster Sergeant Hamblin may have produced a banner that was acceptable to the officers, but the black newspapers nurtured cultural traditions that were independent from, and in some cases alien to, those of the officer corps.[42]

The black newspapers that circulated in the camps had unique cultural traditions. They contained elements from slave folklore and news about the social life of Northern black communities wrapped in the values of Northern society. The editors spread many of the social values of mainstream republicanism, for example, commitment to social respectability, self-reliance, and citizenship. However, these values, which the editors shared with the abolitionist officers, were communicated with great subtlety. Certainly, this appears to have been the case with the regimental newspapers. Their editors wanted not only to amuse and entertain but also to inspire and educate. Their newspapers nurtured the soldiers' cherished ideals and aspirations, and they instructed them in how to survive the harsh military environment. Even a casual glance at the pages of *The Swamp Angel,* the most complete surviving

At left: *The Swamp Angel.* Appleton Collection. Regional History Collection, WVUL.

regimental newspaper, suggests that these were the primary functions of this literary medium.

The 54th Massachusetts Volunteers published *The Swamp Angel*. Named after a "big gun that sent 100 lb. shells into Charleston compelling Charlestonians to leave their luxury homes," the first edition of the paper appeared May 19, 1864, while the regiment was stationed on Morris Island, South Carolina. Supposedly the creation of Col. William Davis, commander of the 104th Pennsylvania Volunteers, the paper was printed by members of Colonel Davis's regiment. However, the real catalyst behind the regimental paper was its editor, an intelligent and politically active noncommissioned officer, Orderly Sgt. John H. W. Collins.[43]

The objectives of the newspaper, which was to appear "semi-occasionally," were outlined in its first edition. It had two mutually dependent functions. On one hand, it would be a source of entertainment and instruction for soldiers during their leisure hours. Hence, it included reports on military affairs, moral advice, and discussion of controversial issues. Commercial advertisements for sutlers' supplies were also found in the newspaper. On the other hand, it was to be a vehicle for the black soldiers' anti-rebel propaganda. In pursuit of these two functions, *The Swamp Angel* was well supported by the significant number of abolitionist officers in the regiment. Certainly, few of these officers objected to Orderly Sergeant Collins's instructing his readers in patriotism, discipline, valor, and racial pride. Moreover, there was something intriguing and appealing about such an able black soldier satirizing the rebels for their "cowardice" and "stupidity."[44]

While no officer objected to the editorial policy of *The Swamp Angel* to provide entertainment and anti-rebel propaganda, few realized that these objectives were rooted in black American folklore. The slave storyteller looked upon his vocation as both artistic entertainment and moral instruction in the war against the enemy. The regimental newspaper editor served a similar cultural function, and, although their roles were not identical, the editor shared the storyteller's expressive tradition. *The Swamp Angel* commented on the harsh reality of military service, and from this perspective the newspaper identified with the black soldiers' experiences.

The first issue of the paper contained numerous exaggerated reports of Union military victories. Under a heading "Latest News from Va. Lee Out generalled, The Rebellion howling and tottering its fall," the editor reported that Union troops had fought courageously near Spotsylvania Court House, but none more so than the black soldiers under the command of General Ambrose Burnside. They had "fought with great desperation and success."

The editor reminded his readers that "Fort Pillow [in Tennessee, captured in April 1864 by Confederates who then murdered dozens of its black defenders] was not forgotten."[45]

The military report in the second edition of the paper, published on May 26, 1864, reinforced the pattern. The newspaper rejoiced in the shelling of Charleston, South Carolina, and the courageous stand taken by a detachment of the 55th Massachusetts Volunteers on nearby Battery Island. Special mention was again made of the Fort Pillow massacre. Soldiers were reminded that although Union victories brought a role reversal, with rebels, once masters, now vanquished, black soldiers were urged to fight according to rules of civilized warfare. The rights of rebel prisoners of war were to be respected.

This advice was consistent with that given by the officers, who encouraged black soldiers to disregard the barbaric practices of slavery. However, it was also consistent with the main tenets of slave folklore. Soldiers serving in Northern black regiments who had experienced slavery firsthand would have been familiar with these folk traditions. In slave folktales, weak and humble animals often triumphed over the strong and powerful, not through brute strength but with subtle intelligence and manipulation. In gaining their victory, the "weak" animals did not acquire the characteristics of the vanquished. The editor's plea to black soldiers to take the high moral ground by showing clemency to rebel prisoners was a humanitarian appeal with a cultural context. By showing mercy and respecting the rights of rebel prisoners of war, the black soldiers accentuated their sense of victory.[46]

The Swamp Angel cultivated the soldiers' feelings of military pride and accomplishment by extolling their high standard of discipline. In addition, it praised the cleanliness and general bearing of the troops on Morris Island.[47] Yet *The Swamp Angel* was more than a vehicle for military comment. War service carried with it an element of adventure and romance. The paper captured this romantic spirit, for instance, by publishing long, artistic descriptions of the geography of Morris Island.[48]

As well as serving the black soldiers' aesthetic appreciation, *The Swamp Angel* helped them place the war in a cultural continuum. In the hands of its editor, it became a powerful weapon for denegrating the rebels. It made intelligent use of satire and symbolic inversion. However, whereas in the past role reversals had been based on the verbal rearrangement of the slave's world, now every Union victory rooted the role reversal in reality. It was not the black soldiers' wishful thinking but the clash of arms that had brought the Confederacy to the brink of defeat. The paper relished the opportunity to describe the plight of the South, and truth was liberally laced with satire and exaggeration. Rebel manhood became a subject of special attack. Under the heading "Southern News," *The Swamp Angel* reported that the rebel manpower shortage was so great that the government treasury had been forced to employ female clerks. Comment was also made about bread riots instigated in Savannah by troublesome Southern belles. However, the crowning piece of satire was a love letter supposedly written by an illiterate rebel soldier. This letter was a testament to the black soldiers' growing confidence and strong sense of identity. The relatively well educated black soldiers who read the amusing love letter could laugh loudly at rebel claims of cultural superiority.[49]

Along with the amusing accounts of the rebels' plight, however, came somewhat disturbing reports of affairs in the South Carolina Sea Islands, reports that may well have disrupted race relations in the black regiments stationed there. In May 1864, *The Swamp Angel* reported that twenty-one laborers from the Quartermaster's Department had been imprisoned in the guardhouse over a pay dispute. This report would have shaken the officers of the 54th Massachusetts Volunteers, because it would have reminded them that their troops had refused to accept their own pay because of the inequitable pay rate. Mutiny then appeared a distinct possibility.[50]

Early in June 1864, *The Swamp Angel* was ordered closed, probably by Gen. Alexander Schimmelfennig, a pragmatic officer and Prussian immigrant who had little sympathy with the abolitionist cause. No reason can be found for discontinuance of the paper after such a short run. However, the fact that by May 1864 the 54th Massachusetts was hovering on the brink of mutiny because of the pay issue may partly explain Schimmelfennig's action. Certainly, he would have had every reason to fear that Orderly Sergeant Collins would use *The Swamp Angel* to air the men's grievances.

Orderly Sergeant Collins was a strong advocate for the black soldier's rights. Indeed, a belief in racial equality formed an integral element of his concept of military service. At about the time of *The Swamp Angel*'s closure, Collins had written to the *Christian Recorder* and earnestly expressed the desire that black soldiers be given commissions. Approximately a year later, he again raised this issue, in the *Christian Recorder*. The poignant comment, "We have got rights that white men are bound to respect," concisely summed up his attitude.[51]

Black soldiers engaged in a great range of leisure pursuits in their off-duty hours. Some were preoccupied with simple pleasures, such as eating and drinking, while others spent hours polishing brass buttons, brushing uniforms, and blacking boots. Others spent their time in more intellectual pursuits, such as debating and newspaper editing. However, regardless of the type of activity, these pastimes enriched their military experience. In a period of traumatic stress, they helped the soldiers to shape their lives and establish their own cultural boundaries.

The stories of "Big Sam" Johnson cannot be dismissed as the idle chatter of an old soldier. They became an essential part of the Union army's narrative, simply because they gave cultural meaning to the black soldiers' war of liberation.

CHAPTER FOUR

"Nearly All the Freedmen Are Eager to Learn"

THE STRUGGLE FOR LITERACY

During the month of November I wrote 150 letters for the Soldiers to their families, and friends, preached on all seasonable occasions, distributed all the reading matter that could be made use of, and spent an average two hours each day in teaching the men to read & write. School books are furnished by Freedmen's Aid Com. and sold at figures which will cover cost. It is thought better to teach the men to spend a part of their money judiciously in buying books &c. than to give books to them. Nearly all the Freedmen are eager to learn to read and write. Many of the 119 have already learned to read, without any instructor, quite a number are advanced to the 2d and 3d Readers, (McGuffies series). The discipline of the Army seems necessary in training them to correct habits.

—Chaplain John R. Reasoner, 119th USCI

Sometime in 1866, Chaplain Thomas Johnson received an undated letter written by a soldier, Tilman Hardy, who had formerly been under his pastoral care. Written from a post hospital in "Brazos desantiago," Texas, the letter opened with conventional pleasantries: "I have the pleasure of addressing you a few lines to-day being at leisure. Nothing to do at present." Hardy then went on to explain the pressing reason behind his correspondence. Tilman Hardy was an earnest scholar who was desperately trying to improve his level of education, and his letter arose out of his efforts at self-improvement. For some time he had been "spelling under a corporal" at the post hospital. However, his progress was being impeded by serious doubts about his teacher's ability. "I don't know whether he is correct or not," wrote Tilman. In order to end his uncertainty, he resolved to "see you [Chaplain Johnson] or the Quarters Master & ask him or you & if so being that he is right why I will continue spelling under him." In order to provide evidence of his teacher's skill, Tilman described his current progress. He was "spelling in the lesson of Cheverilize & peculiarize & allogrize & Enigmatize// characterize// anathematize// and Republicanism// cardinalize." He concluded by asking Chaplain Johnson to check his spelling—"if I spelt the words right please let me know." In a postscript, Tilman added a further request: since he did not have "any pens that is of any count," he "would be glad to get too or three from" his friend.[1]

Tilman Hardy's simple request encapsulates the fundamental elements of a complex process of education that was occurring in the camps, where thousands of illiterate black soldiers went to "school" for the first time. Since literacy was the mark of a free man, the learning process became a ritual that affirmed the soldier's liberated status. School attendance became an expression of liberty and an act of defiance against slavery. The soldiers themselves were the driving force behind this education revolution. The white officers could provide valuable assistance, critical advice, and pens. But the students and their teachers were found within the enlisted ranks. The soldiers learned from one another, from "a corporal here in Hospital." It was a revolution from below, and every soldier who learned to sign his name was engaged in revolutionary activity. In the struggle for citizenship, the pen was a powerful weapon in the hand of the former slave.[2]

Only a small proportion of blacks who enlisted in the Union army were functionally literate. In the Southern states, laws specifically forbade the instruction of slaves. However, in spite of these laws, a small number of slaves had gained a rudimentary education. By 1860 an estimated 5–10 percent of the Southern black population, both free and slave, was at least partially literate. This low level of literacy was reflected in the educational standards of Union army recruits who had been slaves. While few statistics are available, individual assessments from chaplains and regimental commanders suggest that there were wide variations in educational standards among regiments. For example, whereas Chaplain James Gregg believed that only 1 percent of his Maryland ex-slave soldiers could read when they enlisted, Chaplain James Peet believed approximately 16 percent of his men from Louisiana and Mississippi "knew the alphabet or more before enlisting."[3]

The educational standards of black regiments recruited in the North were generally higher than those composed of former Southern slaves. This appears to have been the case with the 127th U.S. Colored Infantry, a regiment composed mainly of Pennsylvania blacks. In his "Register of the Officers and Enlisted Men," the regiment's chaplain, Thomas S. Johnson, noted that according to his subjective ranking scale of 0 to 3, 42.62 percent of the privates were totally illiterate, while approximately 6.06 percent were in the highest ranking, that is, scale 3. In contrast, only 25.00 percent of the noncommissioned officers were illiterate, while 37.50 percent reached the highest level, scale 3 (see table 3). In the elite black regiments formed in Massachusetts and composed mainly of free blacks, the level of educational attainment was probably much higher than that of the 127th U.S. Colored Infantry. Certainly the level of newspaper correspondence from soldiers of the 54th Massachusetts Volunteers and the fact that this regiment supported a regimental newspaper, *The Swamp Angel*, indicates a relatively high level of educational attainment.[4]

Officers had very good military reasons for advocating the education of their troops. Some generals, such as Major General Nathaniel P. Banks and Brig. Gen. James Wadsworth, promoted various schemes to educate their black troops, because they believed that the possession of a formal elementary education significantly increased military effectiveness. Certainly, there was a well-known association of illiteracy with inefficiency and disorder in black army camps. Lt. Lawrence Van Alstyne, for example, discovered that the ignorance of his Louisiana ex-slave soldiers made his task of being officer of the guard an extremely tiresome one. He was forced to repeat the name of each member of each relief party until the illiterate noncommissioned officers had committed them to memory. However, even then there were many "mix ups" that had "to be straightened out." The shortage of literate troops also meant that the quality of the noncommissioned officers' leadership suffered. Lt. Col. Nelson Viall admitted that in his camp some noncommissioned officers "presumed upon their ability." They held their office because of their level of education at a time "when their conduct should have reduced them to the ranks." Low literacy levels also created enormous administrative problems for the officers. Unable to secure an adequate supply of literate noncommissioned officers to act as clerks, many officers were forced to carry out much of the routine administration themselves.[5]

In addition to a desire to improve the military efficiency of their regiments, a minority of officers, especially those with strong abolitionist beliefs, educated their soldiers, because they believed such work was an essential prepa-

Table 3

Literacy Levels in the 127th USCI (Cos. A, B, C, E, F, I) before Enlistment

Noncommissioned Officers

RANKING	NUMBER	PERCENTAGE
Scale 3	24	37.50
Scale 2	10	15.63
Scale 1	5	7.81
Scale 0	16	25.00
No Indication	9	14.06

Privates

RANKING	NUMBER	PERCENTAGE
Scale 3	30	6.06
Scale 2	40	8.08
Scale 1	36	7.27
Scale 0	211	42.63
No Indication	178	35.96

Note: According to Chaplain Johnson's scale, scale 0 indicates illiteracy and scale 3 indicates a high level of literacy. Companies D, G, H, and K have not been included in the table because less than 20 percent of soldiers in these companies had their literacy assessed. Chaplain Johnson had extensive experience as an educator of black troops. Not only did he establish schools in his regiment but he also was responsible for organizing education throughout the entire Twenty-fifth Corps.

Source: "Register of Officers and Enlisted Men of the One Hundred and Twenty-Seventh Regiment of U.S. Colored Troops in the Field," in *Hand Book of the 127th Regiment of Colored Troops, 1864–1866,* Thomas S. Johnson Papers, SHSW.

ration for citizenship. These officers were intent on creating socially responsible citizens as well as brave Union soldiers. Therefore, since they believed that the possession of an elementary education was the hallmark of a free man, they encouraged the teaching of reading, writing, and arithmetic in their camps. They believed a formal elementary education offered the ignorant black soldier an opportunity for moral reform, self-reliant citizenship, and some degree of protection from his enemies in the post–Civil War South.

In Col. Samuel C. Armstrong's camp, the school was open four hours a day. He considered it a "pitiful sight" to see his soldiers "groping after the

Col. Samuel C. Armstrong, 8th USCI. MOLLUS Massachusetts Collection. USAMHI.

very least knowledge." He acknowledged that their enthusiasm for learning was "wonderful" and blamed the institution of slavery for keeping them
in brutal ignorance. For Colonel Armstrong and others like him, the elementary education of the black soldier was an integral part of the process

of citizenship education. Academic education went hand in hand with moral education and military training. Col. Thomas Morgan acted on his belief that these educational processes were inseparable when he organized two USCI regiments, the 42d and 44th, at Chattanooga. "In addition to ordinary instruction in the duties required of the soldier," he established "in every company a regular school, teaching the men to read and write."[6]

Some officers believed that they had a divine duty to make the black soldier an orthodox Christian. "A knowledge of the Holy Scriptures," commented Chaplain Charles Buckley in his chaplaincy report, "at best an ability to read them, must be regarded generally as the basis of an intelligent Christian faith." He believed the best action he could take to improve the spiritual welfare of his men was to establish a school. An additional advantage was that the learning process occupied leisure hours that would "otherwise be wasted in idleness or vice."[7]

Col. Charles Francis Adams Jr. expressed the hope that the Union army would "become for the black race, a school of skilled labor and of self-reliance as well as an engine of war." He believed that if properly organized, the army could produce fifteen to twenty thousand trained, literate black mechanics each year. This aspiration never became a reality, although Col. Samuel Armstrong's military experience with black troops did encourage him to establish the Hampton Institute, a manual arts college for black students, after the Civil War.[8]

The Union army victories during the war gave considerable impetus to the general debate on the future role of the black in the reconstructed South. In the Twenty-fifth Corps, Maj. Gen. Godfrey Weitzel, who established an elaborate system of education, did so partly to prepare his men for life in the liberated South. Charitable and religious agencies also petitioned the government to allow them to expand the educational facilities among black troops. In March 1865, J. W. Alvord, secretary of the American Tract Society, wrote to the U.S. adjutant general, Brig. Gen. Lorenzo Thomas, urging that black troops be taught to read and write. He argued that once the war was over the black soldiers would find "few friends" in the South; instead, many would "stand ready to prey upon their ignorance." Two months earlier, Rev. Samuel Colt, corresponding secretary of the General Assembly of the Presbyterian Church of the United States, wrote to President Lincoln offering aid from his church to open "camp schools during the winter for the freedmen soldiers." He argued that such aid would prove invaluable in that "such instruction" would make the blacks "better soldiers and better men" and "fit them to become safe and useful members of the community after their military service honorably ceases." Lincoln approved Colt's plan and offered support in the form of rations and quarters, provided that such support was not "detrimental to the public service."[9]

Within the army camps, a number of different schooling arrangements operated. In some camps no formal school structure existed. The chaplains and sympathetic officers, rather than being classroom teachers, were simply intermittent purveyors of knowledge. They distributed primers and spelling books, and they occasionally gave instruction to individuals or small groups of soldiers while moving from tent to tent on their pastoral rounds. G. M. Irwin, a U.S. Christian Commission worker, operated in this manner while ministering to the needs of black troops at Wild Station, Virginia.[10]

Sometimes a number of schools sprang up in a camp almost independent of any centralized control. Often these schools were started by overworked company officers, who saw the importance of having literate noncommissioned officers to help them with routine clerical duties. Capt. Etham Earle started one such school at Fort Scott, Kansas, in the winter of 1862. His school appears to have been an outstanding success; he could boast that his school "furnished men for the commissary and quartermaster's department and non-commissioned officers for the company."[11]

Some of the instruction given by officers occurred in an incidental and personal manner, and those who found time to respond to the immediate demands of their soldiers garnered debts of gratitude. Freeman Bowley, for example, developed close friendships with the men in his company, partly because he was prepared to assist them when they wrote letters to their loved ones.[12]

The most usual method of organizing the soldiers' education was simply to establish one large school to cater to all students in the camp. In the camp of the 22d U.S. Colored Infantry, "a big tent almost as long as a meeting house" was used as the schoolhouse. When regiments were located in one place for any length of time, a more substantial wooden building often replaced the large school tent. These schoolhouses, and the tents they replaced, often also served as the camp chapel.[13]

Foremost among the chaplains' allies in the struggle to educate black soldiers were sympathetic officers who were motivated by the same forces that impelled the chaplains. Such company officers as 2d Lt. Rufus Kinsley and Capt. Charles Bowditch spent much of their leisure time teaching ignorant soldiers to read and write. These activities were given official support and blessing by camp commanders, especially those who were themselves ardent abolitionists, such as Cols. Thomas Morgan, James Beecher, and Thomas Higginson.[14]

Officers' wives were another source of teachers who taught significant numbers of black soldiers. Mrs. Frances Beecher Perkins was an active teacher in the camp of her husband, Col. James Beecher.[15]

Northern missionary and freedmen aid society workers' contributions to the education of black soldiers rivaled that of the officers and their wives. Dedicated Yankee "school marms" taught contraband children in the day and black soldiers at specially constituted evening schools. When black soldiers were encamped near large contraband settlements, Northern female teachers were sometimes incorporated into the teaching staff.[16]

One Northern charitable society that was very active in the camps was the U.S. Christian Commission. Formed in New York in November 1861 to promote the spiritual and temporal welfare of Union soldiers and sailors, the society cooperated with chaplains in the distribution of food, clothing, and religious literature. Delegates of the U. S. Christian Commission also embarked upon elementary education campaigns in army camps they visited. Herbert Clapp, a delegate at Wild Station, Virginia, was so moved by the ignorance of the black soldiers that he felt "compelled to go among the men from tent to tent to give instruction."[17]

Operation of the camp school was influenced by two factors: the absence of War Department directives and regulations and the officers' perceptions of slavery and the black character. Although the concept of using the Union army as a vehicle for the formal education of black soldiers had been advocated in Congress (by Representative John Hickman of Pennsylvania) as early as December 1862, the War Department failed to develop any guidelines or regulations for the education of black soldiers. As late as March 1865, the chief of the Bureau of Colored Troops was promising to issue special orders that would regulate the education of the soldiers; these orders were never issued. This lack of War Department direction meant that efforts to educate soldiers generally took place in a haphazard, localized manner. Success, therefore, depended heavily upon the support of empathetic officers and the initiative of the soldiers.[18]

Almost all officers commanding black troops believed that the soldiers' intellectual development had been stunted by the tyranny of slavery and their lack of exposure to the higher elements of Christian culture. Surgeon Seth Rogers expressed this point of view succinctly when he commented that "after centuries of slavery, which utterly shuts the avenue of thought, we should hardly expect rapid development of activity in the superior regions of thought." For Chaplain Philander Read, the years of servitude had cast a "dark cloud of superstition" over the minds of his soldiers.[19]

While most officers agreed on the negative impact of slavery on the soldiers' intellectual development, those closely associated with the teaching process believed that their troops had actually derived a number of indirect benefits from their years of servitude. First, some officers felt that the horror of slavery had taught the soldiers to place a very high premium on education. They attributed the soldiers' great thirst for knowledge to the fact that their pupils believed that literacy was the mark of a truly liberated man. "The fact slavery keeps them in ignorance teaches them that learning is the first importance," wrote 2d Lt. Rufus Kinsley in his diary. Second, the soldiers seemed particularly obedient; years of servitude had apparently made them docile and amenable to teaching. A "Sunday School Teacher" working among the men of the 1st South Carolina Colored Volunteers believed the "honest endeavour of their black faces" was evident because "their docility of character" was "rendering them apt pupils." Surgeon Humphrey H. Hood believed that the men in his regiment made remarkable educational progress, because slavery had taught them to depend on socially superior whites. "They have implicit faith in their teachers. Being white they imagine, or rather are fully convinced, that they are vastly superior. And they receive instruction with the trust of children." Bereft of such higher intellectual faculties as creativity and initiative, the soldiers supposedly survived by exploiting to their limits the more elementary intellectual faculties of imitation and memory recall. Surgeon Hood admitted that black soldiers were "of course, less far less intelligent than our white soldiers and therefore might reasonably be expected to learn with less faculty." Even so, they made good progress in their training, because "it does not require a great amount of brains to learn drill, and the Negroes possess this advantage." The soldiers' "dogged patience" made them good students. Chaplain Thomas S. Johnson, observing the progress of his men learning, believed "the patience and perseverance they exhibit at their adult age in the elemental branches of an English education" was "remarkable."

Finally, some officers believed that the soldiers had certain innate attributes that made them susceptible to the teaching process. Foremost of these attributes, in this view, was a well developed sense of musical rhythm and a deep religious faith.[20] It was the essentially childlike qualities of the black soldier, these officers felt, that made him such an attractive vehicle for instruction. "To learn drill, one does not want a set of college professors," commented Colonel Higginson, "one wants a squad of eager, active, pliant school-boys; and the more childlike these pupils are the better."[21]

A camp school's specific educational function and shape depended very much upon the commitment of the commanding officer; the demands of military duties; the limitations imposed by the physical plant and shortages of equipment and teaching materials; the educational philosophy of the teachers; and, above all, the motivation of the student body. Even though the schools developed somewhat haphazardly, without uniform educational objectives and curriculums, this development generally occurred within a common ideological framework. While most officers supported the education of black troops, for obvious military reasons, literate soldiers and empathetic officers carried out most of the actual teaching. This situation was not surprising, for teaching had to be done by volunteers, mainly in off-duty hours; only officers with strong ideological commitments to blacks were prepared to make the necessary sacrifices. The fact that most of these white teachers believed the Union army could be used as a school to prepare blacks for future citizenship placed certain preconditions on the educative process. This long-term vision gave some sense of meaning and direction to the richly diverse and intermittent educational activity that occurred within the camps.

The elementary textbooks used in Northern common schools were extensively used in the camp schools. Chaplain William Elgin reported that his school used "some 600 Primary Lessons, 400 Spelling Books, 240 First, 200 Second, 60 Third and 100 Bible Readers. Also 36 First Lesson Geography and 60 Mental Arithmetics."[22]

Webster's spelling books and copybooks were widely used to develop writing skills. Extensive use was also made of religious literature. Sometimes this material reflected the teacher's belief that their "naturally religious" students required textbooks that would be morally edifying and spiritually orthodox. However, the selection of educational materials was often governed by factors other than the teacher's educational philosophy and religious beliefs. Unable to secure funds to buy textbooks, pens, slates, or other supplies, teachers became dependent upon the charity of Northern freedmen aid societies. This meant that their schools sometimes became depositories for publications from charitable religious presses.[23]

The subject areas taught depended very much upon the teachers' personal priorities. However, most teachers hoped their students would achieve a degree of mastery in the "three Rs," reading, writing, and arithmetic. This broad educational objective provided the outer limits for curriculum development. Few teachers endeavored to push beyond this boundary, partly because they did not believe the "childlike" soldier was capable of more substantial academic studies. The army itself placed practical limitations on the length and breadth of the curriculum. While the schools proved invaluable aids for the education of illiterate noncommissioned officers, they were not, nor were they ever intended to be, training colleges for black officers. Moreover, the demands of military service, for example, fatigue details and constant troop movements, were constraints.

Although academic subjects were largely excluded from the school curriculum, three distinctive, sequential phases of the learning process may be identified: word recognition, functional literacy, and elementary education. These three phases are a simple and convenient way of describing behavioral changes that occurred while the students were learning. Few schools covered all three stages of the learning process. Transition from one phase to another was not marked by formal examinations because the ad hoc nature of camp school development prevented the introduction of tightly structured curriculums.[24]

In the first phase of the learning process, teachers taught their students to recognize letters of the alphabet. Often this was done by using primers. Lt. Benjamin Kinsley commented in a letter home that he considered "primers with large letters" the best instructional media for the men in his camp. Where primers were not available, the alphabet was often drawn on large cards and hung around the classroom. Once the alphabet letters had been learned, the soldiers were generally taught to spell simple words.[25] Assistant Surgeon James Otis Moore observed this method of instruction being employed in his camp just before the end of the war. In a letter he informed his daughters that the soldiers "read out of a primer just as you used to read when you were little girls. They had a primer and would read p-i-g, h-o-g, c-o-w, o-x, . . . m-a-n, b-o-y." There was something amusing about this pattern of learning. "Shouldn't you think that was funny?" he asked. He answered himself: "Well it was but they never had a chance to go to school when they were young."[26]

This method of instruction created perplexing problems for students who failed to grasp the mysteries of phonetics. Chaplain Arnold Needham observed one student in his class whose face was "gemmed with pearly drops of perspiration" because of his efforts to "solve the perplexing mystery, why k-a-t, won't spell cat, as well as c-a-t."[27]

As well as teaching simple word recognition and spelling skills, students were also taught to copy letters into a copybook or onto a slate. Sometimes apparently remarkable results were achieved. Lt. J. H. Meteer noted that one of his "favorites, an amiable soldierly little black scamp," could with only ten minutes of instruction "make almost any letter better than some learned gentlemen of my acquaintance." He explained this outstanding calligraphic performance by black students' great "power of imitation."[28]

The first phase of the learning process, then, introduced the illiterate soldier to the educational process. Soldiers who graduated from this phase could read simple signposts and affix their names to military documents.

Those students who went on and mastered the second phase of the learning process became functionally literate. Often one of the first exercises attempted was the writing of simple sentences. After three months of teaching, Chaplain James Peet's "boy," [servant] Joseph Socia, had learned to "spell out easy sentences." Color Cpl. Preston Gatewood, the protégé of black chaplain Francis Boyd, also made good progress. After a few months of learning, he was able to perform efficiently such routine clerical duties as writing out the company sick list.

Diligent students who worked through a series of graduated readers often considered each completed reader as a personal milestone on the road to literacy. Lieutenant Meteer once came upon one of his soldiers who had recently been studying under "Mrs. Dr. Ong," the surgeon's wife, and enquired how his studies were progressing. The reply was, "I've done it." Immediately the student produced his reader and proved "he had 'done got it' pretty well." Even to a casual observer like Lieutenant Meteer, it was obvious that many students looked upon their accomplishments with considerable personal pride. In a letter to his friend Caleb Mills, Meteer noted that "it delights them very much to pick up the 2nd. Reader and read off without any trouble."[29]

In the second phase of the learning process, students were also taught simple arithmetic skills that would prove useful in routine military record keeping. Biblical principles, religious stories, and moral fables were also taught, to edify the soul. Lessons included smatterings of geography, history, and English grammar. The level of competence, however, that characterized this phase was only that required for an efficient noncommissioned officer, one who could cope with the clerical demands of the military service.[30]

In a few large, well-established schools, soldiers mastered the third stage of the educative process and acquired a good elementary education that equaled those of their white officers. One such school existed at Fort Pickering at Memphis, Tennessee, under the patronage of Lt. Col. James Harper, 3d U.S. Colored Heavy Artillery. There, the regiment's surgeon, Humphrey Hood, heard an elite band of students deliver outstanding antislavery orations. Such demonstrations of academic achievement were relatively rare, however. The routine hardship and vagaries of military life, shortages of teaching materials, and, above all, the indifference of the officers generally combined to prevent intelligent soldiers from being recognized as serious scholars.[31]

The soldiers' enthusiastic approach to schooling was a great source of encouragement to their teachers. Chaplain George Barnes had "been several years a teacher," but never before had he witnessed a "stronger desire to learn or know more rapid progress." Thomas Higginson observed that in his camp, the desire for "the spelling-book" was "perfectly inexhaustible."[32] Soldiers were motivated to attend camp schools for reasons of pragmatic self-interest. They believed schooling could help to safeguard their freedom, strengthen family ties, and secure citizenship rights.

Some officers accounted for the black troops' seemingly relentless search for knowledge by pointing to their own allegedly powerful educative influence. However, officers who studied the soldiers' responses perceived the origin of this enthusiasm for education in the tyranny of slavery. When James Peet told his "boy" Joseph Socia that he was going to teach him to read and write, the young teenager "grew an inch or two taller" and proudly replied "O'ze had dat idea in my head dis yer long time." Because in the mind of the ex-slave soldier freedom and education were very closely related, soldiers sometimes made very determined efforts to ensure that they and their families could attend school. In November and December 1864, Sgt. J. Harris wrote to Brig. Gen. Daniel Ullmann to rescue his family from Mrs. Marther Turnbuill's plantation at Bayou Sara, Louisiana, so that his children could attend school. Maria Taylor and other wives of soldiers in the 2d South Carolina Volunteers wrote to Maj. Gen. Nathaniel Banks claiming that their husbands' military service in the Union army entitled them to receive federal government aid for the education of their children.[33]

Soldiers attended school because they believed that this was one of the best ways they could safeguard their freedom. "R.H.B." expressed this point of view clearly in a letter to the editor of the *Christian Recorder* in August 1864. He argued that "freedom and education" were "the essential properties to make a great and powerful nation. They are a sure foundation."[34]

Many literate Northern blacks believed the Union army was an excellent school for the education of the black race. Ignorant ex-slave soldiers were a particular focal point of their concern. Black leaders who had suffered under slavery, for example, Chaplains John Bowles and Henry Turner, felt they had a moral duty to enlighten their enslaved brethren. Some soldiers, such as Sgt. James Trotter, even extended this mission to helping local Southern black communities in the vicinity of the camps. (This work did not end when conflict ceased. During Reconstruction a number of freedmen's schools were staffed by Northern black teachers who had once served in the Union army.)[35]

The motivating factors that encouraged white abolitionist officers to educate black soldiers also operated among the soldiers themselves. This was particularly the case in the Northern regiments. There, literate leaders shared many of the ideals of citizenship education with their white abolitionist officers. For example, Chaplain Bowles conducted a literacy campaign among his men, primarily because he wanted to improve the moral standing and religious life of his unit. The soldiers themselves were motivated by a desire to improve their station in life and, therefore, saw school as a valuable vehicle for personal advancement. Sgt. W. Wilberforce Hampton rejoiced that "classes for mental improvement" were held in his camp. He believed they would "tend more than any other step" to improve morals and fit the soldiers "to fill positions which in the past we have been denied." Literate soldiers had a much greater chance of becoming noncommissioned officers, and this fact alone encouraged many scholars to continue their studies.[36]

Some soldiers learned to read and write in order to maintain communication with their loved ones at home. Literacy, therefore, had the effect not only of reaffirming freedom but also of strengthening kinship ties. "H.S.H.," a sergeant, noted with some pride that many of the soldiers in his camp who had entered military service ignorant and illiterate were "now writing their own letters to their families."[37]

As the war progressed, some soldiers became more assertive in their demands for improved educational opportunities. Black chaplain Henry Turner believed all black soldiers should receive elementary educations. He argued that the soldiers' heroic performance on the battlefield had won for them the right to enter the schoolhouse. Further, commissions having been consistently denied them, he argued, the War Department could recompense them by supporting camp schools. To this end he demanded from the adjutant general of the U.S. Army "five hundred advanced spelling books."[38]

The teaching methodologies and curriculums of New England common schools influenced camp schools. However, this influence was mitigated by two factors. The first was the officers' lack of teacher training, and the second was the difficult teaching conditions. Formal, structured, classroom education remained an incidental activity in most camps.[39]

The soldiers were taught moral and political lessons that were deemed appropriate for preparation for citizenship. Surgeon Humphrey Hood visited Fort Pickering "Institoot" on examination day; he discovered that many of its scholars exhibited their educational accomplishments in the form of letters written with antislavery motifs. Less able students wrote simple sentences, such as "we fight for our liberty," and signed their name to them. Two outstanding students gave lengthy orations, including one by Patrick Henry ending "Give me liberty or give me death." Such public demonstrations of educational achievements were used to validate the educational process and show off the teaching skills of the instructors.[40]

Some camp commanders offered prizes for outstanding academic performances. Lt. Col. O. E. Pratt encouraged his men to attend school by publicizing the educational progress of model scholars. First Sgt. Daniel Young was praised in regimental orders not only "for his high proficiency in drill" but also "for the rapid improvement he . . . made in his studies." Illiterate when he enlisted, Young was "now able to make himself an efficient and acceptable 1st Serg." His "success in rising so rapidly from slavery to manhood" was proclaimed as an example that should "incite every man in the regiment to fresh vigor and make them eager after knowledge."[41]

Schooling was essentially a voluntary activity. When elements of compulsion were introduced, school attendance lost some of its appeal. It became another military duty, a command performance, one that by its very nature provoked resistance. As resistance mounted, punitive action increased; recalcitrant students were fined and put on fatigue duty. Some officers even used education as a vehicle for controlling the black leadership. Col. Ladislas L. Zulavsky threatened noncommissioned officers of his regiment who failed to attend school with demotion and fines. Lt. Col. David Branson reduced five noncommissioned officers to the ranks for failing to become literate by a set date.[42]

The soldiers' progress at school owed little to the discipline of slavery but a great deal to their enthusiasm for learning and to the military environment in which schooling took place. Although the officers recognized their soldiers' accomplishments, their assessments were often strongly influenced by their racial views. Chaplain Buckley identified "a deeper interest . . . manifest in writing than ever before," so much so that writing became an important "recreation pastime." However, he attributed the soldiers' success in this area of study to "the power of imitation so peculiar to the colored race." This "power[,] . . . which exhibits itself in learning the manual of arms," was also manifest in the art of writing. At best, this process of drill learning enlarged the students' vocabulary and reinforced correct word and sentence patterns. However, if, as often happened, this instruction was not linked with individual remedial education, learning could be seriously impeded. Arnold Needham observed that one of his students was "astonished that his memory can retain a whole verse of poetry, and yet not remember each individual letter that composed a word."[43]

Teachers also made use of the black students' apparent religious natures and great sense of rhythm in their teaching practice. Chaplain Needham noted that his students had a "strong perchance [*sic*] for religious topics"; therefore, he repeatedly drilled them in the recitation of passages of Scripture. He also employed music as a principal vehicle of instruction. Yet his attempt to employ the soldiers' cultural mediums in the teaching process compounded learning difficulties. Slaves had a tradition of spontaneous creativity; they continually applied new words and phrases to familiar tunes and melodies. This continued in the classroom and marred the learning process. Indeed, Needham complained that "they seem to remember the jingle of poetry so well, that it is no trouble for them to substitute words of their own." In order to correct this "carelessness in remembering the jingle rather than the sense," he made extensive use of the church hymnals. He got his students "to repeat distinctly, each word of some familiar hymn and then explain its meaning." Chaplain Needham left no record of the success of his new teaching strategy. However, it is doubtful whether the students were motivated by having to analyze painstakingly each verse of a "familiar hymn." After all, they had no tradition of examining music in this way.[44]

Something the officers perceived but did not understand was the soldiers' "ritualistic" approach to education. For soldiers in the early stages of education, the writing process was almost as important as the message that the writing conveyed. They affirmed their freedom by making legible marks with pens on slate or paper. Slaves valued writing above all other forms of learning. The written word seemed to have a power of its own; soldiers who had escaped the plantation using a forged pass already knew this. Literacy was a passport to freedom and an expression of power. In the army, this association between freedom and power was reinforced. Order and routine were maintained by written orders. Even the soldiers' individual identities were enveloped in a mass of official documentation. Those in authority who placed their signatures on standing orders thus had the power to command. Those who obeyed were ignorant and poorly educated. Hence, the nexus between power and literacy so clearly present on the plantation emerged again, albeit in a more humane way, in the army.[45]

The soldier's signature symbolized his new status and separated him from other, less fortunate brethren who could only make the "slave's mark." Soldiers who could write their name, who could sign official documents, affirmed their relationship with the republic. Their signatures on muster rolls, marriage certificates, and payrolls signified a new reciprocal relationship that imposed obligations and rights on both parties. Writing, therefore, became a ritualistic process that affirmed the soldier's new identity. In an effort to "stimulate their pride . . . in every way possible," Capt. Joshua Addeman taught his men to "sign their names in our rolls, instead of making their mark." For many officers and soldiers alike, the company roll served as a measure of educational achievement and social progress.[46]

For some soldiers, such as James Jones of the 14th Rhode Island Heavy Artillery, literacy was inseparably linked to the privileges and responsibilities of citizenship. It was the mark of the civilized and self-reliant man. Ever mindful of this aspect of learning, Jones was dismayed to discover that only 250 of the 900 men in his regiment could sign their names for the paymaster. His "face burned with shame" as he witnessed countless free black soldiers born in Indiana, New York, and Ohio "and even in the very cradle of literature and learning[,] Massachusetts[,]" put marks rather than signatures on the payroll.[47]

The soldiers' enthusiasm for schooling was largely sustained by the work of literate comrades, like James Jones, who made up the body of the teaching force in army camps, and, on some occasions, neighbouring black communities. Regiments located in their home areas often made provision for the education of the soldiers' families. These schools were, in fact, community institutions. Whole families attended them, at different times of the day. A common pattern of instruction was for the wives and children to attend during the day and their husbands in the evening. These community schools had the effect of boosting morale in the regiment and cementing family ties. Chaplains and officers believed their support for these schools complemented their support for the holy institution of marriage. In the classroom and at the chapel altar, black soldiers were taught important lessons in parental and matrimonial duty, moral living, and social responsibility.[48]

Some schools were fairly exclusive institutions, which restricted entry to noncommissioned officers or "intelligent" privates. This exclusiveness reflected the urgent need of officers to raise the educational standards of their noncommissioned officers, who were responsible for much routine military administration. It also reflected a demand for education that often outstripped the resources available. Hence, some officers argued that rather than spread the effort over the entire camp, it would be better to concentrate on a few highly talented individuals. "It is useless to teach dunces so long as you can find those who have brilliancy," was the advice Col. Thomas Morgan gave to Maj. Nicholas Vail, who was responsible for educating a detachment of the 14th USCI stationed at Lookout Creek, Tennessee.[49]

Officers who restricted access to schooling often justified their action by claiming that their "elite" schools graduated teachers. Colonel Morgan, for example, advised Major Vail to "organize classes of privates under intelligent N.C.O.'s." Variations of this system of education gained acceptance in a number of camps. Etham Earle successfully used it in his company school. A cacophony emanated from his classroom at Fort Scott, for "all were students and all were teachers, when one had learned the letters, he would teach them to others." In this way, Captain Earle's school became "nearly a self supporting institution."[50]

Most of the instruction that was given by black soldiers was offered on an incidental, casual basis. It occurred outside the classroom walls and was not part of any structured education program. This fact made the literate soldiers the most effective teachers in the army camps.

Literate blacks proved to be more effective teachers than the white officers partly because they were more numerous. However, their communication skills were also vitally important. Effective two-way communication, an essential element in any educational process, was severely restricted in overcrowded schoolhouses. Overworked chaplains and officers had little time to give students individual attention. Yet this is precisely what many students required. Individual instruction occurred naturally within the camp community as part of the normal process of social communication. It did not have to be orchestrated by academically better qualified white officers. Slaves had had a tradition of sharing valuable knowledge through networks of social obligation. In the North, free-Negro schools served as focal points for black communities.[51] While Sgt. Milton Harris praised the teaching of sympathetic officers, he made a special point of mentioning that the educational standing of one company had "improved a great deal by the teaching of the sergeant of that company, Lewis Willis."[52]

Black nurses and soldiers' wives formed another group of very active

The public image of education. This photograph of black soldiers holding books and of their teachers was probably taken in South Carolina. It suggests that the education process was orderly and under the direction of white teachers. However, the informal and intermittent nature of learning meant that the soldiers' most important instructors were their literate comrades. Library of Congress.

teachers. Nurse Susie K. Taylor taught many soldiers in her husband's regiment to read and write. Her husband also taught his comrades, "when it was convenient for him."[53]

Edward Pierce, an agent of the Treasury Department at Port Royal, South Carolina, observed that literate former slaves actively assisted Northern teachers who worked among the freedmen. One assistant, Anthony, established four schools at Hilton Head before he left his teaching occupation to join the Union army. The weight of evidence suggests that Anthony and other former slaves like him continued their teaching activities after they had joined the army.[54]

Literate soldiers formed a very effective teaching body in the camp communities, because they taught their comrades in ways that were culturally consistent and harmonious with their students' background. Thomas Higginson observed his soldiers' "love of the spelling book" and noted that "they stumble on by themselves, or aiding each other, with the most pathetic patience." The colonel seems to have had little direct involvement in the educational process, although he was "getting up a school house," where he intended to "teach them as he gets opportunity."[55]

Of course, there were inherent problems in poorly educated soldiers acting as instructors. However, students were able to check their progress and the standing of their instructors with the knowledge gained at the regimental school. Tilman F. Hardy reflected this strategy when he wrote to a friend, Thomas S. Johnson, asking him to check the spelling and the standing of his instructor. A diligent student, Hardy also sought "homework" from his friend.[56]

In their search for knowledge, the soldiers acted in a self-reliant manner. They raised funds from which they employed teachers and bought textbooks and stationery. Sgt. John Sweeney was so keen to secure a teacher for his regiment that he wrote to Brig. Gen. Clinton B. Fisk, requesting that one be appointed. He believed that the labors of a teacher could make the ex-slave soldiers "a People capable of self support."[57]

Even when extensive education systems were established for black troops, the soldiers continued to play a vital part in the teaching process. The school system operating in Brigadier General Ullmann's brigade in Louisiana during 1863–64 employed many American Missionary Association teachers. Nevertheless, the bulk of the instruction continued to occur outside the classroom, during routine duties or during leisure time. Chaplain Edwin Wheeler observed that the soldiers "regarded their books as an indispensable portion of their equipment." The "spelling book and the cartridge-box are generally attached to the same belt." Soldiers also did what they could to augment their educational facilities. Col. James Clark congratulated the men in his regiment for erecting a schoolhouse with their "own hands" and furnishing it according to their "own tastes." Perhaps the most elaborate system of education was established in the Twenty-fifth Corps during the final months of the war. Even here the dynamism of the education process was dependent upon the soldiers sharing their collective knowledge. Thomas Johnson, superintendent of schools for the Second Division, Twenty-fifth Corps, observed that while the soldiers were on fatigue, picket, or even guard duty, they "would draw from their pocket their treasured book and earnestly study its pages." In his own regiment, Chaplain Johnson appointed "a sergeant and three assistants to be teachers in each of the ten companies."[58]

The soldiers' interest in education extended beyond their own immediate needs. Soldiers from army camps interacted with local black communities and often helped to erect and maintain community schools. Chaplain Asa Randal believed the schools in his regiment stimulated the development of educational facilities in the colored communities of Little Rock, Arkansas. Thomas Montgomery proudly proclaimed that the men in his regiment had pledged five thousand dollars for the Lincoln Institute, a school to be established in Missouri for the benefit of black soldiers and citizens. His company donated to the institute two hundred dollars, half of which was "given by Samuel Sexton," a private "who had bought his freedom in Mo."[59]

Perhaps the greatest obstacle to the learning process was the routine of military service. Few officers were more concerned about the welfare of their troops than Col. Thomas Higginson, and yet even he admitted that "the alphabet must always be a very incidental business in a camp." The constant demands of fatigue and camp duties prevented black troops from receiving systematic instruction. Often schoolhouses had to be abandoned when regiments participated in military operations or permanently moved.[60]

A perennial lack of physical plant, books, slates, and other teaching materials plagued camp schools. Samuel Anderson and Elijah G. Nutting, U.S. Christian Commission agents, taught soldiers in a smoke-filled schoolhouse in the winter of 1865. In many camps, the demands of military service kept schoolhouses from being built.[61]

Racial prejudice was another factor preventing some soldiers from receiving educations. Some officers believed that blacks were so innately inferior that they would not benefit from formal education. "These officers are laying here and learning us nothing," complained an anonymous soldier to the secretary of war in October 1865. "Instead of learning us something," they were robbing the soldiers of their money and rations. Henry Cork and Andrew Jordan both wrote to a friend, Esther Hawks, complaining that their officers were preventing them from attending her school in Jacksonville, Florida. Officers teaching in camp schools were also very conscious of the resistance and general apathy of fellow officers. Chaplain Corydon Millerd complained bitterly to the U.S. adjutant general that he was having great difficulty meeting the educational needs of his men because the other officers were interested solely in their own personal welfare; all the soldiers' leisure time was being spent building comfortable quarters for officers.[62]

Officers, preoccupied with the immediate military advantages to be gained from educating their troops rather than the long-term social goal of elevating the black race, sometimes restricted educational activity in their camps. This was particularly the case if they believed teaching school damaged discipline and morale. The work of civilian teachers was an issue of particular concern. Col. Lauriston Whipple closed the school in his camp, because he feared the activity of teachers. These "persons not assigned by law to the organization" could by their "intimate relations" with the men make "them feel that their duties are irksome and needless." The regiment's chaplain, Joel Grant, did not "doubt the propriety of this feeling" but greatly regretted the impact it had on his education program.[63]

Cultural barriers and social isolation restricted the educational progress of some soldiers. In some camps, the cultural gulf that existed between teacher and student was so great that communication was difficult. Lt. Lawrence Van Alstyne, for example, had so much difficulty understanding the speech of his men that he was forced to employ a soldier to act as an interpreter.[64]

Teachers often explained their failures by pointing to alleged racial traits of the black and cultural deficiencies inherited from slavery. In a June 1865 chaplaincy report, George Shaw noted that the educational progress was limited by the soldiers' "defects." The only real obstacle to the majority of his men's "procuring an education" was "their own fickleness, which so characterizes the whole African race in America." The "moral decadence" of the ex-slave soldier was another factor that frustrated the officers. Chaplain James Peet lamented that the progress of his soldiers was curtailed by the pilfering of spelling books. "Slave habits" persisted in the schoolhouse.[65]

However frustrated officers engaged in educating their soldiers were, they were convinced that their students made excellent progress. However, they found it difficult to measure the extent of this progress, because of a lack of uniform assessment criteria. Methods of student assessment varied almost as much as did teaching methodologies, and this variation made comparison of educational standards among regiments somewhat problematic. For example, whereas Thomas Johnson measured attainment in reading and writing before enlistment on a subjective scale of 0 to 3 (see table 1), James Peet measured the educational progress of his camp in terms of the mastery of specific literary skills, for example, knowledge of the alphabet, ability to write one's name, and ability to produce "easy sentences" and "write readily."[66]

Significant progress appears to have been made in some camps, such as camps of ex-slave soldiers stationed for long periods near large urban centers. Nevertheless, it is probably true that the vast majority of black soldiers remained functionally illiterate at the end of the war in spite of their military experience. Ira Berlin's claim that few ex-slave soldiers from the lower South could sign their names appears valid. Even in camps composed of free blacks recruited in the North, illiteracy was the norm. However, in these camps most noncommissioned officers and a significant minority of privates could sign their names when they were discharged (see table 1). Chaplain Thomas Johnson's subjective analysis of educational progress in the 127th U.S. Colored Infantry suggests that shortly after enlistment, approximately 21 percent of the privates and 61 percent of the noncommissioned officers were literate or semiliterate (see table 3).[67]

After the war, educated black soldiers made a significant impact on educational development in the South. Some soldiers, such as QM Sgt. Greenbury Martin, 39th USCI, sought early discharge from the Union army so that they could teach their recently freed brethren, who were in dire need of "amelioration and enlightenment." Many former slaves who acquired elementary educations in the Union army sought to teach in freedmen schools after the war. When Lymas Andus left the army, he chose to spend his bounty and wages on building a schoolhouse and church in the village of Mitchellville, South Carolina. For Andus and many others like him, the schoolhouse was a visible symbol of their newly won freedom and a vehicle for the realization of future social aspirations.[68]

At right: QM Sgt. Greenbury Martin, 39th USCI, seeks a discharge. Many soldiers waged a war against ignorance in their camps. After they were discharged, a number of soldiers, including Greenbury Martin, worked in freedmen schools in the South. National Archives.

To The Honor E. M. Stanton
Secratary of War

Respected Sir

On the 14th of March in Year 1864, I enlisted in the Service of the United States, and held the position of Quarter Master Sergeant. in which character I am still Serving, having as can be abundantly attested discharged all my du= ties promptly and faithfully.

It is now my purpose with your leave and favor to render what small service I may in another field of duty where my labors may prove advantageous to my own race & color who stand so much in need of amelioration, and Enlightenment. In the South as your Honor is aware there are countless numbers almost of the class referred to who desire and require to be Educated, and I can redily procure a Situation of that character. My ability to instruct in the rudiments of a common English education is ample, having had some experience in that occupation; but unless relieved by my government from the Military obligations by which I am bound to her, I cannot render that aid to my own people, which I am ready and anxious to do, And which your humanity and deep Consi= derations for the colored race induces me to think you will not hesitate to contribute to.

Hopeing your usual favour and kindness will be Extended in my personal behalf and in behalf of the cause in which I am ambitious to Embark by granting me a discharge from the Service

I am most humbly
Your Obedient Servant
Greenbury D Martin Q. M. Seogt, 39th U.S. = C. Infty

Pleas address at my residence No. 30 McClderry st, between Forest and Asquith. Baltimore Md

Few officers could deny the black soldier's tremendous enthusiasm for education. "I have been several years a teacher," wrote George Barnes, "but have never witnessed a stronger desire to learn or know more rapid progress."[69] This enthusiasm appeared to validate the abolitionist officers' faith in the schoolhouse as a primary vehicle for the soldiers' intellectual and moral elevation. Yet in a very real sense, the white officers were deluding themselves. The main focus of the educational activity in the army camp was not the chaplain's schoolhouse but the soldier's tent. It was the soldiers themselves and not sympathetic officers who were primarily responsible for the educational progress that was made. Most of the learning that took place went on outside the classroom while the soldiers were performing monotonous military tasks, such as picket and fatigue duty, or during off-duty hours. The students' instructors were their more literate comrades. Only a few perceptive officers, for example, Thomas Morgan and Etham Earle, actually recognized the dynamics of the learning process and tried to incorporate a monitorial teaching system into their education programs.

The educational process became an expression of racial unity. Men like Chaplain Henry Turner and Sgt. James Trotter shared the objectives of the white abolitionist officers; they too believed that literacy was an essential prerequisite for citizenship. To this end they labored incessantly among their fellow soldiers and recently liberated slaves. However, although their goals were similar to those of their white allies, their teaching was decidedly superior. They had shared the soldiers' life experiences: many had felt the lash of slavery, and all had suffered the sharp barbs of racial discrimination. This experience, together with their common community background, enabled them to tap the social networks that developed in the army. Sharing knowledge became another form of social communication.

On the evening of the January 16, 1864, Lt. Col. Charles Fox decided to visit a school that had been established in the camp by the noncommissioned officers. He "found them fairly hardly organized." Moved by this apparent lack of organization, he felt compelled to give his soldiers some advice. He "told them" his "ideas of how it should be arranged and then stood back and listened to their discussion." The independence and resourcefulness of the noncommissioned officers disturbed him. Therefore, he resolved "to manage this school very carefully," so that it would "not interfere with discipline." Military authority had to be strictly maintained. Clearly, he believed that "the old proverb about giving an inch and taking an ell grows more true as education less perfect, and judgement less acute."[70]

Many officers shared Colonel Fox's deep concern about the function of

Lt. Col. Charles B. Fox, 55th Massachusetts Infantry. MOLLUS Massachusetts Collection, USAMHI.

the camp school. Education enhanced the soldiers' status and enlarged their freedom. Soldiers' signatures were placed on muster rolls, payrolls, petitions, and letters of grievances. In the process of becoming literate, the soldiers were redefining their identities. Now soldiers could define themselves not only through their music and stories but also by documents that listed their rights and proclaimed their grievances. The struggle for literacy made the soldiers more independent and more assertive. Success in this struggle cannot be measured simply in terms of grammatical correctness. Above all else, it was a social movement that strengthened racial unity and challenged white authority. Plantation owners had long known this, but for many Union army officers it was a "lesson" they still had to learn.

CHAPTER FIVE

Godly Correspondents and Military Advocates

BLACK CHAPLAINS AT WORK IN USCT CAMPS

Perhaps the men will compare favorably in a moral sense with other Regiments. Profanity is very prevalent, so is card playing for amusement very common. The Sabbath is somewhat respected and most of the men like to go to meetings.

—Chaplain John R. Bowles, 55th Massachusetts Volunteers

In August 1863, Rev. Henry M. Turner, minister of a large African Methodist Episcopal church in Washington, D.C., wrote to Secretary of War Edwin Stanton seeking to be appointed chaplain of the 1st USCI. In support of his application, he enclosed recommendations from Colonels John Holman, 1st USCI, and William Birney, 2d USCI. Turner informed Stanton that these two officers had "flattered him with the idea" that his "services would be invaluable in giving impetus, impulse and encouragement to the men, as well as stimulating them to brace dangers, responsibilities and hardship of a soldier's life." Two months later, he was officially appointed chaplain to the 1st U.S. Colored Infantry.[1]

During the course of the Civil War, thirteen other black clergymen joined Henry Turner to serve as chaplains in USCT regiments. Though small in number, these clergymen played an important role in USCT camps, for they served as vital links between the men and their home communities and also as military advocates, defending the soldiers' rights and ministering to them.[2]

All Union regiments were extensions of the communities from which they sprang. Reid Mitchell reminds us that "the soldiers saw themselves as better embodying the values of the community than those who selfishly stayed behind." Men were tied to their communities by locality, kinship, friendship, and tradition; strong though these bonds were, however, distance and death tugged hard upon them. The more the composition of the regiment changed and the more the volunteers became veteran soldiers, the more the men grew away from their communities, their values, and their people. Letters home and furloughs helped to maintain the link but could never allay the communities' fears that somehow their boys would be lost to them even if they survived the conflict. The soldiers themselves were equally fearful that their sacrifices would be forgotten and that their places in their home communities would disappear. In these circumstances, the role of the officer corps was vital. More than any other group, it formed an important link in the human chain that tied the men to home, for often officers were leaders in both societies. As community leaders they had recruited local volunteers, and as officers they had helped to transform them into veterans. The tension between these roles weighed heavily upon the officers, particularly the chaplains (who held commissions as officers). Although they played no role in the disciplining and training of the men, it was the chaplains' duty to nurture spiritual values, safeguard community virtues, and assist in the recruitment and organization of the regiment.[3]

Most abolitionists looked upon the organization of black regiments as a bold experiment. No one could predict with any certainty the performance of black troops in training or on the battlefield. If they proved themselves as soldiers, then the abolitionists' claims for emancipation and citizenship would be vindicated. If the black troops performed poorly, proslavery arguments could triumph. Given the high ideological stakes, it is not surprising that abolitionists encouraged the inclusion in the black regiments of responsible community leaders who could exercise authority over the men. Yet herein lay a tension that surfaced in those regiments during the war, for the USCI regiments were like no other regiments in the Union army; they consisted of not one community but two. The white officers and the black soldiers may have fought under the same flag and forged an alliance in battle, but culturally and socially they lived in separate societies. Because black chaplains belonged to both groups, their role was exceedingly difficult, as commissioned officers they embodied the expectations of two distinctly different groups. Soldiers saw them as advocates in the struggle for racial equality and citizenship, while white politicians and officers expected them to be recruiting agents and loyal officers who would help the Negro to adjust to the demands of military service. The task of meeting these differing expectations was particularly burdensome because the chaplain's duties were not clearly defined by army regulations.

General Orders No. 15, issued in May 1861, allotted one chaplain to each regiment. He was to be "appointed by the regimental commander on the vote of the field officers and company commanders on duty with the regiment at the time of the appointment"; he was required to be "a regular ordained minister of a Christian denomination"; and he was to "receive the pay and allowances of a captain of cavalry." The chaplain's duties required him to "report to the colonel commanding the regiment to which he is attached, at the end of each quarter, the moral and religious condition of the regiment, and such suggestions as may conduce to the social happiness and moral improvement of the troops."[4]

Those who were active in the movement to organize black regiments in the Northern states enthusiastically endorsed the employment of black clergy in their recruiting campaigns. They recognized that the recruiting success of Garland H. White, 28th USCI, in Ohio and Indiana; George W. Le Vere, 20th USCI, in New York; Samuel Harrison in Massachusetts with the 54th; and Henry M. Turner, 1st USCI, in Washington, D.C., owed much to their standing and influence in the black communities to which they ministered.[5]

Governor John Andrew of Massachusetts was particularly aware of the important role black clergy could play in the organization of black regiments. When he appointed William Jackson and William Grimes as camp chaplains at Readville, Massachusetts, the rendezvous point for recruitment of the 54th Massachusetts Volunteers, he expected them to make a significant impact on the spiritual and moral lives of the soldiers. They were charged with "the duty of instructing, encouraging and inspiring the men by appeals to their moral sentiments, their hopes and aspirations, as men and citizens." Above all, they were to communicate "with fervor and simplicity the ideas and sentiments of Christian duty." Andrew also expected the "instruction of the chaplains" to "help the men become good soldiers," men who would be "obedient to their proper commanders." It was his firm hope that Jackson and Grimes would help make the 54th Massachusetts Volunteers "a honor to Massachusetts and a means of elevating the position of the people of color hereafter."[6]

Northern black communities repeatedly lobbied the War Department for the appointment of black chaplains to regiments being organized among them. In September 1863, Jeremiah Asher, of Shiloh Church, wrote to President Lincoln on "behalf of the Colored Clergy and Church of Philadelphia" to ask whether any law prohibited the appointment of black chaplains to Negro regiments. Asher was keen to serve as a chaplain primarily because "the soldiers are anxious to have Colored Ministers." Eventually, after protracted negotiations, Asher was appointed chaplain of the 6th USCI.[7]

The forces that motivated men such as Jeremiah Asher went much deeper than a simple desire to serve the men. Indeed, most chaplains were motivated by community, pastoral, and military objectives. They had a strong desire to serve their home communities by seeing to it that the men maintained their links with their loved ones and held on to civic traditions and community ideals. A number kept the Northern black communities informed of their soldiers' progress by writing in two widely circulated and reprinted black newspapers, the *Weekly Anglo-African* of New York and the *Christian Recorder*, the journal of Philadelphia's African Methodist Episcopal church. "I shall try and get a much larger regular subscription for your paper as soon as I can get about from regiment to regiment. Rest assured that I will do all in my power to give your paper as wide a circulation as possible," wrote Chaplain Garland H. White, 28th USCI, to the editor of the *Christian Recorder* in September 1864. To make his task easier, he urged the editor to send "as late [an] issue as possible, and as promptly as you can." Chaplains and soldiers both used black newspapers to communicate the trials and triumphs of military service to their home communities. Often the letters they published in the newspapers had the appearance of progress reports. Some soldiers even took upon themselves the task of promoting correspondence between the soldiers and their relatives. Early in December 1864, the *Christian Recorder* carried on its front page an item indicating that it had "received a note from Sergeant Theo. Rogers," 25th USCI, "which states any person having friends in said regiment can hear from them by writing to him, enclosing a stamp, at Fort Duane, near Beaufort, S.C." Yet such offers remained relatively rare. Throughout the war, it was the black chaplains who most actively coordinated links with the home communities, as this function was an important part of their military duty. Relationships with the home communities were also strengthened by the chaplains who served as their regiments' official postmasters.[8]

The chaplains' various duties seldom existed in isolation. Every chaplain knew that when he lifted the soldiers' morale, he improved his soldiers' health, sharpened battlefield performance, and increased commitment to loved ones at home. White chaplains shared these universal roles, but black chaplains' fervent commitment to the antislavery cause set them somewhat apart from their white brethren. Some of the black chaplains had been slaves, so their hatred of slavery and love of freedom were intense. Moreover, in common with other members of the Northern black communities, they were motivated by a strong desire to uplift their enslaved brethren in the South.[9]

In their reports to newspapers, the black chaplains invariably commented on the combat performance of their men. These reports emphasized the courage of the soldiers and the seemingly relentless advance of the Union army. "We have whipped and driven the enemy in every battle except the first," exclaimed Chaplain Benjamin Randolph in the *Weekly Anglo-African* when commenting on the arrival of Gen. T. Sherman's army in Savannah. The claim that bravery on the battlefield would nullify racial prejudice was repeatedly made. Chaplain William Hunter had no doubt that the performance of black troops in the assault on Petersburg on June 15, 1864, would be "remembered by entire colored race on this continent" as "the day when prejudice died in the entire Army of the U.S. of America," the day when "it was admitted that colored men were equal to the severest ordeal." With a sense of pride, Chaplain Hunter informed the readers of the *Christian Recorder* that the "gallant 4th suffered dreadfully on that day, . . . more than any other regiment in our Division." Hardships of war were described in a way that emphasized the soldiers' personal commitment to liberty and equality. Writing from the Petersburg front, Chaplain Garland White described his men lying in rifle pits full of water. "Although in this situation for more than a week," the soldiers did not complain; indeed, no man "heard a single murmur." This fortitude was the result of the soldiers' "knowing that in these sufferings" their "manhood is thoroughly vindicated." "Give us victory and liberty in the end, and we ask no more," Garland White exclaimed. Soldiers who made the ultimate sacrifice were assured of salvation. In the same report, Chaplain White was "happy to say" that some of his "troops fell in the harness of fa[ith] and hope in Christ" and were now "far away from the land of battle."[10]

This focus on bravery, liberty, and the elimination of racial prejudice made the chaplains particularly sensitive to negative criticism of the soldiers' combat performance. Garland White was incensed by the "large number of cowards at home" who asserted that during the battle of the Crater "colored troops under General Burnside" had acted "cowardly." Keen to set the record straight, White defended the honor of the black soldiers, by accusing the *New York Herald*, "a paper familiar with political corruption," of using "slanderous language" and blaming the disaster on the commanders who had planned the operation. He reported that before the battle the soldiers had pleaded with him, that should they die, he would inform their loved ones that they "died like a man." They had urged him to forward their pay to their kin and to remind earnestly their wives to raise their children "in the fear of the Lord." In short, Chaplain White informed the readers of the *Christian Recorder*, their soldiers were not cowards but heroes fighting for hearth and home. Invariably the casualty lists that concluded the chaplains' reports powerfully endorsed such assertions.[11]

Religious duties weighed heavily on the minds of the chaplains. In December 1864, Chaplain George W. Le Vere reported to the readers of the *Christian Recorder* that it had been his "very anxious desire to have a regimental church and school permanently established for the spiritual and moral condition of our regiment." He "thanked God" that he had "thus far succeeded." Such religious devotion strengthened the relationship between the soldiers and their home communities, because it made both parties feel that they were integral parts of a holy struggle for freedom, a feeling so powerful that it transcended racial boundaries. One white chaplain, Enoch K. Miller of the 25th USCI, wrote numerous letters assuring the readers of the *Christian Recorder* that his soldiers had not forgotten their God. After describing the suffering caused within his regiment by its lack of pay, Miller declared that nonetheless "we are blessed in numberless respects." Stationed at Fort Pickens, Florida, his congregation was "having what our congregation at home would call a revival." There was "scarcely an enlisted man in the fort who does not come to our meetings when off duty." Several "backsliders" had been "reclaimed," "while many sinners had turned to the Lord." This was not exclusively the product of the chaplain's labor, for Miller noted that "Bros. Harris and Turner, Co. B., and also Bro. Mills Co. C., all licensed preachers in the African M.E. Church at home, render us sufficient aid." Such reports provided the soldiers' home communities with positive assurance, especially when they were reinforced by letters from the soldiers themselves. Within a few weeks of Enoch Miller's report on the Fort Pickens revival, soldiers from his regiment wrote to the newspaper praising the work of the "good and kind," "fine" and "noble" chaplain.[12]

One important and generally well publicized duty that chaplains performed was to give comfort to soldiers who faced death by execution. Chaplains White and Le Vere both wrote letters to the editor of the *Christian Recorder* outlining the painful duty they performed in upholding military justice. When White was requested to call upon Pvt. Samuel Mapp, 10th USCI, who was under sentence of death for attempting to kill his captain, he complied earnestly, stating that he "would do all in" his "power to point him to the Lamb of God that taketh away the sins of the world." While comforting the condemned man, White pointed him to the pernicious penalties of sin and God's saving love. He "cited in plain terms the case of the dying thief" on the cross beside the Lord's on Calvary, and "that seemed to give him hope." The death of this condemned man contained implicit warnings on the wages of sin that the readers of the *Christian Recorder* would find difficult to ignore. Certainly, White found the whole episode "the saddest spectacle he had every witnessed," and "he hoped never to witness another." Moral vigilance was also an important message that Chaplain Le Vere carried with him when he comforted James Quinn, who had been condemned for murdering Charles Cisco at Fort Jackson, Louisiana. In his vivid description of the events surrounding the execution Le Vere was careful to note that the condemned man had "a mother living in the city of Baltimore" who was "a member of the A.M.E. Church."[13]

As well as ministering to the needs of all Union soldiers, both the heroes and the condemned, black chaplains carried a heavy burden of concern for Southern slaves. When Chaplain White, a former slave from Richmond, Virginia, observed the doors of the Richmond slave pen being broken open and thousands of liberated slaves coming out "shouting and praising God and father or master Abe, as they termed him," he shed tears of joy and forgot much of the speech he had been asked to deliver to mark this momentous occasion. Touching scenes of family reunion took on spiritual and personal significance. In his letter on the episode to the *Christian Recorder,* he confessed he "could not express the joy" he felt at the meeting of his mother and other friends: "suffice to say, that God" was "on the side of the righteous, and will in time reward them." Yet linked with these feelings of exhilaration was a deep sense of the responsibility that White and other black chaplains shared. All believed they had a divine duty to bring the gospel to the former slaves.[14]

Slavery had left its mark even on former slaves who served in the Union army. Garland White observed that at the battle of the Crater, "the First Division of Colored Troops, who led the charge, were those who were principally raised in Slave States." During the battle, "they did not stand up to the work like those from the Free States." Enoch Miller reported that during an expedition to Pollard, a small town on the Montgomery, Mobile railroad, his troops, "with one exception," behaved "splendidly." This exception "consisted of the killing of prisoners." Chaplain Miller explained this deed by noting that "some of the men who had been slaves" would remember old grievances and "seek to avenge them on such occasions." To all who would violate the rules of war, Miller quoted the Scripture: "Vengeance is mine, I will repay, saith the Lord." The damaging influence of slavery could be detected even at a personal level. When reporting the execution of Private Mapp for the attempted murder of his captain, Garland White was careful to inform his readers that this condemned man had lacked the benefits of Northern culture and guidance from black chaplains. "He was a Virginian, and had never lived in the North. His regiment was raised in Virginia, and has a white chaplain, who is not here at present."[15]

Because the chaplains believed themselves the agents of the soldiers' home communities, they constantly looked there for support. Writing from Camp Parapet in Carrollton, Louisiana, in December 1864, George Le Vere praised the "Ladies Association for the Relief of Sick and Wounded (Colored) Soldiers" of New York for a "well filled box" of medicines. A white chaplain, Enoch Miller, reminded the readers of the *Christian Recorder* that "while absent from our Churches we will endeavor by God's help, to do our duty, both as soldiers and as Christians." However, the soldiers could not do their duty alone: "Let the Church and all true hearted followers of Christ do theirs, by not forgetting to unite their prayers with ours for the defenders of their country." Prayer support was an issue of vital concern for Chaplain Miller. In May 1865 at Fort Barrancas, in western Florida, he organized a Sabbath school for children in the vicinity of the fort. Attendance grew to sixty children, who were "eager" and "hungry" for knowledge. Since the success of the school depended on God's blessing, Miller urged the readers of the *Christian Recorder* to remember the school in their prayers.[16]

Garland White was more aggressive in his appeals for support. At the front before Petersburg, he bemoaned the fact that "we get no books, tracts, periodicals, nor anything at all from our colored religious associations." In addition, "none of the Bishops" paid "the attention which might be extended to us." The net result of this neglect was the absence of chaplains in the brigade of black troops to which White was attached. White informed the *Christian Recorder* that "all the white regiments" were "provided with chaplains and we could have the same if our Bishops and leading men were actively engaged in bringing about such a result." "White friends" had asked, "Why don't some of your people come down here and take part in looking after the welfare of their own people?" To this question White "could not give the requisite answer." In order to meet the pressing needs that confronted him, White turned to Northern black youth. In the same letter in which he blamed the black leadership for its lack of interest in the fate of

Southern blacks, he made a special appeal to "our young people to come out to teach in the contraband regiments." This was not simple charity work, for "any one will pay a dollar a month" for such instruction.[17]

No black chaplain reported more extensively on the war than Henry M. Turner, 1st USCI. A regular correspondent for the *Christian Recorder,* he wrote extensively about his duties as the moral guardian and spiritual pastor of his men.[18] Chaplain Turner embarked on a number of initiatives to improve the moral health of his men. In August 1865, he reported that there were "several company schools in active operation, this employing the leisure hours of soldiers, who are off duty." Excellent educational progress was being made, for the men were learning "with flattering success." He had "never seen the fruits of" his "labor so visibly" since he had been appointed chaplain. Turner repeatedly lobbied the U.S. Army adjutant general for educational supplies, especially spelling books. As well as educating his soldiers, Turner took a keen interest in their spiritual needs. When military duties prevented him from holding church services, he distributed religious literature to the troops. Turner rejoiced when his men found God. On September 24, 1864, he reported to the *Christian Recorder* from Harrison's Landing, Virginia, that "during the entire night, mourners can be heard groaning and praying in every direction for God's saving grace and thank God, several have not mourned in vain." They had "found the Pearl of Great Price." As a minister, Turner saw God's hand at work in the regiment's affairs; light casualties in combat were "thanks to God's Providence." The incidental duties did not escape him; he visited the sick in the hospital, encouraged the fainthearted, and counseled the homesick.[19]

Turner did all he could to keep open the lines of communication between the soldiers and their home communities. Under the bold heading "Everybody Read This" in an issue of the *Christian Recorder,* he urged readers not to forget their men at the front. Nothing did more to lift morale than letters from home. He had "seen soldiers go from day to day, asking for letters, and on a continual answer in the negative, they would look so down hearted, that," he "would feel sorry for them in" his "heart." In contrast, "others, after long suspense, . . . get a letter, and it seemed to have illuminated their very souls with joy." Turner also worked hard at mending ties that kept families together. He blamed the government for indirectly causing family distress by failing to pay the soldiers equitably and on time. He wrote from Goldsboro, North Carolina, in May 1865 that "if our soldiers were paid regularly they would not grieve so often about their wives remarrying and claiming as an excuse that they were compelled by actual necessity." Turner rebuked "any cowardly civilian" who would undermine community moral standards by taking "advantage of a brave soldier's wife, on account of her poverty." Such an individual "ought to have his rotten tongue pulled out by the roots, his throat cut, his heart burned and his infamous carcass devoured by snakes."[20]

Chaplain Turner's accounts of his wartime experiences reassured the readers of the *Christian Recorder* of the benefits of military service. He depicted army life as an edifying experience, one that reinforced basic community values. With well-placed anecdotes, Turner was able to show that army life placed a premium on literacy. For example, in a letter written September 24, 1864, he narrated the amusing incident associated with the distribution of spelling books. When news of the books arrived, his quarters were invaded by hundreds of soldiers, shouting over one another's heads, "Chaplain, for pity's sake if you have a spelling-book, let me have one. No, says another, I am ahead of you."[21]

More than any other of his writings, however, Turner's battle reports reassured the readers that their sons were indeed heroes. Black soldiers were depicted as avenging the massacre of black troops by Maj. Gen. Nathan Bedford Forrest's men at Fort Pillow, Tennessee, in April 1864.[22] In his report of the 1st USCI's charge at Petersburg Heights in June 1864, he wrote: "The bayonets were fixed, and away went Uncle Sam's sable sons across an old field nearly three quarters of a mile wide, in the face of rebel grape and canister and the unbroken clatter of thousand of muskets. Nothing less than the pen of horror could begin to describe the terrific roar and dying yells of that awful and yet masterly charge and daring feat. . . . But onward they went through dust and every impediment, while they and the rebels were crying out 'Fort Pillow.' This seemed to be the battle cry on both sides. But onward they went, waxing stronger and mightier every time Fort Pillow was mentioned."[23]

Examples of individual heroism were cited to show that black troops were courageous fighters. Turner witnessed "one man whose arm was blown off" beg "another soldier to load his gun while he fired." This brave soldier was "only got off the field by persistent measures."[24]

Although he acknowledged that his soldiers were motivated by a desire for revenge, Turner counseled against the killing of Rebel prisoners: "let us disappoint our malicious anticipators, by showing the world that higher sentiments not only prevail, but actually predominate." However, he was not averse to inflicting some forms of revenge on haughty Rebels. "When the rich owners would use insulting language," Turner reported, "we let fire do its work of destruction." While recruiting in Smithville, North Carolina, in February 1865, Turner was insulted by Southern belles who blocked the sidewalk, "frowned," and "poked faces" at him. Two months later, however, he reported that in Raleigh, North Carolina, he had gained personal satisfaction from seeing white Southern ladies and "slave oligarchs" approaching him for government rations. "I know it was all fudge, but it satisfied me to see them crouching before me, and I am a negro." He pointed to the dawning of a new age in the South, an age when the black man would appear not as cringing slave but as noble victor. Liberated slaves welcomed the men of the 1st USCI as divine redeemers, with cries of "Yankees have come! Yankees have come!" and "'Are you the Yankees?" When Turner's men replied "in the affirmative, they would roll their white eyeballs up to heaven, and, in the most pathetic strain," say, "'Oh Jesus, you have answered my prayer at last! Thankee, Thankee, Jesus."[25]

Turner assured the readers that black soldiers could change the course of race relations. To prove this he pointed to the "brilliant achievements of our boys in front of Petersburg." This did "more to conquer the prejudice of the army of the Potomac than a thousand newspaper puffs." After the assault "white and colored soldiers talked, laughed," and ate "together with a friendly regard not surpassed by any previous occasion." Even the rebels now appeared to respect them as soldiers. In September 1864, Turner reported that upon visiting the Petersburg trenches he discovered, to "his great surprise, . . . rebels and the soldiers of my regiment, talking, laughing, exchanging papers, tin cups, tobacco &c." Some of the rebels "deserted and came to our lines, and cursed the rebellion, and thus they had a jolly time with our boys."[26]

Turner's depiction of black military service highlighted the "high ideals" such as a commitment to honor, duty, manhood, and courage that motivated many Civil War soldiers. Although the black soldiers shared these high ideals, in some important ways their motivation was different from that of white soldiers. They were driven by a strong desire to liberate and elevate the Southern slave and an equally strong desire to convert Billy Yank to new notions of racial equality and national citizenship.[27]

Chaplain Turner shared with the white officers in his regiment a desire to destroy slavery. This shared objective enabled him to act effectively as a link and conciliator between the officers and enlisted men. Like most of his fellow officers, he believed that slavery had degraded the Negro and robbed him of his manhood. As a chaplain, he believed it was his divine duty to rescue the Southern former slaves and restore them to true manhood by teaching them the gospel. In this regard, he greatly admired the work of black chaplain William H. Hunter, 4th USCI, who could "take a man from the very rubbish of slavery, and in a few hours infuse into him all the manhood and energy necessary for any purpose of life."[28]

Shortly before the war ended, Turner wrote to the secretary of war requesting that he be appointed colonel in charge of recruiting black soldiers. He gave as his sole motive his desire to serve his "country and to be so situated that" he could "inspire" his race "with those manly principles they are in many respects devoid of owing to their former condition."[29]

White officers had little to fear from the work of Chaplain Turner. From a religious perspective, his work reinforced the discipline and the command structure of the regiment. His regimental church was both hierarchical and well disciplined. The clandestine prayer meetings and emotionally charged religious services commonly found in regiments of liberated blacks were not a feature of the religious life of the 1st USCI. Indeed, Turner actually measured his religious progress by the degree of discipline and order evident in his church services. In August 1865, he informed the adjutant general of the U.S. Army, Gen. Lorenzo Thomas, that he was "proud to say" that the church in his regiment "has as much system and order about it as are generally found in civil life." He accordingly pronounced "the moral and religious condition" of his regiment in "an excellent condition."[30]

Henry Turner believed that his chaplaincy placed him in a spiritual continuum. He endeavored to run his regimental church in a manner that resembled the way he had governed his church in Washington, D.C. The soldiers, some of whom had been part of his Washington congregation, accepted his spiritual discipline because they acknowledged him as their spiritual leader. His preoccupation with order and discipline reflected his determination to maintain his spiritual preeminence and his desire to keep the regiment's religious life safely within the confines of military rules and regulations. Even so, the members of his military congregation sang their hymns with emotional enthusiasm. Although the regiment's church services reflected the salient spiritual values of Northern black community churches, they also contained elements of the slave's African heritage. Some members of Chaplain Turner's flock had had personal experience of slavery; this experience formed part of their religious background.[31]

Even though Chaplain Turner's ministry tended to reinforce the command structure of the regiment, tension did develop between him and fellow officers. While his beliefs and practices were similar to those of other abolitionist chaplains, the color of his skin prevented him and other black chaplains from being incorporated into the social environment of the officer class. Racial prejudice even surfaced among the officers of the 1st USCI. Although Turner praised the "noble example" set by his "most excellent colonel" in "always taking his position at the head of the Regiment during divine service," other officers were far less generous in their support. Chaplain Turner had to abandon the special services he held for the officers because of their insulting behavior. In a report published in the January 7, 1865, edition of the *Christian Recorder,* he explained: "The cause of my stopping the services which I was conducting was not, that I felt myself to be personally insulted, but because I considered their conduct very ungrateful to God." Probably the root cause of the officers' disrespectful behavior was their refusal to acknowledge the black chaplain as their social equal and spiritual adviser.[32]

Even though most officers refused to accept black chaplains as social equals, they generally recognized that they made a valuable contribution. Jeremiah Asher of the 6th USCI, John R. Bowles of the 55th Massachusetts Infantry, and Benjamin F. Randolph of the 26th USCI labored manfully to improve the spiritual welfare of the soldiers in their regiments; eradicate such social vices as gambling, swearing, and drunkenness; and increase the level of literacy of their flock. The white officers appreciated such work, because by improving the regiment's social health and alleviating suffering it greatly strengthened morale and military performance. Furthermore, the white officers knew that the black chaplains were uniquely placed to reinforce, through moral persuasion, the military discipline the officers sought to impose. Although not officially part of the command structures of the regiments, the black chaplains were vital in the maintenance of military order and control. The chaplains willingly accepted this role. Their leadership of well organized black churches in large Northern cities had taught them the value of order and discipline in religious affairs. Moreover, they realized that if they were to maintain their positions in the regiment, military order and discipline had to be maintained. Hence, in this sense, they identified with the officer class to which they officially belonged. Benjamin Randolph, 26th USCI, believed there was a strong positive correlation between the maintenance of strict military discipline and high moral standards. He advocated the use of physical punishment to this end. James Underdue, 39th USCI, had no doubt about the link between military bearing and faith in God. In his July 1864 chaplaincy report, he noted the men who trusted in God had confidence in their commanders. Chaplain Bowles, who endeavored to help the men cope with the injustices they faced, expressed a similar view. In June 1864, he reported that his regiment was near mutiny

Chaplain John R. Bowles, 55th Massachusetts Infantry. MOLLUS Massachusetts Collection, USAMHI.

because of the government's refusal to pay black soldiers at the same rate as white soldiers. In an act of defiance, the black soldiers had stood by their moral principles and refused to accept any pay at the lower rate. In these difficult circumstances, Chaplain Bowles "labored incessantly to prevent so dreadful a calamity" as an outright mutiny. Fortunately, none occurred; "so far God has blessed my labor."[33]

Yet there were limits to the chaplains' influence. When soldiers took a firm stand on matters of principle, not even a chaplain could move them. Approximately nine months earlier, Samuel Harrison had also grappled with the problem of pay inequity. He "tried to persuade" the men to accept the lower rate of pay "on account of their families." However, his efforts at persuasion proved ineffective, because the men were "of a different metal." Since they were indignant, Harrison "desisted" and "promised to lay the matter before the Governor."[34]

Officers harshly condemned chaplains who neglected the welfare of their men. Assistant Surgeon Lewis Whitaker, 26th USCI, thought very little of Chaplain Benjamin F. Randolph. While admitting that it was a "hard matter to find a black man smart enough and every way qualified to be a chaplain," Whitaker complained that Randolph's "greatest fault" was "laziness and self conceit." Apparently he was "too proud to do many of the little things which as a chaplain he might do for the comfort of the men."[35]

William Jackson was harshly criticized for failing to gain the confidence of his men. Jackson had been appointed to the position of post chaplain at Readville, the rendezvous and training camp of the Massachusetts black regiments, but Col. Robert G. Shaw opposed Jackson's appointment to the chaplaincy of his 54th Massachusetts Volunteers, a regiment that included a number of educated soldiers in its ranks. In a letter to Governor Andrew, Colonel Shaw argued that while he wanted a black chaplain for his regiment, William Jackson would not be acceptable, because he was "an ignorant man, and one who does not gain much influence over the soldiers." Other officers in the regiment also opposed his appointment. Andrew apparently complied with Shaw's request, and the 54th Massachusetts sailed for South Carolina without a chaplain.[36]

Criticism of William Jackson persisted after he was appointed to the 55th Massachusetts Infantry. Complaining about Jackson's ignorance in a letter to his wife, Lt. Col. Charles Fox commented that he "did us more harm than good." Fox believe that "a colored man in order to be respected by the men of his own race, of limited education, must show his superiority over them very plainly." A few months after Jackson's departure, Fox welcomed his

Chaplain Samuel Harrison, 54th Massachusetts Infantry. MOLLUS Massachusetts Collection, USAMHI.

successor, John Bowles, as a man "very much superior to Mr. Jackson." Bowles possessed a "good degree of education," "good natural ability," and had "the respect of the men."[37]

While some black chaplains, such as William Jackson, were criticized for ignorance and lack of respect, others created "problems" by rebuking the dissolute behavior of the white officers. Jeremiah Asher and Benjamin

Randolph harshly criticized the officers in their regiments for destroying the moral tone of their units. In their chaplaincy reports, they complained strongly that the officers who played cards, swore, or desecrated the Sabbath by ordering the men to do fatigue duty were attacking the work being done by God's servants. Similar accusations are found in reports made by some white chaplains. However, when black chaplains made these accusations, they tended to reinforce racial barriers and place themselves even more firmly within the social orbit of the enlisted men.[38]

Initially paid at lower rates, sometimes subjected to personal abuse but more often forced to endure subtle discrimination by fellow officers, most black chaplains became social outcasts. Their recruiting activities were accepted, but they were not always welcomed personally as part of the officer corps. For example, Chaplain Francis A. Boyd, 109th USCI, lost his position because his colonel, Orion A. Bartholomew, objected that his appointment had not been voted upon by the officers in the regiment. Chaplain Boyd unsuccessfully presented his case in letters to Lincoln, arguing that his "only dishonor was the color of his skin" and that Colonel Bartholomew had endeavored to degrade him "on account of prejudice alone." Chaplain George Le Vere was initially excluded from the New York Union League Club's celebrations marking the organization of his regiment, even though he had been one of the main recruiting agents; only prompt action by Vincent Colyer, the chief recruiting officer, secured him entry. Even in regiments such as the 1st USCI, with significant numbers of abolitionist officers, black chaplains faced discrimination. In some ways, the social environment that evolved in Northern black regiments reflected the basic social fabric of Northern society. In the North, Negroes were excluded from political office, confined to the lowest socioeconomic strata, and restricted to certain residential areas by poverty and racial discrimination. In the Northern black regiments, similar forces of discrimination were at work. Yet these forces did not prevent the chaplains from defending the rights of the black soldiers.[39]

The extent to which black chaplains could stand between the officers and the enlisted men depended ultimately upon their personal character. The most successful chaplains were those who had sufficient personal magnetism to gain respect from both officers and enlisted men. Like influential slave preachers, they had to walk a social tightrope between the dominant whites and their own black brethren. If the black chaplains lost the respect of either or both parties, their influence declined. This appears to have been the fate of Chaplain Jackson.[40]

On July 29, 1864, Chaplain James Underdue added cryptically to his monthly report, "Every idle moment is employed either by religious or moral lectures, or in social meetings, the men profess unshaken faith in God, and confidence in their commanders." Then he added, "the Colonel has cheerfully led in this part of the work, so we feel 'it is good to be here.'" The phrase "it is good to be here" had resonance in all those USCI regiments with black chaplains as their spiritual leaders. By their efforts, these men made a significant contribution to black soldiers' war effort. Certainly Chaplain William H. Hunter, 4th USCI, could say "it is good to be here" when he visited the Front Street Methodist Church one week after the fall of Wilmington, North Carolina. In an act of symbolic appropriation, Hunter, a former North Carolina slave, brushed aside the vain protests of the church's white minister, the Rev. L. S. Burkhead, made his way to the pulpit, and addressed a predominantly black congregation of 1,600 freedmen.[41] As he preached, the freedmen loudly shouted their approval. "A few short years ago I left North Carolina as a slave. [Hallelujah, oh, yes.] I now return a man. [Amen] I have the honor to be a regular minister of the Gospel in the Methodist Episcopal Church of the United States [Glory to God, Amen] and also a regularly commissioned chaplain in the American Army.[Amen] . . . One week ago you were all slaves; now you are all free. [Uproarious screamings] Thank God the armies of the Lord and of Gideon has triumphed and the Rebels have been driven back in confusion and scattered like chaff before the wind.[Amen! Hallelujah!]"[42]

For Chaplain Hunter and other black chaplains serving in "the armies of the Lord," the Civil War was a holy struggle against slavery. Their presence in the Union army linked Southern and Northern black communities in this struggle for freedom. The congregation of Front Street Methodist Church knew this and so did Chaplain Hunter's home community in the North.

CHAPTER SIX

"God Have Mercy!"

THE RELIGION OF THE FORMER SLAVE

What do you think I saw? In one very large gathering, they were singing and shouting very earnestly, and almost dancing as they sang. I saw there was something of special interest going on, and stood outside. Soon, I saw in the midst a man lying on a litter, and apparently in great mental agony, crying out "God have mercy! God have mercy!" There were three men singing and chanting and praying around this man exorcising him, bringing him through. What do you say to that?

—Chaplain James Schneider

While stationed at Vicksburg in the summer of 1864, Lt. Col. Byron Cutcheon, 27th Michigan Volunteers, observed a division of black soldiers attached to his corps laboring on fortifications. The workers were genuine "down south negroes" who had fled to the safety of Union lines "chiefly in Virginia and North Carolina." Attracted by the "usual good nature and light heartedness of the negro," he witnessed the soldiers calling upon their cultural heritage to ease the pain of labor. The air was filled with "plantation melodies," and these vocal echoes of a past life sustained the soldiers' spirits. Yet what most strongly captivated his interest was not the steady vocal rhythm of the work party but the "emotional tendencies" of the soldiers' religious practices. Soldiers not laboring on the fortifications held regular religious meetings "similar to the down south camp meetings." Preachers moved among their flock, and as they walked they "preached and exhorted and sang with a sort of wild abandon." Winds of spiritual power that had once blown across the plantations now swept through the army camps and renewed the soldiers' spirits. Cutcheon observed soldiers becoming "vividly excited" and some even "get the power." Many became so overwhelmed by feelings of religious ecstasy that they were carried away by comrades "as if dead." On one balmy moonlit night, he counted as many as a dozen soldiers "laid out comatose on the grass." He had "not seen anything like it before"; it was an "interesting phenomena" that could not be easily forgotten.[1]

For many Civil War soldiers, military service was a testing trial, a journey of faith. The extensive religious revivals among the Confederate troops and the religious meetings held in Union camps all bear testimony to the significant role religion played in the soldiers' lives. Religious practices were also an important part of the black soldiers' military experience, just as they had been on the plantation. Byron Cutcheon knew this. He had heard the plantation melodies and had seen the preachers working among the men. He knew religious ritual was a vital vehicle for survival. However, what he did not know and could not experience was the complex interplay of religious conflict and accommodation that was occurring in the army camps.[2]

In the camps, religion acted as an agent of group unity and social cohesion. There, as on many plantations, two churches existed. One was the official, biracial, orderly, well disciplined institutional church under the leadership of the chaplain; it was most visible during the Sabbath church services. The other church was the soldiers' church, which met clandestinely late at night, often under the leadership of preachers who had been slaves themselves. Although this church had many of the features of the slaves' former plantation church, it had its own unique form and function. It was a composite body, made up of a number of eclectic fellowship groups. The soldiers who joined these groups sought to share their faith and adapt their religious experiences to a new age of freedom. Although significantly different, both the chaplain's church and the soldiers' church provided opportunities for the soldiers to reshape their religious experiences.[3]

The religious conflict that developed in the camps was not merely institutional; it went much deeper than that. In essence, every black soldier experienced his own "inner civil war." He was torn between a desire to identify with the Union army, with its badges of rank and church services, and a burning desire to break free, to cast aside the white man's church. This struggle between identification and liberation was ever present in the camp; conflict raged in a variety of circumstances in the fatigue detail, at band practice, and drill. However, the conflict was most clearly visible in religious activities. Yet elements of secrecy and mystery remained. It is these elements that make the study of religious affairs of the black regiments so intractably difficult. The largely illiterate ex-slave soldiers left few written records of their religious rites and doctrines. Nor did they have any desire to explain their sacred affairs to the white officers. The mystery surrounding their faith, its freedom from white domination and direction, gave it authority and deep spiritual meaning. In order to discover the spirituality of the black soldier, one has to examine the reports of the officers, especially the chaplains, which often represent religious developments in the camps simplistically as a struggle between good and evil.

Yet religious life in the camps cannot be viewed purely as a clash between staid Yankee orthodoxy and emotional ex-slave fanaticism. In some camps, the religious picture was complicated by the presence of Northern black soldiers and chaplains. These black troops brought their own religious heritage to the army camps, a heritage that was different from those of the Yankee officers and of the ex-slave soldiers. It contained elements of both but owed allegiance to neither.[4]

Embedded in the rich diversity of the soldiers' religious lives were important elements of compromise and cooperation. Some soldiers became active participants in the chaplain's church, just as they had been actively involved in the biracial plantation churches that had white ministers and racially mixed congregations. Research by John Boles suggests that in the biracial churches on the plantations, the slaves were able to develop their leadership skills and indirectly make claims for equality and freedom. In the regimental churches, these claims were made with even more intensity, as the soldiers began to explore separate forms of religious worship. In some ways, the army heralded religious developments that were to occur in the liberated South. At the end of the war, Southern blacks would begin to withdraw from the white-dominated biracial churches and establish congregations of their own.[5]

Although the religious struggle that surfaced in the Union army shared many of the features of the earlier conflict on the plantation, in some significant ways it was decidedly different. The army chaplain was not "old massa's" minister in a different guise. The enlisted men knew this, and this knowledge enabled them to make compromises and adjustments that would never have been sustained on the plantation. The Yankee chaplains were comrades in arms; they too were waging war against slavery and for the Union. This commonality of purpose enabled the former slaves to express their religious feelings in new, vibrant ways. The soldiers' church became more audible and more visible as the confidence of the soldiers grew. This surge of religious confidence and enthusiasm challenged the authority of the camp chaplains, but ex-slave preachers and their flock never sought to destroy the regimental church. It had its place, on the parade ground. They simply wanted the right to shape their own spiritual lives according to their own religious beliefs. The geographic center of their spiritual activity was not the parade ground but the soldier's tent. In the crusade for freedom, religious experiences could be shared even if white hegemony had to be resisted.

Even though the officers were aware of the presence of the soldiers' church in their camps, they had very little understanding of its function or role. Many officers attributed the ecstatic displays of religious devotion and superstitious ritual to the legacy of slavery and the black's emotional instability. Lt. Thomas Montgomery had no doubt about the latter. Stationed at Morganzia in August 1864, he noticed that the soldiers "nerves" were "easily worked up" to the point that they became oblivious to the vows they had made and "the professions they uttered." In a state of religious ecstasy, they sang "Old Ship Zion" with "fervor, zeal, shaking of hands, jumping and happiness." Another officer experienced a similar display of religious exuberance at a baptism service at Vicksburg. There, he observed the congregation behaving like "crazy persons."[6] "It is good as a play to watch them" at worship, commented Lt. Col. John Bogert, in a letter to his parents. However, these disparaging attitudes were not universally held. After Col. Thomas Higginson heard his soldiers singing spirituals, he commented, "The songs were to the men more than a source of relaxation; they were a stimulus to courage and a tie to heaven." Devout abolitionist Col. James C. Beecher wrote home to his wife stating he had "never preached to so appreciative audience." When U.S. Christian Commission delegate Rev. William Fulton, visited black soldiers encamped at Hampton, Virginia, he was "particularly impressed with the religious morality." While visiting on "the Lord's day," he observed "quietitude, discipline and moral order." During his visit, he heard only one oath uttered "and that oath was sworn in a tent adjoining the first section by a white soldier—an Irish Catholic!"[7]

Most army chaplains believed they had a divine duty to undo the work of the slaveholder. In their official monthly reports to the U.S. adjutant general's office, they repeatedly stated that their vocations extended far beyond the narrow confines of military affairs. Therefore, in their effort to make the soldiers orthodox Christians and respectable citizens, they waged a holy crusade against the "barbaric" superstitions of slavery and the "heresy" of slaveholders' gospel. Chaplain Philander Read was confident that the ex-slave soldiers were amenable to Christian teaching and preaching. In his October 1865 chaplaincy report, he commented that "after the dark cloud of superstition is broken from over their minds," they were the "most teachable men that I ever saw." A fellow chaplain believed that in order to prevent the men falling back upon the evil habits of slavery, they had to be "furnished with the gospel and education."[8]

The alleged moral decadence of the ex-slave soldier disturbed many chaplains. "The men among whom I labor," commented Owen Riedy, "having been brought up under an evil and unjust system of slavery, possess a very limited sense of right and wrong, of duty and honor." Their "immoral and sinful habits" had "grown on them" and become "as it were a second nature." Like most chaplains, Owen Riedy believed that religious conversion and moral reform were part of one spiritual process. Progress in one area would inevitably lead to progress in the other. Therefore, once a former slave became an orthodox Christian, he was expected to espouse middle-class social values of sobriety and self-reliance. Another chaplain observed that his soldiers had a notable "want of respect for one another" and a "want of manly bearing." Nevertheless, he confidently predicted that once they had been exposed to the Christian gospel, they could be "taught self respect and self reliance."[9]

Chaplains committed to religious reform devised a number of strategies to advance the soldiers' spiritual welfare and to cope with the influence of the soldiers' church in their camps.

The first and most important strategy employed was to ensure that the regimental church services were regular, well attended, and, above all, orderly and dignified. In their efforts to root out the evil religious practices of slavery, the chaplains sought to make regimental church worship the antithesis of the emotionally charged slave meeting. The Sabbath service, therefore, became an important vehicle for religious conversion and moral indoctrination. Given this intense devotion to propagating a "pure" form of Christian worship, it is not surprising to find that the chaplains vehemently denounced officers who failed to enforce Sabbath observance. In Chaplain Thomas Johnson's judgment, the "loss of the humanizing elevating influence of the Christian Sabbath" contributed greatly to the demoralization of the regiment. In his July 1864 chaplaincy report, James Peet lamented that in "army life, the Fourth Commandment of the Decalogue appears practically to be nul[l] and void." While admitting that military necessity sometimes forced soldiers to perform duties, he claimed that, in his opinion, "Sunday work might be avoided."[10]

Devout chaplains even condemned officers who weakened Sabbath church attendance by giving their soldiers holidays or furloughs or by allowing them to attend religious services in neighboring towns. Brig. Gen. Morgan Smith became a target of criticism for allowing his black troops holidays at Christmas. Chaplain Thomas Calahan believed this decision was "most injurious," because "it revived their plantation habits, from which it is desirable to wean them as soon as possible."[11]

A second strategy commonly employed by many chaplains was to wage a moral crusade against specific sins. The catalogue of offenses listed in the chaplaincy reports included profanity, gambling, theft, drunkenness, and sexual immorality. Of course, these sins were not peculiar to ex-slave soldiers. The chaplains recognized this fact but argued that slavery had so degraded the black that he was particularly susceptible to these moral vices. Profanity was considered a serious vice not only because it was blasphemous but also because it was a verbal demonstration of the black soldier's emotional instability, his lack of self-control and of self-respect. These were the very moral values the chaplains were trying to inculcate. Similarly, gambling, drunkenness, theft, and sexual immorality were condemned because they broke scriptural injunctions and led to moral degradation.[12]

Chaplains carried out their moral crusade in a number of different ways. Some, for example, Chaplain Charles Buckley, established special prayer meetings for their soldiers. These prayer meetings were used as informal vehicles for religious and moral indoctrination. Other chaplains sought to propagate the gospel by employing the talents of small bands of devout converts. These converts were not difficult to find; many soldiers shared some of the moral values of the chaplains. In this sense, they were not "converts" at all. In the biracial churches of the South, they had sought to curb the evils of drunkenness, profanity, and stealing. Now in the army, they continued to campaign against these social vices. George A. Rockwood rejoiced in the fact that in his camp "a few men have given up their wicked ways and are trying to live better lives." He believed that the small "band of Christians in the regiment" had stood up "nobly against all wickedness" and shown that "the gospel is no hindrance, but a great help in making good soldiers." Chaplains like Rockwood hoped that their recent converts would work among their fellow soldiers as evangelists and role models. In addition, they called upon their fellow officers to assist them with their work. Abolitionist officers generally responded enthusiastically to this call. This was particularly true of a number of camp commanders who had themselves served as ministers of religion or army chaplains. Included in this category were Colonels Thomas Higginson, James Beecher, and John Eaton.[13]

The chaplains expected their fellow officers to be models of Christian virtue who would imprint their noble attributes on the minds of their men. "If the influence of officers, both by precept and example were always on the right side," exclaimed Chaplain Rockwood, "I should have no doubt, but that the good effects desired would follow." The chaplains also sought assistance from Northern charities. The U.S. Christian Commission, for example, provided many chaplains with religious literature, which they distributed among their men. However, the alliance with these civilian allies was somewhat precarious. When the charity workers encroached on the work of the chaplains and sought to win proselytes of their own, conflict ensued.[14]

Finally, the chaplains sought to raise the moral life in their camps by ensuring that the officers maintained strict codes of military discipline. They called upon commanders to actively enforce prohibitions against gambling, drunkenness, stealing, and sexual immorality. Moreover, they were quick to point out the close correlation that existed between moral reform and the maintenance of good military order. They reminded the officers that the honest, thrifty, sober soldier was much more amenable to discipline than the debauched thief. Chaplain Thomas Calahan praised the strict disciplinarians, believing they were creating a social environment that was very conducive for moral reform. Their strict military routine "exposed . . . sneaks" and "brought out in stronger relief the good qualities of others."[15]

In the course of attempting to convert their soldiers to orthodox Christianity, the chaplains often came into conflict with the soldiers' church. In some camps, a spiritual power struggle took place as the chaplains and preachers grappled for the souls of the soldiers. This conflict contained some of the dynamic elements of the conflict that had raged between slaveholders' ministers and the religious leaders of slave communities.[16]

No two spiritual battles were the same. However, the dynamic complexity of the religious conflicts that occurred in some camps may be analyzed by examining the spiritual warfare in the 2d USCI.

Three months after he was appointed chaplain to the 2d USCI, a regiment of former slaves from Maryland, James Schneider found his ministry seriously challenged by the activities of the soldiers' church. In his routine religious duties, Chaplain Schneider attended a religious meeting organized by the men of his regiment. What he saw at this meeting thoroughly disturbed him. "They were singing and shouting very earnestly, almost dancing as they sang." Intrigued that "something of special interest [was] going on," Chaplain Schneider "stood outside" and watched. Soon he "saw in the midst a man lying on a litter." Writhing in "mental agony" the man cried out, "God have mercy! God have mercy!" In an effort to aid the deranged sufferer, "three men [were] singing and chanting and praying, . . . exorcising him, bringing him through." Concluded Schneider in amazement, "What do you say to that?" [17]

Chaplain Schneider believed that "ninety percent of the religious zeal" exhibited at the meeting was "nervous or magnetic excitement." He took no part in the meeting but simply asked Christians present "to pray still more for that man" who had been subject to exorcism. This extraordinary religious service and his routine chaplain's rounds convinced him that the men were "very much attached to these peculiarities of worship." He considered such religious practices as very "injurious"; they threatened his regimental church and military discipline, and he resolved to "use management to eradicate them." [18]

A few days after witnessing the emotionally charged religious meeting, Chaplain Schneider discovered to his dismay that official "statistics" indicated "that not much more than a hundred of nine hundred of the men were Christians, while a little more than half the officers" were Christians. A recent murder committed in the camp appeared to confirm his belief that evil forces gripped his men. In a determined effort to reform the former slaves' religious practices, he decided to preach incessantly on salvation; "Believe in the Lord Jesus Christ" was his text. Within two weeks he had developed a strategy for implementing religious reform. Rather than seek a confrontation, he "called together the Christians of the regiment, to talk with them about matters of religious interest in the regiment." At this meeting he outlined his strategy for reform. He gave his men "suggestions as to the manner of conducting meetings." He admitted that he was "not accustomed to their method of conducting meetings," but he asked them not to "infer that he thought them wrong or inexpedient." Having somewhat allayed their fears, he decided to offer his soldiers a pattern of orthodox worship that could serve as a subsequent model of behavior. However, he had no intention of imposing, on his men, a straightjacket of religious orthodoxy. "I will read the Bible and explain it, and start them with new thoughts," he earnestly claimed; "then they can carry themselves to such a pitch of excitement as they chose." [19]

Chaplain Schneider was forced, by circumstances, to adopt an educational approach to religious reform; no other strategy appeared practical. It would have been impossible for him to eliminate the "peculiarities of wor-ship," because the soldiers' church conducted its worship services in an informal, clandestine way, during off-duty hours. Moreover, these religious customs were supported by a strong tradition of hiding sacred folklore from whites. Unlike most chaplains, James Schneider refused to admit openly that the former slaves' practices were "wrong or inexpedient," for to have done so would have driven the soldiers' church farther underground and thus further outside his sphere of influence. By taking the unusual step of overtly "accepting" the former slaves' religious practices, he was able to act as a religious guide and subsequently lead the soldiers in a new spiritual direction. He realized that his powers of persuasion were limited. He could point his men to new religious horizons, but he could not compel them to follow him. In fact, his impact on the soldiers' church was probably mini-mal. Soldier preachers who had themselves been slaves retained their power and continued to exercise spiritual control over their congregations.[20]

The emotionally charged religious meetings of the soldiers continued in spite of the efforts chaplains made to reform them. Officers were amazed at the spiritual enthusiasm of their troops. Lt. Lawrence Van Alstyne com-plained the nightly prayer meetings soldiers held in his camp were so noisy and disturbing that he was surprised "how they get along with so little sleep." Other officers experienced similar unease from the former slaves' religious practices. Sometimes, the officers took decisive action to dampen the reli-gious enthusiasm of the devout participants. In March 1866, an anonymous Louisiana black soldier wrote to the secretary of war complaining that his officers treated black soldiers cruelly: "They even don't like to hear any meeting."[21]

Officers found their authority challenged and tested by not only the worship of the soldiers' church but also by powerful religious rituals. Some-times the officers' perception of the behavior of the participants in the cer-emonies masked the deep spiritual significance of ritual. Capt. Joseph Scroggs and Lt. Benjamin Mills scoffed at the "amusing antics" of partici-pants in baptismal ceremonies. However, the "comedy" of the ceremony prevented them from understanding that ritual marked the participant's transition from a state of their unbelief into membership of the church. The baptismal ritual was therefore a rite of passage that cushioned the tran-sition process. Moreover, it linked the soldiers to their heritage. Although the environment had changed, with the camp replacing the slave planta-tion, many features of the ritual remained.[22]

Cultural continuity was also evident in the prayer rituals of the soldiers' church. White observers who witnessed them often commented condescendingly on their "childish simplicity." Nevertheless, the officers invariably commented that the prayers were delivered with considerable devotion. Furthermore, the white observers were often deeply moved by the common themes of the soldiers' prayers—the plight of their loved ones in slavery, the destruction of slavery, safety in battle, and freedom from sin.[23]

The devout members for the church were empowered by the prayers they uttered. In times of despair, they could appeal to their heavenly father to protect them from illness and injury, safeguard them in battle, deliver their loved ones still in bondage, and destroy the Confederacy. Prayer was a liberating experience. Yet it was more than this; it was also a vehicle for identification. The soldiers used prayer to ease their transition into the military service and to cement bonds of loyalty with their white officers. They prayed about problems associated with the army, and, in this way, they gave their military service a spiritual dimension.

Moreover, when the soldiers prayed about military affairs it was often for their white comrades. They were convinced that all who served in the black regiments served in Jesus' army. The white officers, serving under the same banner, deserved the prayerful support of their black brethren. Such support deeply affected those few officers who managed to observe the soldiers at prayer. In some cases, this experience greatly strengthened the bond between the soldiers and the officers. Surgeon Seth Rogers witnessed a soldiers' prayer meeting at Camp Saxton, Beaufort, South Carolina. He was "sure the President is remembered more faithfully and gratefully in prayer by these Christian soldiers than by any other regiment in the army." Moreover, he observed, "These men never forgot to pray earnestly for the officers placed over them"; he added as an afterthought, "such praying ought to make us true to them."[24]

Few religious rituals emphasize cultural continuity more than the burying of the dead. Nevertheless, upon entering military service, former slaves appear to have willingly adopted new burial practices. The soldiers demanded that they be buried with military honors, and the officers generally acceded to these requests. The funeral service united the white officers and the black soldiers. In burying a soldier with military honors, the officers and soldiers openly acknowledged the significant change that had occurred in the onetime slave's status. Abolitionists were more aware of this change than most officers.

In a letter to his sister Mela, Col. Samuel Armstrong described in reflective detail the funeral of an enlisted man. In particular, he noted, "It was a strange thing to see a man who had been born a slave and lived the life of a slave, under the lash like a dog, carried to the grave with the Stars and Stripes shrouding his coffin." All the trappings of military ceremonies were present. The funeral procession was led "by a brass band playing a funeral dirge, escorted with a body of soldiers with arms reversed and followed by a procession of comrades in the uniform of U.S. soldiers, under charge of three commissioned officers of the Army." Samuel Armstrong believed that this particular military ritual encapsulated the very essence of the struggle that divided the nation. Indeed, he asserted, "We are fighting for humanity and freedom, the South for barbarism and slavery." He reminded his sister that he was describing "the burial of a private soldier, the humblest man in the army and the funeral of a negro." Upon further reflection, he added a poignant comment: had it "not been for the freedom we gave him," he "might have been beaten to death and tumbled into a pit." The funeral was, according to Armstrong, not a testament to the heroic sacrifice of a black soldier who had died fighting to preserve his liberty but a grand witness to the liberating power of white abolitionists.

Armstrong's experience at the graveside suggests that religious ceremonies and rituals were not always spheres of conflict and struggle. Regardless of the meaning officers such as Colonel Armstrong attached to the funeral service, the soldiers became willing participants in this military ritual. For members of the soldiers' church, the blue uniform became a most acceptable shroud.[25]

Sometimes the officers' authority in the army camp was challenged by the soldiers' belief in powerful supernatural forces. Many soldiers believed that they could use magic and conjuring to bring order to, and control over, the forces of the natural world. It was their way of manipulating their destinies. To officers committed to institutionalized Christianity and serving in an army that was marching in step with an increasingly modern, industrialized society, the soldiers' belief in the supernatural seemed primitive, offensive, and at times exceedingly dangerous. This was particularly the case when the soldiers' beliefs manifested themselves with such force and authority that military discipline disintegrated.

The soldiers' beliefs in malign spirits and the power of the conjurer, ghosts, and the snake god were survivals from a slave culture that had its origin in African religious traditions. Essentially, their religious life was an amalgam of beliefs and religious customs acquired from the official regimental church and those inherited from slave traditions. However, the relationship between acquired beliefs and inherited traditions was not static. At particular times, one of the two elements of the religious equation could dominate. Sometimes when the soldier was subject to trauma, he drew comfort and support from his traditional belief system. When this happened, officers often felt powerless. Ignorant of, and generally hostile to, the "spirit world," the officers had great difficulty devising strategies that would discipline the soldiers' apparently irrational behavior. This difficulty was compounded by the fact that no officer could predict when an outbreak of superstitious behavior would occur.[26]

After Lt. Freeman Bowley joined the 30th USCI in July 1864, he attempted to elevate the former slave by freeing him from his "evil" servile habits. However, his attempts to "civilize" his black soldiers were frustrated; "old superstitions still clung to them." Personal experience had convinced him that these superstitions were a major source of the "difficulties that their white officers had to contend with."

On one occasion, his company was forced to conduct a night march in the vicinity of Petersburg, Virginia. During the march the soldiers thought they saw light following them. Confusion followed this observation, and "it was with difficulty that a general stampede was prevented, so great was the fear among most of the men." Ironically, only a few hours previously his men had "stood their ground bravely against rebel cavalry and bushwhackers"; now they were "ready to fly before an imaginary 'spook.'" To restore order in his company, Bowley was forced to employ tactics that resembled those of a slave conjurer. He told them that "if they scattered, Jack-o-lantern would catch them separately"; if they "kept together, he would not dare to trouble them." His appeal to religious heritage rather than military law proved effective; "an immediate huddling was the result." Yet lacking the mystical authority of the conjurer, he was unable to persuade his men to resume their march. Finally, he admitted defeat and pitched camp, realizing that he had "no alternative but to wait till daylight."[27]

On another occasion, Lieutenant Bowley observed belief in ghosts so strong that it appeared to scatter a whole division of black troops. When a pack mule laden with pans and kettles and flapping pieces of a "shelter tent" stumbled into the lines of the Fourth Division, Ninth Corps, many of the black soldiers fled. Chaos reigned; the officers "were calling and yelling to their men, but none responded." It was over an hour before all the men returned to the line. Once the soldiers realized the true nature of the "ghostly apparition" attacking their lines, they "were much ashamed." In order to prevent further panic, orders were issued to the officers to "shoot down the first man who left the line under such circumstances." Several weeks later, a number of "incipient panics" occurred, but these were soon checked by the officers and the "resolute example of many of the men themselves."[28]

Fear of the awesome power of ghosts and "evil spirits" was one of the most pernicious and persistent religious beliefs that pervaded the black soldiers' camps. The soldiers tended to succumb to this fear when they felt most alone, that is, while doing picket and guard duty. It was then, isolated from the support of their comrades and away from the direct surveillance of their officers, that they were most vulnerable to spiritual attack. Capt. Henry Freeman reported that on many occasions his soldiers, former slaves from Tennessee, while on a picket line that transected a Confederate army graveyard near the Elk River, "saved" the regiment by firing upon advancing lines of rebel "ghosts." Another officer witnessed similar displays of spiritual warfare among black soldiers doing picket duty in the vicinity of Port Hudson, Louisiana.[29]

Lieutenant Van Alstyne had to contend with demonic forces much more visible but no less powerful than those that attacked Elk River and Port Hudson. A fatigue detail digging a ditch around a fort in Louisiana discovered a large snake. Immediately, all the soldiers disobeyed orders and left the detail. The soldiers called the snake a "Congo snake and seemed to have a superstitious dread of it." Their belief in the power of the snake god proved so strong that Van Alstyne was unable to get them back to work. The impasse was finally resolved when he killed the snake and "threw it out of sight. Only then did the soldiers obey the order to return to duty."[30]

Attacks by jack-o'-lantern, ghosts, and Congo snakes were frightening experiences. However, occasionally, serious confrontations between officers and men occurred even over allegedly trivial incidents. For example, when Lieutenant Colonel Viall enforced normal army regulations and commanded a soldier of "Moorish descent" to cut his mass of "coarse black hair," the soldier objected, explaining that it would violate his religious beliefs. The colonel waived aside this objection and had the soldier pinned to the ground and his hair forcibly cut. His locks shorn, the outraged soldier violently attacked an officer.[31]

In many ways, disputes involving the soldiers' hair encapsulated a deeper and more general struggle that was occurring in the army camps. Hair length and hair style were expressions of not only the soldiers' religious beliefs but their individuality and personality. Officers who cruelly sought to impose their will and cultural values on the enlisted men serving under them provoked feelings of resentment, physical resistance, and, above all, religious intransigence. Supernatural forces, ghosts, and spirits moved most freely in camps that most closely resembled slave plantations.

Regional variation, together with differences in prewar family background, led to different strains of religious development. Col. Thomas Higginson noted significant differences between his regiment of South Carolina former slaves, the 1st South Carolina Colored Volunteers, and the 9th U.S. Colored Infantry, which was composed of former slaves from Maryland. The Maryland soldiers had "different songs & ways," and "their type of religious enthusiasm" appeared to be different. Yet the Maryland regiment was not one single, uniform congregation. Colonel Higginson perceived that it was divided into two broad religious divisions, "the Holy Jumpers & the Holy Rollers."[32]

Some regiments that had been organized in the North contained both free blacks and ex-slaves. In these regiments, some Northern blacks considered themselves superior to their ex-slave comrades. Indeed, in common with the abolitionist officers, many of these free Northern blacks felt they had a divine duty to civilize the supposedly degraded slave. When these "enlightened" Northern black soldiers embarked on their civilizing missions, they came into conflict with not only the white officers but also the former slaves, who resented being treated in a condescending manner. Lieutenant Bowley observed friction developing in his company when an "enlightened" noncommissioned officer tried to eradicate the "old superstitions" of the soldiers. A dispute occurred between "Joe Wright, a big, jet-black man," and Sergeant Scott, "a bright intelligent mulatto." Sergeant Scott vainly tried to convince Joe Wright that it was nonsensical to believe in the existence of "Ole Stonewall Jackson's ghos" (the famous Gen. Thomas J. Jackson had been accidentally killed by his own forces in May 1863). Joe had learned of the ghost's existence from "de culled [colored] ladies at de big plantation," and no amount of rational argument by Sergeant Scott or Lieutenant Bowley could shake his belief.[33]

Although most officers were interested in the soldiers' religious beliefs only in so far as they affected military performance, chaplains had a higher calling. They were determined to maintain religious order in the regiment. In pursuit of this objective, they devised strategies that accommodated the soldiers' traditional belief systems. Sometimes this meant giving the ex-slave preachers significant roles in the regiment's church service. The preachers were often asked to lead camps in prayer, and, occasionally, they were permitted to deliver sermons.[34]

Col. Thomas Higginson was not averse to employing loyal black preachers to help him maintain order in church. When the regiment's chaplain was absent, he called upon Cpl. Thomas Long to conduct religious services. Before a battle was to take place, Higginson often called upon an ex-slave preacher to address the troops. His soldiers from South Carolina believed that they formed part of "a religious army," "a gospel army," and Colonel Higginson used this religious allegiance to motivate his men when they faced battle. He observed that those soldiers in his regiment who had a blind faith in God were the most courageous fighters. "Those most reckless and daring fellows" in his regiment "were perfect fatalists in their confidence that God would watch over them, and that if they died, it would be because their time had come."[35]

Chaplain Thomas Calahan believed that his soldiers should be allowed to reform their religious practices in a way that was relevant to their cultural heritage. He thought it was his duty to remove the emotional excesses of plantation religion and to open the black soldiers' eyes to the basic fundamentals of the Christian faith; however, it was the soldiers' duty to take these truths and reinterpret them so as to give them meaning and relevance. "My business is primarily to teach them to read the word of God for themselves," wrote Chaplain Calahan, "and leave them to choose their sectarian ecclesiastical connections as they deem best." He recognized the authority of the ex-slave preachers and allowed them "to conduct that part of their religious services in their own way," provided that they were orderly and all major points of dispute were referred to him for judgment.[36]

The leaders of the soldiers' church acted as mediators. On one hand, they strengthened the soldiers' sense of group loyalty. They settled disputes, acted as role models, and sometimes preached an alternative gospel, one that was not heard at the regimental church. On the other hand, they helped the soldiers to respond creatively to the challenges inherent in the chaplains' gospel.

The process of religious accommodation that occurred in the camps was not simply a response to a challenge issued by the white chaplains. The former slave preachers not only took the white officers' religious knowledge into the company streets and the soldiers' tents, but they also took the soldiers' gospel into the regimental churches. Many ex-slave preachers delivered sermons, said prayers, gave testimony, and sang hymns during official services. Officers who witnessed the contribution of these preachers had their views on black docility and spiritual depravity seriously challenged. In some cases, the soldiers actually changed the way the officers treated their men. Therefore, the process of spiritual accommodation was occurring simultaneously at two levels; soldiers from the enlisted and commissioned ranks were forced to reevaluate their attitudes to each other.

Although most chaplains were acutely aware of the assertiveness of the soldiers' church, they never seriously contemplated abdicating their own religious authority. The struggle to save souls continued with unremitting vigor. Yet their missionary activity met with very little success. In part, their failure resulted from the strength and cultural resilience of the soldiers' church. However, it also resulted from the clandestine nature of the church services. Therefore, chaplains often had little idea of what was actually occurring in the soldiers' worship. What little knowledge they had, gained from their forays into the soldiers' quarters, suggested that the soldiers' church manifested all the emotional exuberance of slave worship. What they heard and saw were the elements of spiritual "defeat": shouting, groaning, dancing, clapping, and waving of arms. What they did not see was the subtle process of religious accommodation that occurred as the preachers reinterpreted the theological knowledge gained in the regimental church. Since worship in the soldiers' church incorporated total congregational involvement, all soldiers had an opportunity to incorporate at least some of the white chaplain's theology into their own spiritual canon. Thus the worship services were vehicles of both resistance and accommodation; they prevented spiritual indoctrination while encouraging theological change.[37]

Many chaplains explained their failure to win converts not by pointing to the strength of the soldiers' church but by drawing attention to the apparent inconsistency in the religious behavior of their fellow officers. The monthly chaplaincy reports contain numerous references to the "evil" habits of dissolute officers. For example, Chaplain Rockwood reported that "in the Colored Service it is highly important that those in authority should set a correct example before the soldiers. . . .[T]hese men are so quick to imitate, that they are very easily influenced by the example of officers either for good or evil." Another chaplain condemned the officers in his camp for behaving in a manner "calculated to retard the progress of truth and righteous among the men." Officers were citicized for failing to attend church, swearing, drinking, gambling, and failing to keep the Sabbath. The officers reacted angrily. Hence, in camps, religious disputes fragmented the commissioned ranks.[38]

Those chaplains who explained their religious failings by pointing to an imperfect witness rather than their own impotent ministry earnestly studied the soldiers' behavior for evidence of moral improvement. The absence of vices such as gambling, profanity, drunkenness, and sexual immorality was seen as indicative of spiritual conversion. Church attendance was considered another important barometer of true spirituality. However, nothing pleased them more than the orderly, dignified nature of the worship.

Chaplain A. C. McDonald proudly reported to the U.S. adjutant general in September 1865 that the religious services in his camp were "improving"; they were not "wild or excitable" in the way that was "usually expected of colored people." Conformity to Northern Protestant worship patterns became, therefore, an important measure of spiritual progress. Praise was heaped on soldiers who appeared to display the acceptable mode of religious behavior. Certainly Lt. Thomas Montgomery had praise for one of his "darkies," who had "made a closing prayer superior to nine-tenths of any" he "had ever heard white men make." The attraction lay in the fact that "the words were correct, the language perfect, and the sense and effect complete." In short: it was a flawless performance, modeled on the best Anglo-American Christian conventions.[39]

In reality, the degree of religious conformity in black regiments depended more on the influence of the black leadership than on the authority of the white officers. The black soldiers were much more likely to avoid the "sins" of gambling, profanity, theft, etc., if warnings emanated from their own leaders. Lt. Thomas Montgomery inadvertently admitted this in a letter to his mother. The moral health of his regiment depended not on his example or on the officers' diligence but on his "very good orderly sergeant." Thanks to the sergeant's efforts, "you will hear no swearing and see no card playing" in the company.

In the last analysis, evidence of "Christian morality" in the company streets and piety in the regiment's church service could not be taken as a conclusive sign that the soldiers had abandoned their "plantation ways." Slaves had a long tradition of masking their true feelings and attitudes by adopting roles that appeared appropriate for particular circumstances. This plantation survival strategy continued to operate, in varying degrees, in the Union army.[40]

The religious rituals and beliefs of the soldiers' church served a variety of functions that enabled the men to face the challenges of military service. Soldiers sometimes coped with the demanding routine of camp life by calling upon God to give them inner strength. The faith of these soldiers was intense and personal. Pvt. Robert Fitzgerald read his Bible regularly and found it "very instructive and interesting." He was "thankful for such a guide." James Payne saw the army as "a great field for the display of Christian benevolence." He urged the readers of the *Christian Recorder* to send him Bibles and religious tracts so that he could convert his comrades.[41]

The horror of battle tested the soldiers' faith, and, while death and suffering made some atheists, it turned others closer to God. Ex-slave preachers sometimes led their men in prayer or delivered inspiring sermons immediately before battle. "Uncle Freddie More" and orderly I. J. Hill challenged the men of the 29th Connecticut Volunteers in this way just before an attack on the defenses of Petersburg in August 1864. In the heat of battle soldiers, looked to God to sustain them. While attacking a fort near Malvern Hill, Sgt. Alexander Newton was constantly in prayer. He "prayed in this battle whenever" he "had opportunity" and looked "to Heaven, for grape and canister and bullets of all shapes and sizes were falling thick and fast about" him. Battlefield experiences reinvigorated the faith of many soldiers. Sgt. James Payne noted that new recruits who spent their time in barracks or in camp would become dissolute and "backslide." However, once they experienced "the horrors of battle they realized the importance of trusting God."[42]

The soldiers attributed theological meaning to the war. Some saw the war as a divine crusade, a holy war of liberation. Religious symbolism and imagery, so frequently used to verbalize slave resistance on the plantation, was employed in the camps to project aggression against the former masters. Drawing upon their knowledge of the Old Testament, knowledge that was encapsulated in many of their spirituals and songs, the soldiers compared their conquest of the South to the Israelites' conquest of Canaan. In both situations, God liberated his enslaved people so they could conquer their Promised Lands. "He will mount his chariots of power, and will draw His sword with vengeance" proclaimed Sgt. Maj. N. B. Storrett. He believed God would "drive out the Hittites, the Canaanites and the Jebusites, viz. the rebels, the slaveholders and the copperheads." A new era of freedom was beginning; the victory cry would ring "from the highest mountain to the lowest valley," because "this world is become the Kingdom of our God and His Christ, for slavery is abolished for ever."[43]

Not all the aggression and anger of the soldiers was directed against their former masters. Their religious practices enabled them to release some of their anger against the injustices inflicted upon them by the federal government. The inequitable rate of pay for black troops was a great provocation. This issue became a spiritual battleground. Indeed, the editor of the *Christian Recorder* warned Congress to "remember the words of the Lord God: 'Thou shalt not muzzle the ox that treadeth out the corn.'"[44]

The shouting, singing, and dancing activities of the soldiers' church also provided an excellent form of social recreation. The religion of the soldiers helped to improve their mental health, because it placed all the tragedy, hardship, and glory of war in a cultural framework that they understood. Camp life bore some of the marks of the plantation regime. Although some of the cruel forms of punishment were absent, the awesome specter of death, by combat or disease, was always present. The long hours of backbreaking fatigue were somewhat reminiscent of the plantation regime. It is not surprising, therefore, to find that former slaves coped with the hardship and trauma of military service in ways consistent with their plantation experiences. The soldiers' church thus acted as a sustaining and survival mechanism. When Lt. Col. Byron Cutcheon observed black soldiers laboring on military fortifications and singing plantation melodies, he was witnessing former slaves using a traditional survival mechanism in a new, but not totally foreign, environment.[45]

Finally, the religious practices of the soldiers' church gave the soldiers a strong sense of cultural and communal unity. This does not mean that there was a common creed in the black camp community. Religious diversity existed, but these differences became part of the rich texture of community life. The trauma of war service encouraged the soldiers to share their faith. Freeman Bowley witnessed this when he accidentally observed a prayer meeting being held by black soldiers among pine trees. Although he had only been with his regiment a week, he was impressed by the soldiers' solid commitment to freedom and family life. While "the cannon were roaring at Spotsylvania and the dropping sound of musketry was heard," he observed "one powerful black soldier" praying "'O Lord Jesus, you know we'se ready an' willing to die for the flag, but O Lord! If we falls comfort de lubbed ones at home.'" This prayer moved Bowley so much that he "turned away with tears in" his eyes; he too was thinking of his home, and "the black soldier had spoken" his "unuttered prayer." Clearly, at times the religious practices of the ex-slave soldiers could act, as Freeman Bowley testified, as bonds of empathy and unity.[46]

The soldiers' traditional religious beliefs were rooted in their African heritage. However, this heritage had changed on the plantation, and it changed again in the Union army. In the process of affirming their identity as free men, the soldiers reworked their religious heritage so they could effectively fulfill their role as patriotic soldiers and future U.S. citizens. On some occasions, their religious and military roles produced tension and conflict between the officers and men. However, because the roles were not mutually exclusive, the conflict was not inevitable, nor did it seriously damage the war effort. Spiritual growth and military performance could occur concurrently. This development was possible because the soldiers saw little distinction between the sacred and secular worlds. They believed that service in the Union army was yet another way of fighting slavery and doing

God's will. Certainly this was the viewpoint of Pvt. Willington Hawkins, 4th Louisiana Native Guard, a former slave who had bought his freedom in Richmond, Virginia, just prior to the outbreak of war. Private Hawkins informed the editor of the *Evening Post,* "We have meeting in or regement often and also as we solgers in the United States we are still trying to be solgers for Jesus Christ."[47]

CHAPTER SEVEN

"The Trumpets Sound"

THE SOLDIERS' MUSIC

The trumpets sound, the armies shout,
    They drive the hosts of hell,
 How dreadful is our God to adore,
    The great Immanuel!
They look like men, They look like men,
    They look like men of war,
All arm'd and dress'd in uniform,
    They look like men of war.
              —"Negro Battle Hymn"

In September 1864, Orrin Densmore made a visit to his elder brother, Daniel, stationed at Fort Pickering near Memphis, Tennessee. The visit excited young Orrin, because he was particularly interested in the plight of the Southern slaves. This interest had been stimulated by a steady stream of letters that flowed back home to Minnesota from his two brothers, who held commissions in black regiments. Now he had an opportunity to observe the "African" race, to watch Daniel's Missouri and Tennessee soldiers make the transition from slavery to freedom. During the course of his visit, Orrin observed the 7th U.S. Colored Heavy Artillery band performing in Court Square in Memphis. These soldiers, whose regiment had fought so gallantly at Fort Pillow only five months previously, played with considerable distinction. However, what impressed him was not so much the repertoire of the band but the spirit of the performance. Court Square, "a resort of the aristocracy," resounded to a defiant blast of martial music. "The fine ladies" who looked on were "quite vexed at what they considered an insult." Unperturbed by their protests, "the band played well." The martial tunes of Union victory filled the air and conveyed the soldiers' feelings of racial pride and love of freedom. The band's music "showed the difference between negroes as soldiers and as slaves a year ago."[1]

Music was a vital element in black culture. On the slave plantation it had enriched the texture of life and acted as an important vehicle for survival. In the army, it served a similar function. It helped the black soldier place his military experience in a cultural continuum, and it eased his transition to freedom and citizenship. Around the campfire the soldiers created new songs for a new world.[2]

Officers commanding black troops often commented on the important role music played in the leisure activities of their men. Capt. George Sutherland expressed this view succinctly when he commented that "the black soldiers' life was full of either music or religion." Many officers endeavored to use the medium of music to train their troops and develop within them martial spirits. To this end, soldiers were encouraged to sing the popular war songs written by white composers. Among the favorites were George Root's "Tramp, Tramp, Tramp" and "Just before the Battle, Mother"; Henry Clay Work's "Marching through Georgia"; and Patrick S. Gilmore's "When Johnny Comes Marching Home." These songs were sung lustily, for they expressed themes common to all soldiers: the hardship of the route march, the dread of battle, the exhilaration of victory, and the joy of returning home. Like troops in all units of the Union army, black soldiers claimed "ownership" of these songs by changing the words and adapting tunes to fit appropriated social occasions. Some popular songs became work songs, marching songs, and camp songs sung for entertainment in off-duty hours.[3]

In many areas of the South, music was used to encourage enlistment. Lt. Oliver Norton observed that his fellow officers employed recently recruited soldiers to act as "musical" recruiting agents. As the "darkies who wanted to enlist" thronged the camp of the 8th U.S. Colored Infantry, the soldiers who had already enlisted sang "Rally round the flag, boys, rally once again, shouting the battle cry of freedom. Down with the traitor, up with the star." The sight of former slaves singing the praises of the Union and urging their brethren to fight for their freedom swelled the ranks. The musical message met a responsive chord; it appealed to the slaves' deepest needs and aspirations. Certainly, Oliver Norton believed that the singing had an "electrifying effect on the crowd of slaves."[4]

ENLISTING SOLDIERS.

(From the African M. E. Church Hymn Book, page 399.)

Hark ! listen to the trumpeters,
    They call for volunteers;
On Zion's bright and flow'ry mount
    Behold the officers :

Their horses white, their armors bright,
    With courage bold they stand,
Enlisting soldiers for their King,
    To march to Canaan's land.

It sets my heart quite in a flame
    A soldier thus to be :
I will enlist, gird on my arms,
    And fight for liberty.

We want no cowards in our bands
    That will their colors fly :
We call for valiant-hearted men,
    Who are not afraid to die

To see our armies on parade.
    How martial they appear !
All arm'd and dress'd in uniform,
    They look like men of war.

They follow their great General,
    The great eternal Lamb,
His garments stain'd in his own blood,
    King Jesus is his name.

The trumpets sound, the armies shout,
    They drive the hosts of hell ;
How dreadful is our God t' adore,
    The great Immanuel !

Published by the Supervisory Committee for Recruiting Colored Regiments.

"Enlisting Soldiers." Free Military School Register, Historical Society of Pennsylvania.

In order to promote enlistment, the Philadelphia-based Supervisory Committee for Recruiting Colored Troops made use of the musical heritage of the free Northern black communities. One popular song that was employed, "Enlisting Soldiers," was taken directly from the African Methodist Episcopal Church hymnbook. The Supervisory Committee published a number of other songs to promote enlistment; however, most of these, for example, "The Original Version of the John Brown Song" and "The Black Regiment" bore the hallmarks of the abolitionist movement (Appendix A: 218–21).[5]

Abolitionists composed songs that celebrated the soldiers' heroism on the battlefield. By publicizing these heroic exploits, they hoped to validate their experiment to arm the blacks. In particular, they sought to ease the entry of blacks into the Union army by counteracting negative stereotyping and allaying racial fears. One song that was widely publicized in the North was George H. Boker's "The Black Regiment" (Appendix A: 219–21), known alternatively as "The Second Louisiana." Written to publicize the heroic attack by the 2d Louisiana Native Guard on Port Hudson, Louisiana, on May 27, 1863, the song endeavored to show that black soldiers fought Johnny Reb because they loved liberty and hated slavery. In the third stanza, the "flag-sergeant" challenges his troops to prove their manhood and demonstrate that they deserve their freedom:

"Now," the flag-sergeant cried,
"Though death and hell betide,
Let the whole nation see
If we are fit to be
Free men in this land; or bound
Down, like the whining hound—
Bound with red stripes of pain
In our old chains again!"
Oh! what a shout there went
From the black regiment![6]

The final stanza lauds the sacrifice of the 2d Louisiana Native Guard. Boker celebrated the death of these black soldiers because he believed they died like heroes, not slaves. Union soldiers were urged to accept the black troops as comrades, to "fight with them side by side" and put away feelings of racial prejudice.

Hundreds on hundreds fell;
But they are resting well;
Scourges and shackles strong
Never shall do them wrong.
O, to the living few,
Soldiers, be just and true!
Hail them as comrades tried;
Fight with them side by side;
Never, in field or tent,
Scorn the black regiment![7]

"The Black Regiment," then, celebrated the black soldiers' fighting prowess in a way that most members of the Northern public would find acceptable. Blacks were depicted as patriotic heroes who would willingly lay down their lives for the Union, in defense of freedom.

Songs were also written in order to "elevate" black culture. The Supervisory Committee for Recruiting Colored Troops published a number of songs, which some officers used to transmit their social values. Abolitionist officers in particular used these songs to inculcate in their soldiers the white abolitionist view of the war and emancipation. Some of these songs contained weighty moral lessons about the social obligations associated with liberty. Included in this collection were some songs "dressed" in slave dialect. For example, "Song of the Negro Boatman" (Appendix A: 221–22) purported to be a black spiritual that celebrated emancipation. In fact, renowned abolitionist hymn writer and poet John G. Whittier had written it. Blacks were told not to fear liberty, for this change in status would herald the dawn of a new era of untold prosperity. Indeed, the chorus claimed,

De yam will grow, de cotton blow,
We'll hab de rice an' corn:
Oh, nebber you fear, if nebber you hear
De driver blow his horn![8]

The soldiers were implicitly reminded that with freedom came responsibility. For the first time they had an opportunity to protect their loved ones and maintain the unity of the family. As future property owners, they had an obligation to become economically self-reliant, to "sell de pig" and "sell de cow."

Ole massa on he trabbles gone;
He leab de land behind:
De Lord's breff blew him furder on,
Like corn shuk in de wind.
We own de hoe, we own de plow,
We own de hands dat hold;
We sell de pig, we sell de cow,
But nebber chile be sold.[9]

The committee also included some allegedly authentic slave songs in its collection. One such song was "Old Shady" (Appendix A: 222–23) which had supposedly been written by ex-slave D. Blakely Durant, who had served as a cook at Union army headquarters during the siege of Vicksburg, Mississippi. Catalogued as "A Contraband Song," "Old Shady" was published with the comment that this "rare Lyric" was a favorite song of the Mississippi contrabands. The "character and enthusiasm" of the song was "great"; "among songs of this kind" it had "no superior."[10]

"Old Shady" appealed to the committee primarily because of the moral precepts it proclaimed. "Old Shady" flees North because he loved liberty and wants to become economically independent. The fourth stanza, for example, points to the attractive working conditions in the North, where honest labor brings a just reward.

Good-bye, hard work, and never any pay
I'm goin' up Norf where de white folks stay;
White wheat-bread and a dollar a day!
    Comin' comin'! Hail, mighty day.[11]

The last stanza describes "Old Shady"'s genuine love for his family.

I've got a wife, and she's got a baby,
Way up Norf in Lower Canady—
Won't dey shout when dey see ole Shady
    Comin', comin'! Hail, mighty day.[12]

"Song of the First Arkansas" (Appendix A: 223–24) is an interesting composition that illustrates the determination of some officers to control and direct the development of black culture for military objectives. Capt. Lindley Miller, 1st Arkansas Volunteers, African Descent, wrote this song for his "boys," and they were required to sing it when on dress parade. The first three lines of the song celebrate the indivisible Union.

> Oh! we're de bully soldiers of de "First of Arkansas."
> We are fightin' for de Union, we are fightin' for de law;
> We can hit a rebel furder dan a white man eber saw.[13]

Captain Miller believed that soldiers who had been slaves had to be taught to be patriotic defenders of the Union. Other, more personal motives, for example, revenge and emancipation were considered of secondary importance. After praising the indivisible Union, the song proceeds to laud the "Africans'" fighting spirit and then describes the social revolution that will occur in the South once the Confederacy has been defeated. It concludes with an appeal to the blacks to enlist and fight for liberty, while they still have an opportunity:

> Father Abraham has spoken, and de message has been sent,
> De prison doors be opened, and out de pris'ners went,
> To join de sable army of de "African descent,"
> As we go marching on.

> Den fall'in colored bredren, you'd better do it soon,
> Don't you hear de drum a beatin' de Yankee Doodle tune?
> We are wid you now dis mornin', we'll be far away at noon,
> As we go marching on.[14]

Conscious of the cruelty of slavery and of the former slaves' supposedly meek disposition, Miller felt some appeal had to be made to the former slaves' pragmatic self-interest. In short, the former slave had to be incited to fight: "While it [the song] is not very conservative, it will do to fight with." Certainly he believed the utopian motif that described Southern whites bowing to Southern blacks was a prophetic vision that black soldiers would fight for.[15]

It is difficult to assess the degree to which officers like Capt. Lindley Miller were able to use the medium of music to inculcate their own social values in their men and also appeal to the soldiers' cultural values. While there is some evidence that music could be a useful aid to military training, the soldiers certainly did not present a blank musical score to their officers. They had their own musical heritage, and this heritage nurtured distinctive cultural values.[16]

Spirituals and secular songs were vital elements of camp culture. Often these songs were sung as a source of relaxation and comradeship. Col. Samuel Armstrong observed that his regiment of Maryland former slaves continually "sang at night around their camp fires." Another officer reported that whereas white troops freely debated "any striking event or piece of news," black troops often put their social comment into song. In the evening, his soldiers sat round the campfires in groups, "'studying'[,] as they call it." While the soldiers ruminated upon important issues, the "spirit moved" individuals to "lead the others in a melodious chant." The singing of spirituals also formed a vital element in the religious meetings of the soldiers' church. They "sing more than they pray," remarked one line officer commanding a company of former Louisiana slaves.[17]

As well as being powerful vehicles of social communication, the camp songs of former slaves served a traditional purpose, helping them cope with the hardship of military service. The songs lightened the burden of arduous fatigue duty by strengthening morale and minimizing the monotony. Time passed quickly for the soldiers of the 1st South Carolina Volunteers, who sang "boating songs" as they rowed among the South Carolina Sea Islands. After a particularly "stormy and comfortless night," Col. Thomas Higginson observed a party of his soldiers wearing blankets, shining from "the rain streaming from these," returning from a "very exposed" picket station, joyfully singing "Hangman Johnny" (Appendix B: 225).[18]

Favorite spirituals became popular marching songs. The soldiers sang these with gusto, adjusting the rhythm of the plantation to match the tempo of the army camp. Higginson noted that his regiment's favorite marching song, "Go in the Wilderness," was "invaluable to lift their feet along." Its rhythm had a kind of "spring and lilt to it, quite indescribable" (Appendix B: 225–26).[19]

Most of the songs recorded as having been sung by the black soldiers were spirituals. This may have been because white observers underestimated the importance of secular songs or attributed spiritual meanings to secular themes. Moreover, black soldiers may have made a point of singing spirituals within hearing range of white officers, because they assumed that the officers favored them. Colonel Higginson believed that he "never overhead in camp a profane or vulgar song." However, spirituals probably did, in fact, dominate the musical repertoire and probably because the soldiers considered them the most significant.[20]

The themes of the spirituals reflect the past experience of the slave plantation, the present challenges of military life, and postwar expectations.[21]

A number of the spirituals sung by the soldiers, for example, "O Yes,

Lord," "Good News," and "The Heavenly Road" (Appendix B: 226–27) point to the soldiers' resilient religious faith. These spirituals tell of God's faithfulness and his deep love for his children.[22] This dominant theme is illustrated in the second stanza of "The Heavenly Road."

> O Satan is a mighty busy ole man,
> And roll rocks in my way;
> But Jesus is my bosom friend,
> And roll 'em out of de way.
> O won't you go wid me? (*Thrice*)
> For to keep our garments clean.[23]

Linked closely to a belief in God's infinite love was a belief in heaven as a glorious refuge from slavery. Higginson's soldiers affirmed this theme in such spirituals as "Fare Ye Well," "Walk 'Em Easy," "O the Dying Lamb," "Cry Holy," and "O'er the Crossing" (Appendix B: 227–30).[24]

Of course, ex-slave soldiers, like all soldiers, had to face the harsh realities of sickness and death. They sought solace in spirituals they had learned on the plantations. "The Baby Gone Home," "Jesus with Us," and "I Know Moon-Rise" were three spiritual laments that Higginson's soldiers sang. Although these spirituals convey sorrow and anguish, they also carry messages of hope and salvation (Appendix B: 230).[25]

A number of spirituals referred to the sufferings of slavery. "I Want to Go Home" (Appendix B: 231) describes heaven as a glorious sanctuary, free from the cruelty of slavery. After each individual hardship of slavery is evoked by its heavenly opposite, for example, "Dere's no rain to wet you," "Dere's no sun to burn you," "Dere's no whips a-crackin'," the refrain, "O, yes, I want to go home," is repeated. Other spirituals express a common hatred of some of the worst features of slavery. For example, "The Driver" (Appendix B: 231) portrays the black slave driver as an object of fear and derision, a "Nigger-driver second devil." Soldiers also sang joyously about their change in status. They celebrated their emancipation by singing spirituals that described how their lives had improved. Capt. James S. Rogers claimed that in one version of "I Want to Go Home," a seventh verse, "No more slavery in de kingdom," was added when the Emancipation Proclamation was issued.

New spirituals were created to celebrate the war against slavery. Colonel Higginson believed that "Many Thousand Go" (Appendix B: 232), the most recent of all the spirituals sung by his troops, was a song "to which the

Rebellion had actually given rise." According to another officer in Higginson's regiment, Lt. Col. Charles Trowbridge, this spiritual was first sung when Confederate general P. G. T. Beauregard took slaves from the Sea Islands to build fortifications at Hilton Head and Bay Point. In "Many Thousand Go," the soldiers rejoiced that there was "No more driver's lash for me" and "No more mistress' call for me." Such refrains reminded them that they were fighting a war of liberation. Moreover, the song enabled them to compare their present status as Union army soldiers with their past experience as slaves.[26] In "Hail Mary" (Appendix B: 232), the soldiers were reminded that they were brothers in arms. In the army camp, as on the slave plantation, survival was a communal operation.

> One more valiant soldier here,
> To help me bear de cross.[27]

As well as lifting morale, the spirituals turned the soldiers' minds to their loved ones still suffering in slavery or resting with Jesus in heaven. Such spirituals included "Room in There" and "Early in the Morning" (Appendix B: 233–34).[28]

Events of army life were sometimes linked to spiritual themes. Old songs were given new meanings. The ritual of the morning roll call impressed many soldiers, because the daily recording of their name and rank on the company roll reaffirmed their new liberated status. A number of songs, for example, "When That General Roll Is Called," evoked the metaphor of the roll call to emphasize the soldier's faith in his heavenly home and his conquest of death.[29]

Some spirituals had as their subjects the triumph of the Union army. In these songs, the soldiers constantly alluded to Old Testament themes. For example, "My Army Cross Over" (Appendix B: 234) refers to the destruction of the pharaoh's army by the Red Sea and the Israelite "army" crossing the Jordan River. The soldiers believed that they were fighting in God's army and that General Jesus was their leader. The images of Jesus as suffering servant and triumphant king were also popular with the soldiers.[30] They too had suffered, like Jesus, but now they were returning to their homeland as conquerors. The first and second stanzas of "Ride In, Kind Saviour" (Appendix B: 234) boldly proclaim Jesus as a triumphant savior.

> Ride in, kind Saviour!
> No man can hinder me.

O, Jesus is a mighty man!
No man can hinder me.[31]

The third and sixth stanzas describe the destruction of the Confederacy: "We're marching through Virginny fields" and "O, old Secesh done come and gone!"[32]

Singing was an important recreational activity for Col. Samuel Armstrong's once-enslaved Maryland soldiers. They would "gather around the camp fire and would sing by the hour the melodies of plantation life." However, not all their songs came directly from the plantation. In fact, the most popular song of the 8th U.S. Colored Infantry was what Colonel Armstrong called the "Negro Battle Hymn" (Appendix A: 215–16).[33] This song links the symbolism of the Old Testament with military language and terminology in order to celebrate the black soldiers' valor.[34]

In the first two stanzas of the song, the soldiers are portrayed as God's avengers, eager to fulfill their apocalyptic mission:

> Hark! Listen to the trumpeters,
>   They called for volunteers,
> On Zion's bright and flow'ry mount
>   Behold the officers.

> *Refrain:* They look like men, they look like men
>   They look like men of war,
> All arm'd and dressed in uniform,
>   They look like me on war.

> Their horses white, their armor bright,
>   With courage bold they stand,
> Enlisting soldiers for their King,
>   To march to Canaan's land.[35]

In stanzas three and four, the soldiers are urged to "fight for liberty" and demonstrate their courage.

> It sets my heart quite in a flame
>   A soldier thus to be,
> I will enlist, gird on my arms,
>   And fight for liberty.

Refrain

We want no cowards in our band,
    That will their colors fly;
We call for valiant-hearted men,
    Who're not afraid to die.[36]

The fifth, sixth, and seventh stanzas appeal to the soldiers' military pride and bearing. The men are reminded that "King Jesus" has given them the final victory.

To see our armies on parade.
    How martial they appear!
All arm'd and dress'd in uniform,
    They look like men of war.

Refrain

They follow their great General,
    The great eternal lamb,
His garments stain'd in his own blood,
    King Jesus is his name.

Refrain

The trumpets sound, the armies shout,
    They drive the hosts of hell,
How dreadful is our God to adore,
    The great Immanuel![37]

Above all else, the "Negro Battle Hymn" appeals to the former slave's new status. A refrain repeated after each stanza reminds the men that they are no longer racial refugees or cringing slaves but proud Union soldiers.

They look like men, They look like men,
    They look like men of war,
All arm'd and dress'd in uniform,
    They look like men of war.[38]

Phrases and lines that celebrate the black soldiers' manhood occur elsewhere in the musical score of other black regiments. For example, when a black brigade learned that it was going to lead the charge at the Battle of the Crater at Petersburg, the men sang a refrain that was strikingly similar to that in the 8th U.S. Colored Infantry "Negro Battle Hymn"—"We-e looks li-ike me-en a-a marchin' on, we looks li-ike men-er war."[39]

Of course, not all the songs of the ex-slave soldiers were loudly proclaimed. Slaves had a long tradition of hiding elements of their musical heritage from whites' ears. Indeed, "a little drummer boy" in Colonel Higginson's regiment informed him that one line in the song "We'll Soon Be Free" (Appendix B: 235) was thought by some South Carolina whites to have a hidden meaning. "De Lord will call us home" was believed to refer to the Yankees; "De tink de Lord mean for say de Yankees," claimed the drummer boy. In the Union army, the soldiers continued to sing songs that either had hidden messages or were not meant for the ears of the white officers. This was particularly the case with songs that verbalized grievances.[40]

These songs emerged from the political experience of the free Northern blacks and the resistance of the plantation slaves. Sometimes even the most empathetic observers of black behavior were unable to comprehend the true nature of black resistance. "Hangman Johnny," a song Higginson's soldiers sang, contained references to the soldiers' inequitable rate of pay and the "mercenary aims they attributed to the white soldiers." However, Higginson was unable to discern the exact nature of the soldiers' complaint, because the men halted their performance when they saw him approaching. In November 1863, however, he heard his soldiers sing a "protest" song about the government's discriminatory pay:[41]

> Ten dollars a month
> Tree ob dat for clothing!
> Gwine to Washington
> To fight for Linkum's darter.[42]

Colonel Higginson dismissed this song: "Their nonsense is as inscrutable as children's." However, in reality, the soldiers were stating their grievances in a way that they could comprehend. Just because the full meaning of the song was hidden from Colonel Higginson, did not make it a meaningless ditty.[43]

The new freedom of the army camp enabled the soldiers to express their grievances in a much more open manner. Soldiers in the 1st U.S. Colored

Infantry did this by subtly linking, in one of their favorite marching songs, the themes of regimental pride, religious devotion, and opposition to the discriminatory policies of some Union generals, who confined them to fatigue duties and denied them combat opportunities. The 1st U.S. Colored Infantry expressed this grievance in the following military marching song:

> We are the gallant First,
> Who slightly have been tried,
> Who order to a battle,
> Take Jesus for our guide.[44]

The musical heritage of the ex-slave soldiers was most evident in the expressive behavior of their musical performance. Those officers who were interested enough observed black troops singing around the campfire and noted that their music had a distinctive quality very different from that of white soldiers. They attributed this distinctiveness to the soldiers' slave experience and, having thus identified its source, labeled it inferior and culturally empty. Generally, these officers found the arrangement of the music, its rhythm and melody, and its accompanying body movement far more offensive than the actual words of the songs. In short, it was the quintessential African character of the ex-slave soldiers' musical heritage, particularly the body movement, that most made it "primitive."

Higginson certainly implied this when describing a musical performance of his soldiers as if it were an African tribal gathering. Returning to his regiment one "starlit evening," he approached the camp to discover a "glimmering fire, round which the dusky figures moved in the rhythmical barbaric dance the negroes call a 'shout.'" These "dusky figures" were "chanting, often harshly, but always in most perfect time, some monotonous refrain." Almost invariably, Higginson observed that the soldiers' singing was accompanied by expressive movements, such as "the measured clapping of hands and the clatter of many feet." One popular song, "Room in There," seemed to evoke in the singers a mood of emotional exuberance; soldiers "from oldest to the youngest, would be wriggling and shuffling, as if through some magic piper's bewitchment." Even soldiers who had shown "contemptuous indifference would be drawn into the vortex erelong."[45]

Some officers believed that the soldiers' song was "a moan," a plaintive cry of pain that came from "the house of bondage, and contained weird and suppressed sadness." Because Capt. George Sutherland was unfamiliar with the melody and rhythm of slave music, he assumed that the singing of his soldiers, who had been slaves in Kentucky, lacked the joy, rich variety, and creativity of his own supposedly superior musical heritage. Essentially, it was the difference in musical form that made the soldiers' singing appear inferior, exclusive, and mournful.[46]

Perhaps nothing did more to confirm Captain Sutherland's illusions about his soldiers' musical heritage than his observations of the "call and response chant form." In this form of singing, the leader, often a preacher, chanted an evocative expression, to which the audience or congregation chanted the answer. The emotional intensity of the music depended primarily upon the leader's striking a responsive chord in the audience. If his song appealed to the audience, its members would join the singing, in ever-increasing numbers. When this happened, the leader was able to shape and reshape the song as the singing grew in emotional intensity. However, sometimes the leader's song had little or no appeal. In these circumstances, the chant was not taken up, and the leader was forced to explore his musical vocabulary until he found more congenial themes or tunes.

Col. George Thomas observed this communal recreation process among his Maryland ex-slave soldiers shortly before the Crater. As the soldiers sat around the campfires, the lead singer "would uplift a mighty voice, like a bard of old, in a wild sort of chant." However, if his chant failed to "strike a sympathetic chord," he would "sing it again and again altering sometimes the words, or more often the music" until it was accepted.[47]

On one occasion, Capt. George Sutherland witnessed a particular song develop into a crescendo of emotion. Standing a "little distance from the campfire" of his Kentucky soldiers, he heard "one deep rich voice" call

> I know moon-rise, I know star-rise,

Then two or three soldiers repeated the refrain (of "I Know Moon-Rise"):

> To lay dis body down.

Then the leader called again:

> I walk in de moonlight, I walk in de starlight,

and the refrain is taken up by half a dozen.

> To lay dis body down.

The leader continued:

I'll walk in de graveyard, I'll walk through de grave yard,

and then you are lifted as by a Creation chorus; for now there are fifty voices, and with such wonderful deep, rich melody, as only the Negro can produce they join in.

Lay dis body down
I go to de judgement in de evenin' of de day,
When I lay dis body down
And my soul and your soul will meet in de day
When I lay dis body down.[48]

This musical performance convinced Captain Sutherland that the call and response chant had on the plantation been an opiate, enabling the slaves to endure the suffering of slavery. Other officers who also measured the soldiers' songs against their own, Northern musical heritage laced their assessments with similar expressions of condescension and cultural superiority. Higginson, for example, concluded the chapter "Negro Spirituals" in his book *Army Life in a Black Regiment* with the comment that "these songs are but the vocal expression of the simplicity of their faith and the sublimity of their long resignation."[49]

Music linked the soldier with his ancestral past. The officers were made aware of this when they observed the distinctive features of their soldiers' music. African survivals were most noticeable not so much in the words and themes of songs as in the modes of their presentation, such as the call-response chant, rhythm, melody, and dances and gestures. However, to some extent, these "peculiar" features of black music masked from the eyes of the officers the high degree of cultural accommodation that was occurring. Slave music had never been a simple vehicle of cultural resistance. On the plantation, slave musicians had blended resistance with accommodation. This process made the soldiers' musical heritage both flexible and creative.[50]

Cultural resistance appeared to wane as the soldiers' military prowess increased. Colonel Higginson observed that at first his soldiers sang church hymns reluctantly and were "always gladly yielding to the more potent excitement of their own 'spirituals.'" As time passed, this attitude appeared to change. In September 1863, he wrote in his journal that he was "in no doubt that as their military habits develope, [*sic*] these chants disappear & the regular Ethiopian melodies of the North become more common." Higginson oversimplified the process of change. It was not a question of the soldiers' leaving one musical tradition and adopting another; like plants in fertile soil, various musical traditions flourished in the camps, in an interdependent relationship. The soldiers adopted melodies of the Northern blacks for public performances, while in privacy they continued to sing African melodies and chants.[51]

The adaptation process was particularly noticeable in marching songs. Officers in all branches of the Union army encouraged the singing of marching songs, because they improved discipline and made drill and training easier. They lifted morale and focused the soldiers' attention on the themes of duty and patriotism. Black soldiers sang marching songs lustily, for they recognized that this military medium cushioned their transition from slavery to freedom. Slaves often sang work songs as they marched to the plantation fields. These songs helped the slaves adjust to the rhythm of plantation work, and they carried in their lyrics the folk wisdom of the slave community. Now, in the army, ex-slave soldiers sang military marching songs to help them adjust to a new and challenging regime.[52]

Although their function was specific to the army, the form of the marching songs owed much to that body of apocalyptic spirituals that predicted an end to slavery. Colonel Higginson observed that a number of these spirituals were sung by the black troops while marching. These spirituals generally placed the struggle in an Old Testament context. "My Army Cross Over" and "Blow Your Trumpet, Gabriel" (Appendix B: 234, 235–36) were two such spirituals; they reassured the black soldiers that God had promised them ultimate victory over slavery. Marching songs that referred to Jesus often pictured him a triumphant, returning king. It would appear, then, that many of the marching songs were modified spirituals. New words were added, and old words were given new meanings in order to make them suitable vehicles of expression.[53]

The soldiers had to reshape their musical heritage from various regional repertoires. It is incorrect to speak of a single slave musical tradition. In reality, there were a number of traditions, reflecting regional differences. During the war, the Union army brought many of these dynamic traditions together for the first time.

Thomas Higginson attributed the constant changes in his soldiers' musical heritage in part to their diverse regional background. Organized in 1863, the 1st South Carolina Volunteers was composed of former slaves from South Carolina, Georgia, and Florida. As the regiment became a unified fighting force, the different regional musical traditions began to coalesce. This musical interaction and amalgamation sometimes caused several versions of the same song to evolve. For example, in Higginson's camp three regional derivations of "The Ship of Zion" appeared (Appendix B: 236–37).[54]

Some spirituals had distinctive features that identified their places of origin. "Hail Mary," a popular spiritual, had purportedly been introduced into the camp of the 1st South Carolina Volunteers by Roman Catholic soldiers from St. Augustine, Florida. Other spirituals lacked a specific origin and were, in fact, cosmopolitan compositions. Higginson observed that in the course of making musical compositions, the soldiers frequently borrowed lines from other songs. The song that was by far the most popular among his soldiers, "Hold Your Light," consisted of a single chorus "with which the verses of other songs might be combined at random." During this process of communal re-creation, the vocabulary of popular songs was also changed, to make them more relevant to the military environment. For example, in "Hail Mary" and "Sweet Music," the word "soldier" was substituted for "soul" and "saviour" (Appendix B: 232, 238).[55]

Much of this syncretic process Higginson attributed to the fact that the soldiers "learned all their songs by ear." This meant that "they often strayed into wholly new versions which sometimes became popular and entirely banished others." Generally, syncretism was governed by the soldiers' sense of rhythm and melody. Therefore, the inherited musical tradition formed the grammar, or mental rules, for the adoption of songs from Billy Yank's musical repertoire. Higginson discovered this when he introduced to his men camp songs popular with white Northern troops. Acting under the colonel's instructions, the regimental quartermaster attempted to teach the soldiers "Marching Along." However, the soldiers found that the words "Gird on the armor" impeded the rhythm. Eventually this "stumbling-block" was overcome by "some ingenious ear" that substituted "Guide on de army."[56]

The army included in its ranks not only slaves from different geographic areas but blacks from radically different social backgrounds. Both Southern former slaves and Northern free blacks served in the Union army, and sometimes this service brought them into very close proximity. When this happened, a certain degree of cultural diffusion occurred. In order to make the adjustment to the demands of military service, the free black and the ex-slave soldier borrowed extensively from each other's musical heritage.

Like white Union soldiers and their former slave comrades, the free black soldiers were also capable of employing their musical heritage to help them adapt to the military environment. For example, the soldiers of the 29th Connecticut Volunteers changed the words of a popular patriotic song, "Hoist Up the Flag," to praise the fighting prowess of black soldiers.[57]

Of course, many of the free black soldiers from the free Union states had at one time been slaves. These men also drew upon their slave traditions to help them adjust to the demands of military service. The songs of the former slave soldiers had, therefore, a special appeal to these free Northern black soldiers. Sgt. Maj. Alexander Newton recorded in his autobiography that when black soldiers from Gen. William Birney's Third Division fought at Petersburg, they sang a song that had hallmarks of a slave spiritual.

> Sure, I must fight if I would win,
> Increase my courage Lord;
> I'll bear the toil, endure the pain,
> Supported by Thy Word.[58]

Ties of blackness gave the Southern ex-slave and the Northern free black soldiers a degree of cultural affinity. Their camps echoed with songs proclaiming the death of slavery and the birth of citizenship. The Civil War brought with it a musical invasion. As the black soldiers marched through the South, they spread their musical heritage and sang their songs of liberty. The echoes of these songs could be heard in the South long after the war ended.[59]

In many camps, singing groups or glee clubs were formed. Similar singing groups had existed on slave plantations and in Northern free black communities. In these two different environments, they had served common functions of providing entertainment and stimulating social communication. Singing groups served similar roles in the Union army, but they developed in a way that had not been possible earlier. Although slaves had a tradition of hiding some elements of their musical heritage from whites, there also existed a tradition of publicly demonstrating the merit of their culture.

Blacks were proud of their musical traditions and through the medium of singing groups displayed their cultural wares. These public performances increased the social status of the singers and strengthened camp unity. When the black singers joined the Union army, they discovered that they had many opportunities to demonstrate their musical talents. As the soldiers became more familiar with the military routine, they became more assertive, and this assertiveness flowed over into their music. The glee clubs promoted friendly rivalry among companies and regiments. As well as providing an important vehicle for social interaction, they also helped the soldiers to increase company funds. However, above all else, the glee clubs became a most effective means of communicating with white officers and soldiers.

For example, Capt. Elliott Grabill reported to his wife in April 1864 that soldiers from his regiment had serenaded their commanding officer, Col. Giles Shurtleff. When such entertainments were made command performances, considerable antipathy developed; the soldiers resented being treated as mere entertainers in uniforms. However, many of the performances given by the soldiers for their officers were voluntary demonstrations of genuine appreciation. Such performances strengthened the social bonds between the two groups. On some occasions, black singing groups performed for white soldiers. Pvt. Warren Goodale, 11th Massachusetts Battery Light Artillery, for example, wrote enthusiastically about black glee clubs that had entertained his regiment.[60]

Choirs celebrated important events in the black soldiers' calendar, for example, the Emancipation Proclamation and the granting of equal pay. Sometimes special songs were composed to mark the significance of the occasion. This appears to have been the case when the 55th Massachusetts Volunteers celebrated the equal-pay decision. Lt. Col. Charles Fox sent to his wife in October 1864, a "hymn," "All Hail," written by "someone unknown" to him, and sung by the men to celebrate the granting of equal pay.[61]

The first stanza of "All Hail" (Appendix A: 216) describes the "glorious morning" that "proclaims a nation's birth." In the second stanza, the "light of victory" is described shining "from Richmond's fen-bound regions" to "above the bastions grey." The third and fourth stanzas describe the "light of victory" burning "through all our northern borders, New England's homes and halls." Soldiers are described joining the "glad hosannah That ring throughout the land" and lifting high the "Union banner." Finally, in the fifth stanza, the soldiers are asked to "stand firm" against the "two-fold foe," that is, rebels and traitors.

> Stand firm, the law's upholder,
>   Against the two-fold foe,
> The rebel who strikes bolder,
>   The traitor's secret blow.
> Fight we like men our conflict,

MORRIS ISLAND, S. C.,
November 10th 1864.

Sir.

At the earnest request of the several Officers in the Northern District, Department of the South, the

SHAW GLEE CLUB,

Will give a Musical Soiree on

Thanksgiving Evening,

November, 25th 1864.

IN THE STOREHOUSE OF THE POST A. A. Q. M.

MORRIS ISLAND. S. C.,

Commencing at 7½
To which your company is respectfully solicited.
In behalf of the Club,

Sergt. Frederic Johnson
Co. C. 54th Mass. Vols.

Please present this circular at the door.

Shaw Glee Club invitation. Formed by the men of the 54th Massachusetts Infantry, the Shaw Glee Club was named after Col. Robert G. Shaw, the commander of the regiment who died leading his men on an assault on Fort Wagner, South Carolina, in July 1863. 54th Massachusetts Infantry Regiment papers. Massachusetts Historical Society.

> Renew our vows to-night,
> For God and for our Country,
> For Freedom and the Right.[62]

The hymn concludes with an ideological reaffirmation. In the last two lines, the solders are asked to pledge their continuing commitment not only to God and the Union but also to preserving liberty and justice.

The soldiers' musical performances reached a crescendo during festive occasions. There was much organized singing during the Christmas and New Year season. During Thanksgiving Day celebrations, the soldiers sang joyfully of their commitment to the Union and the nation. Although many of these celebrations were "official" performances, the organization and program presentation were very much in the hands of the men.[63] For example, when the officers of the Northern District of the Department of the South requested that the Shaw Glee Club give a Thanksgiving Day performance in 1864, the club members in the 54th Massachusetts Volunteers organized the presentation. Sgt. Frederic Johnson organized the distribution of the invitations for the evening and helped to plan the program. The soldiers were keen to join in the Thanksgiving Day celebrations, for their participation indirectly acknowledged their claim to citizenship.[64]

The Shaw Glee Club's distribution of invitations to a "Musical Soiree" on Thanksgiving eve was an important social ritual that highlighted the soldiers' claim to social equality. Invitations to such social events are essentially a dialogue between equals; elements of reciprocity and cultural integrity are symbolically present. The invitation was issued after "several officers" had made an "earnest request." The signature of Sergeant Johnson at the bottom of the invitation was the mark of a liberated man, not a slave. The invitation is, then, documentary evidence of the way blacks were forging their new identity and asserting their newly won independence and freedom. An essential element of this process involved building new relationships with white Americans. Music became an important vehicle for defining this relationship, for the chords of musical appreciation transcended racial boundaries and helped to maintain social harmony between the white officers and the black soldiers serving under them.

Early one evening in September 1864, a contingent of soldiers from a black Union regiment crept close to the rebel lines in the vicinity of Petersburg. As the casual conversation of the rebel pickets drifted through the still night, the Connecticut troops made final preparations for a surprise attack. Preparations complete, the Union soldiers took their instruments in hand and began their assault—a musical one. Patriotic martial tunes wafted triumphantly across rebel positions. Throughout the night, the band of the 29th Connecticut unleashed one patriotic tune after another at rebel lines. Finally, as dawn neared, the bandsmen withdrew. No bodies covered the battlefield, but the soldiers believed a psychological victory had been won. The significance of this victory did not escape the notice of the bandsmen themselves. They knew that their most recent victory over Johnny Reb had ultimately depended upon their ability to adjust their cultural traditions to the rigorous demands of military service.[65]

The recruitment of musicians into the Union army during the Civil War seemed natural and almost inevitable. The association of band music with civic or patriotic demonstrations was commonplace in the decade immediately prior to the Civil War. Throughout the North, military bands had an important function in the formation and development of militia units. Consequently, when war erupted between the states, military bands formed a vital part of the citizen army that was raised to defend the republic.[66]

Bandsmen were more than entertainers. They had essential parts in the regulation of the daily routine of the Union army, from reveille to taps. As part of the machinery of war, bands served a variety of tasks. Military bands were at the forefront of recruiting campaigns; they led troops into major engagements; and their triumphant martial music accompanied soldiers as they marched through conquered Southern cities. On body-strewn battlefields, band music consoled the dying and uplifted the morale of the living. Bandsmen entertained troops and serenaded officers; they drummed in recruits and drummed out miscreants. Their music added dignity to the funeral services of heroes and provided a solemn warning at the execution of mutineers. Their presence in regiments and brigades was both a reflection of military tradition and a testament to the mainstream of American culture from which the citizen army itself had sprung.[67]

As a group, black soldiers stood outside the mainstream of American society. Racial prejudice in the North and slavery in the South had largely prevented blacks from being involved in the organization of militia bands. Many white officers commanding black troops were aware of this apparent weakness in their soldiers' musical heritage but did not despair of raising bands from the ranks. On the contrary, many officers believed that the black soldiers' "peculiar" racial traits made them musical and extremely teachable. Surgeon Seth Rogers believed that officers endeavoring to train black troops had to pay particularly close attention to their soldiers' musical attributes. Observing the behavior of men from South Carolina and Georgia in his regiment, he concluded that "imitation and musical concert" were the "avenues to the minds of these children."[68] Other officers serving in black regiments also thought the black soldiers' sense of rhythm remarkable.[69]

While many officers recognized black troops' apparent senses of timing and rhythm, few were prepared to admit that their music had any cultural value. In part, the officers devalued the black soldiers' musical heritage because it was inextricably linked to the soldiers' religious beliefs. Therefore, it was seen as an audible expression of emotional instability and religious fanaticism.[70]

The essentially African cadence and rhythm of the soldiers' music also alienated officers commanding black troops. To ears accustomed to whites' American melodies, the quintessential African nature of the black soldiers' music was incomprehensible, if amusing. Lt. Col. John Bogert, for example, was bemused by his soldiers at worship because "they made noise enough for a New York fire company."[71]

Not all officers reacted to their soldiers' music with feelings of condescension and amusement. Some, for example, Lt. Col. Charles Adams, saw the musical "decadence" of his soldiers as a matter of grave concern. In his report to the inspector general of the Department of Tennessee, he declared that while the "majority of the negroes had some musical talent," they had "no music worth mentioning." In an effort to rectify this situation, Adams sent a request to the War Department in Washington for "two instructors of music." To Adams, and other officers like him, the granting of such a request appeared imperative, the ex-slave soldiers' music, with its spontaneity, emotionalism, and African rhythm, seemed nothing more than an audible expression of the degrading impact of slavery. If the former slave was to become a Union soldier, all vestiges of slavery had to be cast off. In the process of overseeing the change from degraded slave to citizen soldier, many officers urged their black troops to adopt a new musical repertoire, one that befitted their new status. To this end, bands and band music were promoted by officers such as Colonel Adams not simply because they increased military efficiency but also because they were powerful instruments of acculturation. In short, the exuberant slave musician was to become a disciplined military bandsman.[72]

Officers commanding black troops believed that the presence of musicians in their camps yielded a number of specific benefits. Black musicians were valued entertainers; they served this function in both Union and Confederate armies. Many officers soon realized that their soldiers found it much easier to drill to band music. Recruiting officers and agents knew that military bands were excellent vehicles for promoting black enlistment. Thomas Webster, chairman of the Philadelphia Supervisory Committee for Recruiting Colored Troops, formed numerous black military bands at Camp William Penn for precisely this reason. In conquered regions of the Confederacy, black bands heralding a Union victory gave considerable impetus to the recruitment of former slaves into Federal ranks. A well-turned-out military band was also an excellent public-relations vehicle. Lt. Col. Nelson Viall reported that his band "acquired so much proficiency that in a few months it was sought for to play for private parties, and on public occasions in the city of New Orleans." On such occasions black bands provided social recreation for soldiers and citizens alike. However, more important still, black bands provided audible demonstrations of the edifying impact of military service on blacks. Black military bandsmen, therefore, heralded Union victory in the South in a way that helped to allay Southern fears of social dislocation and anarchy. Black troops could be presented to the Southern population not as conquering avengers but as entertainers. However, unlike the slave musicians, these bandsmen wore Union blue, and Yankee officers, not "old master," called the tune.[73]

Attempts by officers like Lieutenant Colonel Adams to organize military bands within their regiments were met with tremendous enthusiasm by the black soldiers. Unwittingly, these officers were actually reinforcing vital cultural elements in the Southern ex-slave and Northern free black communities.

Black Creoles (with French or Spanish ancestry) living in New Orleans were intensely interested in military band music and organized their own marching bands. On the plantations, slaves possessed a variety of musical instruments, including fiddles, triangles, flutes, clarinets, banjos, and drums. Some of these instruments were made by the slaves themselves; others were given to them by their masters. However, since only a minority of slaves actually possessed musical instruments, their possession became a source of special status within the slave community. Maj. Daniel Densmore, of the 68th USCI, a regiment of former Tennessee slaves, observed that when his regiment was paid, so-called magicians bought "violins, or rather fiddles."[74]

The experience of the soldiers in the 68th USCI suggests that the soldiers responded creatively to the challenge military service posed to their musical heritage. For example, these men, who were stationed at Fort Pickering in Tennessee, not only bought musical instruments with their army pay but formed dance bands and organized dances. Major Densmore noted in a letter home that the effect of these activities "on the disposition of the men generally is very apparent." The music and dancing and the presence of ladies from the surrounding areas created "great merriment" and lifted the morale of the soldiers, who had spent many hours digging in the vicinity of the fort. The music and dancing, therefore, gave the soldiers a temporary release from hard labor and excellent opportunities for socialization. The slaves' music had served the same function on the plantation, but in the army the situation was different; the soldiers had more opportunity for

The regimental band of the 107th USCI. The photograph was taken at Fort Corcoran, on the Arlington Heights outside Washington, D.C., in November 1865. USAMHI.

socialization and access to a greater range of musical instruments. Moreover, the soldiers' social activities received active support from the officers, who knew these activities increased a regiment's morale. The officers' objective of improving military morale had important cultural consequences, for the dance bands that were organized actually widened the musical horizons of the ex-slave soldiers.[75]

The surge of support for the formation of bands in black regiments did not occur simply because band music struck a responsive cultural chord. Some soldiers joined regimental bands because of the relatively high salaries offered to musicians. Yet some soldiers were not attracted by financial gain. When Lieutenant Colonel Viall formed a band in his camp, "nearly all the command were candidates." Sergeants were even willing to be reduced to the ranks to secure membership. Capt. Joseph Scroggs observed similar enthusiasm when a regimental band, the "Ebony Tooters," was formed in his camp.[76]

The limited number of places available also acted as a spur to would-be musicians. Under General Orders No. 48, of July 31, 1861, bands in volunteer infantry and artillery regiments were restricted to a maximum of twenty-four musicians, while the bands of mounted regiments were confined to six-teen members. In July 1862, band sizes were reduced even further. Bands were disbanded in volunteer regiments, and brigade bands were kept to a maxi-mum of sixteen members. Unofficially, however, many regimental bands con-tinued to exist. The fact that many bands continued to flourish in black regi-ments was a testimony to the self-reliant enthusiasm of the black bandsmen and the support and protection of officers who valued their regimental bands and knew how to take advantage of loopholes in regulations.[77]

Military bands were complex organizations. To operate efficiently, the band required a substantial number of sophisticated musical instruments and intensive musical instruction. In many camps the soldiers themselves maintained their bands, at considerable personal sacrifice; Captain Scroggs noted that in his camp the soldiers "expended some of their surplus funds in purchasing brass instruments for a band." However, sometimes influen-tial abolitionists provided valuable assistance. Col. Robert Shaw reported that a special ladies committee supporting black recruitment agreed to pay for a band instructor for the 54th Massachusetts Volunteers. Edward W. Kinsley, an influential member of the "Black Committee," which organized the recruitment of soldiers for Massachusetts black regiments, raised a con-siderable amount of money for the purchase of band instruments. In Au-gust 1864, Sgt. William Logan wrote to Edward Kinsley thanking him for a clarinet he had donated; "It makes great improvement in the music and the boys were very glad to receive it." Sgt. Maj. James M. Trotter expressed similar gratitude when he wrote to Kinsley informing him that "Prof. Moore" and "first Asst. Smith" had proficiently performed "Cottage by the Lea" on two horns that Kinsley had recently donated.

Black band music became, then, a vehicle for unity between the soldiers and their close allies, the Northern abolitionists. Abolitionists provided the instruments and instructors because this assistance helped them to use the Union army as a school for citizenship. Indeed, it gave them an opportunity to improve the black soldiers' military capabilities and, by doing so, prove that blacks were worthy of citizenship. As well as training their black sol-diers for combat duty, the officers endeavored to "elevate" their soldiers' culture. While the soldiers did not accept the cultural hegemony of the abo-litionist officers, they did not spurn their musical instruction. In addition, band music gave them an opportunity to enrich their musical heritage. However, the cultural tide did not flow only one way. Blacks' melodies and tunes were often taken up in the repertoires of military bands in white Union regiments. Black bandsmen gave Union army music a distinctive "African" interpretation. Indeed, Captain Scroggs noted in his diary that the members of the "Ebony Tooters" would "discourse enchanting music, especially when not attempting to play any particular tune."[78]

While black bandsmen received encouragement and support from many officers, from some they received at best harsh criticism and at worst, ruthless exploitation. The bandsmen in the 5th USCI suffered severely at the hands of a group of rogue officers who stole their instruments. Members of the "Ebony Tooters" felt this loss keenly; their instruments had been purchased with nine hundred dollars of their own funds. One bandsman was so aggrieved that he wrote to the secretary of war, declaring that the officers' illicit behavior was "more i [sic] masters would *have done.*"[79]

The musical tradition of the black soldier was not a simple extension of his slave inheritance. In many ways the soldiers' music had a distinctive quality and developed in new directions. In the army camps musical performance was shaped by personal preference and public expectation.

The soldiers made a distinction between private and public performance. Those officers who came close enough to hear the "private music" of the black soldiers as it wafted from the campfire surrounds were sometimes offended by the African melodies, rhythms, and gestures. These officers often found the "public" music of the soldiers more appealing, simply because it contained songs and melodies with which they were familiar. This is not to suggest that the musicians and songsters had two entirely separate repertoires. Nevertheless, they did have musical preferences, and these preferences were guided by their perception of audience expectations. Therefore, most campfire songs appealed to the soldiers' cultural values, their deep spirituality, their desire to express aggression, and their communal feelings. Soldiers' "public" music contained more songs that had the imprint of the Yankee musical tradition. Many of these songs had more immediate military relevance than did the "private" songs.

Soldiers sang these songs lustily, for they too had become part of their musical heritage. They lifted morale of the laborer on the fatigue detail and prepared the veteran for battle. In short, they made him a better soldier. Moreover, these songs forged empathy between the officers and the soldiers. In spite of their diverse social backgrounds, both groups could sing patriotic songs with fervor. The harmony derived from these songs transcended musical performance and helped to alleviate discord in other areas. Although there was some racist antagonism to "African" rhythm and tunes, generally the soldiers' music promoted feelings of mutual respect.

Indeed, it enabled both soldiers and officers to perform the difficult task of expressing their patriotism in a way that minimized racial antagonism. Certainly this was Lt. Palemon Smalley's experience as he marched with his soldiers in the 99th U.S. Colored Infantry during the 1864 Red River expedition in Louisiana: "As we passed through the village on our way, our colored soldiers I thought, took a special delight in singing 'John Brown' and it was a fine sight to see them go swinging along and hear their . . . melodious voices singing a song that meant more to them than to all others."[80]

CHAPTER EIGHT

Married "Under the Flag"

KINSHIP AND GENDER ROLES IN THE CAMPS

> In the afternoon eight couples presented themselves for marriage, most of them pairs, whose marriages have never been solemnized. Their request was to be married "under the flag." A certificate for each pair, was given to the wife, and a record made in a blank book which I preserved.
> —Chaplain Thomas D. Howard, 88th USCI, at Port Hudson

On January 26, 1865, Pvt. Aaron Oats, a former slave from Kentucky, wrote to Secretary of War Edwin Stanton, asking that the government take action to release his wife from bondage. "I am a Soldier willing to lose my life for my Country and the liberty of my fellow men, please be so kind as to attend to this." He enclosed two letters with his correspondence, one from his wife, Lucrethia, telling of the hardship she was experiencing, the other, a bitter, vengeful letter from her master, one Jerry Smith, who accused Oats of betraying his trust. Smith thought he had given Lucrethia to Aaron Oats as a "gift," a reward for service.[1]

Many blacks, like Aaron Oats, joined the Union Army believing that their service would safeguard their loved ones at home. Yet shortly after enlisting they discovered it was an exceedingly difficult task to maintain the integrity and unity of kinship ties while often far removed from the family. This problem was compounded because of the officers' negative views of the soldiers' morality. While the majority of officers were interested in the family affairs of their men only insofar as they affected military performance, a minority of officers, most notably the abolitionists, sought to teach them how to be "good parents" and "responsible citizens." Sometimes these teachers attempted to impose their own rigid models of family life. When this happened, the soldiers responded creatively by developing patterns of resistance and/or accommodation. They had their own concepts of family life, but these concepts were never static or rigidly held. While serving in the army, the soldiers were able to reshape their kinship and gender roles to meet the demands of a new age of freedom.[2]

During the Civil War, black Union soldiers sought to affirm their kinship obligations. Certainly the strength of family ties was seen in the correspondence that flowed between Northern soldiers, their kin, and military authorities. Many of the themes of this correspondence were common to all Civil War soldiers. Soldiers and their loved ones wrote letters to secure leave and permanent release from active service, to escape punishments, and to affirm their patriotism and manhood. Black soldiers also wrote about issues that had special appeal to them. They wrote to seek redress for the poverty forced on their families by their inequitable rate of pay, to demand equitable treatment as prisoners of war, and to protest the hardships inflicted upon them by racist officers. Former slaves wrote letters to military authorities pleading for protection for their families still in bondage and urging the army to mount rescue operations. In their letters the soldiers and their kin revealed their deepest emotional needs, the ties that bound them to hearth and home. These letters provide a rich commentary on family life in that they describe, in a most personal way, the manner in which the war reshaped family relationships.

Many Northern soldiers enlisted in order to provide their families with financial security. Since most black families were at or below the poverty level, questions of pay, clothing allowance, and state and federal bounties were of vital concern. Initially the economic incentives to join the Union army appeared quite strong; the pay of thirteen dollars a month, plus a clothing allowance, was higher and more permanent than laborers' wages. Bounties, in some cases equivalent to a year's wages, were most attractive inducements. These initial financial benefits lost much of their appeal when the black soldiers' pay was lowered to ten dollars a month. The soldiers' wives and mothers responded by seizing the initiative and writing a barrage of letters to influential politicians, the War Department and the president, seeking equal treatment and pay justice for their men and protesting the government's failure to lift them from poverty.

The letter of Mrs. John Wilson, wife of the band leader of the 102d USCI, was typical of such requests. Writing to Stanton from Detroit in May 1865, she complained that her husband had "not received any pay from the government for nine mounths" and that this had left her "compleatly distitute." Moreover, "the relief fund" which she had been receiving had "been cut of through prejudice of Color and it leaves me compleatly distitute of means for my support." She believed Michigan had "no respect for her Colored Soldiers or their famileys." Widow Julia Pimer of Philadelphia wrote to Stanton in August 1864 complaining that because her two stepsons, David T. Jones, 22d USCI, and Joseph V. Pimer, 6th USCI, had not been paid since they enlisted, she had been forced to seek assistance from the Supervisory Committee for the Recruiting of Colored Soldiers and from the Sanitary Commission. In order to alleviate her poverty, she requested that she be paid (and duly was paid) her sons' bounties.[3]

Few black regiments suffered more family hardship than the 54th and the 55th Massachusetts Infantry Regiments. For over a year their men rejected the inequitable pay, surviving on army rations alone. The soldiers' families paid a high price for this struggle for justice. In March 1864, an anonymous soldier wrote to Governor Andrew claiming that his regiment was "entirely discouraged" because of the pay issue. Loved ones "at home" were "suffering for want of support, or taken to the Poor House." The mental stress was so great that he and his comrades had "neither curage to fight for our country and to defend our selves." Sgt. A. S. Fisher, 55th Massachusetts Volunteers, echoed the anonymous soldier's remarks in a letter written from Jacksonville, Florida, addressed to his "Dear Friend," Governor Andrew of Massachusetts, in March 1864. He believed the "horrible sufferings of dear sufferin familys" were "more than manhood can beare." Writing at approximately the same time, another soldier in the 55th Massachusetts Volunteers, Sgt. Maj. James Trotter, informed his friend Edward Kinsley that the men showed resolution and patience in their struggle for equal pay. "The men are not discouraged though often sad when thinking of the necessities of a dear wife and little ones and other beloved ones at home whom they have no power to relieve." Trotter could account for "this great manifestation of patience" only by attributing it to "an inspiration given to them by the great Jehovah, who will not suffer this war to end until every trace of slavery is gone."[4]

In an effort to improve their families' financial positions, soldiers gave their wives detailed instructions about how to secure funds from abolitionist societies and Northern charities. Sgt. H. Golden, 55th Massachusetts Volunteers, wrote to his wife from Folly Island giving her clear instructions on how to send to Governor Andrew for her "lotment." A few weeks later, Sgt. James H. Jackson, a sergeant in Golden's company, wrote to Governor Andrew to inform him of the "sufferings and destitution" of Golden's family.[5]

The inevitable uncertainty that accompanies war service caused considerable distress to many wives and mothers. "Is he alive?" wrote Mrs. Lucy Bailey to Secretary Stanton, asking after the fate of her husband in May 1865. A few days later, Maj. C. W. Foster, chief of the Bureau of Colored Troops, replied that the location of deserter John Bailey, 100th USCI, was unknown. In some camps there was virtually no news from home, and at times this communication breakdown had personally traumatic consequences. Depressed kin accused their loved ones of ignoring their plights and squandering their pay. Mrs. Catherine Massey wrote to Stanton from Hampton, Virginia, in July 1865 pleading for the government to deduct a family allowance from the pay of her "bad," "spendthrift" husband. Such accusations deeply troubled the soldiers. Mental anguish became so great in the camp of the 25th USCI that in April 1865 Chaplain Enoch K. Miller wrote to the editor of the *Christian Recorder* asking him to publicize widely the fact that the regiment had not yet been paid. He assured him that the men would "send the greater share of their money home" when payday arrived.[6]

Pressing money problems were not the only issues worrying loved ones. Mothers and wives also wrote emotionally charged letters pleading for leniency for loved sons and husbands accused of breaking military regulations. Joanna Taylor, a fifty-five-year-old widow from Pittsburgh, Pennsylvania, wrote to plead, unsuccessfully, for a pardon for her son, Sgt. Charles W. Taylor, 6th USCI, on the grounds that when he deserted, he had been "very young" and suffering from a "severe cold" and that the officers from his regiment had not been at his trial. Further, since Charles had not had the articles of war read to him when he enlisted, he did not know he was breaking military law. She pleaded that he be allowed to reenlist in his regiment. The crime of desertion could not easily be dismissed, because it struck hard at family honor. Decades after the war had ended, families continued the struggle to clear the names of loved ones. In July 1884 Willeyan Parker, a poor, eighty-year-old mother, successfully pleaded the case of her son, Elias Queen. His charge of desertion was removed in 1886.[7]

Family members made special requests for furloughs and discharges for their men. In some cases kinfolk pleaded illness or disability as a reason for the return of their loved ones. Mary Bower of Baltimore wrote to Col. O. P. Stearns in June 1865 unsuccessfully seeking a discharge for her son, John Bower, 39th USCI, claiming that she was disabled and her son was "all my support."

Kinfolk pointed to the poor health of their men and argued that their very survival depended on securing a discharge. Sarah Whitfield wrote to Stanton in December 1863 asking for the discharge of her sixteen-year-old son, George, who, suffering from respiratory problems, had run away from home and joined the 14th Rhode Island Heavy Artillery. In some cases correspondents offered to buy substitutes. One, Julia Rowser, wrote unsuccessfully to President Lincoln and Secretary Stanton before her husband was granted a discharge, on the condition that his place be taken by a substitute.[8]

Issues of poverty, punishment, illness, and injury were matters of universal concern for the families of Civil War soldiers. What made the black soldiers' family correspondence unique was how relatives laid claim to the Negroes' changed status. The soldiers' military service enabled families to make powerful claims for equal treatment. When Mrs. Nancy Weir of Rochester, New York, wrote to Lincoln in February 1864 seeking the bounty of her son, Pvt. James S. Weir, 54th Massachusetts Volunteers, so she could support his infirm father, she was careful to note that "he went to the battle field with sorrow of heart because of the Helpless ones dependent on him." Yet "we see drunkards because of their white [skin] receive that which is due to all equal." White drunks could be paid but black heroes could not. In an endorsement on the letter, Private Weir's commanding officer, Col. E. N. Hallowell, admitted the inherent merit of Mrs. Weir's claims, stating, "Private Weir was enlisted under false representations he having been promised by the authorizing agents, the same bounty, pay, rations &c as is given to white soldiers. Many of the families have suffered severely because the government has failed to fulfill its contract with them."[9] Another mother, Hannah Johnson, who also had a son in the 54th Massachusetts, wrote to Lincoln arguing that colored men who were fighting for the nation should be treated as prisoners of war and not be sold as slaves. "You must put the rebels to work in state prisons to making shoes and things, if they sell our colored soldiers till they let them all go. And give their wounded the same treatment. It would seem cruel, but their is no other way, and a just man must do hard things sometimes, that shew him to be a great man."[10]

Hannah Johnson's letter defending the rights of black prisoners of war reinforced the fact that the security and freedom of Northern black communities depended on the defeat of the Confederacy. The soldiers knew this. Many of them had in fact enlisted to save the Union and protect their loved ones from the encroaching power of the Confederacy. For these soldiers the war was a personal challenge to their manhood. Writing in August 1864 from the Petersburg front, Sgt. George De Courcy, 1st USCI, informed the editor of the *Christian Recorder* that he had "left the home of a dear mother and father and many relatives, whom" he loved and respected "next to God." There was nothing unique about this sacrifice; "many other soldiers [had] done the same, to save the country and dear homes from a savage and invading foe." For Cpl. Henry C. Harmon, in camp at Morris Island, South Carolina, it was a question of rights. He praised Congress for allowing the "colored men to do something to elevate our race." This action had enabled "a great many of us to go forth to battle for our country's rights, our rights, our people's rights, and to help the Government preserve the glorious Union."[11]

While regular mail deliveries generally nurtured the soldiers' love of the Union, some mail cast shadows of despair. Stories of poverty and poor health drained the emotional energy of the men and undermined their morale. Some questioned their own manhood, believing they had failed as husbands and fathers. Even when they managed to secure furloughs, they often returned home destitute and in bad health. Some frustrated and disillusioned soldiers blamed their officers for their plight. When on duty at Fort Pickens, Florida, in October 1864, Jacob Johnson complained that the officers had "various loads of punishments, . . . to keep us in subjection." There was "nothing to cheer the poor colored volunteers but privations and excessive fatigue." Yet this suffering was nothing compared to that experienced by loved ones at home. Indeed, the soldiers' minds were "harrowed up with frightful" and "true pictures of their families' destitution." "We have the same feelings for our wifes and children at home and we are study the welfare off them as much as do the white soldiers," wrote Sgt. John H. Morgan, Fourteenth Corps d'Afrique, on behalf of the other sergeants in his regiment to Lincoln in January 1864. Morgan reported that the "majority of men in this Regiment" had "familys in New Orleans[,] and from letters received" they appeared to be "in a starving condition." Arguing for equal pay, he complained that "we cant seport them on seven dollars per month."[12]

Concern about the plight of loved ones did not abate when the fighting stopped. Agitated soldiers pleaded to be allowed to return to civilian life so they could take care of their kin. In July 1865, Sgt. Isaac Watson, 5th Massachusetts Cavalry, wrote to Stanton from Clarksville, Texas, desperately asking that he be allowed to go home so he could care for his sick wife and two children. Fourteen-year-old drummer boy Rezin Brown, 19th USCI, pleaded with the secretary of war to be released from the service, arguing that he had given fourteen months of continuous service and that his mother had written to him asking him to "come home." Since he was a son who "respects his folks," he had unsuccessfully applied to his regiment for furloughs on three occasions. "They have put me off saying that i was nothing but a boy and did not need one." Unwilling to accept failure, Brown "thought he would write to a higher authority."[13]

A great number of soldiers who were former slaves were keen to return home to protect their loved ones who were still living in slavery. Military service gave these men new opportunities to assert their kinship obligations. While serving in the army they made strenuous efforts to communicate with loved ones still in captivity, undertook rescue operations, and provided aid to family members living in contraband camps.[14]

Soldiers from the border states who were aware of their families' suffering often appealed to their officers and to government officials for assistance. One anonymous soldier, writing from Chattanooga, Tennessee, in August 1865, on behalf of soldiers in the 16th, 18th, and 44th USCI Regiments, "late from Mo and Ka" (from Missouri and Kansas), reported their families were "threadless and shoeless without food and no home to go to." In some cases, "their masters run them off." Urgent action was required; the soldier feared that the "hole race will fall back if the U.S. Government doesn't provide for them."[15]

Soldiers from rebel-held regions of the South knew that their military service could compound the suffering of their kin who remained in bondage. In a very real sense, they saw themselves as personal liberators. While at Camp Saxton, Beaufort, South Carolina, in December 1862, Colonel Higginson's men uttered determined prayers for the salvation and relief of their kin.[16] Not even death could separate them from their loved ones. "I hab leff my wife in de land ob bondage, my little ones dey say ebry night where is my fader? But when I die, when de bressed morning rises when I shall stand in de glory, wid one foot on de water & one foot in on de land, den, O Lord, I shall see my wife & my little chil'en once more."[17]

A number of former slaves joined the Union army in order to rescue their loved ones. Capt. Etham Earle reported that his company sergeant, Clement Johnson, a Methodist preacher, had joined the 1st Kansas Colored Volunteers in order to search for his wife and daughter. Unwilling to wait for the Union Army to act, squads of black soldiers on furlough from St. Louis, Missouri, successfully mounted raids into Howard County, Missouri, in March 1864 in order to rescue their families.[18]

Even when black soldiers managed to rescue their families, the operations were not always joyous. This was because plantation owners sometimes took slave children with them when they fled. Mothers and remaining members of the family had then to make the difficult decision of whether to desert their children and gain their freedom or remain on the plantation and hope that the master would return with their children once the Union troops had left. On other occasions, poor health prevented the hazardous journey through rebel-held territory, even with an army escort. In a few cases elderly slaves preferred to stay on the plantation and continue in service. This was some-times the case with house slaves who had "benevolent" masters.[19]

Some families managed to escape intact from slavery, particularly in Vir-ginia and along the coasts of South Carolina and Georgia. On abandoned plantations and on the estates of loyal masters in the Mississippi Valley and Louisiana, slave families also retained their essential integrity. There, how-ever, families located within Union lines and often in close proximity to black troop encampments, created a number of problems for the officers in command of black regiments. Because the federal government lacked any consistent, all-embracing policy of relief for the soldiers' families, the wives and children sometimes survived by working in the army camps as cooks, servants, and laundresses. Susie K. Taylor, a teacher, cook, and nurse, and her friend Mary Shaw gave invaluable service to the men of the 1st South Carolina Colored Volunteers. So too did Nurse "Sister Penny," wife of Tho-mas Penny, 5th USCI. However, the opportunities for paid work within the camps were limited. Families were thrown on their own resources. Women labored tirelessly on abandoned plantations, leased plantations, and lived in contraband camps to make provision for their families. Government ra-tions supplemented their efforts; so too did visits to the army camps.[20]

Like all commanding officers, those commanding black regiments were fearful of the damaging impact the presence of civilians could have on camp morale and discipline. In addition, USCT officers feared that the presence of former slaves in their camps would do much to revive the habits of slavery. This was particularly so with women intruders. Writing in his chaplaincy report from Vicksburg in November 1864, Chaplain Thomas Calahan noted that "very many of the women that have gathered into the camp are the vilest of their sex and only seek marriage as a means of support without work."[21]

The presence of women and children in camp became a pressing prob-lem for USCT commanders in western Tennessee and the Mississippi Valley in the fall and winter of 1864–65. There the freedmen sheltering in contra-band camps found few resources and little protection from exploitation. Capt. William Ferry, 14th Michigan Infantry, observed in February 1864 that the contraband camp near Memphis had become "a scene of prostitu-tion" for white soldiers. Women "were herded together like cattle & sol-diers went among them picking out as they might fancy here & there one to satiate lust." Many of the victims were the wives of soldiers, their "men taken away from their families and sent here and there at the point of the bayonet to work or enlist." The "wives & daughters who were left became the subjects of brutality." Conditions in the contraband camps were so bad that thousands fled to the army camps to seek the protection of their kin.[22]

Many of those seeking shelter in the army camps had been driven off their plantations by rebel masters who were seeking to punish the families of Union soldiers. Lt. Warren Goodale, 114th USCI,[23] reported on this practice in a letter to his children. Commenting on the plight of one of his Kentucky soldiers, he noted, "Last evening I answered a letter from a man's wife who said she had received only one of four he had sent. The white folks had destroyed the rest. She had been driven to leave them at last by the cruelty." Soldiers who were aware of the cruelty of their former masters sought leave to go home to protect their families. Pvt. George Washington, 123d USCI, wrote to "Mr Abraham Lincoln" asking for a discharge to go home and rescue his "Woman" Malindia Iann and four children from "a hard master one that loves the South [and] hangs with it." His former master, "David Sparks in Oldham Co Ky. [County, Kentucky]," refused to give his family sustenance; "he says let old Abe Giv them close [clothes]." Even when the soldiers' families could eke out existences, the poverty caused by the soldiers' lack of pay caused considerable distress. "The regiment has not been paid for six months and the families of the men are all needy and a good deal clamorous," remarked Chaplain Thomas Calahan, 48th USCI, in his November 1864 chaplaincy report from Vicksburg.[24]

In his September 1864 chaplaincy report, Thomas Calahan claimed that the soldiers were continually pointing to the rebel raids in the region of Vicksburg as an excuse for having their families "hanging about camp." Their presence brought "injury" to "good order among the men," led to a "perpetuation of disease and misery" in the camp, and resulted in the "vexing of the officers by annoyance." Other chaplains made similar complaints.[25]

The military and logistical problems created by the soldiers' families were so great that they caused concern at the highest levels. A policy of self-reliance was introduced by Brig. Gen. Lorenzo Thomas during the early stages of black recruitment in the Mississippi Valley. After visiting a number of contraband camps, Thomas wrote to Stanton in September 1863 recommending that women and children "should be made to do such work as is suitable for their sex and age and with this view." He decided to "hire them to Union plantations to gather their crops." Thomas believed that the success of his black recruitment campaign in the Mississippi Valley depended on emphasizing the strong, positive relationship among labor, sustenance, and economic self-reliance. However, he was fearful that "family problems" would wreck his recruitment strategy and turn army posts into overcrowded contraband camps. Therefore, he issued specific directions to Lt. Col. J. Phillips, superintendent of freedmen, in western Tennessee, informing him that while "every company is entitled to a certain number of laundresses," the wives and children of soldiers had "no claim on the government for rations." Indeed, "the families of colored soldiers were on the same footing as other Blacks." They would be required to work. In the interest of military discipline, he was totally "opposed to having large numbers of women and children around stations of Colored Troops." However, the poverty of the soldiers' families and the uncertainty about the exact nature of government regulations induced General Thomas to telegraph the War Department seeking clarification and assistance. Maj. Charles W. Foster, Bureau of Colored Troops, informed Thomas that military law regarding black soldiers made "no provision for their families except freedom to such as owned by disloyal masters."[26]

USCT camp commanders in Tennessee and the Mississippi Valley attempted to solve the problems caused by the soldiers' families in a number of ways. First, some simply placed severe restrictions on women and children entering camp and the soldiers returning home. Second, some USCT commanders moved their camps or relocated the soldiers' families to distant contraband camps. Finally, long-term solutions were attempted by placing the families in self-supporting environments.

Those camp commanders who severely restricted communication between the men and their families actually exacerbated their problems. This policy of social isolation encouraged the soldiers to "run the guard" and, in some cases, desert. In some localities, absentee and desertion rates were so high that officers found it prudent to ignore the problem. Officers even tried to make informal agreements with their men and promised them extra leave if they stopped "running the guard." Capt. Henry Fox, 59th USCI, made this kind of agreement with his company. During their first nine months of service, many soldiers from Captain Fox's company deserted and returned to their home district of Bolivar, Tennessee. According to Fox's commanding officer, Lt. Col. Robert Cowden, "Capt. Fox prevented desertions, and saved many of his men, by making them a promise that he would, at some time, take them in a body, to visit their families." Upon resigning from the service, Fox attempted to fulfill his part of the bargain; however, Brig. Gen. Augustus L. Chetlain, commanding the District of Memphis, would allow Fox's men to be furloughed only in squads of six.[27]

Even when regiments moved away from their home areas, family problems did not disappear. Surgeon Henry Penniman, 1st Mississippi Heavy Artillery, African Descent, blamed "homesickness" as the primary cause of death in his camp. He believed that "the blacks race are greater sufferers both in frequency of cases and mortality from homesickness than whites." This meant that they were "so debilitated in mind and body as to fall easy victims to any disease." Therefore, "many deaths accredited to other causes" could be "more properly be classed under the head of nostalgia." In some cases the families actually followed the soldiers on the march. When military maneuvers made this impossible, final departures were charged with emotion. Feelings of bitterness and betrayal surfaced, since many soldiers believed that they had been recruited specifically on the promise that they would not leave their home areas and that the government would protect their families. In March 1864 Capt. Samuel Barnes, 64th USCI, wrote in his diary that when Col. Samuel Thomas ordered his men to leave Goodrich Landing, Louisiana, "the men thought we had cheated them." Barnes admitted, "They have been deceived it is true," but he excused himself, claiming, "I have not done it, nor could I help it."[28]

One of the most common solutions to the problems caused by the presence of the soldiers' families in camp was simply to transport them to a distant contraband camp. Initially established by Union commanders to shelter ex-slave families, aid employment, and reduce contact between the Union soldiers and the ex-slave population, these camps held thousands of refugees. Although the superintendent of contrabands and Northern freedmen's aid workers did much to alleviate suffering by dispensing rations, providing elementary education, and reuniting families, the camps remained essentially poverty traps that harbored disease. Not surprising, the soldiers strongly objected to their families being moved to them. Soldiers stationed at Vicksburg "complained bitterly" when their families were relocated in early 1864. In some situations, USCT commanders actually argued against relocation, claiming that it would only undermine morale and exacerbate discipline problems. It was for this reason that Col. Ignatz Kappner, sought to prevent the removal of his enlisted men from Fort Pickering, Memphis, to a camp located farther south.[29]

Officers who lacked Colonel Kappner's empathy and insight, and callously removed the soldiers' families to distant locations, invariably compounded the suffering in their camps. This appears to have been the case at Camp Nelson, Kentucky, in November 1864. An important training camp for black soldiers, Camp Nelson attracted hundred of destitute families in the fall and winter of 1864. Confronted by the "Nigger Woman Question," Camp Nelson's commander, Brig. Gen. Speed Smith Fry, feared a breakdown in military discipline, a drain on government rations, and outbreaks of disease. Adhering to government policy, Fry attempted to expel the families from his camp on a number of occasions. In an act of exasperation, he drove approximately four hundred women and children from the camp on November 23, 1864. Exposed to winter climate, the suffering of the families was intense.[30]

One soldier, Joseph Miller, 124th USCI, reported in an affidavit that "the morning was bitter cold. It was freezing hard. I was certain it would kill my sick child to take him out in the cold. I told the man in charge of the guard that it would be the death of my boy. I told him my wife and children had no place to go and I told him that I was a soldier of the United States. He told me that it did not make any difference. He had orders to take all out of Camp."[31] Miller's prediction proved correct. On the night of November 23, he found his wife and children "shivering with cold and famished with hunger. They had not received a morsel of food during the whole day." His "boy was dead." The next morning he "walked to Nicholasville," where he "dug a grave and buried" his son.[32]

The Camp Nelson tragedy was roundly condemned by both the Northern press and military authorities, and it resulted in a refuge home being established at Camp Nelson for the soldiers' families. Perhaps this decisive response occurred because the Camp Nelson incident represented the culmination of a long line of abuses heaped upon the families of black soldiers. Reports of such abuses had appeared in the Northern press. For example, on August 19, 1864, the *Commonwealth* published a letter from "A Colored Soldier" stationed in Louisville, Kentucky, which had first appeared in the *New York Tribune*. The soldier complained that enlisted men had been cruelly treated. "Their wives and children are whipped before their faces because they come to see and encourage their husbands and fathers, who, perhaps, they have not seen for years, to fight for the country."[33]

Although incidents of arbitrary mistreatment were common, efforts were made to find permanent solutions to family sustenance problems by relocating them in self-supporting environments. Generally this meant placing them on "loyal" plantations or establishing self-supporting family colonies. These two solutions to the complex web of "domestic" problems that faced the officers may best be studied in the Mississippi Valley and Louisiana, the regions with the highest contraband populations.

In mid-1863, Lorenzo Thomas implemented an agricultural plan aimed at securing a loyal population along the Mississippi River. The central element of this plan was the movement of the displaced black population, including soldiers' families, from the contraband camps to leased plantations. The lessees, mainly Northern speculators, some "loyal southerners," and a handful of freedmen, agreed to hire the former slaves who had gathered at the contraband camps, pay them wages, and provide for their families. Two special regiments—the 9th and 7th Louisiana Volunteers, African Descent (63d and 64th USCI)—under the command of Col. John Eaton and Col. Samuel Thomas, respectively, were created to administer the scheme and to coordinate the movement of labor. Black soldiers were, therefore, given the unenviable task of emptying the contraband camps and placing loved ones under the "protection" of "benevolent," and supposedly "loyal," employers.[34]

The policy of forcing the soldiers' families to work on leased plantations proved a failure, for a number of reasons. First, many lessees exploited the women and children, paying them very low wages and failing to provide them with adequate shelter. Chaplain George Carruthers commented that the families of his men were treated "as slaves." Fellow chaplain Thomas Calahan discovered that after "the soldiers' families had been defrauded out of their wages by the lessees and turned adrift," they "poured into camp, to the great detriment of good order and the efficiency and steadiness of the troops." In these circumstances, the soldiers who witnessed the plights of their loved ones strove to ameliorate the resettlement policy. In April 1864, supported by a few Northern missionaries, soldiers stationed at Natchez used the threat of desertion, and violence, to win better conditions for their families who had been uprooted and placed on lessee plantations. Indirectly, the soldiers were also instrumental in having those responsible for ruthlessly implementing the family displacement policy relieved of their commands.[35]

Second, lessees and cotton speculators generally required labor only in the busy harvest season; in the slack winter months, labor was readily shed. Chaplain Carruthers, 51st USCI, reporting from his camp near Vicksburg in January 1865, observed that the action of cotton speculators had resulted in "a number of women about camp." He believed that "as long as cotton speculators can pick them up and work them for this interest during the summer and leave them unpaid and destitute in the winter, the matter will be no better." Finally, the plantations were also exposed to rebel raids. The fact that "the rebels are continually raiding the plantations killing and carrying away colored people" was, according to Chaplain Calahan, "a plea" used by the soldiers' families for "hanging about camp." The net impact of all these factors was that the soldiers' families were pushed back to the army camps.[36]

In the Department of the Gulf, Maj. Gen. Nathaniel P. Banks's "free labor system," developed in detail in General Orders No. 23 in February 1864, removed the more odious features of slavery but retained the notion that the Negro had a contractual obligation to labor for the white employer. While the scheme placed mutual obligations on the planters and laborers, it placed much stricter controls on the contracted laborers, who received low wages and were restricted in their freedom of movement. Banks justified these restrictions by claiming that he was elevating the black race by protecting family unity and teaching idle blacks to be self-reliant. In a letter to William Lloyd Garrison, he argued that "the unity of the family is the essential requisite of any system for the elevation of the negro race."[37]

Banks was particularly concerned about the plight of the black soldiers' families. In an 1863 letter written to the Enrollment Commission, which the department established to deal with issues affecting the freedmen, Banks pledged that "no woman nor child" would "be made to suffer in any way whatever on account of their connection with soldiers enrolled in the military service of the United States." Any action taken against the soldiers' families "ought to be, and must be punished with severity." However, "the families of colored men engaged in the service" were not to be "relieved from the necessity of labor, any more than the families of men in the white regiments." They were to be "provided with comfortable places, and protected in their employment by the officers of the government." While pledging assistance for the sick and the infirm, Banks warned that families would be separated from their men, because it was "impossible that they should follow the regiments in which their friends" were "enrolled." "Soldiers separated in this manner" were permitted to visit their families at "proper times, under the protection of passes," but they were not "allowed to interfere with the arrangements made by the Commission of Enrollment for the protection, the support, or the employment of their families."[38]

The implementation of Banks's free labor system had a significant impact on the black soldiers' families that had gathered near the camps for sustenance and protection. Although he was a staunch supporter of Banks's labor system, Chaplain Thomas Conway, 79th USCI (old), believed that his policy of forced resettlement had damaging results on the soldiers at Camp Ullmann, in the Brashear area. As a consequence, he did all he could "to avoid the great evils resulting from this abrupt and cruel separation" of soldiers' families to "some plantation in the distance." In order to maintain family unity, Conway compiled a family "Directory," "embracing the names, residences" of the families "so that the soldiers may, when paid, be able to assist them." The action was taken at the behest of the soldiers who on the morning of their families' departure begged Conway "to keep a record of their wives and children and to prevent such a separation as will result in their not knowing where their families are." A diligent pastor, Conway toured the plantations less than two weeks after the families' departure, "tabling the name and noting the situation of the families of the enlisted men now at Camp Ullmann."[39]

Soldiers' families received the greatest amount of official protection in the Departments of Virginia and North Carolina. There, the families were given special protection from the general sweep of labor policies by Maj. Gen. Benjamin F. Butler's labor system, which was first promulgated in General Orders No. 46 in December 1863. Butler broke new ground by publicizing the special responsibilities the government had to the families of its enlisted men. They were given certificates entitling them to government rations and protection. Yet in spite of these promises, the integrity of the soldiers' family life was often threatened, and, after the war ended, the army violated Butler's agreement.[40]

Aside from these large-scale, regional schemes, a number of small, localized labor arrangements operated to meet the specific needs of the families of men in camps in problem areas. In August 1865, Lt. Col. Robert Cowden, 59th USCI, faced pressing problems providing sustenance for the families of his men who were doing garrison duty at Fort Pickering, Memphis. As a solution, Cowden suggested a number of self-supporting occupations the soldiers' wives could engage in, including domestic work in Memphis, laboring in nearby cotton fields, and doing the "washing or ironing for soldiers and citizens." In order to prevent conflict, he "conversed with" his men and "pointed out to them the consequences of idleness and the reward of industry." The men "seemed pleased and satisfied with that" he said, and "though all of them would prefer their families should remain for the present," they offered "no opposition to other measures."[41]

Because Cowden's employment policy was heavily dependent on the vocational opportunities available in the city of Memphis, its success was somewhat limited. Cities such as Memphis, Nashville, and Vicksburg, with significant contraband populations and large garrisons of black troops, simply lacked the employment and resources necessary to provide permanent sustenance to the soldiers' families. Most USCT commanders realized this and generally sought to solve their logistical problems by returning the families to the land. In some cases this meant encouraging them to establish self-sustaining garden colonies in the vicinity of the camps. An important corollary of this policy was the encouragement of habits of self-reliance in the ex-slave population. Indeed, camp commanders expected the colonies to yield two important moral benefits: the development of self-reliant households and the eradication of female "loafers." In some circumstances the family garden became an extension of the soldiers' camp. Two communities developed that, though separated by distance, were bound together by personal ties of affection and by the officers' commitment to military discipline and to the principles of self-reliance.[42]

A number of soldiers' colonies were established in the vicinity of Vicksburg in the fall and winter of 1864. Surrounded by contraband settlements and garrisoned after its seizure by a large number of black troops, Vicksburg was a city in which the plight of the soldiers' families was acute. Col. Herman Lieb, of the 5th U.S. Colored Heavy Artillery, was well aware of the problems caused by his regiment's close proximity to contraband camps. The camps were sources of disease and drains upon the regiment's resources. Many of the soldiers pilfered army rations in order to provide for their loved ones. Relatives of deceased soldiers, "penniless and thrown out into the world without a friend," were "thrown on the government for support." Moreover, family poverty induced many soldiers to desert.

Colonel Lieb attempted to solve these problems by ordering his men to move their families to the vicinity of Vicksburg. There they erected log cabins and established gardens for their kinfolk. A small squad of soldiers from the regiment protected this "garden colony." However, it was the women who provided the dynamism that made the venture a viable, self-supporting enterprise. Employing skills they had learned during slavery, the women worked together to support their families. Their productive capacity increased as the colony's tenure lengthened. In time they began to support their men and the Union war effort by sending garden produce to Colonel Lieb's camp.[43]

Col. Charles A. Gilchrist adopted a solution similar to that of Colonel Lieb. The wives and daughter of his men took over "three hundred acres of land in the suburbs" of Vicksburg. Chaplain James Peet reported that each family was allocated "about one acre" on which they could "build a house and cultivate a garden." In early November 1864, Peet reported that sixty-four locations had already been taken up, many of the families living in condemned army tents that had been sold to them at cost by Colonel Gilchrist.[44]

Yet not all schemes were successful. Maj. George L. Stearns tried but failed to establish a large family settlement on the Fairview estate, near Gallatin, Tennessee, in the fall of 1863. He proposed to divide the estate into two hundred, two-acre family "lots." Each family would live in a "hut" located on their lot and gain sustenance by working on the estate for six hours a day and by cultivating their family lots. A chaplain would be provided to educate the children and enforce "cleanliness" "in and about the farm." Major Stearns's plans were never implemented, possibly because he was unable to secure the active support of Andrew Johnson, the governor of Tennessee.[45]

Elsewhere in the South, other family settlement schemes were introduced. Brig. Gen. E. A. Wild encouraged his soldiers' wives to create a family colony on Roanoke Island, North Carolina, in June 1863. To help ensure the success of his scheme, General Wild wrote to prominent abolitionists and sent Horace James, the superintendent of freedmen in the Department of North Carolina, into the Northern states in search of funds for "THE NEW SOCIAL ORDER IN THE SOUTH." However, the position of soldiers' families remained precarious. They remained heavily dependent on government rations, and when these were reduced, great hardship ensued.[46]

In South Carolina, Maj. Gen. Quincy Gillmore established soldier settlements on abandoned plantations. In January 1864 he wrote to the secretary of the treasury, Salmon P. Chase, urging that "the families of colored soldiers . . . be provided for by allowing them to locate upon and cultivate lands, in advance of the regular survey and sale thereof." Acting on the authority of Major General Gillmore, Colonel Higginson had his soldiers' families safely relocated on Treasury-owned plantations near Hilton Head in February 1864.[47]

Although the family settlement schemes were established primarily to solve discipline problems, they also reflected some salient aspects of prevailing abolitionist ideology. They were, in effect, efforts to restore the black soldiers' manhood by placing them at the heads of viable family households. Many officers believed that blacks would become a self-supporting, loyal bulwark in the South if they received land to develop small farms or adequate wages for their plantation labor. Certainly this was the viewpoint that Brig. Gen. James Wadsworth presented when testifying before the American Freedmen Inquiry Commission shortly after he had toured the Mississippi Valley inspecting lessee plantations, contraband camps, and Negro troops in the fall of 1863. Principles of self-reliance appeared to be particularly applicable to the families of black soldiers. Freedmen were urged to become industrious workers so that they might become economically independent citizens. This was the basic objective of the "Port Royal Experiment," carried out by Northern abolitionists on abandoned plantations in the Sea Islands of South Carolina. Research by Lawrence Powell has shown that officers commanding black troops often actively participated in plantation agriculture in the South after the war had ended. For these veteran officers, the profit motive was of paramount importance. However, some also believed that their profitable agricultural pursuits could have an edifying impact on the ex-slaves. Certainly this was true of Capt. Henry M. Crydenwise, who worked his land with men who had served under him during the war. Along with education and the ballot, free labor and land ownership formed basic elements in the radical reconstruction of the South.[48]

Family settlements provided the soldiers' families with a degree of economic security. Yet this security did not begin an ideological revolution. It would be incorrect to believe, as did Colonels Lieb, Gilchrist, Higginson, and Cowden, that they had somehow managed to inculcate in the former slaves not only the Protestant work ethic but also the value of land ownership. Their family colonies were successful because they gave black women new opportunities to utilize skills and abilities they had developed on the plantations. Although these colonies were dependent on Union army protection, the women were not passive recipients of military largesse. They carved out their own existences by the labor of their own hands. The vegetables and garments they sent to their loved ones in the army became important in the war effort. These tangible symbols of affection sustained the soldiers physically and emotionally. For illiterate men, the arrival of these goods was just as important as the receipt of letters.[49]

In many camps, campaigns of moral education ran concurrently with efforts to relocate the soldiers' families in self-sufficient colonies. These campaigns endeavored to undo the work of slavery by teaching the soldiers the duties and privileges of family life. Although the officers attributed to the slaves some of the behavior allegedly seen in lower-class Northern whites, they believed that the slaves were much more immoral and demoralized, simply because they were thought to be racially inferior and had been subjected to a cruel labor regime. "Among other infamous outrages committed by the slaveholders," reported Capt. Stanton Weaver, 62d USCI, in a letter to the *National Anti-Slavery Standard,* "is the sundering of family ties and utter disregard of the marriage relation." Casual observations of prenuptial intercourse and pregnancy made the officers' negative perception of slave morality and family life even more firmly entrenched.[50]

Camp chaplains took upon themselves the difficult task of morally reforming the men. For some chaplains this meant little more than preaching against the sins of the flesh, including drunkenness, profanity, and sexual immorality. Others actively probed the private lives of their soldiers. Acting as God's police, they attempted to root out evil and in its place plant seeds of Christian virtue and love. These chaplains began to focus on Christian marriage as the main vehicle for moral reform.[51]

Chaplains saw Christian marriage as the gateway to respectable citizenship, as a religious ritual that was a public affirmation of Christian values. Participants make vows of fidelity and love. Implicit in the ceremony is a commitment to Christian parenthood. Yet the marriages celebrated by the chaplains in the army camps were more than simple religious rituals. They were, in fact, bold social experiments, audacious attempts to reshape the soldier's identity. The crusade for moral reform, therefore, became an opportunity to restore the soldiers' manhood. Issues of morality were inextricably linked to sexuality. The whole process of black enlistment was part of a much wider movement to develop in the Union soldier generally a manly spirit and a new commitment to the nation. Military service became an important vehicle for manhood and citizenship education, and all recruits, from diverse regional, ethnic, and racial backgrounds, experienced this learning process. Because blacks were considered to be racially inferior and corrupted by slavery, they were deemed to be most in need of moral education. The time-honored goals of military service associated with acts of duty, discipline, courage, and patriotism all contained value lessons for the freedman.

Approximately two months after Appomattox, Col. Joseph Jones and the officers of the 6th USCI wrote to Thomas Fletcher, the governor of Missouri, to inform him that their regiment was being demobilized and that the discharged men were now ready to take their place as citizens of the state of Missouri. Military service had prepared the black soldier for this day. Jones assured the governor that while the officers had been "laboring to instruct" the soldiers "in military knowledge," they had "also endeavored to inculcate correct ideas of manliness, and of those things that will be expected of them when they shall come to act for themselves as citizens." War service became the embodiment of masculine virtue. In their training programs and camp routines, the officers endeavored to impart these values to their soldiers. Battle was the ultimate test of manhood. "Prove yourselves men!" cried Col. Robert Shaw just before his regiment began its bloody assault on Fort Wagner. "Now boys, for the honor of the black brigade! Show the Sixth Corps you are men! This is your chance!" cried Colonel Sigfried as he urged his men forward at the battle of the Wilderness.[52]

However, physical courage was not the only measure of manhood. Officers, particularly the chaplains, also sought to instill in their men the traits of true manhood. By employing military training and moral instruction they endeavored to teach their black soldiers to be loyal to their comrades, to do their patriotic duty to the Union, and to uphold the honor of their families. Above all, the soldiers were urged to show manly self-restraint by resisting moral vices and the sins of the flesh. It was Chaplain Walter C. Yancey's "object as far as possible to impress upon" his soldiers "not only the importance of their religious obligations but to inspire them with a proper sense of the true dignity of manhood." Chaplains such as Walter C. Yancey encouraged their men to display moral responsibility, to make provision for their children and wives, to restrain their sexual passions, and to take their kinship obligations seriously. Ultimately this involved becoming the patriarchal heads of households. Those soldiers who accepted this challenge were urged by the chaplains to sign the marriage contract. Moral precepts were thus bound in contractual legal sanctions.[53]

Chaplain George Carruthers, in contrast, used the institution of marriage primarily as a sexual safety valve, to curtail the level of promiscuity in his camp. In his January 1865 chaplaincy report, written near Vicksburg, he admitted that he had "married seventeen couples during the month," even though he "generally discouraged such relations while the soldier" was "in the army." However, he was prepared to override this consideration in order to prevent an increase in sexual immorality. "Rather than see them live in promiscuous adultery," he had "married such as were urgent when there was no other objection." Chaplain Yancey, stationed at St. Charles, Arkansas, in winter 1864, was far less reluctant to marry the couples that came before him. Indeed, he saw the increasing numbers of soldiers wanting to get married as indicative of a "disposition on the part of the troops to conform to the requirements of Christianity and the usages of civilized life." Moral reform appeared to be working.[54]

Chaplains were keen to marry couples who had established lasting relations during slavery. While stationed at Vicksburg in December 1864, James Peet married Jeffrey Cammel, of Company E, and Bertina Thompson, who had "lived together 16 years by slave marriage." Three months earlier he had married "forty couples of this regiment [the 50th USCI], some of whom had lived together according to the slave system thirty years without legal marriage." However, he frowned upon marrying couples who had supposedly struck up casual relationships. Older men, living in permanent relationships and "who already have a family," were considered the most eligible candidates for marriage. Sometimes chaplains refused to marry young men, because they believed it would be far better for them to wait until after the war was over, when their futures would be more secure.[55]

Some chaplains adopted rigid marriage policies because of their very low estimations of the sexual mores of black women. Many saw them as the antithesis of the Northern lady, who exemplified Christian domesticity, displayed feminine virtues such as gentleness and compassion, and nurtured good moral order. Independent, promiscuous black females appeared to flout the code of true womanhood and pose a serious moral danger to the soldiers. Conscious of the influx of "vagrant women" into his camp near Vicksburg in November 1864, Thomas Calahan refused to marry some couples because he believed that the women in the camp were the "vilest of their sex and only seek marriage as a means of support without work." Calahan was "persuaded that neither God's law nor those of the United States, contemplate making marriage a cloak for vagrancy." While serving at Brazos Santiago, Texas, in April 1866, Chaplain Thomas S. Johnson was "very much discouraged sometimes" when he saw his soldiers and their wives "acting so unfaithfully to their marriage vows." This situation was not unexpected, for this was "the regular education of slavery."

He was particularly concerned about the way married women appeared to flout social conventions by engaging in casual relationships with soldiers who were not their husbands. Social horse-riding parties were events of particular concern, because a married woman who engaged in them undermined her husband's role as the "natural guardian and companion for the wife." Johnson was so outraged by open displays of sexual immorality that he accused the women in his camp of destroying family life and "domestic joy." "Most of them" acted "as if they were only pets and dolls for their husbands to fondle and pet." Such overt displays of passion inevitably led to sexual rivalry among the men, "and then too often suspicion, jealousy and unfaithfulness ruin all domestic joy." Army life was not conducive to domestic bliss; it was "all unnatural," with no "good society." Yet unattractive as army life was, he continued to celebrate the institution of marriage in his regiment. He did so primarily because he believed that marriage could restrain the soldiers' sexual appetites. In common with other servants of God, he believed it was better for his men to marry than to burn with lust and live immoral lives. When he discovered in October 1865 that several women in his camp were "living with men who were not lawfully their husbands," he had the regiment's commander issue a special order outlawing "this system of concubinage." The only women he wanted in his camp were those who were under the legal, moral, and religious "protection" of their husbands.[56]

The institution of marriage received official endorsement from the U.S. adjutant general. Brigadier General Thomas, in Special Orders No. 15, authorized "any ordained minister of the gospel to solemnize the rites of marriage among the Freedmen," provided they were "accredited by the General Superintendent of Freedmen." This official government policy reflected a concern to undo the immoral work of slavery and strengthen family ties. However, in addition to these broad social and moral goals, there were practical administrative gains to be made in dispensing aid to soldiers' families.[57]

Chaplains welcomed the government's initiative. Charles Buckley, 47th USCI, experienced the benefits of Special Orders No. 15 while he was struggling to provide aid for the families of his soldiers near Vicksburg in the winter of 1864–65. He believed it would now be easier to dispense aid, because there would be "no difficulty experienced in identifying such wives as have marriage certificates." The marriage certificates would be "a mutual benefit." They would "aid" the settling of relief claims, and "their importance in this connection" would "render them more valuable, and the marriage rite more sacred and binding in the minds of the candidates." Chaplain Peet, 50th USCI, also serving in the vicinity of Vicksburg, likewise recognized the benefits the soldiers gained from matrimony. He witnessed a "very decided improvement in the social and domestic feelings of those married by the authority and protection of the law." It was an affirmation of their manhood, in that "it causes them to feel that they are beginning to be regarded and treated as human beings."[58]

In some camps, marriage and sexual morality became important areas of conflict between devout chaplains and pragmatic officers. Some of these officers opposed the marriage of their troops, because they believed it made soldiers unfit for military service. Chaplain Yancey experienced this opposition in the 66th U.S. Colored Infantry. He believed that his opponents' policy was sacrilegious, "contrary to the spirit and letter of the Bible." Moreover, it promoted immorality in the camp; it was "calculated to encourage fornication and all those practices which degrade rather than elevate the soldier." In short, it crippled the development of the soldier's manhood, an objective "which the service requires."[59]

Even when officers permitted their soldiers to marry, their support for the holy institution of matrimony was often influenced by condescension and racism. Maj. Daniel Densmore and his colonel, attending a wedding in their camp at Fort Pickering, Tennessee, in January 1864, found it a source of comedy and amusement. The "Col." came in "nearly bursting with merriment" and invited Densmore "to a colored wedding to take place in his front room." Colonel Jones had just "been over to the sutler's and brought a twenty cent ring for Mr. Groom to place on the finger of Mrs. to be." Daniel

Densmore's arrival was greeted with enthusiasm by the wedding party, who cried "Hurrah, Major come over!!"[60]

Perhaps the officers were welcomed as wedding guests by the happy couple because they had formed bonds of friendship that transcended differences in rank. However, it is more likely that the rejoicing arose because the officers' presence gave the marriage visible status and official sanction. Slave marriages had no legal standing. The marriage of this particular former slave from Tennessee was different; it was a legally binding contract, promoted and defended by the might of the Union army. Yet it was more than this. It was also a public demonstration of the love and devotion the young couple had for each other. In essence, it was a ritualized vindication of the painfully long struggle for freedom. On the plantation, slaves had been keen to have their marriages recorded in "the book," the plantation journal, ledger, or daybook. This enthusiasm to legitimize a marriage by documenting it continued, with increased fervor, in the army.[61]

Chaplains and their fellow officers sometimes expressed disparaging views about the romantic liaisons that developed in the camp. They accused the soldiers' wives of sexual immorality and of being root causes of insubordination. "Promiscuous" females were "the enemy," unwelcome intruders. Union army commanders, including those commanding black troops, experienced difficulty devising policies to deal with the presence of prostitutes in or near their camps. Appearing before the American Freedman Inquiry Commission in 1863, Capt. E. W. Hooper, aide to Brig. Gen. Rufus Saxton, commanding U.S. forces at Beaufort, South Carolina, in the Department of the South, commented that there were a "great many women" in houses of prostitution located in the town of Beaufort, South Carolina. These women were "encouraged by the soldiers constantly and the officers protect and conceal them." In despair, Hooper admitted that he did not know what to do with them. Camp prostitutes were often the objects of ridicule. In a letter to his wife, Capt. Elliott Grabill noted that "it is a regular joke to speak of Company D's wife and Co. I's wife." Although prostitutes were present in some camps, Captain Grabill's comments ignored the fact that many women contributed to camp life by performing tasks such as cooking, nursing, and laundering. Moreover, some of these women established long-standing relationships with men who later became their husbands. Officers who assumed they were prostitutes failed to comprehend the social dynamics of camp life. Ironically, derogatory comments were sometimes made by officers who had comfortably housed their own wives in regimental quarters. A few unscrupulous officers also saw in the strong marital ties of their black soldiers an opportunity to make monetary gain by selling passes for family visits to their soldiers. In this regard, the soldiers of the 5th USCI, stationed at Bryant Station, near Lexington, Kentucky, suffered more than most. In October 1865 a "Soldier of 5 USCT" wrote to the secretary of war accusing the officers of preventing the soldiers' wives from visiting the camp and of forcing the men "to pay $30 for a 10 day pass" to visit them. The major of the regiment boasted that he would "keep these dam niggers in until" he made "a fortune."[62]

In some camps, conflict occurred between morally dissolute officers and the chaplains, who acted as the "moral guardians" of their men. The chaplains feared that the men would model themselves on these "ungodly degenerates." In their chaplaincy reports they denounced the corrupt officers for betraying their manhood by failing to show responsible leadership. Chaplain George Rockwood, 8th USCI, for example, accused the officers in his camp, located at Yellow Bluff on the St. John's River in Florida, of swearing and failing to curb the indecent and profane language of the soldiers under their command. Bitter experience had taught him that "if an officer profanes God's name it is very difficult to prevent cursing and swearing among the men."[63]

Although the soldiers shared some of chaplains' values, principally the desire to secure family lives and fidelity, they also held views that the chaplains did not fully share or necessarily understand. The soldiers and their wives believed that the marriage ceremony was the ritual culmination of a deliberate and meaningful courtship. On the plantation they had bitterly resented the slaveholders' intrusion in personal affairs. In the army camp they resisted chaplains who arbitrarily interfered in their personal relationships. Women proved strong opponents of the chaplains' intrusion; perhaps this partly explains why they were seen as moral threats. For the ex-slave women, marriage marked the beginning of family life. Marriage and motherhood were inextricably linked. These women cared little for the notions of sexual guilt that weighed so heavily on the minds of the chaplains; prenuptial intercourse had been common in the slave community. Therefore, some opposed the chaplains' matrimonial arrangements simply because they were not ready to have families. Inevitably, the most successful marriages were those that blessed long-standing relationships and gave loving parents legal sanction.[64]

As the number of marriages increased, so did the number of failed unions. Chaplains had considerable difficulty coping with this problem. While stationed at Fort Pickering, Tennessee, in July 1865, Chaplain Chauncey Taylor, reported that during the past year he had "married 300 of the men of his regiment and their wives." The marriage prospects of most celebrants appeared good, because "many of them lived together as husband and wife before the war." Furthermore, "a large number of them were disposed to be faithful to the marriage contract as could be expected under the circumstances." However, some marriage participants were so "dissolute and reckless," that Taylor felt compelled to warn the government that an "additional law" was "needed to provide for divorce in cases of adultery by one of the parties." He had "a great many such cases brought before him," and he did not "know what to do with them." Chaplain Joel Grant, 113th USCI, faced a similar but far less serious problem while serving at De Vall's Bluff, Arkansas, in March 1866. In an account of his activities as a marriage celebrant, Chaplain Grant reported that during the five and a half months he had "labored in this regiment," he had "solemnized 40 marriages, 36 of them of soldiers in this regiment." Over time Grant had developed a system of marriage education that appeared to be very successful. "At first," he "followed the too prevalent practice of marrying those who requested, insisting only on *prima facie* evidence that no objection existed." However, he "soon adopted a different plan." He required "the parties to appear before" him "and give an account of their former marriages (if any) and their present views, and receive instruction respecting the obligations domestic, social, civil, and moral involved in that relation." The education process culminated in the marriage ceremony. Grant required the celebrants "to arrange for a public marriage in the Chapel, or other suitable place." There he "could make the occasion one of more extended instruction" by preaching on the responsibilities of marriage to the assembled congregation.[65]

Although Grant's instructional activities had been "laborious," he was "pleased in the review of it." "The results (only the smallest part of them can yet be seen) have been happy." Of the "40 cases," twenty-five had "every prospect of constancy and happiness," nine were "too recent or too little under my eye to warrant the formation of an opinion," and six had been "more or less unhappy." Of the six failures, "four were married while the more thorough plan had not been adopted." In the majority of these four cases, "detected or publicly assumed (bigamy) guilt" warranted "the sundering of marriage ties." However, in spite of Grant's appeal to the Freedmen Bureau, there appeared "no available resource" "for the parties thus injured." He wanted to take the matter to the civil courts to protect the innocent party, but the regiment's disbanding prevented this course of action.[66]

Even though some camp marriages did fail, the majority survived. Their survival was, in part, evidence of the fact that the soldiers adopted at least some of the chaplains' views on marriage. Joel Grant's program of marriage education produced benefits, because the soldiers shared some of his moral values. They too wanted to establish permanent, legally binding relationships in which they could nurture their children and secure their property rights. Yet most army camp marriages survived simply because the marriage ceremonies and marriage certificates legitimized meaningful relationships that embraced community values. Marriages of this kind became community responsibilities. In the camps the soldiers established their own moral standards, an amalgam of inherited customs and acquired beliefs. The dynamic for enforcing these moral codes rested with the soldiers themselves. Chaplain Calahan saw a powerful demonstration of this fact while he was serving with the 48th USCI, at Vicksburg in June 1864. Soldiers who were elders of the "Baptist Church in the regiment" "turned a soldier out of church because he took up with a woman in stead of marrying her." Calahan "approved their action" and was "persuaded that there is among them a strong element of true religion" that would "appear better when times are more settled." As the war progressed, some soldiers even developed a sense of moral superiority over the poor Southern whites. Sgt. Alexander Newton, serving at Brownsville, Texas, shortly after war ended, noted that the poor whites lived in an uncivilized, degenerate manner. "The houses were little huts, the people dressed in their shirts and draws." The women "dressed in a long shirt with their breasts exposed, seemingly caring nothing for decency or modesty." It appeared that "the people here" had never "known what it was to know or serve the true and living God. They were certainly far from any such practical knowledge, judging from their daily lives."[67]

For soldiers, military service was a romantic adventure, and as they journeyed through the South, they formed romantic attachments at places as far afield as Vicksburg, Tennessee, and Brownsville, Texas. "Every place our regiment goes," remarked Capt. Elliott Grabill, "the boys get themselves wives for the occasion." New liaisons developed as the young soldiers moved with their units, and sometimes these romances resulted in marriage. This was the case with Rufus Wright, 1st USCI, a resident of Edenton, North Carolina, who married Elizabeth Turner in December 1863. The young black soldiers were free men, and for some of them, military service was an exhilarating journey of courtship and romance that culminated in the marriage ceremony, a ceremony that by its very nature reaffirmed the soldiers' new status at least as much as did his blue uniform.[68]

Perhaps the most poignant challenge to the unity of the camp community was the sexual exploitation of black women. Officers who preyed upon black women challenged the inhabitants of their camps to assert their personal freedom in new ways. The sexual exploitation of black women was not confined to officers in black regiments. Reporting to his aunt Hannah, from Memphis in February 1864, Capt. William Ferry, 14th Michigan Infantry, commented that the Negro women living in neighboring contraband camps "were debauched by our soldiers." The exploitation was so bad that "old Jack," a "good," "religious" Negro, voluntarily returned to slavery with his wife and daughters. This brutality cannot be explained by simply pointing to the white soldiers' unrestrained sexual passion. Noted Civil War historian Reid Mitchell suggests that more complex social forces were at work. Black women became rape victims because many soldiers believed they were racially inferior, promiscuous, and had "caused the war." Rape also became a weapon of revenge. By violating black women, white soldiers "appropriated the property" of the Southern ruling class.[69]

Black soldiers also sexually exploited women. Some attacks were made on women found in the vicinity of army camps. On February 18, 1864, three soldiers from the 55th Massachusetts Volunteers were found guilty by drumhead court-martial of raping a "white woman Sarah Hammond" on the road to Camp Shaw, near Jacksonville, Florida. The men were executed one day after the offence was committed. Lt. Col. Charles Fox, a member of the court, was so affected by the seriousness of this crime that when he announced the sentence to the regiment and called "their attention to its effect on them and their good name," he "could not keep [from] showing a little in" his "voice." However, he consoled himself by believing that "the feeling throughout the regiment seems to be in the right side, and the prompt punishment of the offenders" would "prevent much harm." On some occasions soldiers stole away from camp in order to raid neighboring plantations. On April 11, 1865, a party of eight men from the 38th USCI left camp under the cover of darkness, and with the connivance of soldiers on picket duty, in order to plunder the home of Mrs. Crawford, in the vicinity of Richmond, Virginia. During the course of the raid, clothing was taken, and Mrs. Crawford and her fourteen-year-old niece Eliza H. Woodson were raped. The crime was discovered when the men returned to camp; after a general court-martial, two ringleaders were executed. An eyewitness to the execution, Asst. Surg. James Otis Moore, 22d USCI, had little sympathy for the condemned men, because, not content with robbery, "they took turns until all had gratified their desires." These "unhappy men" were, therefore, "victims of their brutal passions."[70]

Some attacks on plantations were motivated by a desire to exact revenge for the pain and suffering of slavery. When twelve soldiers were tried by general courts-martial for murdering Mrs. J. R. Cook and wounding her husband at their plantation four miles east of Vicksburg, on April 3, 1865, they gave as their main line of defense that they had been searching for rebels. "I went out with the intention to catch rebels, I thought the whole party went out for the same purpose. I always like to be in that kind of crowd that goes after rebels," stated Pvt. Baunestor Washington in his own defense. Henry Johnson, a codefendant and former slave of Mr. Cook, explained that he "had nothing personal against Mr. Cook or his family." However, he admitted that "there's always some men in the company who lead some men astray." He reminded the court "that colored soldiers used to be treated badly by the rebels, and that makes them hate the rebels more than the white soldiers do. Its natural that they should feel so." Yet though attacks on plantation mistresses like Mrs. Cook occurred, the majority of the attacks were perpetrated on black women, either living in the vicinity of encampments or visiting army posts.[71]

Sexual crimes perpetrated by white officers on black women caused considerable damage to military discipline. This was because the harassing officers were reenacting the role of the slavemaster. Undergirding the exploitation of black women by white officers was a basic misconception about the degrading influence of slavery. Few officers questioned that the institution of slavery had breached the sanctity of family life and created conditions of debauchery and immorality. A corollary belief, that feminine chastity and modesty had been destroyed, also gained widespread acceptance, hence the image of the black woman contrasted sharply with that of the Northern white lady. Rather than a gentle and passive sexual innocent, the maternal guardian of family virtue, the black woman was seen by many officers as a sexually aggressive amazon. Testifying before the American Freedmen Inquiry Commission in 1863, Major General Butler declared, "The women are all brought up to think that no honor can come to them equal to that of connection with a white man." As an afterthought, Butler added that he was "sorry to say that white men are not all above taking advantage of this feeling."[72]

Men of lower rank who showed little genuine interest in the black soldiers' moral welfare also held General Butler's belief. For example, Captain Grabill confided to his wife that some of the officers in his regiment thought that "no colored woman will deny gratification to a white man especially if he is an officer." Such sexual attitudes enabled the officers to rationalize their exploitation of black women.[73]

Although female visitors to camp were sometimes subject to sexual harassment, it was the camp women who were most vulnerable to attack.

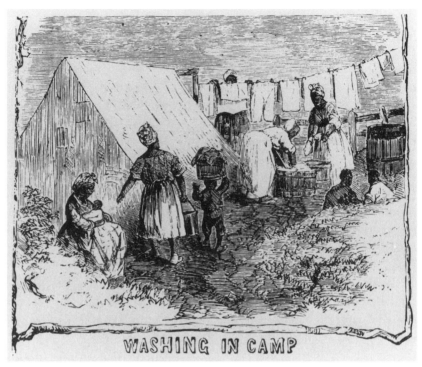

Laundresses Washing in Camp. Wilson, *The Black Phalanx*.

Women worked at a number of camp occupations, including nursing, teaching, cooking, and washing, but those who labored as laundresses were the most numerous and most socially significant. Located in the segregated areas, the women occupied a contested landscape. Both the soldiers and the officers laid claim to their services, militarily, socially, and sexually. Yet these claims fell upon a group of women who were independent and resilient. Of all the work performed on the plantation, washing was most gender specific. It was women's work. On many plantations women had been freed from routine fieldwork on Saturday to carry out their washing duties. During this time, bonds of friendship were formed, and social networks also developed in the army camps. The laundresses were not, therefore, simply refugees of war, vulnerable females seeking male protection in the army camps. On the contrary, they were a resourceful group of women employing their traditional skills in order to survive. Although they shared love, friendship, and kinship with many of the men in the camps, they remained a distinctive and somewhat independent group. This autonomy was revealed not only in the way they resisted sexual exploitation but also in the way they occasionally nurtured feelings of love and affection that transcended racial boundaries.[74]

Not all of the relationships between white officers and black women were based on male coercion. While stationed at Fort Jackson, Louisiana, in December 1863, Capt. William Knapp, 76th USCI, carried on a romantic relationship for some time with a mulatto laundress in his regiment. However, unfortunately for him, this illicit liaison was jeopardized when his friends Capt. Charles Goff, 2d Lt. Henry Blakeslee, and 2d Lt. William Odell tried to force themselves upon other laundresses, referred to as "hags," in the camp.[75]

When officers attempted to coerce women in their camps sexually, they had fights on their hands. The women fought back, and this aggressive resistance repelled some attacks. However, some officers, seeing this spirited opposition as a challenge to their sexuality, persisted. This response disrupted the camp community. This was particularly the case when the victims were married, or bound by close kinship, to men in the regiment. When on December 16, 1863, at Port Hudson, Capt. William H. Daly attempted to "violate the person of a colored woman the reputed wife of a colored man named George," he caused a riot in the camp of the Third Infantry Corps d'Afrique. A similar situation developed in the camp of the 3d U.S. Colored Cavalry, near Memphis in September 1863, when Lt. James S. Matthews attempted to enter the "sleeping department" of Maggie Dixon, the wife of Sgt. James Dixon. Soldiers came from all directions to defend Maggie's honor.[76]

Unshackled by the liberating power of the Union army, the black soldiers carried on a campaign of resistance that was much more openly aggressive than those generally mounted on the plantation. They became, for the first time, the overt protectors and defenders of black women. On January 25, 1864, the harassment of laundresses at Fort Jackson reached a tumultuous climax. When in the evening Capt. Charles Goff and Lieutenants Henry Blakeslee and William Odell invaded the quarters of the laundresses of the 76th USCI, a regiment still recovering from the brutality of Lieutenant Colonel Benedict and the notorious Fort Jackson mutiny of December 1863, the soldiers immediately ran to the women's assistance. In the struggle that ensued, Pvt. Edward Idell was arrested and placed in the guardhouse. At the military commission held to investigate the incident, he argued in his defense that if he had a sister "he would send her away from this Post before she should be so abused by the officers." A strong case was made against the officers, and after considering the evidence of the laundresses, the presiding officer, Brig. Gen. William Dwight, found that the officers had "exposed their persons, used obscene language," and "threatened violence to one negro unless she consented to a proposal of intercourse." During the course of the investigation, it became apparent that the outrage was not an isolated incident; the women reported that this pattern of abuse had occurred frequently in the past. Emotional tensions were, therefore, heightened by past criminal activity. Accusations of sexual harassment were commonplace; even General Dwight came under suspicion.

Ultimately General Dwight recommended the dishonorable discharge of the accused officers, the dismissal of Colonel Drew, the commander of the 76th USCI, and the breakup of the regiment. Yet Dwight's recommendations were not implemented, partly because the Maj. Gen. Nathaniel P. Banks, commander of the Department of the Gulf, did not want to attract further negative attention to the Corps d'Afrique by making more radical changes at Fort Jackson. In addition, the U.S. judge advocate general, Joseph Holt, refused to support Dwight's findings.[77]

It is difficult to evaluate the accuracy of the accusations and counter-accusations made by General Dwight and by the officers under investigation. However, two elements appear well established. First, officers stationed at Fort Jackson sexually harassed black women. Second, black women and black soldiers resolutely resisted these sexual assaults. Evidence contained in the various depositions suggests that sexual harassment in the 76th USCI had a long history. If this was the case, the determination of black soldiers to defend their female relations may have been an important causal factor in the Fort Jackson mutiny, which was one of the most significant challenges to military discipline in the USCT that occurred during the war. The research of Herbert Gutman reveals that black soldiers would threaten mutiny and take up arms to defend their loved ones.[78]

The sexual harassment that occurred in the camp of the 76th USCI encapsulated some of the tensions that were associated with interracial sexual exploitation in the antebellum period. On the plantation and in the camp, rape was more than a vehicle for sexual gratification. The officers of the 76th USCI may have also employed rape as a weapon of psychological intimidation and revenge. The regiment had a history of sexual assaults, but these attacks appeared to have increased in intensity immediately after the Fort Jackson mutiny. The rule of military law had triumphed as a result of the mutiny; Lt. Col. Augustus W. Benedict was dismissed from the service for whipping some of his men like slaves. However, a legacy of recrimination and unease lingered. Racist officers may have felt an even greater need to assert their authority over their men, to teach them a lesson. The sexual harassment of the laundresses may have been a means to this end. While seeking sexual gratification, Captain Goff and his fellow officers may have sought to dramatize the hierarchies of power, to communicate to the men messages of defeat. Laundresses appeared to be particularly attractive targets because they were outside the direct protection of military law. Yet the attacks failed. The women were not violated, and the men were not humiliated. The "hags" fought back fiercely, and the soldiers aided their resistance. Freedom provided the laundresses and the soldiers new opportunities to assert their identities. This determined resistance did not bring justice or even an end to sexual harassment; no officers were convicted of sexual assault. However, the antebellum sexual stereotypes lost some of their potency in the camp of the 76th USCI. The officers learned that it was dangerous to "mess around" with the "hags" who did the washing.[79]

On some occasions, disciplinary action was taken against white officers who engaged in sexual relations with black women. They were accused of weakening military discipline and undermining morale. Dishonorable discharge was the standard penalty imposed by general court-martial, but some officers avoided this penalty by resigning before charges were issued against them. Such relatively light sentences were imposed because the officers were found guilty primarily of association, not of sexual outrage committed on the victim. Furthermore, embodied in these sentences was an implicit belief that the officers had themselves been victims of the lecherously seductive powers of black females. It may have been for these reasons that Capt. De Witt C. Wilson's sentence of dismissal for sharing his bed with "a black concubine" was reduced to "honorable discharge" on the recommendation of both Maj. Charles W. Foster, the chief of the Bureau of Colored Troops, and Edwin Stanton, the secretary of war. Similar considerations may have operated to allow Lt. James Matthews to resign before charges were brought against him for sexually assaulting Sergeant Dixon's wife.[80]

In addition to maintaining the supposedly high moral standard of the officer corps, the machinery of military justice was used to maintain discipline. On September 4, 1863, before a general court-martial held at New Orleans, 1st Lt. F. A. Palmer was accused of having taken "a black woman, known to be a most degraded prostitute, into his private quarters, at a late hour of the evening." He "kept her there without a light burning until disturbed by some officers of his regiment." Such action was "unbecoming to an officer and a gentleman" and jeopardized the military discipline of the regiment. Lt. F. A. Palmer's "licentious practices" were thus deemed to have been "both dangerous and ruinous to the good order and discipline of the regiment, and disgracing to the military service of the United States." He was punished by being dishonorably discharged, with loss of pay and allowances.[81]

Palmer's offence was serious because it had the potential to disrupt the camp community, by implicitly challenging black manhood and embarrassing his fellow officers. His action violated two codes: military law, because it disrupted discipline; and the community moral code, because it raised the specter of slave coercion. The soldiers had long opposed arbitrary physical abuse, such as kicking and whipping, because they saw these practices as legacies of slavery. The soldiers strongly opposed the harassment of female camp workers for similar reasons, and also because such attacks challenged their masculinity in new ways. Freed from the chains of slavery, they now had far more opportunity to assert their manhood by publicly defending black women from attacks from white men. Some soldiers even opposed all social contact between the officers and the black women working in the camps. Their experience of slavery convinced them that such contact was socially dangerous and racially denigrating.[82]

Few soldiers were more aware of the dangers inherent in interracial sexual contact than those who stood accused of raping white women. Black soldiers convicted of sexual offences were treated much more harshly than their officers were. Black rapists faced the likelihood of a solemn march to the gallows. Of the twenty-four soldiers in the Union army executed for rape, fourteen were black. This is a particularly high proportion when one considers that black troops accounted for only 9 percent of the Union army enlistments. The ritual of court-martial and military execution became powerful symbols that publicly endorsed racial stereotypes depicting the black man as a brute.

The soldiers themselves were acutely aware of this unjust caricature, and they protested against the sexual double standards that prevailed in the camps. Some soldiers, like "R.H.B.," openly criticized the morality of their "superiors." In a letter written from Jacksonville, Florida, to the *Christian Recorder* in June 1864, he accused a "set of officers" in his regiment of mingling "with deluded freedwomen" under the cover of darkness and with rebel women by the light of day. The presence of these officers "among us" was "loathsome in the extreme."[83]

Kinship ties gave the black soldiers a variety of roles that military service could not provide. The multifaceted roles of companion, lover, father, protector, brother, and cousin took on another circle of meaning. All soldiers took up at least some of these roles, and this experience molded their attitudes to enlistment and service in the Union army. Above all, these kinship roles enabled them to clarify their identities in an age of freedom. In the army they discovered opportunities to assert their gender and kinship roles in new ways. However, this had to be done within the compass of military law.

The soldiers had bifocal vision. For them, marriage certificates not only reaffirmed the significance of past relationships but pointed to their new status as free men. Few black soldiers would have been more aware of this than the soldiers of the 54th USCI, a regiment of former slaves from Arkansas. On January 17, 1865, a Confederate colonel named Brooks captured a detachment from this regiment. He stripped the soldiers of their arms; when he discovered marriage certificates, he immediately had them destroyed. He then "loudly cursed" the black soldiers "for having such papers in their possession." In Colonel Brooks's eyes, the marriage certificate was anathema: it legitimized a relationship that slaveholders had refused to acknowledge.[84]

Officers laboring in Union regiments to elevate the black soldiers morally also had distorted views of slave kinship relations. They explained the soldiers' eagerness to be bound in holy wedlock in terms of their own alleged powers of moral persuasion and religious reformation. Yet the soldiers' enthusiasm did not imply total acculturation, even though at times the military discipline and bearing of the black troops appeared to give this impression.

This impression was manifested immediately after the fall of Richmond. Black soldiers led the triumphant march into the Confederate capital. Watching and reporting on the parade, Garland White, the black chaplain of the 28th USCI, witnessed recently liberated slaves desperately searching for loved ones among the columns of black soldiers. "Here and there one was singled out in the ranks," and an effort was made "to approach the gallant and marching soldiers who were too obedient to orders to break ranks."[85]

The black soldiers were "obedient to orders" because the action of the Union army did not threaten but actually reinforced those kinship ties that had survived the horrors of slavery. After all, it had been Union soldiers who opened the Richmond slave pens and liberated their loved ones. The black soldiers marched on because they were fighting for their hearths and homes as well as an indivisible Union. Union victory protected family life. The soldiers knew this, and so did the women who cheered them on. In the family gardens, in the camp hospitals and kitchens, and at the camp washtubs, they had labored to support the war effort. Their battleground was different, but their love of liberty was no less intense.

Epilogue

In early September 1999, I visited the Petersburg National Battlefield Park, near Richmond, Virginia, to see what remained of the Crater, the site of a comprehensive Union army defeat. There on July 30, 1864, thousands of white and black Union soldiers were killed or captured as they attempted to pour through a large gap blown in the Rebel lines by Union mining operations. As I gazed into what was left of the Crater and surveyed the ground over which Brig. Gen. Edward Ferrero's black division had pitched their tents only days before their life-and-death struggle, I became acutely aware that my study of camp life was less a research project than a journey through history. History had been made here at the Crater, and the black soldiers who had helped to make it had left behind an indelible record of courage and patriotism, sacrifice and suffering. By analyzing the testimony of white officers, and, especially, the personal records of the black soldiers—their diaries, letters, and memoirs—I entered the world of the soldiers and discerned their martial spirit, the inner strength that enabled them to descend bravely into the hellish pit of the Crater. Such courageous commitment to the Union cause points to the soldiers' love of freedom, their deep commitment to family and home, and to their military training. Yet individuals alone could not have sustained these values and attributes. They were, in essence, the product of shared experiences. In a very real sense they had been nurtured in the unique camp environments that developed in the U.S. Colored Troops regiments. Here communities developed that enabled the soldiers to sustain their cultural lives.[1]

As I stood on the rim of the Crater and looked back across time to the distant campsites of the USCT regiments, the rich array of activities unfolded before me. I could see commanders inspecting their troops and supervising training that would prepare their men for the impending battle. Around the campfires, soldiers were playing cards and laughing as they listened to the storyteller spinning his tales. In quiet seclusion, some soldiers read the regimental newspaper, some labored, with the assistance of the chaplain, to learn the alphabet, and others wrote letters to kinfolk at home. Here and there, small groups of noncommissioned officers gathered to discuss how they would reduce the heavy load of fatigue duty their men had to bear. In some camps former slave preachers called upon God to stand by his soldiers in the forthcoming conflict. In other camps the stillness of the day was broken by the uplifting chorus of soldiers singing the defiant chant, "We-e looks li-ike me-en a-a marchin' on, We looks li-ike me-en-er-war." In the far distance, removed from the bustling center of the camps, the washerwomen were busily soaking and scrubbing the soldiers' clothes by the edge of the Appomattox River.

At Petersburg and at thousands of strategically less significant sites, the men and women of the USCT camps played important roles in the process of cultural change. The camp activities they nurtured helped them to reshape their African heritage, slave traditions, and Northern free black community values in a way that prepared them for their future roles in American society. This change was possible because the vibrant cultural life of the camps enabled the soldiers to place their military service in the context of their ages-long struggle for freedom. Spirituals were modified into marching songs. There was nothing unusual about such changes. Billy Yank and Johnny Reb both changed their music, religious practices, and pastimes to ease the transition from civilian life to military service. However, for black soldiers the transition was much more difficult, because the burdens of slavery and racism had largely divided them from the mainstream of American cultural life. Camp activities helped the soldiers to bridge this divide, and to negotiate the changes necessary to meet the demands of army life. Military service helped to reconfigure race relations and give black people a new definition. Black soldiers used their service in the Union army to challenge existing notions of race and citizenship. On the battlefield and in the camp, they validated their claims to freedom and equality by demonstrating their courage, discipline, and leadership. Military service gave them a profound legacy, one that bound them to the nation and endured long after the last bugle had sounded and the last campfire had died.

The demobilization of black troops began immediately after the end of the war. In July 1865, there were still approximately 123,000 black volunteers serving in the army, but by October 1866 only roughly 13,000 remained. This number diminished further until by the fall of 1867 all volunteer troops had been mustered out of service. Generally the soldiers welcomed their exit from military life. They had yearned for the freedom of being private citizens, of casting votes and purchasing land. Conscious of the turmoil in the war-ravaged South, former slaves were keen to return home to protect their loved ones from the exploitation of their old masters. "I have ben true to my government and I love it dearley now the war is over and I now want to see those who are dearer to me than my life," wrote James Herney, a Missouri soldier, to "Seceretary Stanten." Herney's plea echoed those of the thousands of volunteers still serving in the army after the war had ended. Yet the rush to leave the army was not universal. Some soldiers so enjoyed military life that they joined the six black regiments that became part of the regular army.[2]

Although the black soldiers moved rapidly into the mainstream of civilian life, their allegiance, the Union army and the cause of freedom never wavered. This commitment found its public expression in the activities of veteran societies and in commemorations held to remember the sacrifices of fallen heroes. For the soldiers, few commemorations more powerfully demonstrated their commitment to the Union than the ceremony held in Boston to dedicate Augustus Saint-Gaudens's memorial honoring Col. Robert Gould Shaw and the men of the 54th Massachusetts Volunteers.

As a light rain fell on a gray, dull "Decoration Day" on May 31, 1897, a crowd huddled together on the steps of the Massachusetts Statehouse. The crowd waited in silent expectation, intent on hearing the tramp of feet as the veterans made their way up Beacon Hill. Slowly the muffled sound grew louder, and then they appeared on the crest of the hill men marching in time. Thirty-seven years earlier, they had traveled the same route on their way to war, young men filled with a spirit of adventure and determined to fight for freedom. Now they were old; some were crippled, and some carried bouquets. Their steps were slow and deliberate, their uniforms faded and torn. Yet they marched with pride and resolution, determined to pay their respects to their fallen comrades. Sgt. William Carney held the nation's flag aloft. The war had changed them. On the battlefields of the South they had won their liberty and gained entry into American society. For a few short years, the tent had been their home, the army camp their vibrant community. There they had made the transition from slave to citizen, re-created their identity, and exercised their freedom. Yet now the regular rhythm of camp life was but a cherished memory, the camp songs a distant echo, and the stories a figment, perhaps, of the imagination. However, taps had not yet sounded. For the black soldiers conflict had not ended at Appomattox. In the postwar decades they had continued to fight to preserve their freedom and secure their citizenship.[3]

Almost three years after he carried the battle-torn flag at the solemn dedication of the Saint-Gaudens memorial, Sgt. William C. Carney, Company

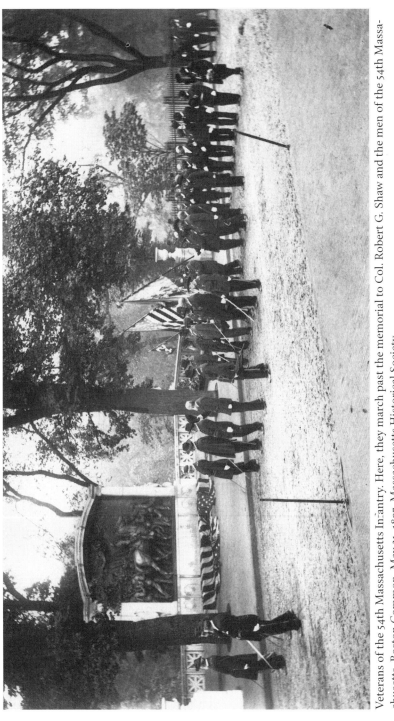

Veterans of the 54th Massachusetts Infantry. Here, they march past the memorial to Col. Robert G. Shaw and the men of the 54th Massachusetts, Boston Common, May 31, 1897. Massachusetts Historical Society.

C, 54th Massachusetts Volunteers, was belatedly awarded the Medal of Honor for outstanding devotion to duty during the attack on Fort Wagner, near Charleston, South Carolina, on July 18, 1863. Although twice wounded, he had rescued the flag in the face of withering enemy fire. "The old flag never touched the ground, boys," cried Sergeant Carney as he limped back to camp. This flag was worth dying for, because it symbolized the black soldiers' aspirations for freedom.[4]

Appendix A

1. NEGRO BATTLE HYMN

Hark! Listen to the trumpeters,
  They call for volunteers,
On Zion's bright and flow'ry mount,
  Behold the officers.

Refrain: They look like men, they look like men,
  They look like men of war,
All arm'd and dress'd in u-ni-form,
  They look like men of war.

Their horses white, their armor bright,
  With courage bold they stand,
Enlisting soldiers for their King,
  To march to Canaan's land.

Refrain

It sets my heart quite in a flame
  A soldier thus to be,
I will enlist, gird on my arms,
  And fight for liberty.

Refrain

We want no cowards in our band,
  That will their colors fly,

We call for valiant-hearted men,
    Who're not afraid to die.

Refrain

To see our armies on parade
    How martial they appear!
All arm'd and dress'd in uniform,
    They look like men of war.

Refrain

They follow their great General,
    The great eternal lamb,
His garment stain'd in his own blood,
    King Jesus is his name.

Refrain

The trumpets sound, the armies shout,
    They drive the hosts of hell,
How dreadful is our God to adore,
    The great Immanuel!

Refrain[1]

2. ALL HAIL

Air: "Greenland's Icy Mountains"
    All hail the glorious morning
That burst o'er the earth,
    The eastern sky adorning
Proclaims a nation's birth.
    Praise to the God of battles;
In joy the day returns
    And o'er the sunlit mountains
The light of victory burns.

From Richmond's fen-bound regions,
    Atlanta traitor hold,
Where freedom's stalwart legions
    The rebel crew enfold.
Along the well-manned trenches,
    Above the bastions grey,
While every foeman blenches,
    The shout rings forth today.

Through all our northern borders,
    New England's homes and halls,
Where patriots stand the warders,
    On freedom's outer walls.
From Alleghania's ramparts,
    Her homes of heroes bold;
From California's gold hills,
    Her heart of purer gold.

Join we the glad hosannah
    That ring throughout the land,
Lift high our Union banner
    Above our Union band.
Yet shout as war-clad heroes,
    Who wave the sword on high,
And know no end of battle,
    Till low the foe doth lie.

Stand firm, the law's upholder,
    Against the two-fold foe,
The rebel who strikes bolder,
    The traitor's secret blow.
Fight we like men our conflict,
    Renew our vows to-night,
For God and for our Country,
    For Freedom and the Right.[2]

3. The Original Version of the John Brown Song

("Words that can be sung to the "Halleujah Chorus"")
Old John Brown lies a-mouldering in the grave,
Old John Brown lies slumbering in his grave—
But John Brown's soul is marching with the brave,
His soul is marching on.
Glory, glory, hallelujah!
Glory, glory, hallelujah!
His soul is marching on.

He has gone to be a soldier in the Army of the Lord,
He is sworn as a private in the ranks of the Lord—
He shall stand at Armageddon with his brave old sword,
When Heaven is marching on.
Glory, etc.
For Heaven is marching on.

He shall file in front where the lines of battle form,
He shall face to front when the squares of battle form,
Time with the column, and charge in the storm.
When men are marching on.
Glory, etc.
True men are marching on.

Ah, foul tyrants! Do you hear him when he comes?
Ah, black traitors! Do ye know him as he comes?
In thunder of the cannon and roll of the drums,
As we go marching on.
Glory, etc.
We all are marching on.

Men may die and moulder in the dust—
Men may die, and arise again from dust,
Shoulder to shoulder, in the ranks of the Just,
When God is marching on.
Glory, etc.
The Lord is marching on.

                                 —H. H. Brownell[3]

4. THE BLACK REGIMENT

May 27th, 1863
Dark as the clouds of even,
Ranked in the western heaven,
Waiting the breath that lifts
All the dread mass, and drifts
Tempest and falling brand
Over a ruined land;—
So still and orderly,
Arm to arm, knee to knee,
Waiting the great event,
Stands the black regiment.

Down the long dusky line,
Teeth gleam and eyeballs shine;
And the bright bayonet,
Bristling and firmly set,
Flashed with a purpose grand,
Long ere the sharp command
Of the fierce rolling drum
Told them their time had come,
Told them what work was sent
For the black regiment.

"Now," the flag-sergeant cried,
"Though death and hell betide,
Let the whole nation see
If we are fit to be
Free in this land; or bound
Down, like the whining hound—
Bound with red stripes of pain
In our old chains again!"
Oh! what a shout there went
From the black regiment!

"Charge!" Trump and drum awake,
Onward the bondmen broke;
Bayonet and sabre-stroke

Vainly opposed their rush,
Through the wild battle's crush,
With but one thought aflush,
Driving their lords like chaff,
In the guns' mouth they laugh;
Or at the slippery brands
Leaping with open hands,
Down they tear man and horse,
Down in their awful course;
Trampling with bloody heel
Over the crashing steel,
All their eyes forward bent,
Rushed the black regiment.

"Freedom!" their battle-cry—
"Freedom! or leave to die!"
Ah! and they meant the word,
Not as with us 'tis heard,
Not a mere party-shout:
They gave their spirits out;
Trusted the end to God,
And on the gory sod
Rolled in triumphant blood.
Glad to strike one free blow,
Whether for weal or woe;
Glad to breathe one free breath,
Though on the lips of death.
Praying—alas! in vain!—
That they might fall again,
So they could once more see
That burst to liberty!
This was what "freedom" lent
To the black regiment.

Hundreds on hundreds fell;
But they are resting well;
Scourges and shackles strong
Never shall do them wrong.
O, to the living few,

Soldiers, be just and true!
Hail them as comrades tried;
Fight with them side by side;
Never, in field or tent,
Scorn the black regiment!
    —George H. Boker[4]

5. SONG OF THE NEGRO BOATMAN

Oh, praise an' tanks! De Lord he come
To set de people free;
An' massa tink it day ob doom,
An' we ob jubilee.
De Lord dat heap de Red Sea waves,
He jus' as 'trong as den,
He say de word: we las' night slaves,
To-day, de Lord's freemen.
De yam will grow, de cotton blow,
We'll hab de rice an' corn:
Oh, nebber you fear, if nebber you hear
De driver blow his horn!

Ole massa on he trabbles gone;
He leab de land behind:
De Lord's breff blew him furder on,
Like corn shuk in de wind.
We own de hoe, we own de plow,
We own de hands dat hold;
We sell de pig, we sell de cow,
But nebber chile be sold.
De yam will grow, de cotton blow,
We'll hab de rice an' corn:
Oh nebber you fear, if nebber you hear
De driver blow his horn!

We pray de Lord: he gib us signs
Dat some day we be free;
De Norf-wind tell it to de pines,

De wild-duck to de sea;
We tink it when de church-bell ring,
We dream it in de dream;
De rice-bird mean it when he sing,
De eagle when he scream.
De yam will grow, de cotton blow.
We'll hab de rice an' corn:
Oh, nebber you fear, if nebber you hear
De driver blow his horn!

We know de promise nebber fail,
An' nebber lie de word;
So like de 'postles in de jail,
We waited for de Lord:
An' now he open ebery door,
An' trow away de key;
He tink we lub him so before,
We lub him better free.
De yam will grow, de cotton blow,
We'll hab de rice an' corn:
Oh, nebber you fear, if nebber you hear
De driver blow his horn!
        —John G. Whittier[5]

6. OLD SHADY

Air: "Away Down South"
Oh! ya! ya! darkies, laugh with me;
For de white folks say old Shady's free!
Don't you see dat de jubilee
    Is comin', comin'! Hail, mighty day!
Chorus.
Den away, den away, for I can't stay any longer;
Hurra, hurra! for I am going home. [Repeat.]

Massa got scared, and so did his lady!
Dis chile broke for ole Uncle Aby;

Open de gates out? here's ole Shady
 Comin', comin'! Hail, mighty day.
Chorus

Good bye, Massa Jeff! good-bye, Missus Stevens,
'Scuse dis nigger for taking his leavins;
'Spec, pretty soon, you'll see Uncle Abram's
 Comin', comin'! Hail, mighty day.
Chorus

Good-bye, hard work, and never any pay
I'm goin' up Norf where de white folks stay;
White wheat-bread and a dollar a day!
 Comin', comin'! Hail, mighty day.
Chorus

I've got a wife, and she's got a baby,
Way up Norf in Lower Canady—
Won't dey shout when dey see ole Shady
 Comin', comin'! Hail, mighty day.
Chorus
   —D. Blakely Durant[6]

7. Song of the First of Arkansas

Oh! we're de bully soldiers of de "First of Arkansas."
We are fightin' for de Union, we are fightin' for de law;
We can hit a rebel furder dan a white man eber saw,
As we go marchin' on.
Glory, glory, hallelujah, &c.

See dar! above de centre, where de flag wavin' bright;
We are goin' out of slavery; we are bound for freedom's light;
We mean to show Jeff Davis how the Africans can fight,
As we go marching on.

We hab done wid hoein' cotton, we hab done wid hoein' corn,
We are colored Yankee soldiers now, as sure as you are born;

When de Massas hear us yellin' dey'll tink its Gabriel's horn,
As we go marching on.

Dey will hab to pay us wages, de wages ob their sin,
Dey will hab to bow their foreheads to their colored kith and kin,
Dey will hab to gib us house-room, or de roof shall tumble in,
As we go marching on.

We heard de proclamation, massa hush it as he will;
De bird he sing it to us, hoppin' on de cotton hill,
And de possum up de gum tree he couldn't keep it still,
As he went climbing on.

Dey said, "Now colored bredren, you shall be forever free,
From the first of January, eighteen hundred and sixty-three."
We heard it in de riber goin' rushin' to de sea,
As it went sounding on.

Father Abraham has spoken, and de message has been sent,
De prison doors be opened, and out de pris'ners went,
To join de sable army of de "African descent,"
As we go marching on.

Den fall'in colored bredren, you'd better do it soon,
Don't you hear de drum a beatin' de Yankee Doodle tune?
We are wid you now dis mornin', we'll be far away at noon,
As we go marching on.

                                   —Capt. Lindley Miller[7]

Appendix B

A SELECTION OF NEGRO SPIRITUALS AND SONGS FROM
THOMAS W. HIGGINSON'S COLLECTION[1]

1. HANGMAN JOHNNY

O, dey call me Hangman Johnny!
O, ho! O, ho!
But I never hang nobody,
O, hang, boys, hang!
O, dey call me Hangman Johnny!
O, ho! O, ho!
But we'll all hang togedder,
O, hang, boys, hang!

2. GO IN THE WILDERNESS

Jesus call you. Go in de wilderness,
Go in de wilderness, go in de wilderness,
Jesus call you. Go in de wilderness
To wait upon de Lord.
Go wait upon de Lord,
Go wait upon de Lord,
Go wait upon de Lord, my God,
He take away de sins of de world.

Jesus a-waitin'. Go in de wilderness,
Go, &c.
All dem chil'en go in de wilderness
To wait upon de Lord.

3. O YES, LORD

O, must I be like de foolish mans?
O yes, Lord!
Will build de house on de sandy hill.
O yes, Lord!
I'll build my house on Zion hill,
O yes, Lord!
No wind nor rain can blow me down,
O yes, Lord!

4. GOOD NEWS

O, good news! O, good news!
De angels brought de tidings down,
Just comin' from de trone.

As grief from out my soul shall fly,
Just comin' from de trone;
I'll shout salvation when I die,
Good news, O, good news!
Just comin' from de trone.

Lord, I want to go to heaven when I die,
Good news, O, good news! &c.

De white folks calls us a noisy crew,
Good news, O, good news!
But dis I know, we are happy too,
Just comin' from de trone.

5. THE HEAVENLY ROAD

You may talk of my name as much as you please,
And carry my name abroad,
But I really do believe I'm a child of God
As I walk in de heavenly road.

O, won't you go wid me? *(Thrice)*
For to keep our garments clean.

O Satan is a mighty busy ole man,
And roll rocks in my way;
But Jesus is my bosom friend,
And roll 'em out of de way.
O, won't you go wid me? *(Thrice)*
For to keep our garments clean.

Come, my brudder, if you never did pray,
I hope you may pray tonight;
For I really believe I'm a child of God
As I walk in de heavenly road.
O, won't you, &c.

6. FARE YE WELL

My true believers, fare ye well,
Fare ye well, fare ye well,
Fare ye well, by de grace of God,
For I'm going home.

Massa Jesus give me a little broom
For to sweep my heart clean,
And I will try, by de grace of God,
To win my way home.

7. WALK 'EM EASY

O, walk 'em easy round de heaven,
Walk 'em easy round de heaven,
Walk 'em easy round de heaven,
Dat all de people may join de band.
Walk 'em easy round de heaven. *(Thrice)*
O, shout glory till 'em join dat band!

8. O THE DYING LAMB!

I wants to go where Moses trod,
O de dying Lamb!
For Moses gone to de promised land,
O de dying Lamb!
To drink from springs dat never run dry,
O, &c.
Cry O my Lord!
O, &c.
Before I'll stay in hell one day,
O, &c.
I'm in hopes to pray my sins away,
O, &c.
Cry O my Lord!
O, &c.
Brudder Moses promised for be dar too,
O, &c.
To drink from streams dat never run dry,
O de dying Lamb!

9. CRY HOLY

Cry holy, holy!
Look at de people dat is born of God.
And I run down de valley, and I run down to pray,
Says, look at de people dat is born of God.
When I get dar, Cappen Satan was dar,
Says, look at, &c.
Says, young man, young man, dere's no use for pray,
Says, look at, &c.
For Jesus is dead, and God gone away,
Says, look at, &c.
And I made him out a liar, and I went my way,
Says, look at, &c.
Sing holy, holy!

O, Mary was a woman, and he had a one Son,
Says, look at, &c.
And de Jews and de Romans had him hung,
Says, look at, &c.
Cry holy, holy!

And I tell you, sinner, you had better had pray,
Says, look at, &c.
For hell is a dark and dismal place,
Says, look at, &c.
And I tell you, sinner, and I wouldn't go dar!
Says, look at, &c.
Cry holy, holy!

10. O'er the Crossing

Yonder's my old mudder,
Been a-waggin' at de hill so long.
It's about time she'll cross over;
Get home bimeby [by and by].
Keep prayin', I do believe
We're a long time waggin' o'er de crossin'.
Keep prayin', I do believe
We'll get home to heaven bimeby.

Hear dat mournful thunder,
Roll from door to door,
Calling home God's children;
Get home bimeby.
Little chil'en, I do believe
We're a long time, &c.
Little chil'en, I do believe
We'll get home, &c.

See dat forked lightnin'
Flash from tree to tree,
Callin' home God's chil'en;
Get home bimeby.

True believer, I do believe,
We're a long time, &c.
O brudders, I do believe,
We'll get home to heaven bimeby.

11. The Baby Gone Home

De little baby gone home,
De little baby gone home,
De little baby gone along,
    For to climb up Jacob's ladder.
And I wish I'd been dar,
I wish I'd been dar,
I wish I'd been dar, my Lord,
    For to climb up Jacob's ladder.

12. Jesus with Us

He have been wid us, Jesus,
He still wid us, Jesus,
He will be wid us, Jesus,
Be wid us to the end.

13. I Know Moon-Rise

I know moon-rise, I know star-rise,
Lay dis body down.
I walk in de moonlight, I walk in de starlight,
    To lay dis body down.
I'll walk in de graveyard, I'll walk through de graveyard,
    To lay dis body down.
I'll lie in de grave and stretch out my arms;
    Lay dis body down.
I go to de judgement in de evenin' of de day,
    When I lay dis body down;
And my soul and your soul will meet in de day
    When I lay dis body down.

14. I Want to Go Home

Dere's no rain to wet you,
O, yes, I want to go home.
Dere's no sun to burn you,
O, yes, I want to go home;
O, push along, believers,
O, yes, &c.
Dere's no hard trials,
O, yes, &c.
Dere's no whips a-crackin',
O, yes, &c.
My brudder on de wayside,
O, yes, &c.
O, push along, my brudder,
O, yes, &c.
Where dere's no stormy weather,
O, yes, &c.
Dere's no tribulation,
O, yes, &c.

15. The Driver

O, de ole nigger-driver!
    O, gwine away!
Fust ting my mammy tell me,
    O, gwine away!
Tell me 'bout de nigger-driver,
    O, gwine away!
Nigger-driver second devil,
    O, gwine away!
Best ting for do he driver,
    O, gwine away!
Knock he down and spoil he labor,
    O, gwine away!

16. Many Thousand Go

No more peck o' corn for me,
No more, no more—
No more peck o' corn for me,
Many tousand go.

No more driver's lash for me,
Twice
No more, &c.

No more pint o' salt for me,
Twice
No more, &c.

No more hundred lash for me
Twice
No more, &c.

No more mistress' call for me,
No more, no more—
No more mistress' call for me,
Many tousand go.

17. Hail Mary

One more valiant soldier here,
    One more valiant soldier here,
One more valiant soldier here,
    To help me bear de cross.
O hail, Mary, hail!
    Hail, Mary, hail!
Hail, Mary, hail!
    To help me bear de cross.

18. Room in There

O, my mudder is gone! my mudder is gone!
My mudder is gone into heaven, my Lord!
I can't stay behind!
Dere's room in dar, room in dar,
Room in dar, in de heaven, my Lord!
I can't stay behind!
Can't stay behind, my dear,
I can't stay behind!

O, my fader is gone! &c.

O, de angels are gone! &c.

O, I'se been on de road! I'se been on de road!
I'se been on de road into heaven, my Lord!
I can't stay behind!
O, room in dar, room in dar,
Room in dar, in de heaven, my Lord!
I can't stay behind!

19. Early in the Morning

I meet little Rosa early in de mornin',
   O Jerusalem! early in de mornin';
And I ax her, How do you do, my darter?
   O Jerusalem! early in de mornin',

I meet my mudder early in de mornin',
   O Jerusalem! &c.
And I ax her, How you do, my mudder?
   O Jerusalem! &c.

I meet Brudder Robert early in de mornin',
   O Jerusalem! &c.
And I ax him, How you do, my sonny?
   O Jerusalem! &c.

I meet Tittawisa early in de mornin',
    O Jerusalem! &c.
And I ax her, How you do, my darter?
    O Jerusalem! &c.

20. MY ARMY CROSS OVER

My army cross over,
My army cross over,
O, Pharaoh's army drownded!
My army cross over.

We'll cross de mighty river,
My army cross over;
We'll cross de river Jordan,
My army cross over;
We'll cross de danger water,
My army cross over;
We'll cross de mighty Myo,
My army cross over. *(Thrice)*
O, Pharaoh's army drownded!
My army cross over.

21. RIDE IN, KIND SAVIOUR

Ride in, kind Saviour!
No man can hinder me.
O, Jesus is a mighty man!
No man, &c.
We're marching through Virginny fields.
No man, &c.
O, Satan is a busy man,
No man, &c.
And he has his sword and shield,
No man, &c.
O, old Secesh done come and gone!
No man can hinder me.

22. We'll Soon Be Free

We'll soon be free,
We'll soon be free,
We'll soon be free,
When de Lord will call us home.
My brudder, how long,
My brudder, how long,
My brudder, how long,
'Fore we don sufferin' here?
It won't be long *(Thrice)*
'Fore de Lord will call us home.
We'll walk de miry road *(Thrice)*
Where pleasure never dies.
We'll walk de golden street *(Thrice)*
Where pleasure never dies.
My brudder, how long *(Thrice)*
'Fore we don sufferin' here?
We'll soon be free *(Thrice)*
When Jesus sets me free.
We'll fight for liberty *(Thrice)*
When de Lord will call us home.

23. Blow Your Trumpet, Gabriel

O, blow your trumpet, Gabriel,
Blow your trumpet louder;
And I want dat trumpet to blow me home
To my new Jerusalem.

De prettiest ting dat ever I done
Was to serve de Lord when I was young.
So blow your trumpet, Gabriel, &c.

O, Satan is a liar, and he conjure too,
And if you don't mind, he'll conjure you.
So blow your trumpet, Gabriel, &c.

O, I was lost in de wilderness,
King Jesus hand me de candle down.
So blow your trumpet, Gabriel, &c.

24. THE SHIP OF ZION

Come along, come along,
    And let us go home,
O, glory, hallelujah!
Dis de ole ship o' Zion,
    Halleloo! Halleloo!
Dis de ole ship o' Zion,
    Hallelujah!

She has landed many a tousand,
She can land as many more.
    O, glory hallelujah! &c.

Do you tink she will be able
For to take us all home?
    O, glory, hallelujah! &c.

You can tell 'em I'm a comin',
    Halleloo! Halleloo!
You can tell 'em I'm a comin',
    Hallelujah!
Come along, come along, &c.

25. THE SHIP OF ZION (SECOND VERSION)

Dis de good ole ship o' Zion,
Dis de good ole ship o' Zion,
Dis de good ole ship o' Zion,
    And she's makin' for de Promised Land.
She hab angels for de sailors, *(Thrice)*
    And she's, &c.

And how you know dey's angels? *(Thrice)*
    And she's, &c.
Good Lord, shall I be one? *(Thrice)*
    And she's, &c.

Dat ship is out a-sailin', sailin', sailin',
    And she's, &c.
She's a-sailin' mighty steady, steady, steady,
    And she's, &c.
She'll neither reel nor totter, totter, totter,
    And she's, &c.
She's a-sailin'away cold Jordan, Jordan, Jordan,
    And she's, &c.
King Jesus is de captain, captain, captain,
    And she's makin' for de Promised Land.

26. THE SHIP OF ZION (THIRD VERSION)

De Gospel ship is sailin',
    Hosann-sann.
O, Jesus is de captain,
    Hosann-sann.
De angels are de sailors,
    Hosann-sann.
O, is your bundle ready?
    Hosann-sann.
O, have you got your ticket?
    Hosann-sann.

27. HOLD YOUR LIGHT

Hold your light Brudder Robert—
    Hold your light,
Hold your light on Canaan's shore.

What make ole Satan for follow me so?
Satan ain't got notin' for do wid me.
    Hold your light,
    Hold your light,
Hold your light on Canaan's shore.

28. SWEET MUSIC

Sweet music in heaven,
    Just beginning for to roll.
Don't you love God?
    Glory, hallelujah!

Yes, late I heard my soldier say,
Come, heavy soul, I am dey way.
    Don't you love God?
    Glory, hallelujah!

I'll go and tell to sinners round
What a kind Saviour I have found.
    Don't you love God?
    Glory, hallelujah!

My grief my burden long has been,
Because I was not cease from sin.
    Don't you love God?
    Glory, hallelujah!

Abbreviations

AAS	American Antiquarian Society
AUL	Atlanta University Library
CHS	Chicago Historical Society
CMSA	Commonwealth of Massachusetts State Archives
CTD	Colored Troops Division
CTHS	Connecticut Historical Society
DCL	Dartmouth College Library
DPL	Detroit Public Library
DUL	Duke University Library
EUL	Emory University Library
HU	Harvard University Library
HHL	Henry E. Huntington Library
HSP	Historical Society of Pennsylvania
HUL	Howard University Library
ISHSL	Illinois State Historical Society Library
IHSL	Indiana Historical Society Library
KSHS	Kansas State Historical Society
LC	Library of Congress
MAHS	Massachusetts Historical Society
MHS	Minnesota Historical Society
MOLLUS	Military Order of the Loyal Legion of the United States
NA	National Archives
NEHGS	New England Historic Genealogical Society
NYHS	New York Historical Society
NYPL	New York Public Library
OBA	Oberlin College Archives
OHS	Ohio Historical Society
RCL	Radcliffe College Library
RG	Record Group
RISSHS	Rhode Island Soldiers and Sailors Historical Society
RIHS	Rhode Island Historical Society
RUL	Rutgers University Library
SUL	Stanford University Library
SHSND	State Historical Society of North Dakota
SHSW	State Historical Society of Wisconsin

SYUL   Syracuse University Library
TTU   Texas Tech University
USAMHI   U.S. Army Military History Institute
UIL   University of Iowa Library
UM   University of Michigan
UMS   University of Missouri
UNC   University of North Carolina
USC   University of South Carolina
UTAL   University of Texas at Austin Library
VHS   Vermont Historical Society
WVUL   West Virginia University Library
WCL   Williams College Library
YUL   Yale University Library

ℳotes

The first attempts to chronicle black military service during the Civil War were made by blacks who had either fought in the Union army or had been actively involved in the abolition movement and the war effort. William Welles Brown, fugitive slave, abolitionist lecturer, and Union army recruitment agent, wrote the first history, *The Negro in the American Rebellion: His Rebellion, His Heroism, and His Fidelity* (Boston: Lee & Shepard, 1867). Two black veterans, George W. Williams (*A History of the Negro Troops in the War of the Rebellion, 1861–1865* [New York: Harper and Bros., 1888]) and Joseph T. Wilson (*The Black Phalanx: A History of the Negro Soldiers of the United States in the Wars of 1775–1812 and 1861–1865* [Hartford, Conn.: American Publishing Company, 1890]), wrote their accounts in the last decades of the nineteenth century.

For many years Dudley Cornish's *The Sable Arm: Negro Troops in the Union Army, 1861–1865* (New York: Longmans, Green, 1956), remained the most comprehensive account of the contribution of black troops during the Civil War. Other accounts of the blacks' role in the war written in the 1950s and 1960s include: Benjamin Quarles, *The Negro in the Civil War* (Boston: Little, Brown, 1953); James M. McPherson, *The Negro's Civil War: How American Negroes Felt and Acted during the War for the Union* (New York: Vintage, 1967).

In recent years a number of important studies of the role of the black soldier have appeared. Joseph T. Glatthaar's *Forged in Battle: The Civil War Alliance of Black Soldiers and White Officers* (New York: Free Press, 1990) is the most comprehensive and analytical account. Other studies include: Hondon B. Hargrove, *Black Union Soldiers in the Civil War* (Jefferson, N.C.: McFarland, 1988); Joe H. Mays, *Black Americans and Their Contributions towards Union Victory in the American Civil War, 1861–1865* (Lanham, Md.: Univ. Press of America, 1984); Noah Andrea Trudeau, *Like Men of War: Black Troops in the Civil War* (Boston: Little Brown, 1998); and Howard C. Westwood, *Black Troops, White Commanders and Freedmen during the Civil War* (Carbondale: Southern Illinois Univ. Press: 1992).

Recent studies of black regiments include: Martin H. Blatt, Thomas J. Brown, Donald Yacovone, eds. *Hope & Glory: Essays on the Legacy of the Fifty-Fourth Massachusetts Regiment* (Amherst: Univ. of Massachusetts Press, 2001); Peter Burchard, *"We'll Stand by the Union": Robert Gould Shaw and the Black 54th Massachusetts Regiment* (New York: Facts on File, 1993); James G. Hollandsworth Jr., *The Louisiana Native Guards: The Black Military Experience During the Civil War* (Baton Rouge: Louisiana State Univ. Press, 1995); Edward A. Miller Jr., *The Black Civil War Soldiers of Illinois: The Story of the*

Twenty-Ninth U.S. Colored Infantry (Columbia: University of South Carolina Press, 1998); and Versalle F. Washington, *Eagles on Their Buttons: A Black Regiment in the Civil War* (Columbia, Missouri: University of Missouri Press, 1999).

A number of important collections of documents, soldiers' letters, and newspaper reports have been published. Of these by far the most important is Ira Berlin, Jospeh Reidy, and Leslie S. Rowland, eds., *Freedom: A Documentary History of Emancipation, 1861–1867*, ser. 2, *The Black Military Experience* (Cambridge: Cambridge Univ. Press, 1982). Other collections include: Virginia M. Adams, ed., *On the Altar of Freedom: A Black Soldier's Civil War Letters from the Front—Corporal James Henry Gooding* (Amherst: Univ. of Massachusetts Press, 1991); R. J. M. Blackett, ed., *Thomas Morris Chester, Black Civil War Correspondent: His Dispatches from the Virginia Front* (New York: Da Capo, 1991); Edwin S. Redkey, ed., *A Grand Army from Black Men: Letters of African-American Soldiers in the Union Army, 1861–1865* (New York: Cambridge Univ. Press, 1992); P. W. Romero, W. L. Rose, eds., *A Black Woman's Civil War Memoirs* (New York: Wiener, 1988); and Donald Yacovone, ed., *A Voice of Thunder: The Civil War Letters of George E. Stephens* (Urbana: University of Illinois Press, 1997).

Important recent publications of officers' diaries and letters include: Russell Duncan, ed., *Blue-Eyed Child of Fortune: The Civil War Letters of Colonel Robert Gould Shaw* (Athens: Univ. of Georgia Press, 1992); John Hope Franklin, ed., *The Civil War Diary of James T. Ayers* (Baton Rouge: Louisiana State Univ. Press, 1999); Charles Looby, ed., *The Complete Civil War Journal and Selected Letters of Thomas Wentworth Higginson* (Chicago: Univ. of Chicago Press, 2000); and C. P. Weaver, *Thank God My Regiment an African One: The Civil War Diary of Colonel Nathan W. Daniels* (Baton Rouge: Louisiana State Univ. Press, 1998).

A number of studies focus on the role of Southern blacks in the Confederate and Union war efforts. Bell I. Wiley's *Southern Negroes, 1861–1865* (New Haven, Conn.: Yale Univ. Press, 1938) remains a valuable analysis. Other helpful studies include: James H. Brewer, *The Confederate Negro: Virginia's Craftsmen and Military Laborers, 1861–1865* (Durham, N.C.: Duke Univ. Press, 1965); and Robert F. Durden's study of the Confederacy's attempt to emancipate and arm the slaves, *The Gray and the Black: The Confederate Debate on Emancipation* (Baton Rouge: Louisiana State Univ. Press, 1972). Ervin L. Jordan provides new insights into the role of Virginia blacks in the Confederacy and Union in *Black Confederates and Afro-Yankees in Civil War Virginia* (Charlottesville: Univ. Press of Virginia, 1995).

1. Alexander H. Newton, *Out of the Briars: An Autobiography and Sketch of the Twenty-ninth Regiment Connecticut Volunteers* (Philadelphia: A.M.E. Book Concern, 1910), 87–88.

2. For the training of recruits and army life as preparation for citizenship, see Reid Mitchell, *The Vacant Chair: The Northern Soldier Leaves Home* (New York: Oxford Univ. Press, 1993), chaps. 1, 2. For how soldiers were socialized and integrated into the Union Army, see Bell I. Wiley, *The Life of Billy Yank: The Common Soldier of the Union* (Baton Rouge: Louisiana State Univ. Press, 1978), chap., 2; J. I. Robertson, *Soldiers Blue & Gray* (Columbia: Univ. of South Carolina Press, 1991), chap. 3; Reid Mitchell, *Civil War Soldiers: Their Expectations and Their Experiences* (New York: Viking, 1988), chap. 3.

3. J. W. Blassingame, *The Slave Community: Plantation Life in the Antebellum South* (New York: Oxford Univ. Press, 1979); Herbert G. Gutman, *The Black Family in Slavery and*

Freedom, 1750–1925 (New York: Pantheon, 1976); Charles Joyner, *Down by the Riverside: A South Carolina Slave Community* (Urbana: Univ. of Illinois Press, 1984); Lawrence W. Levine, *Black Culture and Black Consciousness: Afro-American Folk Thought from Slavery to Freedom* (Oxford: Oxford Univ. Press, 1977); Leslie H. Owens, *This Species of Property: Slave Life and Custom in the Old South* (New York: Oxford Univ. Press, 1976); Thomas L. Webber, *Deep Like the Rivers: Education in the Slave Quarter Community, 1831–1865* (New York: Norton, 1978); Berlin et al., *The Black Military Experience*, xvi.

4. James M. McPherson, *The Struggle for Equality: Abolitionists and the Negro in the Civil War and Reconstruction* (Princeton, N.J.: Princeton Univ. Press, 1964), 192–93; Mitchell, *Civil War Soldiers*, 194–95, 209, and *The Vacant Chair*, 64–65. Mitchell argues that the white Union soldiers saw the war as rite of passage, a way of proving their manhood and validating their citizenship; see *The Vacant Chair*, chaps. 1–3.

5. For reference to citizenship education in flag-presentation ceremonies, see William H.Chenery, *The Fourteenth Rhode Island Heavy Artillery (Colored) in the War to Preserve the Union, 1861–1865* (Providence: Snow and Farnham, 1898), 14–15; [New York] Union League Club, *Report of the Committee on Volunteering* (New York: 1864), 27–28; *National Anti-Slavery Standard*, June 20, 1863.

6. For reference to the Union army as a vehicle for the education and elevation of the freedmen in the Preliminary Report of the American Freedmen's Inquiry Commission, see *The War of the Rebellion: A Compilation of the Official Records of the Union and Confederate Armies*, 128 vols. (Washington, D.C.: GPO, 1880–1901), ser. 3, vol. 3, 435 (hereafter cited as *OR*). For testimony before the American Freedmen's Inquiry Commission advocating the use of the Union army as a vehicle of manhood and citizenship education, see testimonies of B. K. Lee, Judge A. Smith, Col. T. W. Higginson, Gen. J. Wadsworth, J. Eaton, G. L. Stearns, Col. W. A. Pile, American Freedmen's Inquiry Commission, files 3, 5, 7, 0-328, 1863, Letters Received, ser. 12, RG 94.

7. For the work of abolitionists in black recruitment and the motivation of abolitionist officers who joined black regiments, see Glatthaar, *Forged in Battle*, 12–16; McPherson, *The Struggle for Equality*, 192–212; Mitchell, *The Vacant Chair*, chap. 4; Keith Wilson, "Black Bands and Black Culture: A Study of Black Military Bands in the Union Army during the Civil War," *Australasian Journal of American Studies* 8, no.1 (July 1990): 31–37, "'Manhood Education': An Analysis of the Efforts Made by Northern White Army Officers to Educate Black Union Army Soldiers during the Civil War and an Assessment of the Response of the Black Soldiers" (Ph.D. diss., La Trobe University, 1986).

The concept of using the army as a vehicle to educate Americans socially was developed by Thomas Wentworth Higginson. Colonel Higginson, 1st South Carolina Colored Volunteers,was one of the first New England abolitionists to command a regiment of Southern ex-slaves. See "Physical Courage," *Atlantic Monthly* 2 (Nov. 1858): 728–37; "Barbarism and Civilization," *Atlantic Monthly* 7 (Jan. 1861): 51–61; "The Ordeal by Battle," *Atlantic Monthly* 8 (July 1861): 88–95; "Regular and Volunteer Officers," *Atlantic Monthly* 14 (Sept. 1864): 348–57; "Fair Play the Best Policy," *Atlantic Monthly* 15 (May 1865): 623–31; "Our Future Militia System," *Atlantic Monthly* 16 (Sept. 1865): 371–78. For comments by Higginson on manliness and the black character, see Thomas Wentworth Higginson, *Army Life in a Black Regiment* (1869 rpt., Williamstown, Mass.: Corner House, 1971), 10, 29, 44, 265–67. Reid Mitchell has written a perceptive analysis of Higginson's service with his black regiment; see Mitchell, *The Vacant Chair*, chap. 4.

For how wealthy antislavery elites used the war and the Union army to promote their leadership and values, see G. M. Fredrickson, *The Inner Civil War: Northern Intellectuals and the Crisis of the Union* (New York: Harper and Row, 1968), 151–65, 171–74, and *The Black Image in the White Mind: The Debate over Afro-American Character and Destiny, 1817–1919* (New York: Harper and Row, 1971), 167–71. Reid Mitchell argues that "family" communities were established in each regiment and that these communities maintained links with home communities; Mitchell, *The Vacant Chair*, 21–23, 158–59.

8. W. Vaughn to E. Stanton, July 10, 1865, V-64, 1865, Letters Received, ser. 360, CTD, RG 94.

PROLOGUE

1. Berlin et al., *The Black Military Experience* (Cambridge: Cambridge Univ. Press, 1982), 5–6; Mary F. Berry, *Military Necessity and Civil Rights Policy: Black Citizenship and theConstitution, 1861–1868* (New York: Kennikat Press, 1977), 1–33; James M. McPherson, *The Struggle for Equality: Abolitionists and the Negro in the Civil War and Reconstruction,* (Princeton, N.J.: Princeton Univ. Press, 1964), 192–93.

2. Dudley T. Cornish, *The Sable Arm: Negro Troops in the Union Army, 1861–1865* (1956; rpt., New York: W. W. Norton, 1966), 46–47.

3. Berlin et al., *The Black Military Experience*, 9–10.

4. Ibid., 9–10, 75–76, 406–11; John A. Andrew to F. G. Shaw, Jan. 30, 1863, "The Negro in the Military Service, 1639–1886," 1082, ser. 390, CTD, RG 94 (National Archives Microfilm Publication, 1963, no. M858); Luis S. Emilio, *A Brave Black Regiment: The History of the Fifty-fourth Massachusetts Volunteer Infantry, 1863–1865* (Boston: Boston Book Company, 1894), 3–5.

5. Freeman S. Bowley, *A Boy Lieutenant* (Philadelphia: Henry Altemus Co., 1906), 13–14.

6. Cornish, *The Sable Arm*, 148–51; Duncan, *Blue-Eyed Child of Fortune*, 42, 339–54, 356, 364; H. M. Crydenwise to parents, Nov. 28, 1863, Henry M. Crydenwise Letters, EUL.

7. O. W. Barnard to Lincoln, Mar. 3, 1863, B-70 1863; Pvt. W. Freeman to Chief of Bureau, Nov. 11, 1863, F-128 1863; both Applications for Appointments, ser. 370, CTD, RG 94.

8. E. Earle, "Kansas, Colored Volunteer Regiment, 1st Roll, Accounts and History of the First Kansas Colored Volunteer Regiment, 1863–1865," introduction, NEHGS; F. E. Hall to mother, Feb. 1, 1863, Francis E. Hall Papers; E. H. C. Taylor to L. D. Taylor, Apr. 1, 1863, Edward H. C. Taylor Papers, Michigan Historical Collection, UM. Carl E. Hatch, ed., *Dearest Susie: A Civil War Infantryman's Letters to His Sweetheart* (New York: Exposition Press, 1971), 38; George M. Blackburn, ed., "The Negro as Viewed by a Michigan Civil War Soldier: Letters of J. C. Buchanan," *Michigan History* 47 (1963): 75–84; Randall J. Jimerson, *The Private Civil War:Popular Thought during the Sectional Conflict* (Baton Rouge: Louisiana State Univ. Press, 1988), 94–100, 108–11.

9. Joseph T. Glatthaar, *Forged in Battle: The Civil War Alliance of Black Soldiers and White Officers* (New York: Meridian, 1991), 265–70; Keith Wilson, "Thomas Webster and the 'Free Military School for Applicants for Commands of Colored Troops,'" *Civil War History* 29, no. 2 (June 1983): 111–12.

10. *Christian Recorder*, Sept. 10, 1864, 7 Jan., 1865; Cornish, *The Sable Arm*, 108; Emilio,

A Brave Black Regiment, 339, 364; Pvt. S. Joyner to Brig. Gen. E. Wild, Feb. 21, 1864, Edward A. Wild Papers, MOLLUS, Massachusetts Commandery Collection, USAMHI.

11. Col. S. M. Bowman to Maj. C. W. Foster, June 22, 1864, W-500, Letters Received, ser. 360, CTD, RG 94; *Christian Recorder,* Apr. 16, 1864; Berlin et al., *The Black Military Experience,* 186, 656.

12. Berlin et al., *The Black Military Experience,* 37–41; *OR* ser. 3, vol. 2, 53, 56–58; see also 50–60, ser. 3, vol. 2, 147–48, 196–98. Higginson, *Army Life,* 61–130, 167–85; Tilden G. Edelstein, *Strange Enthusiasm: A Life of Thomas Wentworth Higginson* (New York: Atheneum, 1970), 269, 277–80, 287–89.

13. Berlin et al., *The Black Military Experience,* 9; Higginson, Journal, Feb. 4, 15, 1863, Harvard University, *Army Life,* 85–88; Special Orders No. 2, Hd. Qrs. 14th USCI, Jan. 6, 1864, Issuances, 14th USCI, Regimental Books and Papers USCT, RG 94.

14. James I. Robertson, *Soldiers Blue & Gray,* (1988; rpt., New York: Warner Books, 1991), 43.

15. Ibid., 42–47; Bell I. Wiley, *The Life of Billy Yank: The Common Soldier of the Union,* (Baton Rouge: Louisiana State Univ. Press, 1981), 55–65; Inspection Report Maj. Edward Cameron, Inspector Brig. Gen. E. A. Wild's African Brigade, Eighteenth Corps, Aug. 19, 1863,Inspection Reports, RG 94; Glatthaar, *Forged in Battle,* 185–87.

16. Wiley, *Billy Yank,* 57–58.

17. Robertson, *Soldiers Blue & Gray,* 47–48; Wiley, *Billy Yank,* 45–48.

18. Lt. Col. T. J. Morgan to Capt. R. D. Mussey, Dec. 6, 1863, Miscellaneous Records, 14th USCI Regimental Books and Papers USCT, RG 94.

19. James M. McPherson, *For Cause and Comrades: Why Men Fought in the Civil War* (New York: Oxford Univ. Press, 1997), 85–90; Reid Mitchell, *The Vacant Chair,* 21–23, 158–59.

20. Lawrence W. Levine, *Black Culture and Black Consciousness: Afro-American Folk Thought from Slavery to Freedom* (New York: Oxford Univ. Press, 1978), chap. 1; Herbert G. Gutman, *The Black Family in Slavery and Freedom, 1750–1925* (New York: Vintage Books, 1977), chaps. 3, 4; Charles Joyner, *Down by the Riverside: A South Carolina Slave Community* (Urbana: Univ. of Illinois Press, 1984), chaps. 1, 2; John W. Blassingame, *The Slave Community: Plantation Life in the Antebellum South* (New York: Oxford Univ. Press, 1979). See also Eugene D. Genovese, *Roll, Jordan, Roll: The World the Slaves Made* (New York: Vintage Books, 1976); George Rawick, *The American Slave: A Composite Autobiography,* ser. 1, no. 1, *From Sundown to Sunup: The Making of the Black Community* (Westport, Conn.: Greenwood Publishing Company, 1972). I have also found Reid Mitchell's discussion of community life in the Union army very useful. Reid Mitchell argues that since most regiments were formed in a single county or area, the regiment's companies acted as extensions of the soldier's home communities. These military communities maintained links with the home communities; see Mitchell, *The Vacant Chair,* 21–23, 158–59. For the frailty of the slave community and how a slave community may be defined, see Peter Kolchin, *Unfree Labor: American Slavery and Russian Serfdom*(Cambridge, Mass.: Belknap Press, 1987), esp. 199–200; Kolchin, *American Slavery 1619–1877* (New York: Hill & Wang, 1993), 148–55; Kolchin, "Re-evaluating the Antebellum Slave Community," *Journal of American History,* 70 (Dec. 1983): 579–601.

21. Death by disease, battle casualties, desertion, and the War Department policy of organizing new regiments rather than maintaining manpower levels in veteran regiments all contributed to a reduction in regiment size. Nevertheless, even allow-

ing for this numerical decline, the proportion of white officers to black enlisted men probably ranged somewhere between one officer for every twenty to twenty-four men. Robertson, *Soldiers Blue & Gray*, 21; James M. McPherson, *Ordeal by Fire: The Civil War Era and Reconstruction* (New York: Knopf, 1982), 168. For the relationship between plantation size and the creation of social space, see Gutman, *The Black Family*, 102–3; Kolchin, "Re-Evaluating the Antebellum Slave Community," 582–87; Leslie H. Owens, *This Species of Property: Slave Life and Culture in the Old South* (New York: Oxford Univ. Press, 1977), 9.

22. Robertson, *Soldiers Blue & Gray*, 43; C. B. Fox to wife, Nov. 8, 1863, Feb. 23, 1864, Extracts from Letters Written to Wife, vol. 1, 106, 169–71, Chas. B. Fox, Extracts from Letters Written to Wife 1863–65, 3 vols., MAHS.

23. Thomas L. Webber, *Deep Like the Rivers: Education in the Slave Quarter Community* (New York: W. W. Norton, 1978), 3–4; For the relationship between officers and their men in Union army regiments, see Mitchell, *The Vacant Chair*, chap. 3.

24. Berlin et al., *The Black Military Experience*, 433–42; *Christian Recorder*, Jan. 28, July 23, Nov. 12, 1864, Mar. 18, 1865; Christian A. Fleetwood, quoted in Noah A. Trudeau, *Like Men of War: Black Troops in the Civil War 1862–1865* (Boston: Little, Brown, 1998), 290–91.

25. Berlin et al., *The Black Military Experience*, 483–87; William F. Messner, *Freedmen and the Ideology of Free Labor: Louisiana, 1862–1865* (Lafayette: Univ. of Southwestern Louisiana, 1978), 129–32, 136–39; Wiley, *Billy Yank*, 120–21; William Seraile, "New York's Black Regiments during the Civil War" (Ph.D. diss., City University of New York, 1977), 134.

26. A random sampling of approximately 10 percent of U.S. Colored Troops regiments reveals that during the life of a regiment, there was an approximate 94 percent turnover in the personnel of the officers. Promotion, discharge, and resignation accounted for most change in the officer corps; disease, combat casualties, and dismissal accounted for a relatively small number. See regimental register lists for the 5th USCC, 5th USCHA, 9th, 12th, 23d, 33d, 39th, 45th, 56th, 69th, 80th, 89th, 95th, 100th, 110th, 120th, 127th USCI. U.S. Adjutant General's Office, *Official Army Register of the Volunteer Force of the United States Army for the Years 1861–65*, 8 pts., Washington 1865–67, pt. 8, 145, 152–53, 179, 183, 194, 204, 212, 218, 229, 242, 257, 271, 276, 281, 290, 301, 307.

27. McPherson, *Ordeal by Fire*, 165; Reid, *The Vacant Chair*, 46; Wiley, *Billy Yank*, 24–25; General Orders No. 7, Hd. Qrs., 14th USCI, Mar. 1, 1865, Issuances, 14th USCI, Regimental Books and Papers USCT, RG 94; T. J. Morgan, "Reminiscences of Service with Colored Troops in the Army of the Cumberland 1863–1865," RISSHS, ser. 3, no. 13, Providence, R.I., 1887. Lt. Col. T. J. Morgan to G. L. Stearns, Jan. 4, 1864; Col. T. J. Morgan to Brig. Gen. D. Tillson, Mar. 4, 1864; both Letters Received, 14th USCI, Regimental Books and Papers USCT, RG 94. Seraile, "New York's Black Regiments," 92, 241.

28. Higginson, Journal, Dec. 8, 15, 1862, HU. Leon Litwack argues that free Northern blacks believed the religious customs of the slaves had been seriously corrupted by the institution of slavery. During the Reconstruction period, Northern black soldiers became missionaries and worked among the former slaves in an effort to reform their religious practices. Leon F. Litwack, *Been in the Storm So Long: The Aftermath of Slavery* (New York: Vintage Books, 1980), 450–52, 462–63.

29. Bowley, *A Boy Lieutenant*, 80–81.

30. *Christian Recorder,* Mar. 18, 1865.

31. Chenery, *The Fourteenth Rhode Island Heavy Artillery (Colored),* 49.

32. Testimony of Cpl. William Wallace in the proceedings of general court-martial in the case of Cpl. James Morrison et al., 52d USCI, MM-2079, Court-Martial Case Files, ser. 15, RG 153.

1. "There Is No Trouble about the Drill"

1. Higginson, *Army Life,* 14–15.

2. Descriptions of discipline, training, and associated racism in black regiments include: Berlin et al., *The Black Military Experience,* chap. 9; and Glatthaar, *Forged in Battle,* chaps. 5, 6. Published accounts of the regulations, structure, and administration of military justice and discipline in the Union army include: G. B. Davis, *A Treatise on the Military Law of the United States together with the Practice and Procedure of Courts-Martial and Other Military Tribunals* New York: J. Wiley and Sons, 1898; K. W. Munden and H. Beers, *Guide to Federal Archives Relating to the Civil War* (Washington, D.C.: NA, 1962), 326–47; U.S. War Department, *Revised United States Army Regulations, Washington, 1863*; Robertson, *Soldiers Blue & Gray,* chap. 7; Wiley, *Billy Yank,* chap. 8.

3. Glatthaar argues that many USCT officers believed that army training and discipline would do much to negate the damaging impact of slavery. Glatthaar, *Forged in Battle,* 84–85.

4. Higginson, *Army Life,* 253–54.

5. Higginson, Journal, Dec. 3, 1862, *Army Life,* 38, 53, 253–54, 257–58.

6. Testimony of Col. T. W. Higginson before the American Freedmen's Inquiry Commission, File 3, 0-328, 1863, ser. 12 RG 94.

7. Higginson, Journal, Feb. 23, 1863; Higginson, *Army Life,* 53.

8. Higginson, Journal, Dec. 3, 1862; Higginson "Colored Troops under Fire," *Century Magazine* 54 (May 1897): 199.

9. Higginson, "Colored Troops under Fire," 200.

10. Higginson, Testimony.

11. Higginson, Testimony.

12. Higginson, Testimony; Higginson, Journal, Feb. 23, 1863.

13. Higginson, Testimony.

14. General Orders Nos., 24, 38, 54, 98, Hd. Qtrs., 33d USCI, Feb. 13, Apr. 15, June 29, Dec. 31, 1863, Issuances, 33d USCI, Regimental Books and Papers USCT, RG 94.

15. General Orders Nos., 8, 11, Hd. Qtrs., 33d USCI, Dec. 24, 1862, Jan. 1, 1863, Issuances, 33d USCI, Regimental Books and Papers USCT, RG 94.

16. Seth Rogers, "War-Time Letters of Seth Rogers, M.D. Surgeon of the First South Carolina. Afterwards the Thirty-Third USCT, 1862–1863," Jan. 3, 1863, 7, MOLLUS, Massachusetts Commandery Collection, USAMHI; Higginson, Journal, Aug. 26, 1863. General Orders Nos., 27, 28, Hd. Qtrs., 33d USCI, Feb. 21, Apr. 21, 1863, Issuances, 33d USCI; General Orders No. 71, Hd. Qtrs., 33d USCI, Dec. 20, 1863, Miscellaneous Records, 33d USCI; all Regimental Books and Papers USCT, RG 94. Higginson, *Army Life,* 43.

17. Higginson, *Army Life,* 43–44.

18. Ibid., 18; Higginson, Journal, Sept. 12, 1863.

19. Higginson, Journal, Apr. 26, 1863.

20. Higginson, Journal, Feb. 18, May 25, 1864; Col. T. W. Higginson to Brig. Gen.

R. Saxton, Feb. 19, 1864, Letters Received, 33d USCI; General Orders No. 14, Hd. Qtrs., 33d USCI, Feb. 26, 1864, Issuances, 33d USCI, Regimental Books and Papers USCT, RG 94; Higginson, Testimony.

21. Higginson, *Army Life*, 150–51; Higginson, Journal, Feb. 18, 1864; Rogers, "War-Time Letters," Mar. 8, Apr. 15, 1863, USAMHI; M. T. Higginson, ed., *Letters and Journals of Thomas Wentworth Higginson, 1846–1906* (Boston: Houghton Mifflin, 1921), 178.

22. Higginson, Testimony.

23. H. Crydenwise to "parents and all," Jan. 27, 1864, Henry M. Crydenwise Letters, EUL.

24. For a more detailed discussion of the attempts by chaplains to act as the moral guardians of their men, see chap. 5. For the ill feeling and conflict between Chaplain Jones and other officers in the 10th USCI, see Chaplain A. Jones to AAG R. S. Davis, July 12, 1864; General Orders No. 99, H.Q. Dept. Virginia and North Carolina, Aug. 25, 1864, Service Record of Alvah R. Jones, 10th USCI; both Carded Records, Volunteer Organizations: Civil War, ser. 519, RG 94. For Colonel Nelson's inhumane treatment of his soldiers and cruel recruiting methods, see Report of Maj. Gen. B. F. Butler, Commander Department of Virginia and North Carolina, Mar. 15, 1864; Investigation Report, Lt. Col. J. B. Kinsman, Dec. 12, 1863, N-18, 1863; both Letters Received, ser. 360, CTD, RG 94. See also General Orders No. 99, H.Q. Dept. Virginia and North Carolina, Aug. 25, 1864, Service Record of Alvah R. Jones, Carded Records, Volunteer Organizations (hereafter U.S. Vol. Org.): Civil War, ser. 519, RG 94; Chaplain A. R. Jones to Brig. Gen. L. Thomas, July 7, Aug. 31, Oct. 31, Dec. 31, 1864, J-138, J-218, J-286, J-344, Letters Received, ser. 12, RG 94.

25. T. S. Johnson to "My Dear People," Dec. 17, 1864, Thomas S. Johnson Papers, SHSW; *Harper's Weekly*, Nov. 26, 1864.

26. General Orders No. 5, Hd. Qtrs., 5th Mass. Vols., May 3, 1865, Issuances, 5th Mass. Vols., Regimental Books and Papers U.S. Vol. Org., RG 94. Black soldiers in the 5th Mass. Cavalry made a number of protests about the severity of punishments inflicted upon them. See Anon. to Gov. Andrew, July 22, 1865, Exec. Dept. Letters, Letters Received, vol. W-81, no. 236, Andrew Papers, CMSA. *Weekly Anglo-African*, July 16, 1864. Also Maj. H. N. Weld to Provost Marshal, City of New York, Aug. 1, 1864; Maj. H. N. Weld to R. Hamilton, July 18, 1864; both Miscellaneous Records, 5th Mass. Cav., Regimental Books and Papers U.S. Vol. Org., RG 94.

27. C. F. Adams Jr. to father, Nov. 2, 1864; Washington C. Ford, ed., *A Cycle of Adams Letters, 1861–1865* (Boston: Houghton Mifflin, 1920), vol. 2, 216. For Col. Charles Francis Adams's social beliefs and his attitude to service in a black regiment, see Fredrickson, *The Inner Civil War*, 170–72, 206–8.

28. For a discussion on Colonel Adams's views on the use of the Union army as a vehicle for education and a school for blacks, see Dudley T. Cornish, "The Union Army as a School for Negroes," *Journal of Negro History* 37 (Oct. 1952): 368–82; Edwin C. Kirkland, *Charles Francis Adams Jr., 1835–1915: The Patrician at Bay* (Cambridge: Harvard Univ. Press, 1965), 24–35. A mercenary soldier, Col. James Alexander was instrumental in recruiting the 1st Alabama Infantry, African Descent. Colonel Alexander was dismissed from military service for incompetence in drill, purloining supplies, and cruelty. Investigation Report of Maj. I. Pierce, Acting Judge Advocate, Sixteenth Corps, May 10, 1864, A-15, 1863, Letters Received, ser. 360, CTD RG 94; Report Judge Advocate General, J. Holt, June 30, 1864, A-15, 1863, Letters Received, ser. 360, CTD, RG 94.

29. Fredrickson, *The Inner Civil War*, chaps. 10, 11.

30. Samuel M. Quincy, *A Manual of Camp and Garrison Duty* (New Orleans: P. O'Donnell,1 865), 43.

31. Ibid.

32. Chaplain S. L. Gardner to Brig. Gen. D. Ullmann, Dec. 19, 1864, D. Ullmann Letters and Orders, Generals' Papers and Books, ser. 159, RG 94.

33. *Christian Recorder*, Jan. 28, 1865.

34. Ibid., Oct. 10, Nov. 12, 1863; Jan. 16, May 28, Dec. 10, 1864; Jan. 28, 1865. Sgt. William L. Logan to E. W. Kinsley, Aug. 25, [1864], Edward Wilkinson Kinsley Papers, DUL.

35. *Christian Recorder*, Nov. 7, Dec. 26, 1863; May 7, 1864; May 20, 1865. Susie King Taylor, *Reminiscences of My Life in Camp with the 33d United States Colored Troops Late 1st S. C. Volunteers* (Boston: privately published, 1902), 32.

36. *Weekly Anglo-African*, Jan. 7, 1865, in Exec. Dept. Letters, Letters Received, vol. W-100, no. 86, Andrew Papers, CMSA; *Christian Recorder*, Dec. 12, 1863.

37. Sgt. Maj. J. Trotter to E. W. Kinsley, Jan. 29, 1865, Edward Wilkinson Kinsley Papers, DUL. *Christian Recorder*, Oct. 23, Nov. 29, Dec. 12, 1863; May 7, 1864, May 6 and 20, 1865. Taylor, *Reminiscences*, 32;*Weekly Anglo-African*, Jan. 7, 1865, in Exec. Dept. Letters, Letters Received, vol. W-100, no. 86, Andrew Papers, CMSA.

38. *Christian Recorder*, Jan. 28, July 23, Nov. 12, 1864; Mar. 18, 1865. William N. McClintic to E. Stanton, undated, M-437, 1864, Letters Received, ser. 360, CTD, RG 94; *Weekly Anglo-African*, July 16, 1864, in Miscellaneous Records, 5th Mass. Cav., Regimental Books and Papers U.S. Vol. Org., RG 94; E. Barcus to [Gov. Andrew], Oct. 1, 1863, and J. J. Holloway to "Dear Friend," Mar. 7, 1864, Exec. Dept. Letters, Letters Received, vol. 59, nos. 50, 148, Andrew Papers, CMSA.

39. W. Vaughn to E. Stanton, July 10, 1865, V-64, 1865; Anon., 5 USCT, to E. Stanton, Oct. 22, 1865, A-420, 1865; "S.T.D." to S. Casey, June 6, 1864, all C-532, 1864, Letters Received, ser. 360, CTD, RG 94; *Christian Recorder*, Feb. 13, July 9, Nov. 12, 1864.

40. John B. Bowie, Henry W. Butler to U.S. Adj. Gen., Aug. 25, 1865, B-875, 1865; Bvt. Brig. Gen. Llewellyn F. Haskell to Capt. R. C. Shaunon, Sept. 18, 1865, A-321, 1865; Anon., 5 USCT, to E. Stanton, Oct. 22, 1865, A-420, 1865; Anon. private, 10th USCT, to E. Stanton, Dec. 1, 1864, A-423, 1864; John H. Wilkinson to "Hon. Sir.[?]," Nov. 28, 1864, W-945, 1864, Letters Received, ser. 360, CTD, RG 94; Anon., 33d USCT, to Brig. Gen. Gillmore, [Aug. 1865]; all Miscellaneous Records, 33d USCI, Regimental Books and Papers USCT, RG 94. Newton, *Out of the Briars*, 82; *Christian Recorder*, July 30, Aug. 6, 1864; Apr. 22, 1865.

41. *Christian Recorder*, May 27, 1864.

42. Ibid., Aug. 27, 1864.

43. Ibid., Aug. 27, Nov. 12, 1864; Apr. 22, 1865. William N. McClintic to E. Stanton, undated, M-437, 1864; Anon., 4th USCT, to E. Stanton, Oct. 2, 1865, A-396, 1865; both Letters Received, ser. 360, CTD, RG 94.

44. Berlin et al., *The Black Military Experience*, 409–11.

45. *Christian Recorder*, Jan. 28, May 27, 1864; Mar. 25, 1865. Pvt. Alonzo Reed to mother, Alonzo Reed Letters, DUL; Q.M. Sgt. Theodore Sydel to Lt. Col. J. Harper, Nov. 22, 1863, C-26, 1863, Letters Received, ser. 360, CTD, RG 94.

46. *Christian Recorder*, Mar. 25, May 27, 1865.

47. Ibid., Mar. 25, 1865; Sgt. H. Washington to Gen. Ullmann, Aug. 1, 1864, D.

Ullmann Letters and Orders, Generals' Papers and Books, ser. 159, RG 94; Q.M. Sgt. Theodore Sydel to Lt. Col.J. Harper, Nov. 22, 1863, C-26, 1863, Letters Received, ser. 360, CTD, RG 94.

48. "Monstrous Barbarity in the 5th Massachusetts Cavalry," *Weekly Anglo-African*, July 16, 1864, in Miscellaneous Records, 5th Mass. Cav., Regimental Books and Papers U.S. Vol. Org., RG 94; Anon. to E. Stanton, Oct. 2, 1865, A-396, 1865, Letters Received, ser. 360, CTD, RG 94.

49. *Christian Recorder*, Jan. 2, 1864.

50. Ibid.; Berlin et al., *The Black Military Experience*, 484–86.

51. Anon. to Maj. Gen. Gillmore, [Aug. 1865], Miscellaneous Records, 33d USCI, Regimental Books and Papers USCT, RG 94.

52. J. J. Holloway to "Dear Friend," Mar. 7, 1864; "From the 55 Regt. Vol." to Gov. Andrew, May 20, 1864; "Anon., 5 Mass Cav." to Gov. Andrew, July 22, 1864; "Voice of Once Noble, 5 Mass. Col'd" to Gov. Andrew[?], Exec. Dept. Letters; all Letters Received, vol. 59, no. 148, vol. 62, no. 125, vol. W-81, no. 236, vol. 81, no. 7, Andrew Papers, CMSA; *Christian Recorder*, July 23, 1864; Mar. 25, 1865. "Monstrous Barbarity in the 5th Massachusetts Cavalry"; *Weekly Anglo-African*, July 16, 1864, in Miscellaneous Records, 5th Mass. Cav. Regimental Books and Papers, U.S. Vol. Org. RG 94. William N. McClintic to E. Stanton[?], M-437, 1864, Letters Received, ser. 360, CTD, RG 94.

53. *Christian Recorder*, Jan. 28, 1864; "S.T.D." to Maj. Gen. S. Casey, June 6, 1864, C-532, 1864, Letters Received, ser. 360, CTD, RG 94. Sgt. Alexander Newton reported that one officer in his regiment, Captain Clark, "ought to have been with the Greys instead of the Blues, he had so little use for Colored troops. So he Marched them almost to death." The soldiers received temporary respite when Colonel Wooster, "a man without prejudice against the Colored people," arrested Captain Clark for the "outrage perpetuated against" his troops. Newton also complained against callous treatment by hospital staff. See Newton, *Out of the Briars*, 82.

54. Anon. to Gov. Andrew, July 27, 1863, Exec. Dept. Letters, Letters Received, vol. 21b, no. 162, Andrew Papers, CMSA.

55. Sgt. J. M. Trotter to E. W. Kinsley, Nov. 21, 1864, Edward Wilkinson Kinsley Papers, DUL; Sgt. F. Johnson to Gov. Andrew, May 10, 1863, Exec. Dept. Letters, Letters Received, vol. 59, no. 8, Andrew Papers, CMSA.

56. Chaplain B. F. Randolph to Brig. Gen. L. Thomas, Nov. 1, 1864, R-972, 1864; Chaplain J. R. Bowles to Brig. Gen. L. Thomas, Oct. 1, 1864, B-1416, 1864; both Letters Received, ser. 12, RG 94. Newton, *Out of the Briars*, 69–70.

57. *Christian Recorder*, Aug. 27, 1864; Newton, *Out of the Briars*, 70.

58. *Christian Recorder*, Mar. 25, 1865.

59. *Weekly Anglo-African*, July 16, 1864, Miscellaneous Records, 5th Mass. Cav., Regimental Books and Papers U.S. Vol. Org., RG 94.

60. Ibid.

61. *Christian Recorder*, Oct. 10, 1863.

62. S. C. Armstrong to R. B. Armstrong, Feb. 8, 1864; H. Ludlow, ed., "Personal Memories and Letters of General S. C. Armstrong," 5 vols., typescript, Williamsiana Collection, WCL, 363–64.

2. "A MATTER OF PRINCIPLE"

1. Berlin, et al., *The Black Military Experience,* 483–84, 486.
2. Ibid., 484–85.
3. D. Densmore to Benjamin [Dec. 1864], and to "Dear Friends at Home," Dec. 18, 1864, Benjamin Densmore Family Papers, MHS.
4. Col. W. F. Wood to Brig. Gen. W. S. Gorman, Miscellaneous Records, 46 USCI, Regimental Books and Papers USCT, RG 94; D. M. Murray, R. M. Rodney, "Colonel Julian E. Bryant: Champion of the Negro Soldier," *Illinios State Historical Society Journal* 56 (1964): 277–79; *New York Evening Post,* Nov. 17, Dec. 2, 1863; Jan. 20, Feb. 19, 1864. Colonel Bryant served as lieutenant colonel of the 1st Mississippi Volunteers, African Descent, until Sept. 1864, when he was promoted to the rank of colonel and replaced Col. W. F. Wood as commander of the 1st Arkansas Volunteers, African Descent. U.S. Adjutant General's Office, *Official Army Register,* pt. 8, 219, 224.
5. Berlin et al., *The Black Military Experience,* 485–87, 496–98, 513–14; Messner, *Freedmen and the Ideology of Free Labor,* 137–38. Brig. Gen. D. Ullmann to U.S. Adj. Gen., June 30, 1863, U-5, 1863, Letters Received, ser. 360, CTD, RG 94; D. Ullmann Address to Seventh Corps d'Afrique [Nov. 15, 1863], Daniel Ullmann Papers, NYHS.
6. For inspection reports highlighting the poor military appearance and general inefficiency of black troops caused by excessive fatigue duty, see Inspection Report, Col. Theodore H. Harrett, Inspector, Provisional Brigade, Port Hudson, May 25, 1864; Inspection Report, Lt. George F. Welch, Inspector, 20th, 74th, 82d, 96th, 98th USCI, Port Hudson, June 1864; Inspection Report, Lt. Col. W. D. Smith, Inspector, Southern Division of Louisiana, July 1865; all Inspection Reports, RG 94. Like Maj. Daniel Densmore, Maj. Ira Winans, commander of the 26th USCI, in Aug. 1864, felt that his regiment had been unfairly evaluated by inspecting officers who failed to consider the regiment's fatigue duties. W. Seraile, "New York's Black Regiments during the Civil War" (Ph.D. diss., City University of New York, 1977), 154–55.
7. Lt. Col. T. J. Morgan to Capt. R. D. Mussey, Dec. 6, 1863, Miscellaneous Records. Lt. Col. T. J. Morgan to Maj. Gen. J. J. Reynolds, Dec. 6, 1863; Lt. Col. T. J. Morgan to Capt. R. D. Mussey,Dec. 28, 1863; both Letters Received, 14th USCI, Regimental Books and Papers USCT, RG 94. T. J. Morgan, "Reminiscences of Service with Colored Troops in the Army of the Cumberland, 1863–1865," RISSHS, ser. 3, no. 13, Providence, R.I., 1887, 18–19.
8. J. C. Beecher to "Tom," Aug. 8, 1863, to "Frankie," Aug. 28, 1863; Beecher Stowe Papers (microfilm), RCL.
9. Col. J. C. Beecher to Brig. Gen. E. A. Wild, Sept. 13, 1863, Letters Received, 35th USCI, Regimental Books and Papers USCT, RG 94.
10. Berlin et al., *The Black Military Experience,* 493, 503; *National Anti-Slavery Standard,* Dec. 12, 1863.
11. Brig. Gen. L. Thomas to Col. W. W. Sanford, May 19, 1863, General Orders No. 21, June 14, 1864, L. Thomas Letters and Orders, Generals' Papers and Books, ser. 159, RG 94.
12. Anon., 5th USCI, to E. Stanton, Oct. 22, 1865, A-420, 1865, Letters Received, ser. 360, CTD, RG 94; *Christian Recorder,* Aug. 6, 1864. For other protests by black soldiers against fatigue duty, see Isaiah Prince to E. Stanton, July 14, 1865, P-455, 1865; Anon., 4th USCI, to Stanton, Oct. 2, 1865, A-396, 1865; both Letters Received,

ser. 360, CTD, RG 94. *Christian Recorder*, Feb. 13, 1864. One anonymous private of the 10th USCI wrote to Secretary of War Stanton in Dec. 1864 confessing that he "was not quite so silly as to believe that it is all right" for soldiers to pay for clothing worn out during fatigue duty. Private, 10th USCI, to Stanton, Dec. 1, 1864, A-423, 1864, Letters Received, ser. 360, CTD, RG 94.

13. Adams, ed., *On the Altar of Freedom*, 118–20.

14. *Christian Recorder*, Jan. 28, 9, July 30, 1864; Mar. 25, 1865. Isaiah Prince to Stanton, July 14, 1865, P-455, 1865, Letters Received, ser. 360, CTD, RG 94.

15. "S.T.D." to Maj. Gen. Casey, June 6, 1864; Lt. Col. John Wilder to Capt. A. D. Brown, AAG,Oct. 4, 1864, C-532, 1864; both Letters Received, ser. 360, CTD, RG 94.

16. Berlin et al., *The Black Military Experience*, 486–87, 504–14; Inspection Report, Maj. Lewis Mudgett, Inspector, Third Div., Dept. of the Gulf, Dec. 4, 1864; Inspection Report, Lt. Col. J. L. Rice, Inspector, 1st Brigade, First Div., Corps d'Afrique, Nov. 3, 1863; Inspection Report, Capt. H. K. Southwick, Inspector, U.S. Forces District of La Fourche, Louisiana, June 1865; all Inspection Reports, RG 94. For the excessive amount of fatigue duty done by black troops at Morganzia, Louisiana, see Berlin et al., *The Black Military Experience*, 486–87, 504–14. Inspection Report, Maj. George Baldery, Inspector, Col. H. Frisbie's Brigade and Provisional Brigade, U.S. Colored Troops, Morganzia, Aug. 10, 17, Oct. 9, 1864; Inspection Report, Chas. W. Hawes, Inspector, 1st Brigade, First Div., Morganzia, June 3, 19, 1864; Inspection Report, 1st Lt. G. C. Hagerthy, Inspector, Provisional Brigade, Morganzia, July 20, 1864; all Inspection Reports, RG 94.

17. Inspection Report, 1st Lt. G. C. Hagerthy, Inspector, Provisional Brigade, Morganzia, 20 July 1864, Inspection Report, Maj. George Baldey, Inspector, Col. H. Frisbie's Brigade and Provisional Brigade, U.S. Colored Troops, Morganzia, Aug. 10, 17, Oct. 9, 1864, Inspection Report, Chas. W. Hawes, Inspector, 1st Brigade, 1st Div., Morganzia, June 3, 19, 1864, Inspection Reports, RG 94.

Although antislavery officers could alleviate the plight of the black soldier, the heavy burden of fatigue still continued to fall disproportionately on black soldiers, and this situation continued into the immediate postwar period. See Inspection Report, Lt. Col. W. D. Smith, Inspector, Southern Division of Louisiana, July 1865, Inspection Reports, RG 94.

18. Brig. Gen. E. A. Wild to Col. W. Birney, Oct. 20, 1864, Miscellaneous Records, 2d USCI, Regimental Books and Papers USCT, RG 94.

19. *Christian Recorder*, Nov. 7, 1863.

20. Published accounts on the controversy surrounding the payment of black troops include: Adams, *On the Altar of Freedom*, xiii–xiv, 48–49, 82–83, 117–24; H. Belz, "Law, Politics, and Race in the Struggle for Equal Pay during the Civil War," *Civil War History* 22 (Sept. 1976): 197–222; Berlin et al., *The Black Military Experience*, 362–405; Emilio, *A Brave Black Regiment*, 47–48, 109, 130, 142, 179–81, 190–91, 220, 227–28; Cornish, *The Sable Arm*, 181–96; Glatthaar, *Forged in Battle*, 169–76, 195; McPherson, *The Negro's Civil War*, chap. 14, *Ordeal by Fire*, 351, *The Struggle for Equality*, 212–20; Redkey, *A Grand Army of Black Men*, chap. 7; Westwood, *Black Troops, White Commanders*, 11–15, 125–66; Williams, *A History of the Negro Troops*, 151–60; *Statutes at Large*, vol. 12, 592, 599. For the federal government's reasons for changing the black soldiers' rate of pay, see Berlin et al., *The Black Military Experience*, 363. The War Department violated the Mar. 1863 Enrollment Act's guarantee to pay drafted soldiers wages equal to those paid to volunteers. *OR*, ser. 3, vol. 3, 90. By June 1863 some blacks were being drafted.

21. Col. J. C. Beecher to Hon. H. Wilson, Jan. 13, 1864, James C. Beecher Family Papers, RCL; 1st Sgt. J. H. Jackson to Gov. Andrew, Feb. 5, 1865, Exec. Dept. Letters, Letters Received, vol. 62, no. A-99; G. B. Smith to friend Nathan McKay, Aug. 11, 1864, Exec. Dept. Letters, Letters Received, vol. 80, no. 155, Andrew Papers, CMSA; Anon. to E. Stanton, Jan. 24, 1865 A-36, 1865, Letters Received, ser. 360, CTD, RG 94; *Christian Recorder*, Dec. 3, 1864; Mar. 4, May 6, 1865. Emilio, *A Brave Black Regiment*, 130. Discontent over the pay issue led to an upsurge of desertions in some regiments. This was particularly true in South Carolina regiments that had initially been paid at the regular rate of thirteen dollars a month. See Higginson, Journal, Aug. 26, 1863. Discontent over the pay issue also nurtured insubordination. On the day his men received their first pay, Maj. J. C. Chadwick, Ninth Corps d'Afrique, sent copies of protest letters to Maj. Gen. Nathaniel Banks, commander of the Department of the Gulf, Brig. Gen. G. L. Andrews, commander of the Corps d'Afrique, and Major Palmer, department paymaster, complaining about the inequity of the pay. Statement by Maj. J. C. Chadwick, C-242, 1863, Letters Received, ser. 360, CTD, RG 94; Maj. J. J. Comstock to Col. C. E. Bailey, Apr. 16, 1864, Letters Received, 11 USCHA, Regimental Books and Papers USCT, RG 94; N. Viall, "A Brief History of the 14th R.I. Regiment Colored, 1863–65," 17–18, RIHS; Chenery, *The Fourteenth Rhode Island Heavy Artillery*, 66. For the pay controversy in the 14th Rhode Island Colored Heavy Artillery, see Westwood, *Black Troops, White Commanders*, 142–66.

22. The pay rates for enlisted men and noncommissioned officers in white regiments were as follows: $13 a month for privates and corporals, $17 a month for company sergeants, $20 for first sergeants, and $21 for regimental sergeants. Berlin et al., *The Black Military Experience*, 364; Testimony of Col. W. A. Pile before the American Freedmen's Inquiry Commission, file no. 7, 0-328, 1863, Letters Received, ser. 12, RG 94.

23. Testimony of Col. T. W. Higginson before the American Freedmen's Inquiry Commission, file 3, 0-328, 1863 Letters received, ser. 12, RG 94; Lt. Col. R. Cowden to Brig. Gen. L. Thomas, Dec. 1, 1864, Letters Received, 59th USCI, Regimental Books and Papers USCT, RG 94.

24. Col. J. C. Beecher to Hon. H. Wilson, Jan. 13, 1864, James C. Beecher Family Papers, RCL; J. Scroggs, Diary, Mar. 30, 1864, Joseph Scroggs Diary, typescript, Civil War Times Illustrated Collection, USAMHI; Oliver W. Norton, *Army Letters, 1861–1865* (Chicago: Deming, 1903), 214. Two commanders of Massachusetts black regiments, Col. R. G. Shaw of the 54th Massachusetts and Col. A. S. Hartwell of the 55th Massachusetts Volunteers, wanted their regiments mustered out because black soldiers were not paid at the same rate as white soldiers. R.G. Shaw to father, July 1, 1863, Cambridge, Mass., 1864, 314–15; Col. A. S. Hartwell to secretary of war, June 13, 1864, H-407, 1864; both Letters Received, ser. 360, CTD, RG 94. Lt. H. N. Edgerton to T. Webster, June 27, 1864, *Free Military School Register*, HSP.

25. Col. E. N. Hallowell to Gov. Andrew, Nov. 25, 1863, Exec. Dept. Letters, Letters Received, vol. 59, no. 73, Andrew Papers, CMSA.

26. T. Webster to Hon. E. M. Stanton, July 30, 1863, W-68, 1863, Letters Received, ser. 360, CTD, RG 94; Gov. Andrew to Charles Sumner, Apr. 25, 1864, unidentified newspaper extract, Edward Wilkinson Kinsley Papers, DUL (the papers of Edward Wilkinson Kinsley are located in two archives, Massachusetts Historical Society, Edward W. Kinsley Papers, and Duke University Library, Edward Wilkinson Kinsley Papers); *Commonwealth*, Feb. 12, 1864; Gov. Andrew to E. Stanton, July 6, 1864, M-503, 1864,

Letters Received, ser. 360 RG 94; Gov. Andrew to Lincoln, May 27, 1864, Exec. Dept. Letters, Letters Received, vol. W-100, no. 84, Andrew Papers, CMSA; Gov. Andrew to John Wilder, May 23, 1863, John August Wilder–Todd Family Papers, Lomis-Wilder Family Collection, YUL.

27. Berlin et al., *The Black Military Experience*, 362–63; *Christian Recorder*, Sept. 12, 1863; May 17, 29, 1864. Sgt. W. J. Brown to Stanton, Apr. 27, 1864, B-582, 1864; Cpl. James H. Gooding to Abraham Lincoln, Sept. 28, 1863, H-133, 1863; both Letters Received, ser. 360, CTD, RG 94. J. Cross to wife, Dec. 31, 1864, Mar. 6, 1865, Joseph Cross Letters, CTHS; Sgt. J. Morgan to Lincoln, Jan. 16, 1864, M-190, 1864, Letters Received, ser. 360, CTD, RG 94.

28. *Christian Recorder*, Feb. 27, May 17, June 25, Aug. 20, 1864; Sgt. Maj. J. M. Trotter to E. W. Kinsley, Nov. 21, 1864, Edward Wilkinson Kinsley Papers, DUL. Cpl. James H. Gooding to Abraham Lincoln, Sept. 28, 1863, H-133, 1864; 1st Sgt. John H. Morgan, Jan. 16, 1864, B-190, 1864; both Letters Received, ser. 360, CTD, RG 94. *Christian Recorder*, May 21, 1864. For blacksoldiers being paid less than military laborers, see Berlin et al., *The Black Military Experience*, 363. Also Sgt. W. J. Brown to Stanton, Apr. 27, 1864, B-582, 1864; Lt. Col. A. G. Bennett to Brig. Gen. L. Thomas, Nov. 21, 1863, B-439, 1863; both Letters Received, ser. 360, CTD, RG 94

29. *Christian Recorder*, Sept. 12, 1863; Jan. 2, 1864; Berlin et al., *The Black Military Experience*, 365–66; J. Appleton to wife, Mar. 1, Apr. 7, 18, May 20, June 9, 1864, J. W. M. Appleton Letter Book, 210, 213, 226–27, 236 (microfilm), WVUL; Col. E. N. Hallowell to H. Ware, May 28, 1864, Exec. Dept. Letters, Letters Received, vol. 80, no. 7; Col. A. S. Hartwell to Governor Andrew, Apr. 28, 1864, Exec. Dept. Letters, Letters Received, vol. 62, no. 15, Andrew Papers, CMSA; N. Hallowell to Governor Andrew, May 17, 1864, Exec. Dept. Letters, Letters Received, vol. 80, no. 2, Andrew Papers, CMSA; Col. A. S. Hartwell to Gov. Andrew, June 12, 1864, Letters Received, 55th Mass. Vols., Regimental Books and Papers USCT, RG 94; Col. J. Beecher to Hon. Henry Wilson, Jan. 13, 1864, James C. Beecher Family Papers, RCL; Sgt. J. F. Shorter to father, May 29, 1864, S-480, 1864, Letters Received, ser. 360, CTD, RG 94; Westwood, *Black Troops, White Commanders*, 125–66.

30. Stephen Swails, 54th Massachusetts Volunteers, a hero of the battle of Olustee, believed that because the government had "failed to fulfil its part of the agreement" to pay him the "allowance of a sergeant of the regular Army," he "respectfully demanded to be mustered out of the service of the United States." Some black recruiting agents felt guilt and a more acute sense of deception than the soldiers they had enlisted. When John Langston first heard that black troops were going to be paid only ten dollars per month, he enquired in a letter to Governor Andrew whether it was "safe for us to trust future national legislatives for justice in this matter." Sgt. Swails to Col. E. D. Townsend, Jan. 14, 1864, S-97, 1864, Letters Received, ser. 360, CTD, RG 94; J. M. Langston to Gov. Andrew, June 28, 1863, Exec. Dept. Letters, Letters Received, vol. W-100, no. 11, Andrew Papers, CMSA; L. Layden to Gov. Andrew, Apr. 12, 1864, Exec. Dept. Letters, Letters Received, vol. 80, no. 110, Andrew Papers, CMSA; *Christian Recorder*, Dec. 26, 1863; Sgt. J. F. Shorter et al. to president, July 16, 1864, L-211, 1864, Letters Received, ser. 360, CTD, RG 94. Black officers in the 2d Native Guard Regiment also petitioned Edwin Stanton, the secretary of war, for wage justice; Capt. B. S. Pinchback et al. to Hon. Edwin M. Stanton [Oct. 1863] G-104, 1864, Letters Received, ser. 360, CTD, RG 94.

31. Stephen R. Fox, *The Guardian of Boston: William Munroe Trotter*, Studies in American Negro Life (New York: Atheneum, 1970), 3–6; J. Abramowitz, "A Civil War Letter: James M. Trotter to Francis J. Garrison," *Midwest Journal* 4 (1952): 113–22. Sgt. J. M. Trotter to E. W. Kinsley, June 2, Nov. 21, 1864; Jan. 29, 1865 (James Trotter's letter to Edward Kinsley dated June 2, 1864, is unsigned); both Edward Wilkinson Kinsley Papers, DUL. *Christian Recorder*, Feb. 27, May 21, 28, June 25, July 9, Aug. 20, Dec. 3, 1864. James M. Trotter was appointed second lieutenant in the 55th Mass. Inf. in June 1865. U.S. Adjutant General's office, official Army Registry, pt. 8, 315.

32. Pvt. C. Parks to Col. Hartwell, May 2, 1864, Exec. Dept. Letters, Letters Received, vol. 62, no. 111, Andrew Papers, CMSA; Sgt. J. M. Trotter to E. W. Kinsley, Nov. 21, 1864, Edward Wilkinson Kinsley Papers, DUL; *Christian Recorder*, July 30, Aug. 27, Nov. 12, 1864.

33. For evidence of officers encouraging black troops to reject their pay, see Berlin et al., *The Black Military Experience*, 366; P. W. Romero and W. L. Rose, ed., *A Black Woman's Civil War Memoirs, Susie Taylor, Reminiscences of My Life in Camp with the 33d U.S. Colored Troops Late 1st. S. C. Volunteers* (New York: 1988, 1st published, 1902), 42, 48; C. W. Lennox to Gov. Andrew, June 10, 1864, Exec. Dept. Letters, Letters Received, vol. 80, no. 18, Andrew Papers, CMSA; Higginson, Journal, Apr. 17, 1864; J. Appleton to wife, Dec. 11, 13, 1863, AppletonLetter Book, WVUL; Col. N. Hallowell to Gov. Andrew, Dec. 2, 1863, Official Letters, Letters Sent, vol. 44, no. 353, Andrew Papers, CMSA; Fox to wife, Dec. 15, [1863], Extracts from Letters Written to Wife, vol. 1, 131, MAHS; Col. A. S. Hartwell to E. W. Kinsley, Apr. 7, 1864, unidentified newspaper cutting, Edward Wilkinson Kinsley Papers, DUL. For evidence of punitive action and court-martial proceedings taken against soldiers who refused to accept the inferior rate of pay, see Berlin et al., *The Black Military Experience*, 395–97; *Christian Recorder*, July 30, Aug. 27, 1864; N. Viall, "A Brief History of the 14th R.I. Regiment Colored, 1863–65," 17, RIHS; Chenery, *The Fourteenth Rhode Island Heavy Artillery*, 66; Maj. J. J. Comstock Jr., to Col. C. E. Bailey, Apr. 16, Letters Received, 11, USCHA, Regimental Books and Papers USCT, RG 94; G. G. Freeman to U.S. Chief Justice, June 25, 1865, Capt. E. J. McKendrie to Brig. Gen. L. Thomas, Aug. 17, 1865, F-155, 1865, Letters Received, ser. 360, CTD, RG 94; Proceedings of General Court-Martial in the case of Sgt. William Walker, 3d South Carolina Colored Volunteers, MM-1320, Court-Martial Files, ser. 15, RG 153.

34. *Christian Recorder*, July 30, Aug. 9, 1864.

35. Ibid., Sept. 12, 1863; Sgt. J. F. Shorter et al., to the president, July 16, 1864, L-211, 1864, Letters Received, ser. 360, CTD, RG 94.

36. Higginson, Journal, Apr. 17, [1864].

37. *Christian Recorder*, Dec. 26, 1863; Newton, *Out of the Briars*, 36. The "seven dollars a month" was the amount left from ten dollars after three had been deducted for clothing. Fox to wife, Apr. 27, [1864], Extracts from Letters Written to Wife, vol. 2, 57, MAHS; *Christian Recorder*, July 11, 1863; Jan. 2, Feb. 27, May 21, 28, June 11, 25, 1864; Sgt. F. Johnson to Governor Andrew, Aug. 10, 1863, Exec. Dept. Letters, Letters Received, vol. 59, no. 8, Andrew Papers, CMSA; Sgt. Maj. J. M. Trotter to E.W. Kinsley, June 2, Nov. 21, 1864, EdwardWilkinson Kinsley Papers, DUL.

38. For the disruption caused by a breakdown in communications between the officers and the noncommissioned officers, see the analysis of the 14th Rhode Island Colored Heavy Artillery pay dispute in Westwood, *Black Troops, White Commanders*, 142–66.

39. *Christian Recorder*, Aug. 27, Oct. 8, 1864 Jan. 14, 1865.

40. Ibid., Jan. 2, June 11, Sept. 3, Oct. 8, 1864; Jan. 11, 1865; Berlin et al., *The Black Military Experience*, 365–66.

41. *Christian Recorder*, Jan. 2, Feb. 4, June 11, Aug. 27, Sept. 3, 8, Oct. 18, 1864; Jan. 11, 14, 1865.

42. Sgt. F. Johnson to Governor Andrew, Aug. 10, 1863, Exec. Dept. Letters, Letters Received, Vol. 59, no, 8, Andrew Papers CMSA; [Charles B. Fox], *Record of the Service of the Fifty-Fifth Regiment of Massachusetts Volunteer Infantry* (Cambridge, Mass.: John Wilson and Sons,1868), 17–18; Col. N. Hallowell to Gov. Andrew, Dec. 2, 1863, Official Letters, Letters Sent, vol. 44, no. 353, Andrew Papers, CMSA; J. Appleton to wife, Dec. 11, 12, 1863, Appleton Letter Book, 124, 131, WVUL; Fox to wife, Dec. 15, [1863], Extracts from Letters Written to Wife, vol. 1, 131, MAHS.

43. J. Appleton to wife, Mar. 1, Apr. 7, 18, May 20, 1864, J. W. M. Appleton Letter Book, WVUL; Col. E. N. Hallowell to H. Ware, May 28, 1864, Exec. Dept. Letters, Letters Received, vol. 80, no. 7, Andrew Papers, CMSA; Col. E. Hallowell to Gov. Andrew, Oct. 28, 1863, Letters Received, 54th Mass. Vols. Regimental Books and Papers U.S. Vol. Org., RG 94; Col. A. S. Hartwell to E. W. Kinsley, Feb. 9, 1864, Edward W. Kinsley Papers, MAHS; Col. A. S. Hartwell to E. W. Kinsley, Apr. 7, 1864, unidentified newspaper cutting, Edward Wilkinson Kinsley Papers, DUL; Col. A. S. Hartwell to Gov. Andrew, June 12, 1864, Exec. Dept. Letters, Letters Received, vol. 62, no. 134, Andrew Papers, CMSA; [Fox] *Record of Service*, 26–28; C. B. Fox to wife, Apr. 27, 1864, Extracts from Letters Written to Wife, vol. 2, 57, MAHS; J. Appleton to wife, Mar. 1, Apr. 18, May 20, 1864, Appleton, Letter Book, 186, 213, 226–27, WVUL; *OR*, ser. 3, vol. 4, 448, 490–93, 564–65. Equal pay for black troops did not come until the military appropriations bill of June 1864. Payment was retroactive to Jan. 1, 1864, for all soldiers, but those free at the onset of the war, Apr. 19, 1861, were entitled to back pay from their enlistments. Black noncommissioned officers were paid at the same rate as white noncommissioned officers. Early in Mar. 1865 the last vestiges of legislative discrimination were finally removed when Congress granted equitable back pay for all black troops who had been enlisted under a promise of equal pay. *OR*, ser. 3, vol. 4, 448; Glatthaar, *Forged in Battle*, 174–75. Attorney General Bates announced his decision on July 14, 1864. On Aug. 1, War Department Circular No. 6 implemented the new pay policy. *OR*, ser. 3, vol. 4, 490–93, 564–65.

44. Sgt. Maj. J. M. Trotter to E. W. Kinsley, Nov. 21, 1864, Edward Wilkinson Kinsley Papers, DUL; C. B. Fox to wife, Oct. 16, 1864, Extracts from Letters Written to Wife, MAHS. *OR*, ser. 3, vol. 4, 490–93, 564–65; Glatthaar, *Forged in Battle*, 174–75.

45. [Sgt. Maj. J. M. Trotter] to E. W. Kinsley June 2, 1864, Edward Wilkinson Kinsley Papers, DUL.

3. "THIS IS THEIR UNIVERSITY"

1. Testimony of Capt. R. J. Hinton before the American Freedmen's Inquiry Commission, File 8, 0-328, 1863 Letters Received, ser. 12, RG 94.

2. There is no adequate work on black soldiers' use of leisure time. However, the followingcomment on certain recreational activities: Berlin et al., *The Black Military Experience*, chaps. 13, 14; Glatthaar, *Forged in Battle*, 224–27. For the allegedly devastating impact of slavery on the blacks' character, see S. C. Armstrong to R. B. Armstrong, Feb. 8, 1864, in H. Ludlow, ed., "Personal Memories," 363–64, WCL; Chap-

lain J. A. Hawley to Brig. Gen. L. Thomas, Aug. 15, 1864, H-110, 1864; Chaplain A. R. Randall to Brig. Gen. L. Thomas, Oct. 31, 1863, R-1131, 1864; Chaplain D. Reedy to Brig. Gen. L. Thomas, Jan. 4, 1865, R-55, 1864; all Letters Received, ser. 12, RG 94.. G. M. Blackburn, ed., "The Negro as Viewed by a Michigan Civil War Soldier: Letters of John C. Buchanan," *Michigan History* 47 (1963): 82–83; S. Rogers, "War-Time Letters of Seth Rogers, M.D. Surgeon of the First South Carolina. Afterward the Thirty-Third USCT, 1862–1863," Jan. 13, Apr. 7, May 22, 1863, 13–14, 88, 98–100. MOLLUS, Massachusetts Commandery Collection, USAMHI; G. S. Shurtleff to wife, Jan. 14, 1864, Giles W. Shurtleff Papers, OBA.

3. S. C. Armstrong to R. B. Armstrong, Feb. 8, 1864, in H. Ludlow, ed., "Personal Memories," 363–64, WCL; James Walvin divides leisure into "sinful recreations" and "useful pleasures." See J. Walvin, *Leisure and Society: 1830–1950* (London: Longman, 1978), 33–57. For republican recreation and virtue, see Tom P. Dunning's excellent "Convict Leisure and Recreation: The North American Experience in Van Diemen's Land, 1840–1847," *Sporting Traditions* 9, no. 2 (May 1993): 3–15. Gordon S. Wood describes artisan attitudes toward work, leisure, and the aristocracy in *The Radicalism of the American Revolution* (New York: Knopf, 1992). For leisure and the development of civic virtue, see Peter Bailey, *Leisure and Class in Victorian England: Rational Recreation and the Contest Control, 1830–1885* (London: Routledge and Kegan Paul, 1978). For officers' endeavors to elevate black soldiers, see Glatthaar, *Forged in Battle*, 39–40, 84–85, 224–30; K. Wilson, "Thomas Webster and the 'FreeMilitary School for Applicants for Commands of Colored Troops,'" *Civil War History* 29, no. 2 (June 1993): 104–8, 113–14; "Black Bands and Black Culture," 31–37, "'Manhood Education.'"

4. For the role of leisure activities, such as religious worship, musical performance, storytelling, and dance, in the slave community, see Blassingame, *The Slave Community*, chap. 3; Joyner, *Down by the Riverside*, chaps. 4, 5, 6; Levine, *Black Culture*; Owens, *This Species of Property*, chaps. 7, 8; S. Stuckey, "Through the Prism of Folklore: The Black Ethos in Slavery," *Massachusetts Review* 9 (Summer 1968): 417–37; Webber, *Deep Like the Rivers*, 80–90, 118–38, 180–84, 207–23, 215–23, 234–36. For a more general discussion on the way leisure pursuits can help to create new symbolic worlds and violate accepted social structures, see Victor Turner, *From Ritual to Theatre: The Human Seriousness of Play* (New York: Performing Arts Journal Publications, 1982), 36–37.

5. Although black soldiers did more fatigue work than did white soldiers, their general camp routine followed the general pattern common in the Union army. For camp routine, see Roberstson, *Soldiers Blue and Gray*, 47–48; Wiley, *Billy Yank*, 45–48.

6. Col. T. J. Morgan, "Reminiscences of Service with Colored Troops in the Army of the Cumberland, 1863–1865," RISSHS, ser. 3, no. 13, Providence, R.I., 1887, 20; Col. H. Lieb, "Soldier," Address, Hd. Qtrs., 5th USCHA, Aug. 1863, Issuances, 5th USCHA, Regimental Books and Papers, USCT, RG 94; R. G. Shaw to C. F. Morse, Feb. 24, 1863, Robert G. Shaw Papers, MAHS.

7. For the slave's care of clothing, see Genovese, *Roll, Jordan, Roll*, 550–61; Joyner, *Down by the Riverside*, 106–17.

8. Inspection Report, Lt. V. B. M. Bergen, Inspector, U.S. Forces La Fourche District, Apr. 6, 1864, Inspection Reports, RG 94. See also Inspection Report, Col. John V. Du Bois, Inspector General, Dept. of Missouri, Oct. 6, 1863, Miscellaneous Records, 79th (new) USCI, RG 94; General Orders No. 25, Hd. Qtrs., 36th USCI, Nov. 14, 1864, Issuances, 36th USCI, Regimental Books and Papers USCT, RG 94.

9. Inspection Report, Maj. Edward Cameron, Inspector, Brig. Gen. E. A. Wild's "African Brigade," Eighteenth Corps, Aug. 19, 1863, Inspection Reports; Maj. Q. McNeil to Brig. Gen. J. A. Rawlings, Aug. 13, 1864, Miscellaneous Records, 39th USCI, Regimental Books and Papers USCT, RG 94; George W. Buswell, Journal, May 22, 1864, HHL; D. Matson, "The Colored Man in the Civil War," MOLLUS, Iowa Commandery, *War Sketches and Incidents*, vol. 2 (Des Moines: Kenyon Press, 1898), 244; Brig. Gen. C. C. Andrews to Col. J. Eaton, Dec. 14, 1864, Christopher C. Andrews Papers, MHS; Norton, *Army Letters*, 8–9; Cyrus Sears, *The Battle of Milliken's Bend and Some Reflections Concerning the "Colored Troops," the Debt We Owe Them, and How We Paid It* (Columbus, Ohio: F. J. Heer, 1909), 8–9; J. Beecher to wife, Mar. 16, 1864, James C. Beecher Family Papers, RCL; Patrick Egan, "The Florida Campaign with the Light Battery C, Third Rhode Island Heavy Artillery," RISSHS, ser. 3, no. 13, Providence, R.I., 1887, 14; Brig. Gen. W. Birney to Maj. C. W. Foster, June 2, 1864, W-190, 1863, Letters Received, ser. 360, CTD, RG 94.

10. Brig. Gen. W. Birney to Maj. C. W. Foster, June 2, 1864, W-190, 1863, Letters Received, ser. 360, CTD, RG 94.

11. J. M. Meteer to C. Mills, Mar. 8, 1864, Caleb Mills Papers, IHSL. Lawrence Levine argues that "among a slave population whose daily rations were at best rather stark fare and quite often a barely minimal diet, it is not surprising that food proved to be the most common symbol of enhanced status and power." Lawrence W. Levine, *The Unpredictable Past: Explorations in American Cultural History* (New York: Oxford Univ. Press, 1993), 67.

12. Robertson, *Soldiers Blue & Gray*, 96–101; Wiley, *Billy Yank*, 252–54; J. M. Addeman, "Reminiscences of Two Years with the Colored Troops," RISSHS, ser. 2, no. 7, Providence, R.I., 1880, 28; Rufus Kinsley, Diary, 19 [July 1864], VHS; General Orders No. 28, Hd. Qtrs., 35th USCI, Nov. 17, 1865, Issuances, 35 USCI, Regimental Books and Papers USCT, RG 94. Colonel Beecher restricted provision of whisky from the Commissary Department to troops returning from fatigue duty. General Orders No. 74, Hd. Qtrs., 35th USCI, Nov. 16, 1863, Issuances, 35th USCI, Regimental Books and Papers USCT, RG 94.

13. C. B. Fox to wife, 3 Feb. Oct. 6, 1864, Extracts from Letters Written to Wife, vol. 2, 154, vol. 3, 30–33, MAHS; R. G. Shaw to Gov. Andrew, May 14, 1863, Exec. Dept. Letters, Letters Received, vol. 21b, no. 116, Andrew Papers, CMSA; J. Appleton to wife, May 29, 1863, Appleton Letter Book, WVUL.

14. Robertson, *Soldiers Blue & Gray*, 96–101; Wiley, *Billy Yank*, 252–54. William Burton argues that Irish regiments had serious drinking problems that were greater than those experienced by other Union regiments *Melting Pot Soldiers: The Union's Ethnic Regiments* (New York: Fordham Univ. Press, 1998), 153. Opinion is divided over the slaves' level of alcohol consumption. See Joyner, *Down by the Riverside*, 102–3; Kenneth M. Stampp, *The Peculiar Institution: Slavery in the Ante-Bellum South* (New York: Vintage Books, 1964), 370–71; Brenda E. Stevenson, *Life in Black and White: Family and Community in the Slave South* (New York: Oxford Univ. Press, 1996), 255.

15. Glatthaar, *Forged in Battle*, 221, 237–38, 334, 19; Investigation Report Maj. I. O. Pierce, Acting Judge Advocate, Sixteenth Corps, May 10, 1864, Report, Judge Advocate General J. Holt, June 30, 1864, A-15, 1863, Letters Received, ser. 360, CTD, RG 94; Investigation Report, Lt.Col. J. B. Kinsman, Dec. 12, 1863, Report of Maj. Gen. B. F. Butler, Mar. 15, 1864, N-19, 1863, Letters Received, ser. 360, CTD, RG 94. For drunken-

ness as a problem in the Union army, see Robertson, *Soldiers Blue & Gray*, 96–101; Wiley, *Billy Yank*, 252–54.

16. Brig. Gen. E. A. Wild to Maj. Gen. B. F. Butler, "Private," no date [Feb. 186?], Edward A. Wild Papers, MOLLUS Massachusetts Commandery Collection, USAMHI; Higginson, *Army Life*, 38, 257; Higginson, Journal, Dec. 3, 1862; *National Anti-Slavery Standard*, Aug. 15, 1863; Chaplain G. A. Rockwood to Brig. Gen. L. Thomas, May 31, 1864, R-412, 1864, Letters Received, ser. 12, RG 94.

17. W. Seraile, "New York's Black Regiments during the Civil War," 128; General Orders No. 11, Hd. Qtrs., 14th USCI, Mar. 4, 1864, Issuances, 14th USCI, Regimental Books and Papers USCT, RG 94; Report Capt. C. M. Blake, Aug. 30, 1863, James Montgomery Papers, KSHS.

18. General Orders No. 9, Hd. Qtrs., 54th Mass. Vols., Aug. 29, 1864, Issuances, 54th Mass. Vols., Regimental Books and Papers U.S. Vol. Org., RG 94; Wiley, *Billy Yank*, 249–52; General Orders No. 78, Hd. Qtrs., 55th Mass. Vols., Sept. 28, 1864, Issuances, 55th Mass. Vols., Regimental Books and Papers U.S. Vol. Org., RG 94; General Orders No. 9, Hd. Qtrs., 75th USCI, Aug. 5, 1865, Issuances, 75th USCI, Regimental Books and Papers USCT, RG 94.

19. Chaplain C. Bristol to Brig. Gen. L. Thomas, July 1, 1864, B-850, 1864; Chaplain G. A. Rockwood to Brig. Gen. L. Thomas, Dec. 3, 1864, R-1128, 1864; both Letters Received, ser. 12, RG 94. James Peet, Diary, Mar. 14, 1864, James Peet Family Papers, MHS (hereafter Peet, Diary). (The papers of James Peet are located at the Minnesota Historical Society [James Peet Family Papers] and the State Historical Society of Wisconsin [James Peet Diary].)

20. General Orders No. 2, Hd. Qtrs., 79th (new) USCI, May 21, 1864, Issuances, 79th (new) USCI, General Orders No. 9, Hd. Qtrs., 35th USCI, May 28, 1865, Issuances, 35th USCI, Regimental Books and Papers USCT, RG 94.

21. General Orders No. 2, Hd. Qtrs., 75 USCI, June 20, 1864, Issuances, 75 USCI, Regimental Books and Papers, USCT, RG 94.

22. Increase N. Tarbox, *Missionary Patriots: Memoirs of James H. Schneider and Edward M. Schneider* (Boston: Massachusetts Sabbath School Society, 1867), 146; Chaplain G. A. Rockwood to Brig. Gen. L. Thomas, May 31, 1864, R-412, 1864, Letters Received, ser. 12, RG 94. Chaplain G. A. Rockwood to Brig. Gen. L. Thomas, Sept. 30, 1865, Miscellaneous Records, 8th USCI, Regimental Books and Papers USCT, RG 94.

23. Tarbox, *Missionary Patriots*, 146; Chaplain G. A. Rockwood to Brig. Gen. L. Thomas, May 31, 1864, R 412, 1864, Letters Received, ser. 12, RG 94; Chaplain G. A. Rockwood to Brig. Gen. L. Thomas, Sept. 30, 1865, Miscellaneous Records, 8th USCI, Regimental Books and Papers USCT, RG 94; Brig. Gen. L. Thomas to J. W. Atwood, Apr. 25, 1865, L. Thomas Letters and Orders, Generals' Papers and Books, ser. 159, RG 94; Maj. A. Wells to sister, May 14, 1865, Amos Potter Wells Letters, Hagadorn-Wells Collection, RIHS; Capt. D. Foster et al., to Brig. Gen. E. A. Wild, June 14, 1864, and endorsements, Lt. Col. A. C. Chamberlain, Brig. Gen. E. A. Wild, Letters Received, 37th USCI, Regimental Books and Papers USCT, RG 94.

24. Testimony of Capt. E. W. Hooper before the American Freedmen's Inquiry Commission, File 3(A), 0-328 Letters Received, ser. 12, RG 94; W. De Blois Briggs, *Civil War Surgeon in a Colored Regiment* (Berkeley: Univ. of California Press, 1960), 137; General Orders No. 5, Hd. Qtrs., 1st Kansas Colored Volunteers, July 17, 1863, Issuances, 79th (new) USCI, Regimental Books and Papers USCT, RG 94.

25. Roberston, *Soldiers Blue & Gray*, 104–10; Wiley, *Billy Yank*, 183–90.

26. *National Tribune*, May 11, 1899; [Anon.] to Stanton, Aug. 22, 1865, A-345, 1865, Letters Received, ser. 360, CTD, RG 94; Berlin et al., *The Black Military Experience*, 613.

27. *Christian Recorder*, Dec. 10, 1864; M. L. Mainn to Gov. Andrew, June 9, 1863, Exec. Dept. Letters, Letters Received, vol. 84, no. 111, Andrew Papers, CMSA; *Christian Recorder*, July 16, 1864.

28. Pvt. S. Joyner to Brig. Gen. E. Wild, Feb. 21, 1864, Edward A. Wild Papers, MOLLUS Massachusetts Commandery Collection, USAMHI. *The Black Military Experience*, 657–58; Chaplain J. Gregg to Brig. Gen. L. Thomas, Feb. 28, 1865, G-239, 1865, Letters Received, ser. 12, RG 94; C. L. Wagandt, "The Army versus Maryland Slavery, 1862–1864," *Civil War History* 10 (June 1964): 141–48; *Christian Recorder*, Apr. 16, 1864; Lt. W. H. Hurd to Capt. W. C. J. Hall, Mar. 1, 1865, H-150, 1864, Letters Received, ser. 360, CTD, RG 94; J. Payne to Stanton, July 6, 1865, P-358, 1865, Letters Received, ser. 360, CTD, RG 94; Cpl. G. Delavan to E. Hawks, Mar. 17, 1864, J. M. and Esther Hawks Papers, vol. 2, 329–30, LC. Sgt. H. Golden to wife, May 19, 1864; Sgt. J. H. Jackson to Gov. Andrew, May 30, 1864; both Exec. Dept. Letters, Letters Received, vol. 62, nos., 136a, 136b, Andrew Papers, CMSA. For evidence of the soldiers' wives' strenuous efforts to secure funds for their families, see F. L. Sims to Gov. Andrew, July 2, 1863, Exec. Dept. Letters, Letters Received, vol. 21b, no. 154, Andrew Papers, CMSA. S. A. Whitfield to Stanton, Dec. 8, 1863, W-37, 1864; M. Burn to Stanton, Jan. 18, 1864, B-132, 1864; J. Primer to Stanton, Aug. 12, 1864, P-274, 1864; J. Welcom to Lincoln, Nov. 21, 1864, W-934, 1864; S. Brown to Stanton, Jan. 6, 1865, B-25, 1865; J. Wilson to Stanton, May 27, 1865, W-416, 1865; M. Johnson to Stanton, Aug. 12, 1865, J-124, 1865; all Letters Received, ser. 360, CTD, RG 94.

29. *Christian Recorder*, Feb. 13, 1864; Anon. to Gov. Andrew, July 22, 1865, Exec. Dept. Letters, Letters Received, vol. W-81, 236, Andrew Papers, CMSA. See also Anon., [5th USCI], toE. Stanton, Oct. 22, 1865, A-420, 1865, Letters Received, ser. 360, CTD, RG 94; *Christian Recorder*, Dec. 26, 1863; May 21, Aug. 6, 1864. For protests by black soldiers against excessive fatigue duty, see Isaiah Prince to E. Stanton, July 14, 1865, P-455, 1865; Anon., [4th USCI], to Stanton, Oct. 2, 1865, A-396, 1865; both Letters Received, ser. 360, CTD, RG 94. *Christian Recorder*, Feb. 13, 1864.

30. Higginson, *Army Life*, 13, see also 11–14;Higgonson, Journal, Nov. 27, 1862; Chenery, *The Fourteenth Rhode Island Heavy Artillery*, 73. For discussion on the role of the storyteller in the slave community as an agent of entertainment, social criticism, and social solidarity, see Blassingame, *The Slave Community*, 127–30; Joyner, *Down by the Riverside*, 172–95; Levine, *The Unpredictable Past*, 59–77, *Black Culture*, 81–135; Stuckey, "Through the Prism of Folklore," 433–35.

31. J. McMurray, *Recollection of a Colored Troop* (Brookville, Pa.: privately published, 1916), 21–22.

32. Ibid.

33. For antebellum antislavery political activities and the cultural interests of free blacks in the Northern states, see I. Berlin, "The Structure of the Free Negro Caste in the Antebellum United States," *Journal of Social History* 9 (Spring 1976): 300–314; Leonard Curry, *The Free Black in Urban America, 1800–1850: The Shadow of the Dream* (Chicago: Univ. of Chicago Press, 1981), 196–238; L. F. Litwack, *North of Slavery: The Negro in the Free States, 1790–1860* (Chicago: Univ. of Chicago Press, 1968), chaps. 6, 7, 8; B. Quarles, *Black Abolitionists* (London: Oxford Univ. Press, 1969).

34. Berlin et al., *The Black Military Experience*, 25, 28, 612. For the role of debating

and literary societies in the antebellum free black communities, see Curry, *The Free Black in Urban America*, 204–8; Quarles, *Black Abolitionists*, 90–106. Born in 1837, in New Bern, North Carolina, of a slave father and a free mother, Alexander Newton worked as a bricklayer in New Bern. Even while he was working in North Carolina, he actively opposed slavery by helping runaway slaves escape north via the Underground Railroad. In 1858 he escaped to New York and there continued his trade as a bricklayer. While in New York he married Olivia A. Hamilton, the daughter of Robert Hamilton, the editor of an influential black newspaper, the *Weekly Anglo-African*. After being chased through New York City during the draft riots, Alexander Newton moved to New Haven, Conn., and from there joined the 29th Connecticut Volunteers, in Dec. 1863. Newton, *Out of the Briars*, 19–22, 25–28, 31–32.

35. *Weekly Anglo-African,* Jan. 7, 1865, in Exec. Dept. Letters, Letters Received, vol. W-100, no. 86, Andrew Papers, CMSA.

36. *Weekly Anglo African,* Jan. 7, 1865.

37. *Christian Recorder,* Mar. 4, 1865. Ira Berlin argues that the antislavery movement forged a vital link between white and black communities in the North. Abolitionist politics gave some black community leaders an opportunity to gain high wages and secure national political prominence. Berlin, "The Structure of the Free Negro Caste in the Antebellum United States," 303.

38. *Christian Recorder,* Apr. 16, Nov. 14, 1864. For the contribution of black newspapers to the development of the free black communities in the North and the growth of black abolitionism, see Litwack, *North of Slavery*, 232, 238–42; Quarles, *Black Abolitionists*, 84–89.

39. *Christian Recorder,* Nov. 27, Dec. 26, 1863.

40. *Union,* Apr. 9, 1864.

41. *Christian Recorder,* Mar. 26, Aug. 6, Oct. 8, 1864; Berlin et al., *The Black Military Experience*, 25, 28–29.

42. Chenery, *The Fourteenth Rhode Island Heavy Artillery*, 49.

43. *The Swamp Angel,* May 19, 26, 1864, in Appleton, Letter Book, 224–25, 230–31, WVUL.

44. Ibid., May 19, 1864, in Appleton, Letter Book, 224, WVUL.

45. Ibid. For the educative role of the storyteller in the slave community, see Joyner, *Down by the Riverside*, chap. 6.

46. *Swamp Angel,* May 26, 1864, Appleton Letter Book, 230–31, WVUL.

47. Ibid., May 19, 1864.

48. Ibid.

49. Ibid., May 26, 1864.

50. Ibid., May 19, 1864.

51. Ezra J. Warner, *Generals in Blue: Lives of the Union Commanders* (Baton Rouge: Louisiana State Univ. Press, 1964), 423–24; Mark M. Boatner, *The Civil War Dictionary*, 725–26. In his letter book, Maj. John Appleton does not explain why *The Swamp Angel* stopped publication, merely commenting that "the General orders the discontinuance of our little paper the Swamp Angel." Appleton, Letter Book, June 2, 1864, 233, WVUL; *Christian Recorder,* Apr. 15, June 25, 1865. In Sept. 1864 John Collins and John Shaffer wrote to the secretary of war, Edwin Stanton, and offered to raise a light artillery battery, provided that black officers commanded it. Sgts. J. H. W. Collins, J. Shaffer to Stanton, Sept. 11, 1864, C-789, 1864, Letters Received, ser. 360, CTD, RG 94.

4. "Nearly All the Freedmen Are Eager to Learn"

1. T. F. Hardy to Chaplain T. S. Johnson [1866], Thomas S. Johnson Papers, SHSW.

2. For the education of black soldiers in the Union army during the Civil War, see Warren B. Armstrong, "Union Chaplains and the Education of the Freedmen," *Journal of Negro History* 52 (Apr. 1967): 104–15; R. S. Bahney, "Generals and Negroes: Education of Negroes by the Union Army, 1861–1865" (Ph.D. diss., University of Michigan, 1965); Berlin et al., *The Black Military Experience*, 611–32; J. W. Blassingame, "The Union Army as an Educational Institution for Negroes, 1862–1865," *Journal of Negro Education* 34 (Spring 1965): 152–59; D. T. Cornish, "The Union Army as a School for Negroes," *Journal of Negro History* 37 (Oct. 1952): 368–82; Glatthaar, *Forged in Battle*, 226–28.

3. For the impact of Southern state laws prohibiting the education of slaves, see Bahney, "Generals and Negroes," 26–28; Genovese, *Roll, Jordan, Roll*, 561–63. For the number of Southern blacks, both slave and free, who were literate in the antebellum period, see Genovese, *Roll, Jordan, Roll*, 563; Rawick, *From Sundown to Sunup*, 108–9; W. Vaughan, *Schools for All: The Blacks and Public Education in the South, 1865–1877* (Lexington: Univ. Press of Kentucky, 1974), 2. Slaves were often taught to read and write by other slaves, black freedmen, indulgent masters, the masters' children, and clergymen who wanted the slaves to learn the Scriptures. See Genovese, *Roll, Jordan, Roll*, 563–65; L. F. Litwack, *Been in the Storm So Long: The Aftermath of Slavery* (New York: Knopf, 1980), 472–73; Webber, *Deep Like the Rivers*, 131–36. For the slaves' struggle for literacy, see J. D. Cornelius, *"When I Can Read My Title Clear": Literacy, Slavery and Religion in the Antebellum South* (Columbia: Univ. of South Carolina Press, 1991). For African American efforts to gain literacy skills in the 1860s and 1870s, see K. C. Chambers, "'The Alphabet Is an Abolitionist': Literacy and African Americans in the Emancipation Era," *Massachusetts Review* 32, no. 4 (1991–92): 545–80. Chaplain J. Gregg to Brig. Gen. L. Thomas, Nov. 30, 1864, G-891, 1864, Letters Received, ser. 12, RG 94; "Memoranda. School Report, 50th Reg. U.S. Colored Infantry," 82, Peet, Diary [no date].

4. Chaplain T. S. Johnson, "A Register of the Officers and Enlisted Men of the One Hundred and Twenty Seventh Regiment of U.S. Colored Troops in the Field," in *Hand Book of the 127th Regiment of Colored Troops, 1864–1866*, Thomas S. Johnson Papers, SHSW.

5. Berlin et al., *The Black Military Experience*, 611; Lawrence Van Alstyne, *Diary of an Enlisted Man* (New Haven, Conn.: Tuttle, Morehouse, and Taylor, 1910), 216; General Orders No. 25, Hd. Qtrs., 36 USCI, Nov. 14, 1864, Issuances, 36th USCI, Regimental Books and Papers USCT, RG 94; N. Viall, "A Brief History of the 14th R.I. Regiment Colored, 1863–65," 22, RIHS. Brig. Gen. John Hawkins was particularly disturbed by illiteracy of ex-slaves under his command. Brig. Gen. J. Hawkins to Brig. Gen. L. Thomas, Aug. 19, 1864, H-48, 1864, Letters Received by Adj. Gen. L. Thomas, ser. 363, CTD, RG 94; Brig. Gen. John Hawkins to Maj. Gen. A. T. T. Dana, Sept. 15, 1964, H-614, 1864, Letters Received, ser. 360, CTD, RG 94.

6. Col. S. C. Armstrong to R. B. Armstrong, Feb. 8, 1864, H. Ludlow, ed., "Personal Memories," 363–64, WCL; Chaplain T. S. Johnson to Brig. Gen. L. Thomas, Feb. 28, 1865, Thomas S. Johnson Papers, SHSW; Rufus Kinsley, Diary, Mar. 6, 1865, Rufus Kinsley Diary, VHS; Col. T. J. Morgan to Maj. N. J. Vail, Oct. 11, 1865, Letters Received, 14th USCI, Regimental Books and Papers USCT, RG 94; J. M. Mickley, *The Forty-Third Regiment United States Colored Troops* (Gettysburg, Pa.: J. E. Wible, 1866),

22; I. S. Bangs, "The Ullmann Brigade," MOLLUS, Maine Commandery, *War Papers*, vol. 2, Portland, 1902, 301; T. J. Morgan, "Reminiscences of Service with Colored Troops in the Army of the Cumberland, 1863–1865," RISSHS, ser. 3, no. 13, Providence, R.I., 1880, 23–24.

7. Chaplain C. W. Buckley to Lt. A. R. Mills, July 1, 1864, B-949, 1864; Chaplain T. S. Johnsonto Brig. Gen. L. Thomas, June 30, 1864, J-37, 1864; both Letters Received, ser. 12, RG 94. In spring 1864, Congress ordered all Union army chaplains to report each month to the U.S. Army adjutant general on the spiritual and moral conditions of their regiments and posts. *OR*, ser. 3, vol. 4, 227–28.

8. Ford, ed., *A Cycle of Adams Letters*, vol. 2, 217–18; R. Schneider, "Samuel Chapman Armstrong and the Founding of the Hampton Institute" senior honors thesis (Williams College, 1973); Address of Col. J. C. Clark, Feb. 10, 1864, unidentified newspaper cutting, D. Ullmann, Letters and Orders, Generals' Papers and Books, ser. 159, RG 94. Chaplain C. W. Buckley to Lt. A. R. Mills, July 1, 1864, B-949, 1864; Chaplain C. N. Carruthers to Brig. Gen. L. Thomas, Aug. 31, 1865; both C-141, 1865, Letters Received, ser. 12, RG 94. General Orders No. 6, Hd. Qtrs., 7th USCI, May 1, 1865, Issuances, 7 USCI, Regimental Books and Papers, USCT, RG 94. Those officers who promoted the army as an industrial school for blacks could build upon a nucleus of skilled and semiskilled blacks who had worked on the plantations and in the cities of the South. Genovese, *Roll, Jordan, Roll*, 388–98; Owens, *This Species of Property*, 177–81; Robert S. Starobin, *Industrial Slavery in the Old South* (Oxford: Oxford Univ. Press, 1970); I. Berlin, *Slaves without Masters: The Free Negro in the Antebellum South* (New York: Random House, 1974), 217–49. Northern teachers working in the Freedmen's Bureau schools during Reconstruction, like some of their predecessors working in black regiments, emphasized self-reliance and the acquisition of vocational skills. Robert C. Morris, *Reading, 'Riting and Reconstruction: The Education of Freedmen in the South, 1861–1870* (Chicago: Univ. of Chicago Press, 1981), 154–62; S. E. Small, "The Yankee Schoolmarm in the Freedmen's Schools: An Analysis of Attitudes," *Journal of Southern History* 45 (Aug. 1979): 359–400; H. L. Swint, *The Northern Teacher in the South, 1862–1870* (Nashville, Tenn.: Vanderbilt Univ. Press, 1941), 82–83.

9. Berlin et al., *The Black Military Experience*, 612; J. W. Alvord to L. Thomas, Mar. 8, 1865, M-37, 1865, Letters Received by Adj. Gen. L. Thomas, ser. 363, CTD, RG 94; S. F. Colt to Lincoln, endorsement of Lincoln, Jan. 12, 1865, P-1024, 1865, Letters Received, ser. 12, RG 94.

10. H. C. Clapp, G. M. Irwin, Diary Wild Station, Feb. 23, 25, 1865, Diaries, ser. 757, U.S. Christian Commission, RG 94.

11. M. S. Hall, "Reminiscences," 10, Morris S. Hall Papers, UM; Capt. W. A. Prickett, 25 USCI, started a school because he lacked literate noncommissioned officers. *Christian Recorder*, Dec. 24, 1864; E. Earle, "Kansas, Colored Volunteer Regiment, 1st Roll, Accounts and History of the First Kansas Colored Volunteer Regiment, 1863–1865," 10, NEHGS.

12. *National Tribune*, May 11, 1899

13. Chaplain F. Boyd to Brig. Gen. L. Thomas, Dec. 31, 1864, B-1861, 1864, Letters Received, ser. 12 RG 94; J. O. Moore to daughters, Aug. 9, 1865, James Otis Moore Papers, DUL; Higginson, *Army Life*, 25; Higginson, Journal, Dec. 19, 1863; Tarbox, *Missionary Patriots*, 180–81; T. S. Johnson to "Folks," Dec. 27, 1864, Thomas S. Johnson Papers, SHSW; T. Montgomery to parents, Mar. 8, 1865, Thomas Montgomery Papers (microfilm), MHS.

14. *National Tribune*, May 11, 1899; T. D. Howard, "Charles Howard Family Domestic History," 176, typescript, Southern Historical Collection UNC; Tarbox, *Missionary Patriots*, 180–81, 214; Chaplain C. E. Bristol to Brig. Gen. L. Thomas, July 1, 1864, B-850, 1864; Chaplain T. Stevenson to Brig. Gen. L. Thomas, Oct. 6, 1865, S-2387, 1865; both Letters Received, ser. 12, RG 94. Berlin et al., *The Black Military Experience*, 612; Wilson, *The Black Phalanx*, 507; Higginson, *Army Life*, 25; Rufus Kinsley, Diary, Mar. 6, 1865, VHS; Col. T. J. Morgan to Maj. N. J. Vail, Oct. 11, 1865, Letters Received, 14th USCI, Regimental Books and Papers USCT, RG94. Chaplain C. W. Buckley suggested that a civilian teacher would render invaluable assistance in his regiment; Chaplain C. W. Buckley to Lt. A. R. Mills, Feb. 26, 1864, B-339, 1864, Letters Received, ser. 12, RG 94. Brig. Gen. Daniel Ullmann made extensive use of civilian teachers in his brigade; C. Peter Ripley, *Slaves and Freedmen in Civil War Louisiana* (Baton Rouge: Louisiana State Univ. Press, 1976), 120.

15. Joel Williamson, *After Slavery: The Negro in South Carolina during Reconstruction, 1861–1877* (Chapel Hill: Univ. of North Carolina Press, 1965), 26; F. B. Perkins, "Two Years with a Colored Regiment: A Woman's Experience," *New England Magazine* 17 (Jan. 1898): 536.

16. J. H. Meteer to C. Mills, Aug. 8, 1864, B. M. Mills to C. Mills, Apr. 15, 1864, Caleb Mills Papers, IHSL; Maj. G. L. Paddock, Inspection Report, 100th USCI, July 22, 1864, C-803, 1864, Letters Received, ser. 12, RG 94; Col. R. Mussey to Maj. C. W. Foster, Oct. 10, 1864, *OR*, ser. 3, vol. 4, 771–72; Peet, Diary, 12 [Jan. 1865], 4; SHSW; Chaplain C. W. Buckley to Lt. A. R. Mills, Feb. 26, 1864, B-339, 1864, Letters Reveived, ser. 12, RG 94. C. Peter Ripley, *Slaves and Freedmen in Civil War Louisiana* (Baton Rouge: Louisiana State Univ. Press, 1976), 120.

17. L. H. Pease, G. M. Irwin, Diary, Nineteenth Corps, Sept. 22, 1864, Feb. 25, 1865, H. C. Clapp Report, Diary Wild Station, Feb. 23, 1865; S. Anderson, E. G. Nutting, Reports, Diary Nineteenth Corps, Mar. 1865, Diaries, ser. 757, U.S. Christian Commission, RG 94. Chaplain C. E. Bristol to Brig. Gen. L. Thomas, July 1, 1864, B-850, 1864; Chaplain T. Stevenson to Brig. Gen. L. Thomas, Oct. 6, 1865; both S-2387, 1865; both Letters Received, ser. 12, RG 94.

18. Representative John Hickman of Pennsylvania proposed in Dec. 1862 a large black army. An integral part of Hickman's recommendation was that one teacher or "chaplain's clerk" be assigned to each regiment. Bahney, "Generals and Negroes," 24–26; S. F. Colt to Stanton, Mar. 3, 1865, endorsement by Maj. C. W. Foster, C-206, 1865, Letters Received, ser. 360, CTD,RG 94. Samuel Colt wrote on behalf of the General Assembly of the Presbyterian Church of the United States requesting information on the facilities available to support a teacher for each black regiment. Two months earlier, Samuel Colt had proposed to Lincoln to establish camp schools for black troops. In his endorsement of Colt's letter, Maj. Charles W. Foster, chief of the Bureau of Colored Troops, promised to issue a special order to provide teachers for black regiments.

19. Higginson, *Army Life*, 10, 259–60; Testimony of Col. T. W. Higginson and J. Eaton before the American Freedmen's Inquiry Commission, Files 3, 6, O-328, 1863 Letters Received, ser. 12, RG. 94; N. Hallowell, *Selected Letters and Papers of N. Hallowell* (Peterborough, N.H.: privately published, 1896), 43–46. "By an Officer of the Regiment [Joseph M. Carliff]," *Of the Services of the Seventh Regiment, U.S. Colored Troops, from Sept. 1863 to Nov. 1866* (Providence, R.I.: E. L. Freeman, 1878), 19. S. Rogers, "War-Time Letters of Seth Rogers M.D. Surgeon of First South Carolina, Afterwards

the Thirty-Third USCT, 1862–1863," Feb. 20, 1863. See also Jan. 16, 1863, typescript, MOLLUS, Massachusetts Commandery Collection, USAMHI; Chaplain Read to Brig. Gen. L. Thomas, Oct. 2, 1865, R-900, 1865, Letters Received, ser. 12, RG 94.

20. For the claim that slavery made black soldiers easy to teach, see Higginson, *Army Life*, 10, 259; T. W. Higginson to Andrew, Jan. 19, 1863, unidentified newspaper cutting, Exec. Dept. Letters, Letters Received, vol. 21b, no. 10, Andrew Papers, CMSA; L. Thomas to Sen. Wilson, May 30, [1864], unidentified newspaper cutting, J. W. M. Appleton, Letter Book (microfilm), 289, WVUL; Hallowell, *Selected Letters*, 43–46; J. Peet to wife, children, Jan. 20, 1864, James Peet Family Papers, MHS; Rufus Kingsley, Diary, Mar. 6, 1865, VHS; *National Anti-Slavery Standard,* July 26, 1862. H. H. Hood to wife, July 1, 1863, Humphrey H. Hood Papers, ISHSL; Hallowell, *Selected Letters*, 34; Higginson, Journal, Feb. 15, 1863; Higginson, *Army Life*, 30; G.E. Sutherland, "The Negro in the Late War," MOLLUS, Wisconsin Commandery, *War Papers*, vol. 1, Milwaukee, 1891, 180, 182–83; J. H. Meteer to C. Mills, Mar. 8, Aug. 8, 1864, Caleb Mills Papers, IHSL. Chaplain T. S. Johnson to Brig. Gen. L. Thomas, Feb. 28, Mar. 31, 1865, Thomas S. Johnson Papers, SHSW; Hallowell, *Selected Letters*, 46. S. Rogers, "War-Time Letters," Feb. 20, 1863, USAMHI. Northern teachers working in the South during Reconstruction also commented on their black students' ability to excel in music; Litwack, *Been in the Storm So Long,* 483.

21. Higginson, *Army Life*, 10. For the "childlike" nature of blacks, see R. Shaw to Annie, Oct. 16, 1863, *RGS*, 309; J. H. Meteer to C. Mills, Mar. 8, 1864, Caleb Mills Papers, IHSL; H. H. Hood to wife, July 1, 1864, Humphrey H. Hood Papers, ISHSL; S. Rogers, "War-Time Letters," Feb. 20, 1863, USAMHI; A. W. Greely, *Reminiscences of Adventure and Service: A Record of Sixty-Five Years* (New York: C. Scribner's Sons, 1927), 98; Hallowell, *Selected Letters*, 43–46. For Northern racial ideology and the abolitionists' image of the black, see E. Foner, *Free Soil, Free Labor, Free Men: The Ideology of the Republican Party before the Civil War* (New York: Oxford Univ. Press, 1970), 295–300; Fredrickson, *The Black Image in the White Mind*; Litwack, *North of Slavery,* 216–30, and *Been in the Storm So Long,* 477–78; McPherson, *The Struggle for Equality,* 134–53; W. H. and J. H. Pease, "Anti-slavery Ambivalence: Immediatism, Expediency, Race," *American Quarterly* 17 (1965): 682–95; Forrest G. Wood, *Black Scare: The Racist Response to Emancipation and Reconstruction* (Berkeley: Univ. of California Press, 1970), 13–14, 30–31; C. Vann Woodwood, *American Counterpoint: Slavery and Racism in the North South Dialogue* (Boston: Little, Brown, 1971), 14–45.

22. Chaplain W. Elgin to Brig. Gen. L. Thomas, June 30, 1864, E-6, 1864, Letters Received Relating to Recruiting, ser. 366, CTD, RG 94; Chaplain F. Boyd to Brig. Gen. L. Thomas, Dec.31, 1864, B-1861, 1864, Letters Received, ser. 12, RG 94; Rufus Kinsley, Diary, Mar. 6, 1865, VHS.

23. For the use of copybooks, Webster's spellers and religious reading material, see I. Prince, Report, Aug. 7, 1864, vol. 4, 223, Scrapbooks, ser. 791, U.S. Christian Commission, RG 94; Chaplain J. B. Bowles to Brig. Gen. L. Thomas, Sept. 1, 1864, B-1214, 1864, Letters Received, ser. 12, RG 94; M. S. Hall, "Reminiscences," 10, Morris S. Hall Papers, UM. For the difficulties of securing appropriate texts, see Chaplain C. E. Bristol to Brig. Gen. L. Thomas, July 1, 1864, B-850, 1864; Chaplain T. Stevenson to Brig. Gen. L. Thomas, Oct. 6, 1865, S-2387, 1865; both Letters Received, ser. 12, RG 94. Also L. H. Pease, Diary Nineteenth Corps, Sept. 22, 1864, Diaries, ser. 757, RG 94. No special teaching texts were devised for the education of black soldiers. However, special texts were written and circulated in Freedmen's Bureau schools during Reconstruction. These

texts suggest many of the moral values and some of the academic exercises imparted to black troops. For texts used in Freedmen Bureau schools, see Jacqueline Jones, *Soldiers of Light and Love: Northern Teachers and Georgia Blacks, 1865–1873* (Chapel Hill: Univ. of North Carolina Press, 1980), 126; Morris, *Reading 'Riting and Reconstruction*, 188–201.

24. Jacqueline Jones has identified a graduated form of instruction in the Freedmen's Bureau schools in Georgia, which faced difficulties similar to those in the black Union army schools. J. Jones, *Soldiers of Light and Love*, 111–13. For the slaves method of learning, see Cornelius, *"When I Can Read My Title Clear,"* 68–70.

25. B. F. Kinsley to E. W. Kinsley, Sept. 29, 1863, Edward Wilkinson Kinsley Papers, DUL; Howard, "Charles Howard Family Domestic History," 176, UNC; M. S. Hall, "Reminiscences," 10, Morris S. Hall Papers, UM.

26. J. O. Moore to daughters, Apr. 9, 1865, James Otis Moore Papers, DUL.

27. Chaplain Arnold T. Needham, 13th Illinois Volunteers, taught a school of black cooks. A. T. Needham to Rev. W. W. Patton, Mar. 8, 1864, Arnold T. Needham Papers, CHS.

28. J. H. Meteer to C. Mills, Mar. 8, 1864, Caleb Mills Papers, IHSL.

29. J. Peet to wife, Apr. 6, 1864, James Peet Family Papers, MHS; Chaplain F. Boyd to L. Thomas, Dec. 31, 1864, B-1861, 1864, Letters Received, ser. 12, RG 94; J. H. Meteer to C. Mills, Aug. 8, 1864, Caleb Mills Papers, IHSL.

30. M. S. Hall, "Reminiscences," 10, Morris S. Hall Papers, UM; B. F. Kinsley to E.W. Kinsley, Sept. 29, 1863, Edward Wilkinson Kinsley Papers, DUL.

31. H. H. Hood to wife, Aug. 15, 1864, Humphrey H. Hood Papers, ISHSL.

32. Chaplain G. L. Barnes to Brig. Gen. L. Thomas, Mar. 31, 1865, B-726, 1865; Chaplain T. S. Johnson to Brig. Gen. L. Thomas, June 30, 1865, T-37, 1865; both Letters Received, ser. 12, RG 94. Chaplain T. M. Rae to Brig. Gen. L. Thomas, R-40, 1864, Letters Received Relating to Recruiting, ser. 366, CTD, RG 94; Higginson, *Army Life*, 25; Rufus Kinsley Diary, Mar. 6, 1865, VHS. For comments by other officers on the ex-slaves' zeal for education, see T. Montgomery to Alexander, Jan. 30, 1866, Thomas Montgomery Papers (microfilm), MHS; L. Weld to Mason, Feb. 8, 1864, Lewis Weld Family Papers, YUL; J. H. Meteer to C. Mills, Aug. 8, 1864, Caleb Mills Papers, IHSL.

33. Chaplain T. S. Johnson to Brig. Gen. L. Thomas, June 30, 1864; Chaplain O. Reedy to Brig. Gen. L. Thomas, Oct. 31, 1865, R-924, 1865; both Letters Received, ser. 12, RG 94; Mickley, *The Forty-Third Regiment*, 22; Rufus Kinsley Diary, Mar. 6, 1865, VHS; J. Peet to wife, Apr. 6, 1864, James Peet Family Papers, MHS; Sgt. J. J. Harris to Brigadier General Ullmann, Nov. 26, Dec. 27, 1864, D. Ullmann Letters and Orders, Generals' Papers and Books, ser. 159, RG 94; M.Taylor et al. to Maj. Gen. N. Banks, Jan. 17, 1864, Nathaniel Banks Papers, LC. The efforts of Southern whites to prohibit the education of slaves actually increased their desire to learn. Blassingame, *The Slave Community*, 312; Litwack, *Been in the Storm So Long*, 473; Rawick, *From Sundown to Sunup*, 109; Webber, *Deep Like the Rivers*, 135.

34. *Christian Recorder*, Aug. 6, 1864.

35. Chaplain J. R. Bowles to Brig. Gen. L. Thomas, Sept. 1, 1864, B-1214, 1864, Letters Received, ser. 12, RG 94; *Christian Recorder*, Jan. 9, Oct. 8, 1864; Sgt. J. M. Trotter to Edward Wilkinson Kinsley, July 1, 1865, E. W. Kinsley Papers, DUL; Litwack, *Been in the Storm So Long*, 450–52, 499, Morris, *Reading 'Riting and Reconstruction*, 104–7,

112–13; Cornelius, *"When I Can Read My Title Clear,"* 82–84. For the contribution of Southern free blacks to slave literacy, see Cornelius, 78–82.

36. Chaplain J. R. Bowles to Brig. Gen. L. Thomas, Sept. 1, 1864, B-1214, 1864, Letters Received, ser. 12, RG 94; *Weekly Anglo-African,* Jan. 7, 1864, in Exec. Dept. Letters, Letters Received, vol. 62, no. 86, Andrew Papers, CMSA; *Christian Recorder,* Feb. 13, May 20, 1865. Literate slaves, like literate black soldiers, became purveyors of knowledge and information. Blassingame, *The Slave Community,* 312; Owens, *This Species of Property,* 154; Webber, *Deep Like the Rivers,* 136–38.

37. *Christian Recorder,* Dec. 10, 1864.

38. Chaplain H. Turner to Brig. Gen. L. Thomas, Aug. 14, 1865, T-59, 1865. See also June 29, Aug. 31, 1865, T-695, T-736, 1865, Letters Received, ser. 12, RG 94; *Christian Recorder,* Jan. 9, Oct. 8, 1864.

39. Robert Morris and Jacqueline Jones find that Northern teachers working in the Freedmen's Bureau schools in the Reconstruction period based their curriculums and teaching methods, to a significant extent, on those of the New England common schools. J. Jones, *Soldiers of Light and Love,* 110–16; Morris, *Reading 'Riting and Reconstruction,* 211–12.

40. *Christian Recorder,* June 29, 1865; Sarg. H. H. Hood to wife, Aug. 15, 1864, Humphrey H. Hood Papers, ISHSL; Chaplain C. N. Carruthers to Brig. Gen. L. Thomas, Aug. 31, 1865, C-1411, 1865, Letters Received, ser. 12, RG 94.

41. Berlin et al., *The Black Military Experience,* 620; *Christian Recorder,* June 29, 1865; General Orders No. 6, Hd. Qtrs., 7th USCI, May 1, 1865, Issuances, 7th USCI, Regimental Books and Papers USCT, RG 94.

42. Col. T. J. Morgan to N. J. Vail, Oct. 11, 1864, Letters Received, 14th USCI. General Orders No. 18, Hd. Qtrs., 7th USCI, Aug. 15, 1865, Issuances, 7th USCI; General Orders No. 39, Hd. Qtrs., 127th USCI, May 8, 1865, Issuances, 127th USCI; all Regimental Books and Papers USCT, RG, 94. Berlin et al., *The Black Military Experience,* 616–17.

43. Chaplain C. W. Buckley to Lt. A. R. Mills, Oct. 1, 1864, B-1460, 1864, Letters Received, ser. 12, RG 94; Report of Lt. W. B. Stickney, superintendent of colored schools, New Orleans, Dec. 30, 1863, G-2, 1864, Letters Received, ser. 360, CTD, RG 94; J. H. Meteer to C. Mills, Mar. 8, Aug. 8, 1864, Caleb Mills Papers, IHSL; Howard, "Charles Howard Domestic History," 176, UNC; Chaplain A. T. Needham to Rev. W. W. Patton, Mar. 8, 1864, Arnold T. Needham Papers, CHS.

44. Chaplain C. W. Buckley to Lt. A. R. Mills, July 1, 1864, B-949, 1864, Chaplain J. B. Bowles to Brig. Gen. L. Thomas, Sept. 1, 1864, B-1214, 1864; both Letters Received, ser. 12, RG 94. A. T. Needham to Rev. W. W. Patton, Mar. 8, 1864, Arnold T. Needham Papers, CHS.

45. Cornelius, *"When I Can Read My Title Clear,"* 71–73.

46. Quoted in Chenery, *The Fourteenth Rhode Island Heavy Artillery,* 114.

47. *Christian Recorder,* Feb. 13, 1864. Some free blacks, such as James F. Jones, felt culturally superior to slaves, because they were literate. This sense increased their feeling of moral obligation toward their ex-slave comrades. *Commonwealth,* Mar. 27, 1863; *Christian Recorder, Aug.* 6, 1864, June 3, 1865.

48. General Orders No. 10, Hd. Qtrs., 5th USCHA, Feb. 21, 1865, Issuances, 5th USCHA; General Orders No. 39, Hd. Qtrs., Second Div., Twenty-fifth Corps, May 8, 1865, Issuances, 127th USCI; General Order No. 6, Hd. Qtrs., 7th USCI, May 1, 1865,

Issuances, 7th USCI; General Orders No. 7, Hd. Qtrs., 14th USCI, Feb. 21, 1864, Issuances, 14th USCI; all Regimental Books and Papers USCT, RG 94. D. T. Allen to Col. C. C. Andrews, Feb. 1, 1864, A-63, 1864, Letters Received, ser. 360, CTD, RG 94; Chaplain E. S. Wheeler to Brig. Gen. D. Ullmann, Apr. 8, 1864, D. Ullmann Letters and Orders, Generals' Papers and Books, ser. 159, RG 94; B. Mills to C. Mills, Apr. 19, 1864, Caleb Mills Papers, IHSL.

49. General Orders No. 18, Hd. Qtrs., 7th USCI, Aug. 15, 1865, Issuances, 7th USCI, Regimental Books and Papers USCT, RG 94; Chaplain A. R. Randal to Brig. Gen. L. Thomas, June 30, 1865, R-556, 1865, Letters Received, ser. 12, RG 94; Tarbox, *Missionary Patriots*, 180–81; Col. T. J. Morgan to Maj. N. J. Vail, Oct. 11, 1864, Letters Received, 14th USCI, Regimental Books and Papers USCT, RG 94. Samuel Hunt, a U.S. Christian Commission teacher, established a special school among the "sharpshooters" of the Twenty-fifth Corps and found in these talented soldiers a remarkable proficiency in learning. S. Hunt, Report, *Weekly Reports of Delegates*, ser. 755, U.S. Christian Commission, RG 95.

50. Col. T. J. Morgan to Maj. N. J. Vail, Oct. 11, 1864, Letters Received, 14th USCI, Regimental Books and Papers USCT, RG 94. For the operation and effectiveness of the monitorial system, see E. Hall, "Reminiscences," 10, Morris S. Hall Papers, MU; Earle, "Kansas Colored VolunteerRegiment," 9, NEHGS.

51. Janet Cornelius argues that slaves shared their learning. Cornelius, *"When I Can Read My Title Clear,"* 2–3, 77–78. Herbert Gutman believes that in the slave community, fictive or quasi kinship ties had not only prepared slave children for adult roles but enlarged social obligations. Gutman, *The Black Family*, 220–29. C. Peter Ripley, "The Black Family in Transition: Louisiana, 1860–1865," *Journal of Southern History* 41 (Aug. 1975): 369–80. For the socially cohesive nature of free black urban education, see Curry, *The Free Black in Urban America*, 147–73.

52. *Christian Recorder*, Dec. 17, 1864.

53. Romero and Rose, eds., *A Black Woman's Civil War Memoirs*, 52.

54. E. L. Pierce, "The Freedmen at Port Royal," *Atlantic Monthly* 12 (Sept. 1863): 310. Chaplain G. L. Barnes to Brig. Gen. L. Thomas, Feb. 28, 1865, B-396, 1865; Chaplain G. A. Rockwood to Brig. Gen. L. Thomas, May 28, Dec. 31, 1864, R-412, R-1128, 1864: both Letters Received, ser. 12, RG 94.

55. *Christian Recorder*, Dec. 17, 1864; Chaplain A. R. Randal to Brig. Gen. L. Thomas, June 30, 1865, R-556, 1865, Letters Received, ser. 12, RG 94; Higginson, Journal, Dec. 11, 1862.

56. T. F. Hardy to Chaplain T. S. Johnson, Nov. 12, 1865 [1866], Thomas S. Johnson Papers, SHSW.

57. Chaplain J. Lawrence to Brig. Gen. L. Thomas, Jan. 31, 1865, J-64, 1865; Chaplain J. Peet to Brig. Gen. L. Thomas, Nov. 30, 1864, P-1534, 1864; both Letters Received, ser. 12, RG 94; Wilson, *The Black Phalanx*, 504–5; Berlin et al., *The Black Military Experience*, 615.

58. Brig. Gen. D. Ullmann, Generals' Reports of Service, vol. 14, 58, ser. 160, RG 94; Ullmann, *Address*, 6; S. S. Jocelyn to Brig. Gen. D. Ullmann, Mar. 5, 1864, D. Ullmann Letters and Orders,Generals' Papers and Books, ser. 159, RG 94; J. W. Blassingame, *Black New Orleans, 1860–1880* (Chicago: Univ. of Chicago Press, 1973), 46; Messner, *Freedmen and the Ideology of Free Labor*, 167; Ripley, *Slaves and Freedmen in Civil War Louisiana*, 120; Chaplain E. S. Wheeler to Brig. Gen. D. Ullmann, Apr. 8, 1864, D. Ullmann Letters and Orders, Generals' Papers and Books, ser. 159, RG 94;

Address of Col. James C. Clark, Feb. 10, 1864, unidentified newspaper cutting, in Chaplain T. W. W. Conway to Brig. Gen. D. Ullmann, Letters and Orders, Generals' Papers and Books, ser. 159, RG 94. T. S. Johnson, Chaplaincy Reports, Feb. 28, Mar. 31, 1865, Thomas S. Johnson Papers, SHSW; General Orders No. 39, Hd. Qtrs., Second Div., Twenty-fifth Corps, May 8, 1865, Issuances, 127th USCI, Regimental Books and Papers USCT, RG 94.

59. Chaplain A. R. Randal to Brig. Gen. L. Thomas, Mar. 31, 1865, R-285, 1865, Letters Received, ser. 12, RG 94; T. Montgomery to mother, May 11, 1866, Thomas Montgomery Papers (microfilm), MHS; J. M. Trotter to E. W. Kinsley, July 1, 1865, Edward Wilkinson Kinsley Papers, DUL. For the role of the Union army, black soldiers, and veterans in stimulating black self-reliance in education, see Litwack, *Been in the Storm So Long*, 499–501; Morris, *Reading 'Riting and Reconstruction*, 104–7, 112–13.

60. Higginson, *Army Life*, 25; T. S. Johnson, Chaplaincy Reports, Mar. 31, 1865, Thomas S. Johnson Papers, SHSW; Chaplain A. D. Olds to Brig. Gen. A. L. Chetlain, Jan. 10, 1865, Miscellaneous Records, 59th USCI, Regimental Books and Papers USCT, RG 94; Chaplain T. Calahan to Brig. Gen. L. Thomas, Nov. 1, 1864, C-1560, 1864, Letters Received, ser. 12, RG 94; D. T. Allen to Col. C. C. Andrews, Feb. 1, 1864, A-63, 1864, Letters Received, ser. 360, CTD, RG 94.

61. S. Anderson, E. G. Nutting, Diary Wild Station, Mar. 1865, Diaries, ser. 757, U.S. ChristianCommission, RG 94; Chaplain B. R. Catlin to Brig. Gen. L. Thomas, Aug. 31, 1865, C-1413, 1865, Letters Received, ser. 12, RG 94.

62. "Soldiers, 5 usct" to Stanton, Oct. 2, 1865, A-420, 1865, Letters Received, ser. 360, CTD, RG 94. A. Jordan to E. Hawks, Apr. 10, 1864; H. Cork to E. Hawks, Apr. 14, 1864, vol. 2, 348, 351; both J. M. and Esther Hawks Papers, LC. Chaplain C. Millerd to Brig. Gen. L. Thomas, Mar. 1, 1865, M-536, 1864, Letters Received, ser. 12, RG 94; J. Cory to Lincoln, Apr. 15, 1865, C-331, 1865, Letters Received, ser. 360, CTD, RG 94.

63. Berlin et al., *The Black Military Experience*, 631–32.

64. Van Alstyne, *Diary*, 216; Capt. Henry G. Marshall, 29th Connecticut Volunteers, found that while he could understand the speech of "Northern darkies" perfectly well, that of the former South Carolina slaves was incomprehensible. See Capt. H. G. Marshall to Hattie, Apr. 17, May 9, 1864, Henry G. Marshall Papers, Schoff Civil War Collection, UM.

65. Chaplain G. S. Shaw to Brig. Gen. L. Thomas, June 30, 1865, S-179, 1865; Chaplain J. Peet to Brig. Gen. L. Thomas, July 12, 1864, P-810, 1864; Chaplain C. Taylor to Brig. Gen. L. Thomas, May 31, 1865, T 424, 1865; all Letters Received, ser. 12, RG 94. Chaplain J. Witted to Brig. Gen. L. Thomas, Sept. 30, 1865, Miscellaneous Records, 58th USCI, Regimental Books and Papers USCT, RG 94.

66. Chaplain T. S. Johnson, "Register of Officers and Enlisted Men of the One Hundred and Twenty Seventh Regiment of U.S. Colored Troops in the Field," Thomas S. Johnson Papers, MHS; General Orders No. 7, Hd. Qtrs., 14th USCI, Feb. 21, 1864, Issuances, 14th USCI, Regimental Books and Papers USCT, RG 94; Chaplain W. Elgin to Brig. Gen. L. Thomas, Aug. 31, Sept. 30, 1864, E-424, 1864, E-476, 1864, Letters Received, ser. 12, RG 94; Chaplain W. Elgin to Brig. Gen. L. Thomas, June 30, 1864, E-6, 1864, Letters Received Relating toRecruiting, ser. 366, CTD, RG 94; Chaplain J. Peet, "School Report, 50th Reg. U.S. Colored Infantry," Diary, 1865, Memoranda, 81, Peet, Diary, SHSW; Chaplain J. Gregg to Brig. Gen. L. Thomas, Nov. 30, 1864, G-891, 1864, Letters Received, ser. 12, RG 94.

67. Berlin et al., *The Black Military Experience*, 613; Chaplain T. S. Johnson, "Register

of Officers and Enlisted Men of the One Hundred and Twenty Seventh Regiment of U.S. Colored Troops in the Field," Thomas S. Johnson Papers, MHS.

68. Qm. Sgt. G. D. Martin to Stanton, [no date], M-142, 1865, Letters Received, ser. 12, RG 94; [W. C. Gannett, E. E. Hale], "The Education of the Freedmen," *North American Review* 101 (Oct. 1865): 537.

69. Chaplain G. L. Barnes to Brig. Gen. L. Thomas, Mar. 31, 1865, B-726, 1865, Letters Received, ser. 12, RG 94.

70. Lt. Col. C. B. Fox to wife, Jan. 17, 1864, see also Lt. Col. C. B. Fox to wife, Jan. 16, 1864, vol. 1, 144, Chas. B. Fox, Extracts from Letters Written to Wife, MAHS.

5. GODLY CORRESPONDENTS AND MILITARY ADVOCATES

1. H. M. Turner to E. Stanton, 24 Aug. 1863, T-18, 1863, Letters Received, ser. 360, CTD, RG 94. Filed with Turner's letter are letters of support by the secretary of the treasury, Salmon Chase, and Congressman Owen Lovejoy. Col. William Birney was the son of James Birney, former executive secretary of the American Anti-Slavery Society and the presidential nominee of the Liberty Party. Boatner, *The Civil War Dictionary*, 65.

2. For discussion of the role of black chaplains in the Union army during the Civil War, see Berlin et al., *The Black Military Experience*, 309–11, 348–54, 358–61; John W. Blassingame, "Negro Chaplains in the Civil War," *Negro History Bulletin* 27 (Oct. 1963):23–24; Edwin S. Redkey, "Black Chaplains in the Union Army," *Civil War History* 33 (1987): 331–50; Edward A. Miller Jr., "Garland H. White, Black Army Chaplain," *Civil War History* 43 (1997): 201–18. Black chaplains who served included Jeremiah Asher, 6th USCI; John R. Bowles, 55th Mass. Vols.; Francis A. Boyd, 109th USCI; Samuel Harrison, 54th Mass. Vols.; William H. Hunter, 4th USCI; William Jackson, 55th Mass. Vols.; Chauncey B. Leonard, L'Ouverture Hospital, Alexandria, Va.; George W. Le Vere, 20th USCI; Benjamin F. Randolph, 26th USCI; David Stevens, 36th USCI; Henry M. Turner, 1st USCI; James Underdue, 39th USCI; William Waring, 102d USCI; Garland H. White, 28th USCI. U.S. Adjutant General's Office, *Official Army Register*, pt. 8, 169, 172, 175, 191, 197, 207, 212, 283, 289, 313, 315, 652–53.

3. Mitchell, *The Vacant Chair*, 19–37, esp. 32.

4. General Orders No. 15, May 4, 1861, No. 49, Aug. 3, 1861, *OR* ser. 3, vol. 1, 154, 382. Toward the end of the war, the qualifications necessary for admission to the rank of chaplain were more clearly defined. See Miller, "Garland H. White, Black Army Chaplain," 202.

5. Berlin et al., *The Black Military Experience*, 348–49, 483; Blassingame, "Negro Chaplains in the Civil War," 23; Seraile, "New York's Black Regiments during the Civil War," 102–3; Redkey, "Black Chaplains in the Union Army," 334–36.

6. "Official Order of the Governor," Mar. 23, 1863, Issuances, 54th Mass. Vols., Regimental Books and Papers U.S. Vol. Org., RG 94. For discussion of Andrew's involvement in black enlistment, see Henry G. Pearson, *The Life of John A. Andrew, Governor of Massachusetts 1861–1865*, 2 vols. (Boston: Houghton Mifflin, 1904), vol. 2, 63–121; Richard H. Abbott, "Massachusetts and the Recruitment of Southern Negroes, 1863–1865," *Civil War History* 14 (Sept. 1968): 197–200.

7. J. Asher to Lincoln, Sept. 7, 1863; Col. J. W. Ames to Maj. C. W. Foster, Mar. 14, 1864; both A-54, 1863, Letters Received, ser. 360, CTD, RG 94. *Christian Recorder*, Jan. 16, 1864.

8. *Christian Recorder,* Sept. 17, Dec. 10, 1864.

9. For the chaplain's role in the Union army, see Warren B. Armstrong, *For Courageous Fighting and Confident Dying: Union Chaplains in the Civil War* (Lawrence: Univ. Press of Kansas, 1998), and "Union Chaplains and the Education of Freedmen," *Journal of Negro History,* 52 (Apr. 1967): 104–15; Rollin W. Quimby, "The Chaplain's Predicament," *Civil War History* 8 (1962): 25–37, and "Congress and the Civil War Chaplaincy," *Civil War History* 10 (1964): 246–59; Bell Irvine Wiley, "'Holy Joes' of the Sixties: A Study of Civil War Chaplains," *Huntington Library Quarterly* 26 (May 1953): 287–305. For comment on the black chaplain's role, see Redkey, "Black Chaplains in the Union Army," 337, 345–46, 349; Berlin et al., *The Black Military Experience,* 31; Glatthaar, *Forged in Battle,* 180–83; Litwack, *Been in the Storm So Long,* 450–55. Chaplains Samuel Harrison, William H. Hunter, and Garland H. White were former slaves; Redkey, "Black Chaplains in the Union Army," 350.

10. *Weekly Anglo-African,* Jan. 7, 1865; *Christian Recorder,* July 16, Aug. 20, 1864.

11. *Christian Recorder,* July 16, Aug. 20, 1864; Feb. 4, 1865.

12. *Christian Recorder,* Dec. 24, 31, 1864; Feb. 4, 18, Mar. 4, 18, 1865; Chaplain J. Underdue to Brig. Gen. L. Thomas, Dec. 1, 1864, U-21, 1864; Chaplain John Bowles to Brig. Gen. L. Thomas, Sept. 1, 1864; both B-1214, 1864, Letters Received, ser. 12, RG 94.

13. *Christian Recorder,* Dec. 31; May 6, 1864; Robert I. Alotta, *Civil War Justice: Union Army Executions under Lincoln* (Shippensburg, Penn.: White Mane, 1989), 24, 27, 65, 136–37, 206, 208.

14. *Christian Recorder,* Apr. 22, 1864.

15. Ibid., Aug. 20, 1864; Feb. 4, May 6, 1865.

16. Ibid., Dec. 24, 31, 1864; June 10, 1865.

17. Ibid., Aug. 8, Sept. 17, 1864; Mar. 25, 1865.

18. For discussion of Henry Turner's contribution to the struggle for black freedom and equality, see Stephen W. Angell, *Bishop Henry McNeal Turner and African-American Religion in the South* (Knoxville: Univ. of Tennessee Press, 1992); Edwin S. Redkey, *Black Exodus: Black Nationalism and Back-to-Africa Movements, 1890–1910* (New Haven, Conn.: Yale Univ. Press, 1969).

19. Chaplain H. Turner to Brig. Gen. L Thomas, June 30, 1864, T-33, 1864; Aug. 12, 1864, T-428, 1864; Sept. 24, 1864, T-518, 1864; June 29, 1865, T-736, 1865; Aug. 14, 1865, T-59, 1865; Aug. 31, 1865, T-695, 1865; all Letters Received, ser. 12, RG 94; *Christian Recorder,* Oct. 8, 1864; July 16, 1865.

20. Ibid., July 16, Sept. 24, 1864; May 6, 1865.

21. Ibid., Oct. 8, 1864.

22. For the Fort Pillow massacre, see John Cimprich, Robert C. Mainfort Jr., "Fort Pillow Revisited: New Evidence about an Old Controversy," *Civil War History* 28 (Dec. 1982): 293–386.

23. *Christian Recorder,* July 9, 1864.

24. Ibid.

25. Ibid., July 9, 1864; Feb. 25, Apr. 15, May 6, 1865.

26. Ibid., July 9, Sept. 17, 1864.

27. McPherson, *For Cause and Comrades,* 13, 89; Mitchell, *The Vacant Chair,* chap. 2, esp. 25–26, 32.

28. After the war, Turner served in Georgia as a bishop in the African Methodist Episcopal Church and as a Republican member in the state legislature. Litwack, *Been in the Storm So Long,* 471; *Christian Recorder,* June 25, 1865.

29. H. Turner to E. Stanton, Apr. 3, 1865, T-18, 1865, Letters Received, ser. 360, CTD, RG 94.

30. H. Turner to Brig. Gen. L. Thomas, Aug. 31, 1865, T-695, 1865, Letters Received, ser. 12, RG 94.

31. Henry Turner had no personal slave heritage, having been born a free man in South Carolina in 1831. Robert E. Green, *Black Defenders of America 1775–1973* (Chicago: Johnson Publishing, 1974), 94.

32. Chaplain H. Turner to E. Stanton, June 30, 1864, T-334, 1864; Chaplain H. Turner to Brig. Gen. L. Thomas, Aug. 14, 1865, T-59, 1865; both Letters Received, ser. 360, CTD, RG 94. Redkey, "Black Chaplains in the Union Army," 344; *Christian Recorder,* Jan. 7, 1865.

33. Chap J. Asher to E. D. Townsend, Sept. 4, 1864, A-1000, 1864; Chaplain B. F. Randolph to Brig. Gen. L. Thomas, Nov. 1, 1864, R-972, 1864; Chaplain J. Underdue to Brig. Gen. L. Thomas, July 29, 1864, U-21, 1864; Chaplain J. Bowles to Brig. Gen. L. Thomas, June 30, 1864, B-887, 1864; Sept. 1, 1864, B-1214, 1864; all Letters Received, ser. 12, RG 94.

34. Chaplain S. Harrison to Gov. J. Andrew, Sept. 15, 1863, Exec. Dept. Letters, Letters Received, vol. 59, no. 43, Andrew Papers, CMSA.

35. L. J. Whitaker to wife, Mar. 11, 1865, Lewis J. Whitaker Papers, Southern Historical Collection, UNC.

36. Col. R. G. Shaw to Gov. Andrew, May 15, 1863, Exec. Dept. Letters, Letters Received, vol. 216, no. 118, Andrew Papers, CMSA.

37. C. B. Fox to wife, Apr. 17, July 31, 1864, vol. 2, 41–42, 126, Chap. B. Fox, Extracts from Letters Written to Wife, MHS.

38. Chaplain J. Asher to Col. E. A. Townsend, Sept. 4, 1864, A-1000 1864; Chaplain B. F. Randolph to Brig. Gen. L. Thomas, Nov. 1, 1864, R-972; both Letters Received, ser. 12, RG 94.

39. Sgt. F. A. Boyd to Lincoln, Jan. 12, 1865; Col. O. A. Bartholomew to Brig. Gen. L. Thomas, Jan. 12, 1865, V-134, 1864; both Letters Received, ser. 360, CTD, RG 94. Maj. Gen. B. F. Butler had appointed Boyd to the position of chaplain. The War Department revoked this appointment after Colonel Bartholomew complained that the regiment's officers had not elected him. "In Nov. 1865, the officers elected him chaplain, but, because the regiment had fallen below strength, he could not be mustered into office. Boyd left service with his regiment in March 1866, still ranked as a private." Berlin et al., *The Black Military Experience,* 350–54; Redkey, "Black Chaplains in the Union Army," 335–36; Blassingame, "Negro Union Army Chaplains," 23; George Bliss, "Autobiography," 176, typescript, NYHS; [New York] Union League Club, *Report of the Committee on Volunteering,* New York, Union League Club, 1864, 41. For the position of the Negro in Northern society, see Berlin, "The Structure of the Free Negro Caste in the Antebellum United States," 297–318; Leon F. Litwack, *North of Slavery: The Negro in the Free States, 1790–1860* (Chicago: Univ. of Chicago Press, 1965); Benjamin Quarles, *Black Abolitionists* (New York: Oxford Univ. Press, 1969).

40. Blassingame, *The Slave Community,* 131–32; Eugene D. Genovese, "Black Plantation Preachers in the Slave South," *Louisiana Studies* 11 (Fall 1972): 188–214; Albert J. Raboteau, *Slave Religion: The "Invisible Institution" in the Antebellum South* (New York: Oxford Univ. Press, 1978), 231–33, 238–39.

41. Chaplain J. Underdue to Brig. Gen. L. Thomas, July 29, 1864, U-21, 1864, Let-

ters Received, ser. 12, RG 94; Litwack, *Been in the Storm So Long*, 465–66. Chaplain William H. Hunter's visit to the Front Street Methodist Church, Wilmington, North Carolina, was described by "Arnold," probably a soldier in the 4th USCI, in the *Christian Recorder*, Apr. 15, 1865. A number of Union generals were present, including Joseph R. Hawley, Henry Abbot, John Schofield, and Alfred Terry. "Arnold" claims that Hunter was accompanied by Chaplain Jeremiah Asher, 6th USCI, and his description of Hunter's preaching suggests that he saw it as a symbolic act of appropriation. The freedmen were claiming the Front Street Methodist Church as their own. See Redkey, *A Grand Army of Black Men*, 165–66, 168–70.

42. Quoted in Litwack, *Been in the Storm So Long*, 465–66.

6. "GOD HAVE MERCY!"

1. B. Mac. Cutcheon, "Reminiscences," 3–4, Byron Mac. Cutcheon, "Reminiscences," Michigan Historical Collection, UM.

2. For religion in black Union regiments, see Berlin et al., *The Black Military Experience*, 309–10, 348–53, 358–61, 606–10; Blassingame, "Negro Chaplains in the Civil War," 23–24; W. B. Armstrong, "Union Chaplains and the Education of the Freedmen," 104–15; Glatthaar, *Forged in Battle*, 15–16, 224–26; Redkey, "Black Chaplains In the Union Army," 331–50, "They Are Invincible," *Civil War Times Illustrated* 28, no. 2 (1989): 32–37. Also Higginson, Journal, Jan. 12, 1863; Chaplain C. W. Buckley to Lt. A. R. Mills, B-949, 1864, Letters Received, ser. 12, RG 94; Rev. W. Fulton, Report, *Presbyterian Standard*, Feb. 16, 1865, Scrapbooks, vol. 3, 113, ser. 791, U.S. Christian Commission, RG 94. For other comments on the black soldiers' deep religious commitment, see Rogers, "War-Time Letters," Feb. 7, 1863, 40, typescript, MOLLUS, Massachusetts Commandery Collection, USAMHI; E. H. Powell, "The Colored Soldier in the War of Rebellion," MOLLUS, Vermont Commandery, *War Papers*, vol. 3, 1893, 16; T. S. Johnson to sister Susie, Mar. 3, 1865, Thomas S. Johnson Papers, SHSW; T. Montgomery to parents, May 10, 19, 1864, Thomas Montgomery Papers (microfilm), MHS; Chaplain T. Calahan to Brig. Gen. L. Thomas, Jan. 2, 1865, C-144, 1865; Chaplain W. C. Yancey to Brig. Gen. L. Thomas, Aug. 31, 1864, Y-38, 1864; both Letters Received, ser. 12, RG 94.

3. Studies of religion in the slave community emphasizing religious beliefs and practices as defenses against personal degradation, as aids to personal autonomy, and as sources of cultural independence and strength include. Blassingame, *The Slave Community*, 130–48; M. W. Creel, *"A Peculiar People": Slave Religion and Community—Culture among the Gullahs* (New York: New York Univ. Press, 1988), 180–85, 231–38, 248–51, 295–97; Joyner, *Down by the Riverside*, 141–71; Levine, *Black Culture*, 3–80; Owens, *This Species of Property*, 148–63; A. J. Raboteau, *Slave Religion;* Rawick, *From Sundown to Sunup*, 31–52; Mechal Sobel, *Trabelin' On: The Slave Journey to an Afro-Baptist Faith* (Westport, Conn.: Greenwood Press, 1979), 157–58, 169–73; Webber, *Deep Like the Rivers*, 81–89, 191–206. For the relationship between the master's church and the slave's clandestine church on the plantation, see Genovese, *Roll, Jordan, Roll*, 202–9, 236–37; Joyner, *Down by the Riverside*, 141–43, 154–63, 169–71; Levine, *Black Culture*, 41–42; Owens, *This Species of Property*, 152–56; Raboteau, *Slave Religion*, 212–38; Webber, *Deep Like the Rivers*, 191–95, 205–6. For the slaves' role in biracial Southern churches, see K. K. Bailey, "Protestantism and Afro-Americans in the Old South,"

Journal of Southern History 41 (Nov. 1975): 451–72; John B. Boles, *Religion in Antebellum Kentucky* (Lexington: Univ. Press of Kentucky, 1976), 80–100, *Black Southerners, 1619–1869* (Lexington: Univ. Press of Kentucky, 1984), 156–68.

4. For the religious developments in Northern free black regiments, see Berlin et al., *The Black Military Experience*, 309–10, 348–53, 358–61; Blassingame, "Negro Chaplains in the Civil War," 23–24; Redkey, "Black Chaplains in the Union Army," 331–50.

5. Boles believes that as many as a quarter of the slave population may have worshipped in biracial churches before the war. See Boles, *Black Southerners*, 157. For slaves benefiting from the shared worship, see Boles, *Black Southerners*, 158–68, and J. B. Boles, ed., *Masters and Slaves in the House of the Lord: Race and Religion in the American South, 1740–1870* (Lexington: Univ. Press of Kentucky, 1988), esp. intro., chaps. 2, 3. For the black exodus from biracial churches after the war, see Boles, *Black Southerners*, 201–2; Boles, ed., *Masters and Slaves*, 77–78, 96–98, 150–51, 182–91.

6. T. Montgomery to mother, Aug. 22, 1864, Thomas Montgomery Papers (microfilm) MHS; B. M. Mills to father, Nov. 29, 1864, Caleb Mills Papers, IHSL; Raboteau, *Slave Religion*, 231; Scroggs, Diary Apr. 10, 1864, USAMI. During Reconstruction, Northern white missionaries also failed to see the vital significance of the emotional element in the worship of the freedmen; Litwack, *Been in the Storm So Long*, 460–61.

7. Lt. Col. J. Bogert to parents, Feb. 17, 1864, John S. Bogert Letters, USC; Chaplain J. Gregg to Brig. Gen. L. Thomas, Nov. 30, 1864, G-891; Chaplain Z. K. Hawley to Brig. Gen. L. Thomas, Sept. 8, 1865, H-1317, 1865; Chaplain A. C. MacDonald to Brig. Gen. L. Thomas, Sept. 30, 1865, M-2171, 1865; Chaplain W. C. Yancey to Brig. Gen. L. Thomas, Aug. 31, 1864, Y-38, 1864; all Letters Received, ser. 12, RG 94; Higginson, *Army Life*, 221; Col. James Beecher quoted in Glatthaar, *Forged in Battle*, 225; Rev. W. Fulton, Report, *Presbyterian Standard*, Feb. 16, 1865, Scrapbooks, vol. 3, 113, ser. 791, U.S. Christian Commission, RG. 94.

8. On Apr. 9, 1864, Congress passed legislation directing Union army chaplains to submit monthly reports on the health, religious, and moral condition of their regiments and posts. This report became part of War Department regulations with General Orders No. 158, Adjutant General's Office, Apr. 13, 1864. Berlin et al., *The Black Military Experience*, 613; *OR*, ser. 3, vol. 4, 227–28. For typical examples of chaplaincy reports, see Chaplain P. Read to Brig. Gen. L. Thomas, Oct. 2, 1865, R-900, 1865; Chaplain G. A. Rockwood to Brig. Gen. L. Thomas, May 31, 1864, R-412, 1864; Chaplain J. Warren to Brig. Gen. L. Thomas, May 31, 1864, W-860, 1864; Chaplain J. B. McAffee to Brig. Gen. L. Thomas, Aug. 1, 1864, M-1604, 1864; Chaplain T. Calahan to Brig. Gen. L. Thomas, Feb. 28, 1865, C-494, 1865; all Letters Received, ser. 12, RG 94. Northern abolitionist missionaries, both white and black, working in the South among freedmen believed that their "primitive" and "corrupt" religious practices had to be reformed. For the white missionaries, this meant making the emotionally charged slave religion conform to the norms of Protestant worship. For the black missionaries, the Northern black community church became the religious model. Litwack, *Been in the Storm So Long*, 450–52, 458–61.

9. Chaplain O. Riedy to Brig. Gen. L. Thomas, Jan. 4, 1865, R-55, 1865; Chaplain L. M. Hobbs to Brig. Gen. L. Thomas, Aug. 31, 1864, H-987, 1864; Chaplain G. A. Rockwood to Brig. Gen. L. Thomas, May 31, 1864, R-412, 1864; all Letters Received, ser. 12, RG 94.

10. Chaplain T. S. Johnson to Brig. Gen. L. Thomas, July 31, 1865, J-30, 1865; Chap-

lain J. Peet to Brig. Gen. L. Thomas, July 1, 1864, P-810, 1864; both Letters Received, ser. 12, RG 94.

11. For the dangers of holidays and city church attendance, see Chaplain T. Calahan to Brig. Gen. L. Thomas, Jan. 2, 1865, C-144, 1865; Chaplain G. N. Carruthers to Brig. Gen. L. Thomas, Dec. 31, 1864, C-1836, 1864; Chaplain A. C. McDonald to Brig. Gen. L. Thomas, Nov. 30, 1865, M-2443, 1865; all Letters Received, ser. 12, RG 94. For criticism of Sabbath observance, see Chaplain J. Peet to Brig. Gen. L. Thomas, July 1, 1864, P-810, 1864; Chaplain B. H. Shepherd to Brig. Gen. L. Thomas, July 16, 1864, S-1257, 1864; Chaplain J. Asher to Brig. Gen. L. Thomas, Sept. 4, 1864, A-1000, 1864; Chaplain T. Stevenson to Brig. Gen. L. Thomas, Aug. 1, 1865, S-1917, 1865; Chaplain B. R. Catlin to Brig. Gen. L. Thomas, Sept. 29, 1865, C-1506, 1865; Chaplain W. Wilson to Brig. Gen. L. Thomas, Dec. 31, 1865, W-2256, 1865; all Letters Received, ser. 12, RG 94.

12. Chaplain G. A. Rockwood to Brig. Gen. L. Thomas, May 31, 1864, R-412, 1864; Chaplain J. Peet to Brig. Gen. L. Thomas, July 1, 1864, P-810, 1864; Chaplain B. H. Shepherd to Brig. Gen. L. Thomas, July 16, 1864, S-1257, 1864; Chaplain A. R. Randall to Brig. Gen. L. Thomas, Oct. 31, 1864, R-1131, 1864; Chaplain S. S. Higginson to Brig. Gen. L. Thomas, Jan. 31, 1864, H-184, 1865; Chaplain T. S. Johnson to Brig. Gen. L. Thomas, July 31, 1865, J-30, 1865; all Letters Received, ser. 12, RG 94. Chaplain T. S. Johnson to Brig. Gen. L. Thomas, Jan. 31, 1865, Thomas S. Johnson Papers, SHSW.

13. Chaplain C. W. Buckley to Brig. Gen. L. Thomas, July 1, 1864, B-949, 1864; Chaplain G. A. Rockwood to Brig. Gen. L. Thomas, May 31, 1864, R-412, 1864; Chaplain S. Merrill to Brig. Gen. L. Thomas, Jan. 31, 1865, M-376, 1864; all Letters Received, ser. 12, RG 94. For slaves sharing some of the moral values of whites in biracial churches, see Boles, *Black Southerners*, 166; Boles, ed., *Masters and Slaves*, 13–14, 72–74. Before commanding black troops, Thomas Higginson had served as a Unitarian pastor in Massachusetts at churches in Newburyport and Worcester; John Eaton had served as chaplain of the 27th Ohio Infantry; and James Beecher had served as chaplain of the 67th New York Infantry. Edelstein, *Strange Enthusiasm*, 73–77, 129–32; Boatner, *The Civil War Dictionary*, 56, 259.

14. Chaplain G. A. Rockwood to Brig. Gen. L. Thomas, May 31, 1864, Feb. 28, 1865, R-412, 1864, R-168, 1865; Chaplain G. L. Barnes to Brig. Gen. L. Thomas, Jan. 2, 1865, B-78, 1865; Chaplain W. Wilson to Brig. Gen. L. Thomas, Aug. 31, 1865, W-, 1984, 1865; all Letters Received, ser. 12, RG 94. B. D. Ames, Report, *Christian Times*, Sept. 15, 1864, Scrapbooks, vol. 4, 235; Rev. W. Fulton, Report, *Presbyterian Standard*, Feb. 16, 1865, Scrapbooks, vol. 3, 113, ser. 791, U.S. Christian Commission, RG 94; G. W. Ballon, Diary Eighteenth Corps, Nov. 20, 1864, ser. 757, U.S. Christian Commission, RG 94.

15. Chaplain C. E. Bristol to Brig. Gen. L. Thomas, May 31, 1864, B-657, 1864, Letters Received, ser. 360, CTD, RG 94; Chaplain E. R. Pierce to Brig. Gen. L. Thomas, Aug. 31, 1864, P-1052, 1864, Letters Received, ser. 12, RG 94; Chaplain T. Calahan to Brig. Gen. L. Thomas, Sept. 1, 1864, C-1234, 1864, Letters Received, ser. 12, RG 94.

16. For the relationship between the masters' sanctioned religious leaders and those of the "invisible church," see Genovese, *Roll, Jordan, Roll*, 203–8, 236–38, 255–79; Joyner, *Down by the Riverside*, 144–50, 169–71; Levine, *Black Culture*, 47–49; Owens, *This Species of Property*, 152–56; Raboteau, *Slave Religion*, 212–13, 229–39; Webber, *Deep Like the Rivers*, 191–95.

17. Tarbox, *Missionary Patriots*, 151.

18. Ibid.

19. Ibid., 152–55.

20. For the covert nature of slave religion, especially magic and conjurers, and the role religion played in minimizing conflict within the slave community, see Gutman, *The Black Family*, 277–83; Creel, *"A Peculiar People,"* 54–58; Sobel, *Trabelin' On*, 41–43, 68, 169–73; Joyner, *Down by the Riverside*, 144–53.

21. Van Alstyne, *Diary*, 214; T. Montgomery to mother, Aug. 22, 1864, Thomas Montgomery Papers, MHS; Henry V. Freeman, "A Colored Brigade in the Campaign and Battle of Nashville," MOLLUS, Illinois Commandery, *Military Essays and Recollections*, vol. 2 (Chicago: A. C. McClury, 1891), 403; Greely, *Reminiscences*, 91–92; Powell, "The Colored Soldier"; Berlin etal., *The Black Military Experience*, 424–25, 516.

22. B. M. Mills to father, Nov. 29, 1864, Caleb Mills Papers, IHSL. For the socio-religious significance of baptism and other religious rituals in slave society, see Raboteau, *Slave Religion*, 231; Scroggs, Diary, Apr. 10, 1864, USAMHI.

23. For the "amusing" nature of the soldiers' prayers, see Lt. Col. J. Bogert to parents, Feb. 17, 1864, John S. Bogert Letters, USC; A. M. Brigham to Caroline, Sept. 6, 1863, Alfred M. Brigham Letters, EUL; Van Alstyne, *Diary*, 214, 241. For officers being deeply moved by the soldiers' prayers, see *New England Loyal Publication Society Pamphlet*, no. 175, Mar. 19, 1864, Edward A. Wild Papers, MOLLUS, Massachusetts Commandery Collection, USAMHI; Luther G. Bingham, *The Young Quartermaster: The Life and Death of Lieut. L. M. Bingham of the First South Carolina Volunteers* (New York: 1863), 83–84. For the context of the black soldiers' prayers, see Higginson, *Army Life*, 25–26, Higginson, Journal, Mar. 31, 1864; Bowley, *A Boy Lieutenant*, 64–67.

24. Rogers, "War-Time Letters," Jan. 13, 1863, 13, typescript, MOLLUS, Massachusetts Commandery Collection, USAMHI.

25. *Christian Recorder*, Oct. 23, 1863; C. W. Buckley to Brig. Gen. L. Thomas, July 1, 1864, B-949, 1864; J. Peet to Brig. Gen. L. Thomas, Aug. 1, 1864, P-945, 1864; both Letters Received, ser. 12, RG 94; S. C. Armstrong to Mela, Dec. 27, 1863, in H. Ludlow, ed., "Personal Memories," 356, WCL. Funerals showed respect for the dead and the status of the living, and they merged African traditions with Christianity. Sobel, *Trablin' On*, 196–200. For how the funeral derived its impetus from the slave community and the vitality of African traditions, see David R. Roediger, "And Die in Dixie: Funerals, Death and Heaven in the Slave Community, 1700–1865," *Massachusetts Review* 22 (Spring 1981): 163–83. Some planters treated the slave funerals dismissively. See Boles, ed., *Masters and Slaves*, 125; Roediger, "And Die in Dixie," 164–68; Elliot J. Gorn argues that "belief in returning spirits was enhanced by the large number of blacks interred without proper burial." Here the plantation experience contrasted sharply with that of the army camp. For ghostlore and slave burials, see Elliott J. Gorn, "Black Spirits: The Ghostlore of Afro-American Slaves," *American Quarterly* 46 (Fall 1984): 561.

26. Joyner, *Down by the Riverside*, 141–71. For how slave ghostlore acted as a survival mechanism on the plantation, see Gorn, "Black Spirits," 549–65; Gutman, *The Black Families*, 277–83; *National Anti-slavery Standard*, Aug. 29, 1863.

27. Bowley, *A Boy Lieutenant*, 80–81, and "A Dark Night on Picket," *Overland Monthly and Out West Magazine* 5 (July 1870): 35. On many plantations, conjurers coexisted with preachers. This was probably because the conjurer was able to "explain" the mysteries of evil and supposedly exercise control over evil spirits and forces. Al-

though he may not have known it at the time, Lt. Freeman Bowley's explanation of the "Jack-o-Lantern" phenomenon was consistent with the conjurer's method of exercising power in the slave community. Organized at Camp Stanton, Maryland, in Feb. and Mar. 1864, the 30th USCI contained a significant number of ex-slaves. U.S. Adjutant General's Office, *Official Army Register*, pt. 8, 201. For the role of the conjurer in the slave community, see Blassingame, *The Slave Community*, 109–13; Genovese, *Roll, Jordan, Roll*, 222–24; Joyner, *Down by the Riverside*, 144–50; Levine, *Black Culture*, 73–75; Raboteau, *Slave Religion*, 275–88. During Reconstruction, the Ku Klux Klan used religion as a vehicle for social control. It manipulated the ex-slaves' fear of supernatural forces in an effort to keep the black population "under control." See Gladys Marie Fry, *Night Riders in Black Folk History* (Knoxville: Univ. of Tennessee Press, 1975).

28. Bowley, *A Boy Lieutenant*, 84. For the slaves' belief in ghosts and spirits, see Genovese, *Roll, Jordan, Roll*, 219–20; Joyner, *Down by the Riverside*, 141–53; Levine, *Black Culture*, 78–79; Raboteau, *Slave Religion*, 284–85. Creel, *"A Peculiar People,"* 312–17; Sobel, *Trablin' On*, 46–48.

29. Freeman, "A Colored Brigade," 403; H. Soule, Diary, Nov. 12, 1863, 53–55, Harrison Soule Papers, Michigan Historical Collection, UM.

30. Van Alstyne, *Diary*, 338; Joyner, *Down by the Riverside*, 145–46.

31. Chenery, *The Fourteenth Rhode Island Heavy Artillery*, 42–43; B. M. Mills to father, Jan. 20, 1865, Caleb Mills Papers, IHSL.

32. Higginson, Journal, Mar. 15, 1864.

33. Bowley, *A Boy Lieutenant*, 80–81; Newton, *Out of the Briars*, 86; Higginson, Journal, Mar. 15, 1864.

34. T. Montgomery to mother, July 18, 1864, Thomas Montgomery Papers, MHS; Newton, *Out of the Briars*, 44; Higginson, Journal, Apr. 19, [1863]. The masters on plantations had allowed religious leaders a degree of religious freedom, in order to gain leverage over the black community. For this strategy and how black preachers asserted the slaves' relative autonomy, see Blassingame, *The Slave Community*, 331–32; Boles, *Black Southerners*, 159–60; Genovese, *Roll, Jordan, Roll*, 255–63, and "Black Plantation Preachers in the Slave South," *Louisiana Studies* (Fall 1972): 188–214; Joyner, *Down by the Riverside*, 170–71; Levine, *Black Culture*, 47–49; Raboteau, *Slave Religion*, 231–32, 237–38.

35. Higginson, *Army Life*, 93, 255; Higginson, Journal, Jan. 12, Apr. 19, 1863.

36. Higginson, *Army Life*, 255 56; Chaplain T. Calahan to Brig. Gen. L. Thomas, Nov. 1, 1864, C-1560, 1864, Jan. 2, 1965, C-144, 1865, Letters Received, ser. 12, RG 94.

37. Slaves had a tradition of hiding their religious practices from whites' eyes. Genovese, *Roll, Jordan, Roll*, 236–37; Levine, *Black Culture*, 41–42; Owens, *This Species of Property*, 155–56; Webber, *Deep Like the Rivers*, 194–95.

38. Chaplain G. A. Rockwood to Brig. Gen. L. Thomas, Feb. 28, 1865, Letters Received, ser. 12, RG 94. Chaplain T. Stevenson to Brig. Gen. L. Thomas, Aug. 1, 1865, S-1917, 1865; Chaplain A. R. Jones to Brig. Gen. L. Thomas, Aug. 31, 1864, J-218, 1864; Chaplain J. Peet to Brig. Gen. L. Thomas, Nov. 30, 1864, P-1534, 1864; Chaplain T. Calahan to Brig. Gen. L. Thomas, C-144, 1865; all Letters Received, ser. 12, RG 94. Chaplain S. A. Hodgeman to Maj. Gen. N. Banks, Aug. 5, 1863, Letters Received, 74 USCI, Regimental Books and Papers, USCT, RG 94.

39. Chaplain C. E. Bristol to Brig. Gen. L. Thomas, May 31, 1864, Letters Received, ser. 360, CTD, RG 94. Chaplain A. C. McDonald to Brig. Gen. L. Thomas, 31

Sept. 1865, M-2171, 1865; Chaplain E. R. Pierce to Brig. Gen. L. Thomas, Aug. 31, 1864, P-1052; Chaplain W. C. Yancey to Brig. Gen. L. Thomas, Aug. 31, 1864, Y-38, 1864; all Letters Received, ser. 12, RG 94. Lt. T. Montgomery to mother, July 18, 1864, Thomas Montgomery Papers, MHS; N. Winne, Diary, Nineteenth Corps, Dec. 16, 1864, ser. 757, U.S. Christian Commission, RG 94.

40. Lt. T. Montgomery to mother, Dec. 25, 1864, Thomas Montgomery Papers, MHS.

41. Pvt. Robert G. Fitzgerald, Diary, May 21, July 12 and 13, 1864, Fitzgerald Family Collection (microfilm), Southern Historical Collection, UNC; *Christian Recorder*, Sept. 17, 1864.

42. Newton, *Out of the Briars*, 43–44; Higginson, Journal, Apr. 19, 1863; *Christian Recorder*, Sept. 17, 1864.

43. *Christian Recorder*, Feb. 14, 1865. See also *Christian Recorder*, Jan. 4 and 23, 1864, Feb. 4, Apr. 2, 1865. Albert Raboteau claims that the religious imagery in the slave spirituals had more than one level of meaning. For example, images of freedom could speak of liberty from physical as well as spiritual bondage. Raboteau, *Slave Religion*, 246–50; Blassingame, *The Slave Community*, 141–45; Levine, *Slave Culture*, 6–14, 49–51.

44. *Christian Recorder*, Apr. 16, May 28, Sept. 10, 1864.

45. B. Mac. Cutcheon, "Reminiscences," 3–4, Byron Mac. Cutcheon, Michigan Historical Collection, UM.

46. Bowley, *A Boy Lieutenant*, 64–67; Van Alstyne, *Diary*, 241; Higginson, *Army Life*, 25–26; *New England Loyal Publication Society Pamphlet*, no. 25, Mar. 19, 1864, Edward A. Wild Papers, MOLLUS, Massachusetts Commandery Collection, USAMHI; Rev. W. Fulton Report, *Presbyterian Standard*, Feb. 16, 1865, Scrapbooks, vol. 3, 113, ser. 791, U.S. Christian Commission, RG 94.

47. *National Anti-Slavery Standard*, Aug. 29, 1863. The *National Anti-Slavery Standard* carried the letter of Pvt. Willington Hawkins, first published in the *Evening Post*, Aug. 19, 1863.

7. "THE TRUMPETS SOUND"

1. O. Densmore to "friends at home," Sept. 6, 1864, Benjamin Densmore Family Papers, MHS.

2. For the black soldiers' music, see Eileen Southern, *The Music of Black Americans: A History*, 2d ed. (New York: Norton, 1983), 204–16; Wilson, "Black Bands and Black Culture," 31–37, and "'Manhood Education,'" chap. 8. For the importance of music in the slave community, see Blassingame, *The Slave Community*, 114–27, 135–47; Dena J. Epstein, *Sinful Tunes and Spirituals: Black Folk Music to the Civil War* (Urbana: Univ. of Illinois Press, 1977); LeRoi Jones, *Blues People: Negro Music in White America* (New York: W. Morrow, 1963); Joyner, *Down by the Riverside*, 163–71; Levine, *Black Culture*, chaps. 3, 4, and *The Unpredictable Past*, chap. 3; B. A. MacLeod, "Quills, Fifes, and Flutes before the Civil War," *Southern Folklore Quarterly* 42, nos. 2–3 (1978): 201–8; Owens, *This Species of Property*, 164–77; Raboteau, *Slave Religion*, 243–66; Webber, *Deep Like the Rivers*, chap. 16.

3. S. C. Armstrong, "Southern Workmen and Hampton School Record," Mar. 1883, in Ludlow, ed., "Personal Memories," 491, WCL; Norton, *Army Letters*, 196; Van Alstyne, *Diary*, 214, 241; Capt. George E. Sutherland, "The Negro in the Late War,"

MOLLUS, Wisconsin Commandery, *War Papers*, vol. 1 (Milwaukee: Burdick, Aarmita, and Allen, 1891): 182; Southern, *The Music of Black Americans*, 209.

4. Norton, *Army Letters*, 196.

5. "Enlisting Soldiers," "The Original Version of the John Brown Song," "The Black Regiment," *Free Military School Register*, HSP.

6. "The Black Regiment," *Free Military School Register*, HSP. For Northern white compositions of "black" and "contraband" songs, together with the use of supposed "black dialect," see Willard A. Heaps and Porter W. Heaps, *The Singing Sixties: The Spirit of Civil War Days Drawn from the Music of the Times* (Norman: Univ. of Oklahoma Press, 1960), 268–88.

7. "The Black Regiment," *Free Military School Register*, HSP. For songs composed by Northern whites praising the black soldiers, see Heaps and Heaps, *The Singing Sixties*, 277–80.

8. "Song of the Negro Boatman," *Free Military School Register*, HSP. When the Port Royal Experiment was in its early stages, the renowned abolitionist poet and hymn writer John Greenleaf Whittier wrote to another noted abolitionist, Lydia Maria Child, "I wish somebody would write a song worthy of the people [the blacks] and the cause; I am not able to do it." However, Whittier did write a poem, "At Port Royal, 1861," which was published in the *Atlantic Monthly* in Feb. 1862. The first four stanzas of "At Port Royal, 1861" were written in standard English, but the remaining stanzas, the "Song of the Negro Boatman," were written in what was purported to be slave dialect. Dena J. Epstein, *Sinful Tunes*, 257–58.

9. "Song of the Negro Boatman," *Free Military School Register*, HSP.

10. "Old Shady," *Free Military School Register*, HSP. "Old Shady" was also known as "Ole Shady," "The Song of the Contraband," and "Day of Jubilee." The composer, Benjamin R. Hanby, also wrote the music for "Darling Nelly Gray." For the origin of "Old Shady," see Heaps and Heaps, *The Singing Sixties*, 287.

11. "Old Shady," *Free Military School Register*, HSP.

12. Ibid.

13. "Song of the First Arkansas," *Free Military School Register*, HSP.

14. Ibid.

15. Ibid.

16. Eileen Southern finds that when black regiments were being formed, white military bands and "special drum corps composed of young black boys" played during drill. Southern, *The Music of Black Americans*, 207.

17. Henry G. Thomas, "The Colored Troops at Petersburg," *Century Magazine* 12 (Sept. 1887): 777–78; Armstrong, "Southern Workmen and Hampton School Record, Mar. 1883, H. Ludlow, ed., "Personal Memories," 491, WCL; Higginson, *Army Life*, 197–98, 221–22; Sutherland, "The Negro in the Late War," 182; Van Alstyne, *Diary*, 241.

18. Higginson, *Army Life*, 201–4, 220–21; William Francis Allen, Charles Pickard Ware, Lucy McKim Garrison, *Slave Songs of the United States* (1867; rpt. New York: P. Smith, 1951), xvi–xviii; B. Mac. Cutcheon, "Reminiscences," 3–4, Michigan Historical Collection, UM.

19. Higginson, *Army Life*, 211–12.

20. Ibid.; Levine, *Black Culture*, 17–18; Dena J. Epstein, *Sinful Tunes*, 217–29, 241–302; Levine, *The Unpredictable Past*, 48.

21. Levine, *Black Culture*, 17–18; Southern, *The Music of Black Americans*, 207–16; Joyner, *Down by the Riverside*, 163–69.

22. Higginson, *Army Life*, 208, 216–17.

23. Ibid.

24. Ibid., 204–7, 213–14; Allen et al., *Slave Songs*, 72.

25. Higginson, *Army Life*, 209–10.

26. Higginson, *Army Life*, 203, 218–19; Allen et al., *Slave Songs*, 46, 48; Levine, *The Unpredictable Past*, 55.

27. Higginson, *Army Life*, 200–201; Allen et al., *Slave Songs*, 45.

28. Higginson, *Army Life*, 200, 211.

29. For the use of military imagery in slave songs, with particular reference to the roll call, see William E. Barton, "Hymns of the Slave and the Freeman," in Bernard Katz, ed., *The Social Implications of Early Negro Music in the United States* (New York: Arno Press, 1969), 98–102.

30. Higginson, *Army Life*, 201; Allen et al., *Slave Songs*, 38.

31. Higginson, *Army Life*, 202.

32. Ibid.

33. H. Ludlow, ed., "Personal Memories," 491, 507–8, WCL. Eileen Southern believes that "The Negro Battle Hymn" was popular with black troops. It was also known as "They Look Like Men of War"; Southern, *The Music of Black Americans*, 210. The Philadelphia-based Supervisory Committee for Enlistment of Colored Troops published another version, entitled "Enlisting Soldiers"; see *Free Military School Register*, HSP.

34. Ludlow, ed., "Personal Memories," 491, 507–8, WCL.

35. Ludlow, ed., "Personal Memories," 508, WCL.

36. Ibid.

37. Ibid.

38. Ibid.

39. Thomas, "The Colored Troops," 778; Epstein, *Sinful Tunes*, 293–94.

40. Higginson, *Army Life*, 217. For clandestine slave singing and songs with hidden meanings, see Levine, *Black Culture*, 41–42, 51–52; Blassingame, *The Slave Community*, 139.

41. Higginson, Journal, Nov. 6, 1863; Higginson, *Army Life*, 220–21, 252.

42. Higginson, Journal, Nov. 6, 1863.

43. Ibid.

44. *Christian Recorder*, Apr. 16, 1864.

45. Higginson, *Army Life*, 197–200. For body movement as an integral part of the musical process, see Olly Wilson, "The Association of Movement and Music as a Manifestation of a Black Conceptual Approach to Music-Making," in Irene V. Jackson, ed., *More than Dancing: Essays on Afro-American Music and Musicians* (Westport, Conn.: Greenwood Press, 1985), 1–23.

46. Sutherland, "The Negro in the Late War," 183.

47. For the "call and response chant form," see Dena J. Epstein, *Sinful Tunes*, 163–68, 172–73; LeRoi Jones, *Blues People*, 26–27; Joyner, *Down by the Riverside*, 160–63; Owens, *This Species of Property*, 171; Southern, *The Music of Black Americans*, 207–08; Thomas, "The Colored Troops," 777. For communal recreation, see Levine, *Black Culture*, 29–30, *The Unpredictable Past*, 42.

48. Sutherland, "The Negro in the Late War," 184.

49. Ibid., 183–84; Higginson, *Army Life*, 222; Levine, *Black Culture*, 29–30; Levine, *The Unpredictable Past*, 42, 56.

50. For the creative and adaptive character of the slaves' musical culture to react creatively, see Dena J. Epstein, *Sinful Tunes*, 161–237, 247; Joyner, *Down by the Riverside*, 160–69; Levine, *Black Culture*, 5, 15–30, 52–53, 189–91; Raboteau, *Slave Religion*, 243–66.

51. Higginson, *Army Life*, 222. John Blassingame argues that slaves seldom modeled their songs on those of whites. When they did, they changed them radically. Blassingame, *The Slave Community*, 137–38; Higginson, Journal, Sept. 12, 1863.

52. Blassingame, *The Slave Community*, 122–23; LeRoi Jones, *Blues People*, 28.

53. Higginson, *Army Life*, 201–2, 212; Southern, *The Music of Black Americans*, 210; Levine, *The Unpredictable Past*, 55.

54. Higginson, *Army Life*, 214–15; Allen et al., *Slave Songs*, 102.

55. Higginson, *Army Life*, 198–201, 214–15, 221; Allen et al., *Slave Songs*, 45.

56. Higginson, *Army Life*, 221; LeRoi Jones, *Blues People*, 22–23.

57. H. Brown to mother, May 15, 1864, Henry Harrison Brown Papers, CTHS.

58. Newton, *Out of the Briars*, 53.

59. Southern, *The Music of Black Americans*, 205, 210. Southern argues that many black musicians of the postwar period first developed their talent in the Union army.

60. Heaps and Heaps, *The Singing Sixties*, 13–14, 132. For singing groups on the plantations, see Owens, *This Species of Property*, 165–69; Levine, *Black Culture*, 192–95; [C. B. Fox], *Record of the Service*, 2; E. Grabill to wife, Apr. 27, 1864, Elliott F. Grabill Papers, OBA; Pvt. W. Goodale to children, Nov. 10, 1864, Warren Goodale Papers, MAHS. LeRoi Jones finds that in the early years of slavery, the slaves' secret chants were about their desire to return to Africa. LeRoi Jones, *Blues People*, 39.

61. C. B. Fox to wife, Oct. 16, 1864, vol. 3, 44, Chas. B, Fox, Extracts from Letters Written to Wife, MAHS; *Christian Recorder,* Nov. 12, 1864.

62. C. B. Fox, Extracts from Letters Written to Wife, vol. 3 back cover, MAHS.

63. Chaplain T. S. Johnson to Folks, Dec. 27, 1864, Thomas S. Johnson Papers, SHSW; D. Densmore to "friends at home," Dec. 25, 1864, Benjamin Densmore Family Papers, MHS; *Christian Recorder,* Feb. 18, 1865; Peet, Diary, Jan. 2, 1865, SHSW; Col. E. Martindale to wife, Nov. 18, 1864, Edward Martindale Papers, SUL.

64. Shaw Glee Club Invitation, Nov. 10, 1864, 54th Mass. Inf. Reg. Papers, MAHS; J. W. M. Appleton, Letter Book, Nov. 26, 1863, 111, WVUL.

65. H. Brown to "friends at home," Sept. 21, 1864, Henry Harrison Brown Papers, CTHS. For the role of military bands in the Civil War, see Francis A. Lord and Arthur Wise, *Bands and Drummer Boys of the Civil War* (1966; reprint New York: Decapo Press, 1979); Kenneth E. Olson, *Music and Musket Bands and Bandsmen of the American Civil War* (Westport, Conn.: Greenwood Press, 1981). Olson, and Lord and Wise make only brief reference to black bandsmen and the influence of band music on Southern blacks. See Lord and Wise, *Bands and Drummer Boys*, 47, 55, 216; Olson, *Music and Musket Bands*, 103, 153, 163–64. For detail on the role of black bands during the Civil War, see Wilson, "Black Bands and Black Culture," 31–37. (The present discussion of black band music is a revision of this article.) Olly Wilson argues that the Afro-American concept of music making made marching bands especially appealing. Olly Wilson, in I. V. Jackson, *More than Dancing*, 18, 20, 21.

66. Olson, *Music and Musket Bands*, 33, 36, 66.

67. Ibid., 36–37, 61, 188–89, 242.

68. S. Rogers, "War-Time Letters," Feb. 20, 1863, 44, typescript, MOLLUS, MassachusettsCommandery Collection, USAMHI.

69. T. W. Higginson to James [Rogers], Nov. 24, 1862, Thomas Wentworth Higginson Papers, AAS; Rogers, "War-Time Letters," Feb. 20, 1863, 55, USAMHI; J. Shaw, "Our Last Campaign and Subsequent Service in Texas," RISSHS, ser. 6, no. 9, Providence, R.I., 1905; Sutherland, "The Negro in the Late War," 182; L. Thomas to Senator Wilson, May 30, [1864], unidentified newspaper cutting, in J. W. M. Appleton Letter Book, 289 (microfilm), WVUL.

70. B. M. Mills to father, Nov. 29, 1864, Caleb Mills Papers, IHSL; Montgomery to mother, Aug. 22, 1864, Thomas Montgomery Papers, MHS.

71. Lt. Col. J. Bogert to parents, Feb. 17, 1864, John S. Bogert Letters, USC; Chaplain J. Gregg to Brig. Gen. L. Thomas, Nov. 30, 1864, G-891, 1864; Chaplain Z. K. Hawley to Brig. Gen. L. Thomas, Sept. 8, 1865, H-1317, 1865; Chaplain A. C. MacDonald to Brig. Gen. L. Thomas, Sept. 30, 1865, M-2171, 1865; all Letters Received, ser. 12, RG 94. For the difficulties of Europeans comprehending African musical rhythm, see LeRoi Jones, *Blues People*, 26.

72. Lt. Col. C. H. Adams to Lt. Col. J. H. Wilson, Sept. 1, 1863, Miscellaneous Records, 4 USCHA, Regimental Books and Papers USCT, RG 94. There was nothing unusual about Colonel Adams's belief that black music was culturally inferior to that of the white American. Most Northern white observers assessed slave music by their own cultural standards and concluded that it was primitive or barbaric. Epstein, *Sinful Tunes*, 274–75, 283, 290, 296–300.

73. Southern, *The Music of Black Americans*, 207; T. W. Higginson to James [Rogers], Nov. 24, 1862, Thomas Wentworth Higginson Papers, AAS; R. G. Shaw to father, Apr. 17, 1863, *RGS*, 285; T. Webster to Maj. C. W. Foster, Feb. 18, 1864, W-142, 1864, Letters Received, ser. 360, CTD, RG 94; N. Viall, "A Brief History of the 14th R.I. Colored Regiment, 1863–65," 23–24, RIHS. A black newspaper correspondent, Thomas Morris Chester, felt that Capt. Joseph Anderson, 8th USCI, had trained his regiment's band to a very high standard of performance. Captain Anderson was appointed by the government to train black bands at Camp William Penn, Pennsylvania. R. J. M. Blackett, ed., *Thomas Morris Chester*, 121–22.

74. LeRoi Jones, *Blues People*, 73–75; Some plantation owners had slave bands for their own entertainment. Dena J. Epstein, *Sinful Tunes*, 155–58. For the musical instruments used by slaves, see Blassingame, *The Slave Community*, 126; Levine, *Black Culture*, 15; MacLeod, "Quills, Fifes, and Flutes," 201–8; Dena J. Epstein, *Sinful Tunes*, 139–60. D. Densmore to "friends at home," Dec. 25, 1864, Benjamin Densmore Family Papers, MHS.

75. Ibid.

76. Even after pay for blacks was equalized with that of whites in mid-June 1864, pay for privates still lagged behind that for musicians. General Orders No. 231, July 18, 1864, stipulated that half the members of a military band were to receive seventeen dollars a month, one-quarter twenty dollars, and one-quarter thirty-four; Lord and Wise, *Bands and Drummer Boys*, 135; Viall, "A Brief History," 23–24, RIHS; Scroggs, Diary, Jan. 2, 1865, USAMHI.

77. Lord and Wise, *Bands and Drummer Boys*, 28; Olson, *Music and Musket Bands*, 67, 70–72.

78. Lord and Wise, *Bands and Drummer Boys*, 214; Southern, *The Music of Black Americans*, 207; Shaw, *RGS*, 285; Sgt. W. Logan to E. W. Kinsley, Aug. 25, 1864, Sgt. Maj. J. M. Trotter to E. W. Kinsley, June 2, July 18, 1864, Edward Wilkinson Kinsley Papers, DUL; Scroggs, Diary, Jan. 2, 1865, USAMHI. Black newspaper correspondent

Thomas Morris Chester reported that the band of the 8th USCI could "execute, to the satisfaction of competent judges, some forty pieces of scientific music." Blackett, ed., *Thomas Morris Chester*, 122.

79. [Anon.], 5th USCI, to E. Stanton, Oct. 22, 1865, A-420, 1865, Letters Received, ser. 12, RG94.

80. Palemon J. Smalley, "Dad's Memoirs," 98, typescript, MHS. Even in the early years of the war, "John Brown's Body" was very popular among the ex-slaves of the South Carolina Sea Islands; Dena J. Epstein, *Sinful Tunes*, 259, 281, 297, 299. Eileen Southern believes "John Brown" was the black soldiers' "all-time favorite," their "unofficial theme song"; Southern, *The Music of Black Americans*, 209–10. Ervin L. Jordan notes that black troops sang "John Brown's Body" as they marched into Richmond on Apr. 3, 1865; Jordan, *Black Confederates and Afro-Yankees in Civil War Virginia*, 292.

8. "Married 'Under the Flag'"

1. Pvt. A. Oats to E. Stanton, Jan. 26, 1865, O-6, 1865, Letters Received, ser. 360, CTD, RG 94. Published accounts that discuss the black soldiers' involvement in family affairs during the Civil War include Ira Berlin, Francine C. Cary, Steven F. Miller, and Leslie Rowland, "Black Family and Freedom: Black Families in the American Civil War," *History Today* 37 (Jan. 1987): 8–15; Ira Berlin, Steven F. Miller, and Leslie S. Rowland, "Missing: A Freedman Seeks His Family," *American Visions* 3 (Feb. 1988): 8–9; Ira Berlin, Steven F. Miller, and Leslie S. Rowland, "Afro-American Families in the Transition from Slavery to Freedom," *Radical History Review* no. 42 (1988): 89–121; Ira Berlin and Leslie S. Rowland, eds., *Families and Freedom: A Documentary History of African-American Kinship in the Civil War Era* (New York: New Press, 1997); Berlin et al., *The Black Military Experience*, 656–730; N. Frankel, "The Southern Side of 'Glory': Mississippi African-American Women during the Civil War," *Minerva: Quarterly Report on Women and the Military* 8, no. 3 (1990): 28–36; Ripley, "The Black Family in Transition," 369–80; Gutman, *The Black Family*.

2. The officers' views of slave morality and family life were influenced by abolitionist ideology and prevailing Northern images of the degrading nature of slavery and plantation life. See Gutman, *The Black Family*, 60–79, 88–89, 154–55; McPherson, *The Struggle for Equality*, 150–53, and *Battle Cry of Freedom*, 37–39; Mitchell, *The Vacant Chair*, 92–93.

Contemporary Northern views on ideal family life are discussed in N. F. Cott, *The Bonds of Womanhood: "Woman's Sphere" in New England, 1780–1835* (New Haven, Conn.: Yale Univ. Press, 1977); B. L. Epstein, *The Politics of Domesticity: Women, Evangelism, and Temperance in Nineteenth-Century America* (Middletown, Conn.: Wesleyan Univ. Press, 1981). For a discussion of the slave family in the Civil War era, see Berlin, *Families and Freedom*, 3–11. Historians who have discussed the role women played in slave families include Elizabeth Fox-Genovese, *Within the Plantation Household: Black and White Women of the Old South* (Chapel Hill: Univ. of North Carolina Press, 1988); J. Jones, *Labor of Love, Labor of Sorrow;* Ann Patton Malone, *Sweet Chariot: Slave Family and Household Structure in Nineteenth-Century Louisiana* (Chapel Hill: Univ. of North Carolina Press, 1992); Deborah Gray White, *Ar'n't I a Woman? Female Slaves in the Plantation South* (New York: W. W. Norton, 1985).

3. Berlin et al., *The Black Military Experience*, 656–57; Berlin and Rowland, eds.,

Families and Freedom, 64–65. Mrs. J. Wilson to E. Stanton, May 27, 1865, W-416, 1865; Mrs. J. Pimer to E. Stanton, Aug. 12, 1864, P-274, 1864; both Letters Received, ser. 360, CTD, RG 94.

4. [Anon.] to Governor Andrew, Mar. 25, 1864, Exec. Dept. Letters, Letters Received, vol. 61, no. 101, Andrew Papers, CMSA; Sgt. A. S. Fisher to Governor Andrew, Mar. 14, 1864, Exec. Dept. Letters, Letters Received, vol. 80, no. 9, Andrew Papers, CMSA; Sgt. Maj. J. M. Trotter to E. W. Kinsley, Mar. 13, 1864, Edward Wilkinson Kinsley Papers, DUL.

5. Sgt. H. Golden to wife, May 19, 1864; Sgt. J. H. Jackson to Governor Andrew, May 30, 1864; both Exec. Dept. Letters, Letters Received, vol. 62, nos. 136A, 136B, Andrew Papers, CMSA.

6. Mrs. L. Bailey to E. Stanton, May 11, 1865; Maj. C. W. Foster to Mrs. L. Bailey, May 16, 1865, B-313, 1865; Mrs. C. Massey to E. Stanton, July 10, 1865, M-291, 1865; all Letters Received, ser. 360, CTD, RG 94. *Christian Recorder*, May 6, 18, 1865.

7. Mrs. J. Taylor to Maj. Gen. B. F. Butler, Feb. 7, 1864, General Correspondence, B. F. Butler Papers, Library of Congress; Mrs. W. Parker to [?], M-14, 1865, ser. 360, CTD, RG 94.

8. Mrs. M. Bower to Col. O. P. Stearns, June 22, 1865, B-525, 1865; M. Johnson to E. Stanton, Aug. 12, 1865, J-124, 1865; M. Douglass to War Dept., July 6, 1865, D-222 1865; Mrs. S. A. Whitfield to E. Stanton, Dec. 8, 1863, W-37, 1864; J. Rowser to Lincoln, Sept. 24, 1864; Mrs. J. Rowser to E. Stanton, Dec. 14, 1864, R-389, 1864; all Letters Received, ser. 360, CTD, RG 94.

9. Mrs. N. Weir to Lincoln, Feb. 8, 1864, endorsement of Col. E. N. Hallowell, Mar. 3, 1864, W-
264, 1864, ser. 360, CTD, RG 94.

10. Mrs. H. Johnson to Lincoln, July 31, 1863, J-17, 1863, ser. 360, CTD, RG 94.

11. Christian Recorder, Nov. 7, 1863, Sept. 10, 1864.

12. M. L. Mainn to Governor Andrew, June 9, 1863, Exec. Dept. Letters, Letters Received, vol. 84, no. 111, Andrew Papers, CMSA; *Christian Recorder*, Nov. 12, 1864; May 27, 1865; Sgt. J. H. Morgan to Lincoln, Jan. 16, 1864, filed with B-190, 1864, Letters Received, ser. 360, CTD, RG 94.

13. Sgt. I. Watson to E. Stanton, July 21, 1865, W-671 1865; R. Brown to E. Stanton, Feb. 21, 1865, B-126, 1865; Pvts. G. and W. Cufey to E. Stanton, Oct. 5, 1864, C-1088, 1864; all Letters Received, ser. 360, CTD, RG 94.

14. Berlin et al., *The Black Military Experience*, 656–58; Chaplain J. Gregg to Brig. Gen. L. Thomas, Feb. 28, 1865, G-239, 1865, Letters Received, ser. 12, RG 94; Charles L. Wagandt, "The Army versus Maryland Slavery, 1862–1864," *Civil War History* 10 (June 1964): 141–48; *Christian Recorder*, Apr. 16, 1864.

15. Berlin et al., *The Black Military Experience*, 657–58; Berlin and Rowland, eds., *Families and Freedom*, 95–104, 109–14; [Anon.] to E. Stanton, Aug. 22, 1865, A-345, 1865, Letters Received, ser. 360, CTD, RG 94.

16. Higginson, Journal, Dec. 14, 1862, HU; 2d Lt. W. Goodale to children, Apr. 20, 1865, Warren Goodale Papers, MAHS; Peet, Diary, Nov. 8, 1864, SHSW.

17. Higginson, Journal, Dec. 14, 1862, HU.

18. Capt. E. Earle, "Kansas, Colored Volunteer Regiment, 1st Roll, Accounts and History of the First Kansas Colored Volunteer Regiment, 1863–65," 5, 17, NEHGS; Berlin and Rowland, eds., *Families and Freedom*, 35–36, 39; I. Berlin, B. J. Fields, S. F.

Miller, J. P. Reidy, L. S. Rowland, *Free at Last: A Documentary History of Slavery, Free-dom, and the Civil War* (New York: New Press, 1992), 480–82; Higginson, Journal, Feb. 18, 1864, HU; T. Montgomery to father, Oct. 6, 1864, Thomas Montgomery Papers (microfilm), MHS; *Christian Recorder*, Sept. 24, 1864; Pvt. S. Joyner to Brig. Gen. E. Wild, Feb. 21, 1864, Edward A. Wild Papers, MOLLUS, Massachusetts Commandery Collection, USAMHI.

19. Briggs, *Civil War Surgeon*, 154; Rogers, "War-Time Letters," Feb. 12, 1863, 43, USAMHI; Ripley, "The Black Family in Transition," 372.

20. Clarence L. Mohr, "Before Sherman: Georgia Blacks and the Union War Effort, 1861–1864," *Journal of Southern History* 45 (Aug. 1979): 331–52. For the role of black women in the black regiments, see Frankel, "The Southern Side of 'Glory,'" 28–33; J. Jones, *Labor of Love, Labor of Sorrow*, 49–51; Taylor, *Reminiscences*, 21, 34–35; *Christian Recorder*, Jan. 7, 1865; Berlin et al., *The Black Military Experience*, 659.

21. Chaplain T. Calahan to Brig. Gen. L Thomas Nov. 1, 1864, C-1560, 1864, Letters Received ser. 12, RG 94. For officers' comments on slave "immorality" and the negative impact of plantation "vices" on the behavior of black soldiers, see testimonies of Capt. E. W. Hooper, Col. W. A. Pile before the American Freedmen Inquiry Commission, file nos. 3A, 7, O-328, 1863; Letters Received, ser. 12, RG 94. Chaplain T. Calahan to Brig. Gen. L. Thomas, Nov. 1, 1864, Jan. 2, 1865; Chaplain C. Taylor to Brig. Gen. L. Thomas, July 31, 1865; both C-1560, 1864, C-144, 1865, T-6, 1865, Letters Received, ser. 12, RG 94. Chaplain T. S. Johnson to sister, Apr. 23, 1866, T. S. Johnson Correspondence, 1862–1866; Thomas S. Johnson to Brig. Gen. L. Thomas, Oct. 31, 1865, 127, USCT Handbook, Thomas S. Johnson Papers, SHSW. For stereotypes that depicted female slaves as lustful jezebels, see White, *Ar'n't I a Woman?* 29–34; Fox-Genovese, *Within the Plantation Household*, 291–92.

Abolitionists depicted female slaves as the victims of sexual repression. In her study of antislavery iconography, Jean F. Yellin claims that American antislavery women "adopted the emblem" of the chained "female supplicant as their own." Since abolitionists formed only a small portion of the U.S. Colored Troops officer corps, such antislavery stereotypes had limited appeal. Yellin, *Women and Sisters*, 15, 3–26; J. F. Yellin, J. C. Van Horne, eds., *The Abolitionist Sisterhood: Women's Political Culture in Antebellum America* (Ithaca, N.Y.: Cornell Univ. Press, 1994), 5–6.

Slaves had their own moral codes. The sexual mores of the slave community were enforced by peer group pressure, religious customs, and folk beliefs. For slave sexual morality see Gutman, *The Black Family*, 63–73, Genovese, *Roll, Jordan, Roll*, 458–75; Blassingame, *The Slave Community*, 153–54; Owens, *This Species of Property*, 192–93.

22. Berlin and Rowland, eds., *Families and Freedom*, 73–77; Capt. W. M. Ferry to Aunt Hannah, Feb. 29, 1864, William M. Ferry Papers, Michigan Historical Collection, University of Michigan (hereafter UM); Wiley, Billy Yank, 259. For the sexual exploitation of black women as victims of rape, see Mitchell, *The Vacant Chair*, 106–10; Thomas Lowry, *The Story the Soldiers Wouldn't Tell: Sex in the Civil War* (Mechanicsburg, Pa.: Stackpole Books, 1994), 130–31.

23. Lt. Warren Goodale also served as a private in the 11th Massachusetts Battery of Light Artillery. See chap. 7.

24. Lt. W. Goodale to children, July 12, 1865; see also to children, Apr. 20, 1865; both Warren Goodale Papers 1847–65, MAHS. Pvt G. Washington to Mr. Abraham Lincoln, Dec. 4, 1864, W-953 1864, ct. 1864; [Anon.] to E. Stanton, Aug. 22, 1865, A-345,

1865; both Letters Received, ser. 360, CTD, RG 94. Chaplain T. Calahan to Brig. Gen. L. Thomas, Nov. 1, 1864, C-1560, 1864, Letters Received, ser. 12, RG 94.

25. Chaplain T. Calahan to Brig. Gen. L. Thomas, Sept. 1, 1864; Nov. 1, 1864; Jan. 2, 1865, C-123, 1864, C-1506, 1864, C-144, 1865. Chaplain C. W. Buckley to Lt. A. R. Mills, B-1607, 1864; Chaplain G. N. Carruthers to Brig. Gen. L. Thomas, Jan. 31, 1865, C-287, 1865; all Letters Received, ser. 12, RG 94. Peet, Diary, Nov. 8, 1864, SHSW.

26. Brig. Gen. L. Thomas to E. Stanton, Sept. 5, 1863, A-447, 1863, Letters Received, ser. 12, RG 94; circular, Lt. Col. J. Phillips, Apr. 4, 1864, endorsement Brig. Gen. L. Thomas, Miscellaneous Records, 59th USCI, Regimental Books and Papers USCT, RG 94; Brig. Gen. L. Thomas to AAG E. L. Townsend, July 27, 1864; telegram, Maj. C. W. Foster to Brig. Gen. L. Thomas, July 28, 1864, filed with A-257, 1864; both Letters Received, ser. 360, CTD, RG 94.

27. Lt. Col. R. Cowden to Bvt. Brig. Gen. W. H. Morgan, June 2, 1865, Miscellaneous Records, 59th USCI, Regimental Books and Papers USCT RG 94; Capt. J. R. Graton to wife, June 10, 1863, John R. Graton Papers (microfilm), KSHS; Col. W. W. Marple to Lt. Col. E. W. Smith, Nov. 12, 1863, Miscellaneous Records, 34th USCI, Regimental Books and Papers USCT, RG 94.

28. Surgeon H. H. Penniman to Lt. R. B. Neal, Feb. 9, 1864, Letters Sent, 5th USCHA, Regimental Books and Papers USCT, RG 94; Capt. S. D. Barnes, Diary, Mar. 22, 1864, Samuel D. Barnes Diary, LC; Van Alstyne, Diary, 207–8; Frankel, "The Southern Side of 'Glory,'" 29–30; J. Jones, *Labor of Love, Labor of Sorrow*, 49–51; Chaplain T. S. Conway to Brig. Gen. L. Thomas, May 17, 1865, C-365 1865, Letters Received, ser. 360, CTD, RG 94.

29. Berlin et al., *Free at Last*, 185–86; Gutman, *The Black Family*, 22, 370–74; Col. I. J. Kappner to Lt. G. A. Mason, Mar. 4, 1864, Miscellaneous Records, 3d USCHA, Regimental Books and Papers USCT, RG 94; J. Jones, *Labor of Love, Labor of Sorrow*, 50–51; R. M. Reid, "Black Experience in the Union Army: The Other Civil War," *Canadian Review of American Studies* 21, no. 2 (1990): 152.

30. Gutman, *The Black Family*, 370–74; Berlin and Rowland, eds., *Families and Freedom*, 199–201; *Commonwealth*, Dec. 10, 1864.

31. Quoted in Berlin and Rowland, eds., *Families and Freedom*, 200.

32. Ibid., 201.

33. Ibid.; *Commonwealth*, Aug. 16, Dec. 10, 1864.

34. Brig. Gen. Lorenzo Thomas's leasing plan was replaced by one implemented by the Treasury Department in Oct. 1863 under the agency of William Mellen. It was changed again in early 1864 to a scheme modeled very closely on General N. Banks's "free labor system," which operated in the Department of the Gulf. However, the essential character of General Thomas's leasing plan did not change. Agricultural self-reliance was continually promoted as a vehicle for sustaining the black population and creating social order. Louis S. Gerteis, *From Contraband to Freedmen: Federal Policy toward Southern Blacks, 1861–1865* (Westport, Conn.: Greenwood Press, 1973), 119–26, 135–43, 146–49, 155–57; Berlin et al., *Free at Last*, 268; Col. John Eaton, 63d USCI, the superintendent of freedmen, based in Memphis and Col. Samuel Thomas, 64th USCI, provost marshal general of freedmen, based at Vicksburg, administered freedmen affairs throughout the Mississippi Valley. Gerteis, *From Contraband to Freedmen*, 155–57.

35. Chaplain G. N. Carruthers to Brig. Gen. L. Thomas, Dec. 31, 1864, Jan. 31, 1865, C-1836, 1864, C-287, 1865, Chaplain T. Calahan to Brig. Gen. L. Thomas, Dec. 1,

1864, Jan. 2, 1865, C-1813, 1864, C-144, 1865 Letters Received, ser. 12, RG 94; Gutman, *The Black Family*, 21–24.

36. Chaplain G. N. Carruthers to Brig. Gen. L. Thomas, Jan. 31, 1865, C-287, 1865; Chaplain T. Calahan to Brig. Gen. L. Thomas, Sept. 1, 1864, C-1234, 1864, Letters Received, ser. 12, RG 94.

37. Maj. Gen. N. P. Banks to W. L. Garrison, Jan. 30, 1865, in *Liberator*, 24 Feb. 1865. For discussion of General Banks's free labor system see: Gerteis, *From Contraband to Freedmen*, chaps. 4–6; Ripley, *Slaves and Freedmen*, esp. chaps. 3–5; Messner, *Freedmen and the Ideology of Freed Labor*, chaps. 6–7. For a discussion of the relationship between Banks's labor system and his provision for black education see Keith Wilson, "Education as a Vehicle of Racial Control: Major General N. P. Banks in Louisiana, 1863–64," *Journal of Negro Education* 50, no. 2 (Spring 1981): 156–70. For comment on black family life in the Department of the Gulf under Banks, see Ripley, *Slaves and Freedmen*, chap. 8, "The Black Family in Transition," 369–80.

38. Maj. Gen. N. Banks to Enrollment Commission, Sept. 2, 1863, N. Banks Papers, LC; Ripley, *Slaves and Freedmen*, 113–14.

39. Chaplain T. Conway to Brig. Gen. D. Ullmann, May 15, 27, 1863, D. Ullmann Letters and Orders, Generals' Papers and Books, ser. 159, RG 94; Chaplain T. Conway to Brig. Gen. L. Thomas, May 17, 1863, C-365, 1865, Letters Received, ser. 12, RG 94; Thomas Conway was appointed superintendent of negro labor by Banks to monitor the planters' contractual obligations. Ripley, *Slaves and Freedmen*, 61.

40. For comment on General Butler's General Orders No. 46, see Berlin et al., *The Black Military Experience*, 658–59.

41. J. Jones, *Labor of Love, Labor of Sorrow*, 44–46, 51; Lt. Col. R. Cowden, to Capt. W. W. Deane, Aug. 29, 1865, Miscellaneous Records, 59th USCI, Regimental Books and Papers USCT, RG 94.

42. J. Jones, *Labor of Love, Labor of Sorrow*, 44–46, 51.

43. Col. H. Lieb to E. Stanton, Nov. 17, 1864, L-338, 1864, Letters Received, ser. 360, CTD, RG 94. Col. H. Lieb to Capt. N. H. Randall, Apr. 15, 1864; Surgeon H. H. Penniman to Col. H. Lieb, Apr. 19, 1864; Lt. E. N. Owen to Col. [Lieb], May 2, 1864; Col. H. Lieb to Lt. Col. H. C. Rogers, Sept. 19, 1864; all Letters Received, 5th USCHA, Regimental Books and Papers USCT, RG 94. Female slaves developed social networks through work and community activity. These networks help them develop survival skills and gave them degrees of independence; see Fox-Genovese, *Within the Plantation Household*, 172–78, 318; White, *Ar'n't I a Woman?* 22, 94–95, 119–23, 137–41.

44. Chaplain J. Peet to Brig. Gen. L. Thomas, Nov. 1, 1864, P-1316, 1864, Letters Received, ser. 12, RG 94.

45. Testimony of Maj. G. L. Stearns before the American Freedmen Inquiry Commission, file no. 7, O-328, 1863, Letters Received, ser. 12, RG 94.

46. J. Jones, *Labor of Love, Labor of Sorrow*, 51; H. James, "To the Public," printed circular, June 27, 1863, Exec. Dept. Letters, Letters Received, vol. W-102, no. 85, Andrew Papers, CMSA; Brig. Gen. E. A. Wild to E. W. Kinsley, July 28, [1863], Edward Wilkinson Kinsley Papers, DUL; Berlin and Rowland, eds., *Families and Freedom*, 122–26; Col. J. Beecher to Frankie, June 26, 1863, James C. Beecher Family Papers, RCL.

47. Maj. Gen. Q. Gillmore to S. Chase, Jan. 31, 1864, Q. Gillmore Letters and Orders, Generals' Papers and Books, ser. 159, RG 94; *Army and Navy Journal*, May 21, 1864; Col. T. W. Higginson to Brig. Gen. R. Saxton, Feb. 19, 1864, Letters Received,

General Orders No. 14, Hd. Qtrs., 33d USCI, Feb. 14, 1864, Issuances, 33d USCI, Regimental Books and Papers USCT, RG 94; White, *Ar'n't I a Woman?* 137–41.

48. Testimony of Brig. Gen. J. S. Wadsworth before the American Freedmen Inquiry Commission, file no. 5, O-328, 1863, Letters Received, ser. 12, RG 94; Gerteis, *From Contraband to Freedman,* 97; Willie L. Rose, *Rehearsal for Reconstruction: The Port Royal Experiment* (New York: Vintage Books, 1967); Lawrence N. Powell, *New Masters: Northern Planters during the Civil War and Reconstruction* (New Haven, Conn.: Yale University Press, 1980), 10, 26, 28, 29; McPherson, *The Struggle for Equality,* 246–59, and *Ordeal by Fire,* 396–98; Litwack, *Been in the Storm So Long,* 399–406; Foner, *Free Soil, Free Labor, Free Men,* 295–300.

49. J. Jones, *Labor of Love, Labor of Sorrow,* 51. For the development of female survival skills and female work patterns on the slave plantation and during the early years of Reconstruction, see White, *Ar'n't I a Woman?* 22, 94–95, 119–23, 137–41.

50. National Anti-Slavery Standard, Sept. 10, 1864. For slave morality, slave family life, and Northern white perceptions of slave immorality, see Gutman, *The Black Family,* 60–79,88–89, 154–55; Malone, *Sweet Chariot,* 259; White, *Ar'n't I a Woman?* 29–34, 106–11.

51. Chaplain C. W. Buckley to Lt. A. R. Mills, Dec. 1, 1864, B-1841, 1864; Chaplain J. Gregg to Brig. Gen. L. Thomas, Nov. 30, 1864, Feb. 28, 1865, G-819, 1864, G-239, 1865; Chaplain T. H. Hall to Brig. Gen. L. Thomas, Mar. 31, 1865, H-585, 1865; Chaplain W. C. Yancey to Brig. Gen. L. Thomas, Nov. 30, 1864, Y-59, 1864; all Letters Received, ser. 12, RG 94.

52. Col. J. Jones et al., to Gov. T. Fletcher, June 6, 1865, P-359, 1865, Letters Received, ser. 360 CTD, RG 94; J. Appleton to wife, J. W. M. Appleton Letter Book, 57 (microfilm), WVUL; For military service, the concept of manhood, and the inculcation of manly qualities in black troops, see Mitchell, The Vacant Chair, 4–18, 55–69, 127–30. Elizabeth Fox-Genovese comes close to claiming that slavery "unmanned" male slaves; Fox-Genovese, *Within the Plantation Household,* 49, 193–94, 294, 296–97, 326–28. This view sits oddly with the exemplary war records of many black soldiers. For attempts by the officers to use the army as a school of manhood education, see comments by generals: General Orders No. 17, Hd. Qtrs., Dept. of the South, Mar. 6, 1863, United States Army Papers, Department of the South, South Carolina Library, USC; Brig. Gen. L. Thomas to E. Stanton, Nov. 7, 1864, Oct. 5, 1865, L. Thomas Letters and Orders, Generals' Papers and Books, ser. 159, RG 94; Brig. Gen. L. Thomas to Hon. H. Wilson, May 30, 1864, in *National Anti-Slavery Standard,* June 8, 1864; For manhood education by the commanders of regiments, see Higginson, Army Life, 34; Col. J. Beecher, excerpts of letter, June 15, 1863, in New England Loyal Publication Society, no. 175, Mar. 19, 1864, Edward A. Wild Papers, MOLLUS, Massachusetts Commandery Collection, USAMHI; S. C. Armstrong to R. B. Armstrong, Feb. 8, 1864, editorial, *Southern Workman,* Jan. 1884, H. Ludlow ed., "Personal Memories and Letters of Gen. S. C. Armstrong," 5 vols., 363–64, 496–97,typescript, Williamsiana Collection, WCL.

53. McPherson, *For Cause and Comrades,* 6, 13, 25–27, 31; Mitchell, *The Vacant Chair,* 4–5, 8–10, 13–18; Chaplain W. C. Yancey to Brig. Gen. L. Thomas, Nov. 30, 1864, Y-59, 1864, Letters Received, ser. 12, RG 94. Most of the chaplains working in black regiments believed in a concept of Christian marriage, which focused upon legal, contractual sanctions and patriarchal dominance. For mid-nineteenth-century attitudes on family life, marriage, and slavery, see Gutman, *The Black Family,* 62–64.

54. Chaplain G. N. Carruthers to Brig. Gen. L. Thomas, Jan. 31, 1865, C-287, 1865; Chaplain W. C. Yancey to Brig. Gen. L. Thomas, June 30, Nov. 31, 1864, Y-23, Y-60, 1864; both Letters Received, ser. 12, RG 94.

55. Peet, Diary, Dec. 27, 1864; Chaplain J. Peet to Brig. Gen. L. Thomas, Aug. 31, Sept. 30, 1864, P-1039, P-1230 SHSW 1864; Chaplain A. B. Randall to Brig. Gen. L. Thomas, Feb. 28, 1864, R-189, 1865; Chaplain C. Taylor to Brig. Gen. L. Thomas, July 31, 1865, T-6, 1865; all Letters Received, ser. 12, RG 94. Thomas D. Howard, "Charles Howard Family Domestic History," 174, typescript, Southern Historical Collection, UNC; Frankel, "The Southern Side of 'Glory,'" 30–31; Gutman, *The Black Family*, 18–22; Ripley, "The Black Family in Transition," 374, 377–78.

56. Chaplain T. Calahan to Brig. Gen. L. Thomas, Nov. 1, 1864, Jan. 2, 1865, C-1560, 1864, C-144, 1865, Letters Received, ser. 12, RG 94; T. S. Johnson to sister, Apr. 20, 23, 1866, Chaplain T. S. Johnson to Brig. Gen. L. Thomas, Oct. 31, 1865, Hand Book of the 127th Regiment of Colored Troops, 1864–1866, Thomas S. Johnson Papers, SHSW. Mitchell, *The Vacant Chair*, 74, 80, 106–10.

57. Orders No. 15, Mar. 28, 1864, L. Thomas Letters and Orders, Generals' Papers and Books, ser. 159, RG 94; Berlin et al., *The Black Military Experience*, 712 n.

58. Chaplain C. W. Buckley to Lt. A. R. Mills, Nov. 1, 1864, B-1607, 1864; Chaplain J. Peet to Brig. Gen. L. Thomas, Sept. 30, 1864, P-1203, 1864; Chaplain A. B. Randall to Brig. Gen. L. Thomas, Feb. 28, 1865, R-189, 1865; all Letters Received, ser. 12, RG 94. Ripley, "The Black Family in Transition," 374.

59. Chaplain W. C. Yancey to Brig. Gen. L. Thomas, Nov. 30, 1864, Y-59, Letters Received, ser. 12, RG 94.

60. D. Densmore to father, Jan. 28, 1864, Benjamin Densmore Family Papers, MHS.

61. The ex-slaves were keen to confirm their slave marriages legally. See Berlin and Rowland, eds., *Families and Freedom*, 154–55, 164–70. For the slave's view of marriage, see Creel, "A Peculiar People," 247; Malone, *Sweet Chariot*, 224–26; White, *Ar'n't I a Woman?* 99, 105–06, 108–10, 149–51, 153–55.

62. For the stereotype of the Northern Christian lady as a paragon of compliant domesticity and moral virtue, see McPherson, *Battle Cry of Freedom*, 34–35; Mitchell, *The Vacant Chair*, 74–75; testimony of Capt. E. W. Hooper before the American Freedman Inquiry Commission, file no. 3A, O-328, 1863, Letters Received, ser. 12, RG 94; Mitchell, *Civil War Soldiers*, 122; Capt. E. Grabill to wife, June 20, 1865, Elliott F. Grabill Papers, OBA. For prostitution in the Civil War, see Lowry, *The Story the Soldiers Wouldn't Tell*, 61–92; "Soldier of 5 USCT" to Stanton, Oct. 22, 1865, A-420 1865, Letters Received, ser. 360, CTD, NA.

63. Chaplain G. A. Rockwood to Brig. Gen. L. Thomas, May 31, 1864, R-412, 1864; Chaplain J. Peet to Brig. Gen. L. Thomas, Sept. 30, 1864, P-1203, 1864; Chaplain A. R. Jones to Brig. Gen. L. Thomas, Dec. 31, 1864, J-344, 1864; Chaplain T. Stevenson to Brig. Gen. L. Thomas, May 10, Aug. 1, 1865, S-1146, S-1817, 1865; all Letters Received, ser. 12, RG 94. J. Cory to A. Lincoln, Apr. 15, 1865, Letters Received, ser. 360, CTD, RG 94.

64. Slaves accepted prenuptial sex, favored "slow" courtships, and greatly resented the intrusion of the master in their intimate affairs. J. Jones, *Labor of Love, Labor of Sorrow*, 34–36; Malone, *Sweet Chariot*, 41–43; White, *Ar'n't I a Woman?* 97–98, 103–06, 108–11. Marriage sanctioned parenthood and not sexual intercourse. Motherhood gave the female slave more independence and strengthened her bonds

with other women. See J. Jones, *Labor of Love, Labor of Sorrow*, 34–36; Malone, *Sweet Chariot*, 224–29; White, *Ar'n't I a Woman?* 103–18, 140–41, 152–58.

65. Chaplain C. Taylor to Brig. Gen. L. Thomas, July 31, 1865, T-61, 1865; Chaplain Joel Grant to Brig. Gen. L. Thomas, Mar. 31, 1866, W-836, 1866; both Letters Received, ser. 360, CTD, NA.

66. Chaplain Joel Grant to Brig. Gen. L. Thomas, Mar. 31, 1866, W-836 1866, Letters Received, ser. 360, CTD, NA.

67. Chaplain T. Calahan to Brig. Gen. L. Thomas, June 18, 1864, C-859, 1864, Letters Received, ser. 12, RG 94; Newton, *Out of the Briars*, 81. For the dissolution of soldiers' marriages, see Berlin and Rowland, eds., *Families and Freedom*, 140–47; Berlin et al., "Afro-American Families," 97; Berlin et al., *The Black Military Experience*, 660–61; Capt. E. Grabill to wife, 20 June 1865, Elliott F. Grabill Papers, OBA. Sexual fidelity was important to slave couples. See Berlin and Rowland, eds., *Families and Freedom*, 182–83.

68. Capt. E. Grabill to wife, June 20, 1865, Elliott F. Grabill Papers, OBA.

69. W. M. Ferry to Aunt Hannah, Feb. 2, 9, 1864, William M. Ferry Papers, Michigan Historical Collection, UM; Wiley, *Billy Yank*, 259. For the sexual exploitation of women during the Civil War and black women as victims of rape, see Susan Brownmiller, *Against Our Will: Men, Women, and Rape* (Harmondsworth: Penguin Books, 1986), 88; Mitchell, *The Vacant Chair*, 104–10; Michael Fellman, *Inside War: The Guerrilla Conflict in Missouri during the American Civil War* (New York: Oxford Univ. Press, 1989), 193–230; Lowry, *The Story the Soldiers Wouldn't Tell*, 123–31.

70. Service Records of John W. Cook [Cork], 55th Massachusetts, Spenser Loyd, 55th Mass. Vols., John M. Smith, 55th Mass. Vols. Carded Records, Volunteer Organizations, Civil War, ser. 515, RG 94; Robert I. Alotta, *Civil War Justice: Union Army Executions under Lincoln* (Shippensburg, Penn.: 1989), 97–99, 172. Alotta argues that although John M. Smith listed by the U.S. Adjutant General's Office as being executed for rape, he was actually executed for desertion; C. B. Fox to wife, Feb. 18, [1864], Extracts from Letters Written to Wife, vol. 1, 164–65, MHS; Judge Advocate A. A. Hosmer to President, May 15, 1865, filed with proceedings of general courts-martial in the case of Sgt. Dandridge Brooks et al., 38th USCI, MM-1972, Court-Martial Case files, ser. 15, RG 153; J. O. Moore to Lizzie, 30 July 1865, James Otis Moore Papers, DUL.

71. Proceedings of general courts-martial in the case of Cpl. James Morrison et al., 52d USCI, MM-3192, Court-Martial Case files, ser. 15, RG 153. There is no evidence that Mrs. J. R. Cook was raped before she was murdered. Alotta, *Civil War Justice*, 168; Lowry, *The Story the Soldiers Wouldn't Tell*, 130–31.

72. Testimony of Maj. Gen. B. F. Butler before the American Freedmen Inquiry Commission, file no. 5, see also testimony of J. Redpath, file no. 9, Capt. E. W. Hooper, file no. 3A, O-328, 1863, Letters Received, ser. 12, RG 94. For a discussion of abolitionist views on sexually depravity in the South and the immorality of female slaves, see Mitchell, *The Vacant Chair*, 108–09; Walters, *The Antislavery Appeal*, 70–110. For comment on the role of women as the guardians of domestic virtue, see McPherson, *Battle Cry of Freedom*, 34–35; Mitchell, *The Vacant Chair*, 74–75. For a description of antebellum stereotypes of black female slaves, see Fox-Genovese, *Within the Plantation Household*, 291–93; White, *Ar'n't I a Woman?* 29–34, 46–50.

73. Capt. E. Grabill to wife, June 20, 1865, Elliott F. Grabill Papers, OBA; Gutman, *The Black Family*, 385–402, 613–14.

74. For comment on the role of laundresses on the plantation, see J. Jones, *Labor of Love, Labor of Sorrow,* 30; White, *Ar'n't I a Woman?* 122–23.

75. Brig. Gen. W. Dwight to Brig. Gen. C. P. Stone, Jan. 27, 1864, Miscellaneous Records, 76th USCI, Regimental Books and Papers USCT, RG 94.

76. In addition to rape, Captain Daly was charged with drunkenness, breaking arrest, and abusing Col. Henry Fuller. Daly was dishonorably dismissed from the service by Special Orders No. 45, Feb. 19, 1864. See Investigation, Col. H. W. Fuller, into charges against William H. Daly, 3d Inf. Corps d'Afrique, Dec. 18, 1863, filed with G-81, 1864, Letters Received, ser. 360, CTD, RG 94. In addition to sexual assault, 1st Lt. James S. Matthews was charged with illegally selling forage, failing to act on complaints of stealing, and harboring large numbers of Negro women in the quarters of his company. Matthews appears to have escaped conviction and sentencing by resigning from the service. See charges and specifications against 1st Lt. James S. Matthews, 3d U.S. Col. Cav., filed with M-175, 1863, Letters Received, ser. 360, CTD, RG 94.

77. Brig. Gen. W. Dwight to Brig. Gen. C. P. Stone, Jan. 27, 1864, Miscellaneous Records, 76th USCI, Regimental Books and Papers USCT, RG 94; Fred H. Harrington, "The Fort Jackson Mutiny," *Journal of Negro History* 27 (Oct. 1942): 426–30. Brigadier General Dwight was accused of having an illicit relationship with Mrs. Rose Plumber, a laundress in the 76th USCI. The charges against Brigadier General Dwight appear to have been dropped. See charges and specifications against Brig. Gen. W. Dwight, Letters and Orders, Generals' Papers and Books, ser. 159, RG 94; Judge Advocate General I. Holt to Lincoln, Apr. 2, 1864, N-20 1864, Letters Received, ser. 360, CTD, RG 94. Harrington, "The Fort Jackson Mutiny," 420–31; Messner, *Freedmen and the Ideology of Free Labor,* 157–63; Ripley, *Slaves and Freedmen,* 115–16

78. Gutman, *The Black Family,* 22–28.

79. For comment on the sexual exploitation of female slaves and the ways female and male slaves endeavored to resist this form of exploitation, see Fox-Genovese, *Within the Plantation Household,* 49, 294, 296–97, 326–28, 373–74; J. Jones, *Labor of Love, Labor of Sorrow,* 34–38; Malone, *Sweet Chariot,* 221–24; White, *Ar'n't I a Woman?* 77–86, 152–53. For a discussion of the relationship among women, rape, and racial violence in the South, see J. D. Hall, "'The Mind That Burns in Each Body': Women, Rape, and Racial Violence," *Southern Exposure* 12, no. 6 (1984): 61–71.

80. Charges and specifications against 1st Lt. James S. Matthews, 3d U.S. Col. Cav., filed with M-175, 1863; W. D. McInden to Stanton, Feb. 19, 1866, W-12, 1863; both Letters Received, ser. 360, CTD, RG 94.

81. General Orders No. 76, Hd. Qtrs., Dept. of the Gulf, P-157, 1863, Letters Received, ser. 360, CTD, RG 94.

82. Malone, *Sweet Chariot,* 221.

83. List of U.S. Soldiers Executed by United States Military Authorities during the Late War, 5981-A-85, Letters Received, ser. 409, Enlistment Branch, RG 94; *Christian Recorder,* Aug. 6, 1864.

84. Chaplain A. Randall to Brig. Gen. L. Thomas, Feb. 28, 1865, R-189, 1865, Letters Received, ser. 12, RG 94.

85. *Christian Recorder,* Apr. 22, 1865. For a discussion on the black soldiers' entry into Richmond, see Litwack, *Been in the Storm So Long,* 167–70. Leon Litwack argues that black soldiers were deliberately prevented from becoming the first Union troops

to enter the rebel capital. However, he claims that they did help to free slaves from the Richmond slave pens.

EPILOGUE

1. Brig. Gen. Edward Ferrero's Fourth (Colored) Division, consisting of two brigades and numbering 43,000 men, was part of Maj. Gen. Ambrose Burnside's Ninth Corps. During June and July 1864, men from a regiment in the Ninth Corps, the 48th Pennsylvania Volunteers, tunneled under Confederate lines and filled the galleries they had dug with eight thousand pounds of gunpowder. Burnside's objective was to blow a breach in rebel defenses large enough for his divisions to pour through and capture Cemetery Hill. Once this strategic position was captured, it was envisaged, Gen. Robert E. Lee would be forced to abandon Petersburg and Richmond. Early in the morning of July 30, 1864, the explosive charge was detonated, and a huge crater was blown in the rebel lines. A combination of mismanagement, incompetent leadership, and resolute defense by the Confederate soldiers turned the Federal assault into a bloody defeat. Denied a promised opportunity to lead the attack, the Fourth Division fought bravely, suffering 1,269 casualties, including 436 killed or mortally wounded. Recent research by Bruce A. Suderow suggests that the rebel defenders massacred many black soldiers after they had surrendered or had been wounded. The Ninth Corps as a whole suffered 4,000 casualties. See Bryce A. Suderow, "The Battle of the Crater: The Civil War's Worst Massacre," *Civil War History* 43 (Sept. 1997): 219–24; McPherson, *Battle Cry of Freedom*, 758–60. The most comprehensive study of the Battle of the Crater is Michael A. Cavanaugh, William Marvel, *The Petersburg Campaign: The Battle of the Crater "the Horrible Pit," June 25–August 6, 1864*, Virginia Civil War Battles and Leaders Series (Lynchburg, Va.: H. E. Howard, 1989).

2. Berlin et al., *The Black Military Experience*, 733, 765; *OR*, ser. 3, vol. 5, 114, 138, 1029, 1047; James Herney's letter to "Secretary Stanten" is quoted in Berlin et al., *The Black Military Experience*, 778–79; Glatthaar, *Forged in Battle*, 234–35.

3. B. Benson and L. Kirstein, *Lay This Laurel*, pt. 6.

4. Emilio, *A Brave Black Regiment*, frontis., 84, see also 67–104; Burchard, *One Gallant Rush*, 1–2, 141; Quarles, *The Negro in the Civil War*, 15–16; Petitions, C. A. Fleetwood, Jan. 15, 1900, Pvt. C. H. Harrison, Jan. 8, 1900, in Supplemental Report of Chief of the Record and Pension Officer to the Secretary of War, in *Documents Relating to the Military and Naval Service of Blacks Awarded the Congressional Medal of Honor from the Civil War to the Spanish-American War*, National Archives (microfilm), M929, roll 1; Sgt. W. H. Carney to Col. M. S. Littlefield, Oct. 13, 1863, Exec. Dept. Letters, Letters Received, vol. 59, no. 53, Andrew Papers, CMSA.

APPENDIX A

1. Ludlow, ed., "Personal Memories," 507–8, WCL.
2. Chas. B. Fox, Extracts from Letters Written to Wife, vol. 3, back cover, MAHS.
3. *Free Military School Register*, HSP.
4. Ibid.
5. Ibid.

6. Ibid.

7. Ibid.

APPENDIX B

1. All songs from T. W. Higginson, *Army Life in a Black Regiment* (Boston: 1869), 199–221.

Bibliography

BIBLIOGRAPHICAL ESSAY ON PRIMARY SOURCES

In my study of camp life, I have examined a great variety of primary records. These records fall into two groups: official Union army records and private recollections. Official records include muster rolls, inspection reports, chaplaincy reports, military correspondence, orders books, and courts-martial proceedings. This vast array of official documents yields much useful information on the organization of camp life, though they contain all the defects of official documents, especially stylized form and standardized military vocabulary. However, if one reads the text carefully and searches diligently for the imprint of personality, cultural values emerge.

The official Union army war records of the black soldiers' military service are found principally in the Adjutant General's Office, Record Group 94, in the U.S. National Archives, Washington, D.C. Within this record group, the Colored Troops Division is the main source area. While Joseph B. Ross's *Tabular Analysis of the Records of the U.S. Colored Troops* gives the best brief account of the Colored Troops records, a study edited by Ira Berlin, Joseph P. Reidy, and Leslie S. Rowland, *Freedom: A Documentary History of Emancipation, 1861–1867*. Series 2, *The Black Military Experience*, provides the most comprehensive and critical evaluation of the National Archives' holdings of the black soldiers' records. Only one state, Massachusetts, holds relatively extensive records of black soldiers' military service. Many of these records are located in the Andrew Papers in the Commonwealth of Massachusetts State Archives.

The second group of records emanating from the camp are essentially personal interpretations of military experience. Included in this category are recollections, memoirs, regimental histories, monographs, and eulogies. Much of this material represents published records of achievement, personal celebrations of the glorious adventure of war. Beyond this relatively accessible material is a range of sources that are intensely personal. Letters to family and friends, diaries, journals, prayers, poems, and anecdotal scribblings form the main body of this reflective literature. These records enable us to penetrate the mind of the soldier and delineate his cultural world. Finally, there is that great body of witnesses that we may loosely classify as "outsiders," camp visitors and temporary residents. Although their presence in the camps was only transitory, their testimony was not inconsequential. Military personnel from outside the command, newspaper reporters, aid workers, Freedmen Bureau officials, Yankee "school marms," and hawkers were all attracted to camps, for a plethora of reasons. Each visitor gazed upon camp life from a different perspective. Studied in isolation, the testimonies of these visitors are anecdotal and fragmentary; when examined as a collective whole, they yield insights into the dynamics of camp life.

At this point something needs to be said about the inherent problems of using the primary record. The great bulk of it comes from Northern, white witnesses, and most of it reflects the white observers dominating military authority and literacy skills. Put simply, white officers' descriptions of camp life counted for far more than the narratives of the more numerous, but illiterate, soldiers. Of course, much of the officers' testimony is imbued with barbs of racism. The focus of these writings is primarily the officers' own wartime experiences. Many of these officers were acutely aware of their audience, and their testimony conveys the triumph of republican values through personal recollection.

Edwin Main's *Story of the Marches*, Col. Edward Bouton's *Events of the Civil War*, and Lt. Joseph Carliff's *Of the Service of the Seventh Regiment* are all typical studies that take up these themes. These officers sought to explain the deeper meanings of the national conflict by describing its impact on their own personal narratives. Their descriptions of soldiers' behavior are, at times, condescending. The private correspondence of the officers is also marked with elements of racial and cultural superiority. "It is as good as a play to watch them" during their prayer meetings, commented Lt. Col. John S. Bogert in a letter to his parents. Capt. Elliott F. Grabrill wrote home ridiculing the sexual morals of his men. There is nothing surprising about these attitudes, for the vast majority of officers who accepted assignments in U.S. Colored Troops regiments did so for career motives. They were not ardent racists intent on subjugating the soldiers serving under them; they were preoccupied with making the black a good soldier, nothing more. After all, their careers were inextricably linked to the performance of their men.

The testimony of one group of officers deserves special attention. Unlike their careerist comrades, a small but influential band of abolitionist officers attached themselves to black regiments primarily for ideological reasons. Committed to a creed of racial justice, these officers were intensely interested in the soldiers' military performance and leisure activities. Indeed, they were committed to using the Union army as a vehicle for the general elevation and edification of the ex-slave.

Abolitionist officers like Colonels Thomas Wentworth Higginson and James Beecher and Major John W. M. Appleton commented upon the social dimensions of soldiers' lives. They documented slave stories, songs, customs, and pastimes, along with such more routine military activities as weapon training and drill on the parade ground. Intensely proud of their own leadership, these officers produced records that largely validated their military experiences. Their commentaries, while rich in detail, are also culturally biased. In short, their record is tainted by the officers' unwavering faith in the presumed superiority of Northern cultural values and by their distorted images of plantation slave quarters. Black soldiers emerge from these records as victims who have to be rescued from the moral morass of slavery. Yet although imperfect witnesses, the abolitionist officers came closer to the black soldier than any other group of white observers. The bonds of genuine friendship that existed between Shaw, Higginson, and Beecher and their men, at times, transcended racial barriers. The records compiled by these empathetic allies cannot be simply dismissed as the rhetoric of zealots; when read with care and understanding, they yield rich veins of information on even the most personal aspects of the soldiers' lives.

Finally, and most important, there are the records generated by the soldiers and camp workers. These descriptions of camp life are not as numerous as those generated by the officers. Two factors account for this—the illiteracy of the former slaves and the long hours of routine labor and drill imposed on them. The written testimony of the blacks may be divided into two major groups. One group of writers held the pen firmly, scratching simple but profound messages of freedom on the blank page. These were the semiliterate ex-slave soldiers who had largely acquired their literary skills either clandestinely on the plantation or in the army. The second group wrote freely, in literary styles that were almost as good as those of their commanding officers. These free Northern black soldiers, among them, produced a rich and abundant record of life in the Union army camp.

Unlike the literate officers who commanded them, the ex-slave soldiers had little time for written reflection. Theirs was essentially an oral tradition; they passed on knowledge by song, story, or prayer. However, service in the Union army offered the slave an opportunity to acquire numeracy and literacy skills; in the slave's mind, freedom and literacy were inextricably linked. Possession of one seemed to lead inevitably to possession of the other. Why else would their masters have denied them even a rudimentary education? Not surprising, as slaves the soldiers had had a great thirst for "knowledge" and "book learning"; this thirst continued unabated in the army. By the light of the campfire, they poured over simple primers in order to become acquainted with knowledge and skills that had been so long denied them.

Therefore, the written records generated by these diligent scholars were essentially artifacts of freedom. Although relatively few in number, they point poignantly to the soldiers' heritage of bondage and to their aspirations to citizenship. Given their close association of literacy with freedom, it is not surprising to find that much of the written testimony of the ex-slave soldiers was generated by incidents that threatened their status as free men—a record of protestation and affirmation. Within the bulk of Bureau of Colored Troops records are numerous letters, petitions, and grievances protesting excessive fatigue duty, inequitable pay, curtailment of religious freedoms, and the imposition of servile modes of punishment and discipline. Even if the expression is weak and the handwriting a smudged scrawl, the emotional intent is strong, and the affirmation of freedom is very clear.

"I drop thes fewlines [few lines] asking fer Jested [Justice]," wrote bugler David Washington to President Abraham Lincoln. Hoping to overturn a sentence of a year's imprisonment for desertion, Washington unsuccessfully pleaded cruel victimization by his captain: "I ought not to be in prson if I had Jested done to me." Washington was seemingly in a powerless position; "I have no education I dont know nothing at all abought law." However, his low level of education and his ignorance of the law did not prevent this Southern ex-slave soldier from asserting his rights and appealing to the commander in chief of the U.S. military forces.

Another group of black witnesses produced a fragmentary and anecdotal record. Cooks, officers' servants, nurses, laundresses, and drivers were in a transitory civilian workforce. These camp workers stood, vocationally, between the officers and the enlisted men; they ministered to the needs of both. Camp layouts generally reflected their intermediate status. In the camp of the 55th Massachusetts Volunteers, the officers' servants were located between the officers' tents and the company streets. Socially, however, the workers owed their loyalties to the enlisted men. Some were, in fact, bound to the soldiers by kinship. The civilian workers left only meager records, partly because they lacked official military standard and also because they were largely illiterate.

If the first group of soldiers was only semiliterate, the second group of soldiers—the free Northern blacks—generated fairly comprehensive accounts of their military experiences. Although not nearly as extensive as those of the white officers, the free Northern blacks' records covered a similar range of literary forms. These soldiers produced diaries, journals, personal letters, and newspaper correspondence while in the field, as well as reflective records such as autobiographies, histories, and monographs in the postwar period. During the course of the war, Pvt. Robert Fizgerald kept his diary during Grant's Virginia campaign; Chaplain Henry Turner and Cpl. James H. Gooding wrote extensive newspaper copy for, respectively, the *Christian Recorder* and the *Mercury*. After the war, Alexander Newton published his Civil War memoir, *Out of the Briars;* and George W. Williams and Joseph T. Wilson wrote comprehensive histories of the black soldiers' military service.

Although often found in the same archival location, the Northern black soldiers' commentaries on camp life are much richer and more varied than those produced by the Southern ex-slave soldiers in the Union army. In part, this situation derived from their superior educational status. Yet there was much more at work than this. Like their brothers from the plantation, these soldiers generated a body of polemic against violations of their rights and freedoms; they were translators and publicists as well. They wrote extensively for a civilian readership. They interpreted the conflict for loved ones at home, and they publicized the significance of the black soldier's military experience in newspapers.

During the war, this public interpretative function was less important for the Southern ex-slave soldiers, largely because they were poorly educated, lacked a receptive readership in the South, and had little access to Northern black communities and Northern newspaper and book publishers who could have promoted their stories. The extensive proliferation of the Northern soldiers' rich record has, to some extent, obscured the meager and fragmentary but no less important record of the Southern ex-slaves. Obviously both must be carefully examined if the soldiers' military experience is to be accurately assessed.

In spite of this, the differences between the Northern and Southern soldiers must not be exaggerated. Bonds of racial solidarity were much stronger than cultural differences. Indeed, many Northern soldiers, such as Sergeants James Trotter and Alexander Newton, were "Northern" in name only. Before they had fled north to freedom, they too had experienced the cruelty of slavery. Slavery had left an indelible mark on almost all black soldiers, and their commentaries of camp life and military service bear testimony to this searing experience. Moreover, all soldiers, whether Northern or Southern, suffered from racial prejudice. The written records of the black soldiers clearly document the fact that in the eyes of many officers and civilians the soldiers remained "niggers." Racial attitudes changed, but for the black soldiers the change was painfully slow.

PRIMARY SOURCES

MANUSCRIPTS: NATIONAL ARCHIVES, WASHINGTON, D.C.
Record Group 94: Adjutant General's Office
General Records of the Adjutant General's Office:
  Series 9: Letters and Telegrams sent by L. Thomas, Adjutant General, 1863
  Series 12: Letters Received. Included in these records are the monthly chaplaincy reports sent to the adjutant general of the U.S. Army and the testimony and reports of the American Freedmen Inquiry Commission.
Regimental Books and Papers USCT and U.S. Volunteer Organizations
Inspection Reports
Series 159: Generals' Papers and Books
Series 160: Generals' Reports of Service
Records of Divisions of the Adjutant General's Office:
  Colored Troops Division
    Series 360: Letters Received 1863–88 and later
    Series 363: Letters Received by Adjutant General L.Thomas 1863–65
    Series 366: Letters Received Relating to Recruiting
    Series 370: Applications for Appointments 1863–65
    Series 383: Proceedings of Examining Board, Cincinnati, Ohio, 1863–64
    Series 384: Proceedings of Examining Board, St Louis, Mo., 1863–65
    Series 390: The Negro in the Military Service of the United States, 1639–1886
  Enlisted Branch
    Series 409: Letters Received 1862–December 1889
Records of the Record and Pension Office:
  Series 519: Carded Records, Volunteer Organizations: Civil War
Records of the War Records Office:
  Series 729: Union Battle Reports, 1861–65
Other Records: U.S. Christian Commission, 1861–66:
  Series 755: Weekly Reports of Delegates
  Series 757: Diaries 1862–65
  Series 791: Scrapbooks 1862–65
Record Group 153: Records of the Office of the Judge Advocate (Army)
  Series 15: Court-Martial Files

MANUSCRIPTS: OTHER COLLECTIONS
American Antiquarian Society, Worcester, Massachusetts
  Thomas Wentworth Higginson Papers
Atlanta University Library, Atlanta, Georgia
  John W. Phelps Papers, Henry P. Slaughter Collection

Chicago Historical Society, Chicago, Illinois
    Arnold T. Needham Papers
    William H. Ross Papers
Commonwealth of Massachusetts State Archives, Boston
    Exec. Dept. Letters, Letters Received, Andrew Papers
    Official Letters, Letters Sent, Andrew Papers
Connecticut Historical Society, Hartford
    Henry Harrison Brown Papers
    Joseph Cross Letters
Dartmouth College Library, Hanover, New Hampshire
    Joseph M. Clough Papers, typescript
    Claude Goings Civil War Papers, typescript
    Elias C. Mather Civil War Papers
    Albert M. Putnam Papers, typescript
    William H. Thayer Papers, typescript
Detroit Public Library, Detroit, Michigan
    Frank E. Lansing Papers
Duke University Library, Durham, North Carolina
    John Snider Cooper Papers
    Frederick Cutler and Sarah (Munroe) Cutler Papers
    Joseph N. Hayes Papers
    Edward Wilkinson Kinsley Papers
    James Otis Moore Papers
    Alonzo Reed Letters
    Harvey F. Taft Papers
    Henry J. Thompson Papers
    United States Army Orders
Emory University Library, Atlanta, Georgia
    Alfred M. Brigham Letters
    Henry M. Crydenwise Letters
    William M. Parkinson Letters
    Charles B. Thurston Papers
      Union Miscellany Collection
        Ephraim L. Girdner Papers, microfilm
Harvard University Library, Cambridge, Massachusetts
    Thomas Wentworth Higginson Journal
Henry E. Huntington Library, San Marino, California
    George W. Buswell Journal
    Abraham B. Dalton Letter
Historical Society of Pennsylvania, Philadelphia
    Free Military School Register
Howard University Library, Washington, D.C.
    Pickney B. S. Pinchback Papers
Illinois State Historical Society Library, Springfield
    Thomas B. Borne Papers

Humphrey H. Hood Papers
August V. Kautz Papers, typescript
Henry M. Newhall Papers
John D. Strong Papers
Indiana Historical Society Library, Indianapolis
Chapin Family Papers, microfilm
John H. Ferree Papers
George W. Grubb Diary, typescript
Kinder Papers
Andrew J. McGarrah Papers
Caleb Mills Papers
Charles W. Smith Civil War Letters
Julietta Starbuck Papers, microfilm
William R. Stuckey Papers
Wayne County Manuscripts, Civil War Collection no. 9
Stephen A. Miller Letters, microfilm
Kansas State Historical Society, Topeka
John R. Graton Papers, microfilm
James Montgomery Papers
Private Papers of Charles and Sara T. D. Robinson, microfilm
George L. Stearns Papers, microfilm
James M. Williams Papers
Library of Congress, Washington, D.C.
Nathaniel P. Banks Papers
Samuel D. Barnes Diary
Benjamin F. Butler Papers
Frederick Douglass Papers
Christian A. Fleetwood Papers
J. M. and Esther Hawks Papers
Low-Mills Family Collection
George H. Putnam Letters
MMC Collection
George O. Jewett Papers
George W. Morgan Memoirs
William W. Wright Papers
Massachusetts Historical Society, Boston
John A. Andrew Papers
Edward Atkinson Papers
Fifty-Fourth Massachusetts Volunteers Papers
Chas. B. Fox, Extracts from Letters Written to Wife
Warren Goodale Papers
Norwood P. Hallowell Papers
Edward W. Kinsley Papers
Amos A. Lawrence Papers
Horace Mann III Papers

Norcross Papers
Robert G. Shaw Papers
Minnesota Historical Society, St. Paul
Christopher C. Andrews Papers
James M. Bowler Family Papers
James Christie Family Papers
Benjamin Densmore Family Papers
William H. C. Folson Family Papers
Henry N. Herrick Family Papers
Thomas Montgomery Papers, microfilm
James Peet Family Papers
William W. Pendergast Family Papers
Palemon J. Smalley, Dad's Memoirs, typescript
Charles H. Watson Papers
New England Historic Genealogical Society, Boston
Accounts and History of the First Kansas Colored Volunteer Regiment, 1863–65
Etham Earle, Kansas Colored Volunteer Regiment, 1st Roll, Accounts and History of the First Kansas Colored Volunteer Regiment, 1863–65
New York Historical Society, New York
William H. Aldis Papers
George Bliss Autobiography, typescript
Miscellaneous Collection
Howard C. Wright Letters
Porter Chandler Papers
Charles Wadsworth Correspondence
Robert F. Wilkinson Letters
Daniel Ullmann Papers
New York Public Library, New York City, New York
John W. Phelps Papers
Cabot J. Russell Papers
United States Army Collection, 1863
Eben T. Colby Letters
United States Sanitary Commission Files
Oberlin College Archives, Oberlin, Ohio
Elliott F. Grabill Papers
Giles W. Shurtleff Papers
Ohio Historical Society, Columbus
Albert Rogall Diary, typescript
Radcliffe College Library, Cambridge, Massachusetts
James C. Beecher Family Papers
Beecher-Stowe Papers, microfilm
Albert G. Browne Family Papers
Rhode Island Historical Society, Providence
Hagadorn-Wells Collection
Amos Potter Wells Letters

Nelson Viall, "A Brief History of the 14th R.I. Regiment Colored 1863–65"
Rutgers University Library, New Brunswick, New Jersey
  Henry Whitney Diary
Stanford University Library, Stanford, California
  Edward Martindale Papers
  William R. Shafter Papers
State Historical Society of North Dakota, Bismark
  John W. Burnham Papers
State Historical Society of Wisconsin, Madison
  Frank D. Harding Papers
  Harrison Family Papers
    Samuel A. Harrison Letters
  Thomas S. Johnson Papers
  John Knaus Letters
  James Peet Diary
Syracuse University Library, Syracuse, New York
  John A. Bogert Papers
Texas Tech University, Lubbock
  Southwest Collection
    Austin Wiswall Papers
U.S. Army Military History Institute, Carlisle Barracks, Pennsylvania
  Bailey-Stroud Papers
  Civil War Miscellaneous Collection
    John B. Wilson Letters
  Civil War Round Table Collection
    Harvey J. Covell Letters
  Civil War Times Illustrated Collection
    Joseph G. Hamlin Letters
    Joseph Scroggs Diary, typescript
    William Seagrave Diary
    Eben Sturges Letters
    Benjamin W. Thompson, Personal Narrative, typescript
  Rudolph Haerle Collection
    Samuel W. Campbell Diary
  Earl M. Hess Collection
    John C. Haskhuser Letters
  August V. Kautz Papers
  MOLLUS, Massachusetts Commandery Collection
    Seth Rogers, "War-Time Letters of Seth Rogers, M.D. Surgeon of the First South
      Carolina, Afterwards the Thirty-Third usct, 1862–1863," typescript
    Henry Rust Jr. Diary
    Edward A. Wild Papers
    William Winkelman Papers
University of Iowa Library, Iowa City
  Mead Family Papers

University of Michigan, Ann Arbor
   Michigan Historical Collection
   Calvin Ainsworth Diary
   William Baird Diary
   William Boston Diary
   William C. Caldwell Papers
   Orlando Carpenter Diary, typescript
   William L. Clements Library
   Ferdinand Davis Reminiscences
   William M. Ferry Papers
   Jenny Fyfe Papers
   Phineas A. Hagar Papers
   Francis E. Hall Papers
   Morris S. Hall Papers
   Charles B. Haydon Diary
   Byron Mac. Cutcheon Reminiscences
   Wayne E. Morris Papers
   Charles H. Moulton Papers
   Ness Collection
      Judson L. Austin Papers
   George T. Shaffer Papers
   Harrison Soule Papers
   Edward H. C. Taylor Papers
   Edward M. Watson Papers
   John Weissert Papers
   C. Butler Collection
      Charles Horace Papers
   William H. Withington Papers
      Wash Vosburgh Papers
      Phineas Collection
         William H. White Papers
      Schoff Civil War Collection
         Henry G. Marshall Papers
      Weissert Collection
      Jerome Bussey Papers
University of Missouri, Columbia
   Alley-Brewer Family Papers
   F. F. and Harriet E. Audsley Civil War Letters
   Odon Guitar Papers
   John G. Hudson Papers, microfilm
      Western Historical Collection
University of North Carolina, Chapel Hill
   Southern Historical Collection
   Silas E. Fables Papers
   Fitzgerald Family Collection

Robert G. Fitzgerald Diary, microfilm
Thomas D. Howard, Charles Howard Family Domestic History, typescript
Lewis J. Whitaker Papers
University of South Carolina, Columbia
South Caroliniana Library
John S. Bogert Letters
Alice Boozer Papers
B. Hood Letters
Charles F. Lee Letters
R. Saxton, To the Colored Soldiers and Freedmen
Edward M. Stoeber Papers
United States Army Papers, Department of the South
University of Texas at Austin Library
Obadiah M. Knapp Papers
Vermont Historical Society, Montpelier
Rufus Kinsley Diary
West Virginia University Library, Morgantown
J. W. M. Appleton Letter Book, microfilm
Williams College Library, Williamstown, Massachusetts
Williamsiana Collection
Armstrong Collection
Samuel C. Armstrong Family Papers
Yale University Library, New Haven, Connecticut
Lomis-Wilder Family Collection
John August Wilder-Todd Family Papers
Lewis Weld Family Papers

FEDERAL GOVERNMENT PUBLICATIONS

The Statutes at Large, Treaties, and Proclamations of the United States of America, vol. 12.
    Boston: Little, Brown, 1863.
U.S. Adjutant General's Office. *Official Register of the Volunteer Force of the United States
    Army for the Years 1861–65*, 8 pts. Washington, D.C.: 1865–67, pt 8.
[U.S. Commission for United States Colored Troops]. *Orders Relating to Colored Men
    and Colored Troops*. Nashville, Tenn., 1863.
U.S. Congress. *Report of the Joint Committee on the Conduct of the War*, 38th Cong., 2
    sess., no. 1.
———. *House Reports*, 38th Cong., 1st sess., no. 63.
———. *Senate Reports*, 38th Cong., 1st sess., no. 65.
U.S. War Department. *Revised United States Army Regulations*. Washington, D.C., 1863.
———. *The War of the Rebellion: A Compilation of the Official Records of the Union and
    Confederate Armies*, 128 vols. Washington, D.C.: GPO, 1880–1901.

JOURNALS AND NEWSPAPERS

Army and Navy Journal, 1865
Atlantic Monthly, 1861–65
Christian Recorder, 1862–65
Commonwealth, 1863–65
Douglass' Monthly, 1862–65
Harper's Weekly Magazine, 1861–65
Liberator, 1862–65
National Anti-Slavery Standard, 1862–65
National Tribune, 1899
New York Evening Post, 1862–65
North American Review, 1863–65
Union, 1863–64
Weekly Anglo-African, 1863–65

ARTICLES IN JOURNALS, MAGAZINES, AND HISTORICAL PROCEEDINGS

Abramowitz, Jack. "A Civil War Letter: James M. Trotter to Francis J. Garrison." *Midwest Journal* 4 (1952): 113–22.

Appleton, John W. "That Night at Fort Wagner by One Who Was There." *Putnam's Magazine of Literature, Science, Art and National Interest* 4 (July 1869): 9–16.

Blackburn, George M., ed. "The Negro as Viewed by a Michigan Civil War Soldier: Letters of John C. Buchanan." *Michigan History* 47 (1963): 75–84.

Bowley, Freeman, S. "A Dark Night on Picket." *Overland Monthly and Out West Magazine* 5 (July 1870): 31–37.

[Duren, Charles M.]. "The Occupation of Jacksonville, February 1864 and the Battle of Olustee. Letters of Lt. C. M. Duren, 54th Massachusetts Regiment, U.S.A." *Florida Historical Quarterly* 32 (1953/54): 262–87.

Ellis, Richard N., ed. "The Civil War Letters of an Iowa Family." *Annals of Iowa* 39 (1969): 561–86.

Gannett, William C. "The Freedmen at Port Royal." *North American Review* 101 (July 1865): 1–28.

[Gannett, William C., and Edward E. Hale]. "The Education of the Freedmen." *North American Review* 101 (October 1865): 529–49.

Harwell, Richard B., ed. "Edgar Dinsmore Letters." *Journal of Negro History* 25 (1940): 363–71.

Haygood, Johnson. "Letter to Thomas Wentworth Higginson, dated Columbia, South Carolina, September 21, 1881 on the burial of Col. Robert G. Shaw, at Battery Wagner, 19 July 1863." *Massachusetts Historical Society Proceedings* 47 (1914): 341–43.

Hayne, Paul H. "The Defence of Fort Wagner." *Southern Bivouac* (February 1886): 599–608.

Higginson, Thomas W. "Physical Courage." *Atlantic Monthly* 2 (November 1858): 728–37.

———. "Barbarism and Civilization." *Atlantic Monthly* 7 (January 1861): 51–61.

————. "The Ordeal by Battle." *Atlantic Monthly* 8 (July 1861): 88–95.

————. "Regular and Volunteer Officers." *Atlantic Monthly* 14 (September 1864): 348–57.

————. "Fair Play the Best Policy." *Atlantic Monthly* 15 (May 1865): 623–31.

————. "Our Future Militia System." *Atlantic Monthly* 16 (September 1865): 371–78.

————. "Colored Troops under Fire." *Century Magazine* 54 (May 1897): 194–200.

Hodges, Almon D., Jr. "James Swift Rogers." *New England Register* 60 (January 1906): 11–15.

Hunt, Sanford B. "The Negro as a Soldier." *Anthropological Review* 7 (January 1869): 40–54.

"Is this Lt. John Campbell's Letter?" *Annals of Iowa* 39 (1969): 542–45.

Johnson, Mary E., ed. "Letters from a Civil War Chaplain." *Journal of Presbyterian History* 46 (1968): 219–35.

Kilmer, George L. "The Dash into the Crater." *Century Magazine* 12 (September 1887): 774–76.

Levstik, Frank R., ed. "From Slavery to Freedom: Two Wartime Letters of One of the Conflicts' Few Black Medal Winners." *Civil War Times Illustrated* 11 (1972): 10–15.

Montgomery, Horace. "A Union Officer's Recollections of the Negro as a Soldier." *Pennsylvania History* 28 (1961): 156–86.

Perkins, Frances B. "Two Years with a Colored Regiment: A Woman's Experience." *New England Magazine* 17 (January 1898): 533–43.

Pierce, Edward L. "Contrabands at Fortress Munroe." *Atlantic Monthly* 8 (November 1861): 626–40.

————. "The Freedmen at Port Royal." *Atlantic Monthly* 12 (September 1863): 291–315.

Root, L. Carroll, ed. "Private Journal of William H. Root, Second Lieutenant Seventy-Fifth New York Volunteers, April 6–June 14, 1863." *Louisiana Historical Quarterly* 19 (July 1936): 365–67.

[Shaw, Robert G.]. "Letters from Camp Written by Robert Gould Shaw." *Magazine of History* 18 (1914): 104–10, 226–31.

————. "How Colonel Shaw Fell." *Magazine of History* 19 (1914): 25–31.

Straudenraus, P. J., ed. "Occupied Beaufort, 1863: A War Correspondent's View." *South Carolina Historical Magazine* 64 (1963) 136–45.

Thomas, Henry G. "The Colored Troops at Petersburg." *Century Magazine* 12 (September 1887): 777–82.

Wilder, Burt G. "Two Examples of the Negro's Courage, Physical and Moral." *Alexander's Magazine* (January 1906): 23–26.

MOLLUS PUBLICATIONS

Abbott, Abial, R. "The Negro in the Rebellion." In Illinois Commandery, *Military Essays and Recollections*, vol. 3. Chicago: Dial Press, 1899.

Armstrong, William H. "The Negro as a Soldier." In Indiana Commandery, *War Papers*. Indianapolis: Indiana Commandery, 1898.

Bangs, I. S. "The Ullmann Brigade." In Maine Commandery, *War Papers*, vol. 2. Portland, 1902.

Bissell, J. W. "The Western Organization of Colored People for Furnishing Information to United States Troops in the South." In Minnesota Commandery, *Glimpses of the Nation's Struggle,* series 2. St. Paul: St. Paul Book and Stationery, 1890.

Carter, Selden. "The Colored Troops." In Maine Commandery, *War Papers,* vol. 3. Portland: Lefavor, 1908.

Carter, Solon. "Fourteen Months Service with Colored Troops." In Massachusetts Commandery, *Civil War Papers,* vol. 1. Boston: Massachusetts Commandery, 1900.

Freeman, Henry V. "A Colored Brigade in the Campaign and Battle of Nashville." In Illinois Commandery, *Military Essays and Recollections,* vol. 2. Chicago: A. C. McClury, 1894.

Hall, Henry Seymour. "Mine Run to Petersburg." In *Kansas Commandery: War Talks in Kansas.* Kansas City, Kansas: Franklin Hudson, 1906.

Higginson, Thomas Wentworth. "The Re-occupation of Jacksonville in 1863." In Massachusetts Commandery, *Civil War Papers,* vol. 1. Boston: Massachusetts Commandery, 1900.

James, Garth W. "The Assault on Fort Wagner." In Wisconsin Commandery, *War Papers,* vol. 1. Milwaukee: Burdick, Armitage, and Allen, 1891.

Matson, Daniel. "The Colored Man in the Civil War." In Iowa Commandery, *War Sketches and Incidents,* vol. 2. Des Moines: Kenyon Press, 1898.

Norton, Henry A. "Colored Troops in the War of the Rebellion." In Minnesota Commandery, *Glimpses of the Nation's Struggle,* vol. 5. St. Paul: Review, 1903.

Powell, Edward H. "The Colored Soldier in the War of Rebellion." In Vermont Commandery, *War Papers,* vol. 3. Montpelier: Vermont Commandery, 1893.

Smith, Charles W. "Light and Shadows: A Sketch of Five Sundays." In Indiana Commandery, *War Papers.* Indianapolis: Indiana Commandery, 1898.

Sutherland, George E. "The Negro in the Late War." In Wisconsin Commandery, *War Papers,* vol. 1. Milwaukee: Burdick, Armitage, and Allen, 1891.

REUNION SOCIETY OF VERMONT OFFICERS' PROCEEDINGS

Gould, Joseph H. "Col. Goulding's Address: The Colored Troops in the War of Rebellion." In *Reunion Society of Vermont Officers' Proceedings,* vol. 2, 1885–1917, 137–54.

RHODE ISLAND SOLDIERS AND SAILORS HISTORICAL SOCIETY

Addeman, J. M. "Reminiscences of Two Years with the Colored Troops." series 2, no. 7, Providence, R.I., 1880.

Egan, Patrick. "The Florida Campaign with the Light Battery C, Third Rhode Island Heavy Artillery." series 6, no. 10, Providence, R.I., 1905.

Morgan, Thomas J. "Reminiscences of Service with Colored Troops in the Army of the Cumberland 1863–1865." series 3, no. 13, Providence, R.I., 1887.

Personal Narratives of Events in the War of Rebellion, Being Papers Read before the Rhode Island Soldiers and Sailors Historical Society, Providence, R.I., 1880–1905.

Rickard, James H. "Services with Colored Troops in Burnside's Corps." series 5, no. 1, Providence, R.I., 1894.

Shaw, James. "Our Last Campaign and Subsequent Service in Texas." series 6, no. 9, Providence, R.I., 1903.

Sherman, George R. "The Negro as a Soldier." series 7, no. 7, Providence, R.I., 1905.

PUBLISHED DIARIES, MEMOIRS, AUTOBIOGRAPHIES, TRAVEL ACCOUNTS, DOCUMENTS, LETTERS, AND PAMPHLETS

Adams, Charles, F., Jr. *Charles Francis Adams 1835–1915: An Autobiography, with a Memorial Address delivered November 17, 1915 by Henry Cabot Lodge.* Boston: Massachusetts Historical Society, 1916.

Adams, Julius W. *Letter to the Honorable Secretary of War, On the Examination of Field Officers for Colored Troops: Enclosed in a Letter to the Officers of the Army of the Potomac.* 2d ed. New York: privately published, 1863.

Adams, Virginia M. *On the Altar of Freedom: A Black Soldier's Civil War Letters from the Front—Corporal James Henry Gooding.* Amherst: Univ. of Massachusetts Press, 1991.

Allen, William Francis, Charles Pickard Ware, and Lucy McKim Garrison. *Slave Songs of the United States.* 1867; reprint, New York: Peter Smith, 1951.

"An officer of the Ninth Corps." *Notes on Colored Troops and Military Colonies on Southern Soil.* New York, 1863.

Andrews, Christopher C. *History of the Campaign of Mobile: Including the Co-operative Operations of Gen. Wilson's Cavalry in Alabama.* New York: D. Van Nostrand, 1889.

Babcock, Willoughby M., Jr. *Selections from the Letters and Diaries of Brevet-Brigadier General Willoughby Babcock of the Seventy-Fifth New York Volunteers: A Study of Camp Life in the Union Armies during the Civil War.* New York: Univ. of the State of New York, 1922.

Baird, George W. *The Thirty-Second Regiment U.S.C.T. at the Battle of Honey Hill.* [Boston], 1889.

Basler, Roy P., ed. *The Collected Works of Abraham Lincoln.* 9 vols. New Brunswick, N.J.: Rutgers Univ. Press, 1953–55.

Baxter, James H. *Statistics Medical and Anthropological of the Provost-Marshal-General's Bureau, Derived from Records of the Examination for Military Service in the Armies of the United States during the Late War of the Rebellion, of over a Million Recruits, Drafted Men, Substitutes and Enrolled Men, Conscripted under the Direction of the Secretary of War.* 2 vols. Washington, D.C.: GPO, 1875.

Beale, Howard K., ed. *The Diary of Edward Bates 1859–1866.* New York: Da Capo Press, 1971.

Beatty, John. *Memoirs of a Volunteer 1861–1863.* New York: W. W. Norton, 1946.

Berlin, Ira, Joseph P. Reidy, and Leslie S. Rowland, eds. *Freedom: A Documentary History of Emancipation, 1861–1867.* Series 2, *The Black Military Experience.* Cambridge: Cambridge Univ. Press, 1982.

Berlin, Ira, Barbara J. Fields, Steven F. Miller, Joseph P. Reidy, and Leslie S. Rowland, eds. *Free at Last: A Documentary History of Slavery, Freedom, and the Civil War.* New York: New Press, 1992.

Berlin, Ira, and Leslie S. Rowland, eds. *Families and Freedom: A Documentary History of African-American Kinship in the Civil War Era*. New York: New Press, 1997.

Bingham, Luther G. *The Young Quartermaster: The Life and Death of Lieut. L. M. Bingham, of the First South Carolina Volunteers*. New York: Board of Publication of the Reformed Protestant Dutch Church, 1863.

Birney, William. *General William Birney's Answer to Libels Clandestinely Circulated by James Shaw Jr., Collector of the Port, Providence R.I., with a Review of the Military Record of the said James Shaw Jr., Late Colonel of the Seventh U.S. Colored Troops*. Washington, D.C.: Stanley Snodgrass, 1878.

Blackett, R. J. M., ed. *Thomas Morris Chester, Black Civil War Correspondent: His Dispatches from the Virginia Front*. New York: Da Capo Press, 1991.

Blake, Sarah S. W. *Diaries and Letters of Francis Minton Weld M.D. with a Sketch of his Life and a Brief History and Genealogy of the Family of Weld*. Boston: privately published, 1925.

Boney, F. N., ed. *A Union Soldier in the Land of the Vanquished: The Diary of Sergeant Matthew Woodruff, June–December 1865*. Tuscaloosa: Univ. of Alabama Press, 1969.

Bossom, Charles P. *History of the Forty-Second Massachusetts Volunteers*. Boston: Mills, Knight, 1886.

Bouton, Edward. *Events of the Civil War*. Los Angeles: Kingsley, Moles, and Collins, 1906.

Bowley, Freeman S. *A Boy Lieutenant*. Philadelphia: Henry Altemus, 1906.

Briggs, W. DeBlois. *Civil War Surgeon in a Colored Regiment*. Berkeley, Calif.: privately published, 1908.

Brown, William W. *The Negro in the American Rebellion*. Boston: Lee and Shephard, 1867.

Browne, Frederick W. *My Service in the U.S. Colored Cavalry*. N.p.: privately published, 1908.

Butler, Benjamin F. *Butler at Home*. N.p.: n.d.

Butler's Book: Autobiography and Personal Reminiscences of Major General Benjamin F. Butler. Boston: A. M. Thayer, 1892.

Byrne, Frank L., ed. *The View from Headquarters: Civil War Letters of Harvey Reid*. Madison: State Historical Society of Wisconsin, 1965.

[Carliff, Joseph M.]. By an Officer of the Regiment. *Of the Service of the Seventh Regiment, U.S. Colored Troops, from September, 1863 to November, 1866*. Providence, R.I.: E. L. Freeman, 1878.

[Casey, Silas]. U.S. War Department, *U.S. Infantry Tactics, for . . . the Use of Colored Troops*. New York: D. Van Nostrand, 1863.

Chenery, William H. *The Fourteenth Rhode Island Heavy Artillery (Colored) in the War to Preserve the Union 1861–1865*. New York: Snow and Farnham, 1898.

Chetlain, Augustus L. *Recollections of Seventy Years*. Galena, Ill.: Gazette Publishing Co., 1899.

Cowden, Robert. *A Brief Sketch of the Organization and Services of the Fifty-Ninth Regiment of United States Colored Infantry, and Biographical Sketches*. Dayton, Ohio: United Brethren Publishing House, 1883.

Dana, Charles A. *Recollections of the Civil War*. New York: Collier Books, 1963.

Dennett, George M. *History of the Ninth U.S.C. Troops from Its Organization Till Mustered Out, with List of Names of All Officers and Enlisted Men, Who Have Ever Belonged to the Regiment, and Remarks Attached to Each Name, Noting All Changes, Such as Promotions, Transfers, Discharges, Deaths, etc.* Philadelphia: John A. Black, 1866.

Donald, David H., ed. *Gone for a Soldier: The Civil War Memoirs of Private Alfred Bellard.* Boston: Little, Brown, 1975.

Dow, Neal. *The Reminiscences of Neal Dow: Recollections of Eighty Years.* Portland, Me.: Evening Express, 1898.

Duncan, Russell, ed. *Blue-Eyed Child of Fortune: The Civil War Letters of Colonel Robert Gould Shaw.* Athens: Univ. Press of Georgia, 1992.

Eaton, John, Jr. *Grant, Lincoln and the Freedmen: Reminiscences of the Civil War with Special Reference to the Work for Contrabands and Freedmen of the Mississippi Valley.* New York: Longmans, Green, 1907.

Emerson, Edward W., ed. *Life and Letters of Charles Russell Lowell.* Boston: Houghton Mifflin, 1907.

Emerson, Ralph W. *Poems, Complete Works of Ralph Waldo Emerson.* Vol. 9. Boston: Houghton Mifflin, 1904.

Emilio, Luis F. *A Brave Black Regiment: The History of the Fifty-Fourth Massachusetts Volunteer Infantry 1863–1865.* Boston: Boston Book Company, 1894.

Fleetwood, Christian A. *The Negro as a Soldier.* Washington, D.C.: Howard Univ. Print, 1895.

Ford, Worthington C., ed. *A Cycle of Adams Letters, 1861–1865.* 2 vols. Boston: Houghton Mifflin, 1920.

[Fox, Charles B.]. *Record of the Service of the Fifty-Fifth Regiment of Massachusetts Volunteer Infantry.* Cambridge, Mass.: John Wilson and Sons, 1868.

Franklin, John H., ed. *The Diary of James T. Ayers Civil War Recruiter.* Springfield: Illinois State Historical Society, 1947.

Gould, Benjamin A. *Investigation in the Military and Anthropological Statistics of American Soldiers.* New York: Hurd and Haughton, 1869.

Grant, Ulysses S. *Personal Memories of U.S. Grant.* 2 vols. Hartford, Conn.: Charles L. Webster, 1885–1886.

Gray, John C., and John G. Ropes. *War Letters, 1862–1865.* Boston: Houghton Mifflin, 1927.

Greely, Adolphus W. *Reminiscences of Adventure and Service: A Record of Sixty-Five Years.* New York: Charles Scribner and Sons, 1927.

Gregg, John C. *Life in the Army in the Departments of Virginia, and the Gulf, including observations in New Orleans, with an Account of the Author's Life and Experience in the Ministry.* Philadelphia: Perkins, Pine and Higgins, 1868.

Halowell, Nathaniel P. *Selected Letters and Papers of N. P. Hallowell.* Peterborough, N.H.: privately published, 1896.

Halpine, Charles G. *Baked Meats of the Funeral: A Collection of Essays, Poems, Speeches, Histories and Banquets.* New York: New York Herald, 1866.

Hatch, Carl E., ed. *Dearest Susie: A Civil War Infantryman's Letters to His Sweetheart.* New York: Exposition Press, 1971.

Higginson, Mary T., ed. *Letters and Journals of Thomas Wentworth Higginson 1846–1906.* New York: Houghton Mifflin, 1921.

Higginson, Thomas W. *Army Life in a Black Regiment.* Williamstown, Mass.: Corner House, 1971.

————. *Black Rebellion: A Selection from Travellers and Outlaws*. New York: Arno Press, 1969.

————. *Part of a Man's Life*. Boston: Houghton Mifflin, 1905.

Hoffman, Wickham. *Camp Court and Siege: A Narrative of Personal Adventure and Observation during Two Wars, 1861–1865, 1870–1871*. London: Sampson Low, Marston, Searle, and Rivington, 1877.

Holland, Rupert S., ed. *Letters and Diary of Laura M. Towne: Written from the Sea Islands of South Carolina 1862–1884*. Cambridge, Mass.: Riverside Press, 1912.

Hosmer, James K. *The Color-Guard: Being a Corporal's Notes of Military Service in the Nineteenth Army Corps*. Boston: Walker, Wise, 1864.

Howe, Mark De Wolf, ed. *Touched with Fire: Civil War Diary of Oliver Wendell to Holmes Jr., 1861–1864*. Cambridge, Mass.: Harvard Univ. Press, 1946.

Johns, Henry T. *Life with the Forty-Ninth Massachusetts Volunteers*. Pittsfield, Mass.: Ramsey and Bisbee, 1890.

Johnson, Robert U., and Clarence C. Buel, eds. *Battles and Leaders of the Civil War*. 4 vols. New York: Century, 1887–88.

Katz, Bernard, ed. *The Social Implications of Early Negro Music in the United States*. New York: Arno Press, 1969.

Knox, Thomas W. *Camp-fire and Cotton-field: Southern Adventure in Time of War. Life with the Union Armies and Residence on a Louisiana Plantation*. New York: Blelock, 1865.

Langston, John M. *From the Virginia Plantation to the National Capital, Or the First and Only Negro Representative in Congress from the Old Dominion*. Hartford, Conn.: American, 1894.

Looby, Christopher, ed. *The Complete Civil War Journal and Selected Letters of Thomas Wentworth Higginson*. Chicago: Univ. of Chicago Press, 2000.

Main, Ed. M. *The Story of the Marches, Battles and Incidents of the Third United States Colored Cavalry. A Fighting Regiment in the War of the Rebellion 1861–65 with Official Orders and Reports Relating Thereto, Compiled from the Rebellion Records*. Louisville, Ky.: Globe, 1908.

Marshall, Jessie A., ed. *Correspondence of Gen. Benjamin F. Butler during the period of the Civil War*. 5 vols. Norwood, Mass.: Plimpton Press, 1917.

McKaye, James. *The Mastership and Its Fruits: The Emancipated Slave Face to Face with His Old Master. A Supplemental Report to Hon. Edwin M. Stanton, Secretary of War*. New York: Wm. C. Byrant, 1864.

McMurray, John, *Recollection of a Colored Troop*. [Brookville, Pa.]: privately published, 1916.

McPherson, James M., ed. *The Negro's Civil War: How American Negroes Felt and Acted during the War for the Union*. New York: Random House, 1965.

Mickley, Jeremiah M. *The Forty-Third Regiment United States Colored Troops*. Gettysburgh, Penn.: J. E. Wible, 1866.

Moore, Frank, ed. *The Rebellion Record: A Diary of American Events, with Documents, Narratives, Illustrative Incidents, Poetry, etc.* Vols. 1–12. New York: G. P. Putnam, 1861–71.

[New York] Union League Club. *Report of the Committee on Volunteering*. New York: Union League Club House, 1864.

Newton, Alexander H. *Out of the Briars: An Autobiography and Sketch of the Twenty-Ninth Regiment Connecticut Volunteers*. Philadelphia: A.M.E. Book Concern, 1910.

Norton, Oliver W. *Army Letters 1861–1865*. Chicago: O. L. Deming, 1903.

O'Reilly, Henry. *First Organization of Colored Troops in the State of New York to Aid in Suppressing the Slaveholders' Rebellion*. New York: Union League Club House, 1864.

Pearson, Elizabeth W., ed. *Letters from Port Royal Written at the Time of the Civil War*. Boston: W. B. Clarke, 1906.

Pearson, Henry O. *The Life of John A. Andrew, Governor of Massachusetts, 1861–1865*. 2 vols. Boston: Houghton Miffllin, 1904.

Quincy, Samuel M. *A Manual of Camp and Garrison Duty*. New Orleans, La.: Peter O'Donnell, 1865.

Redkey, Edwin S., ed. *A Grand Army of Black Men*. Cambridge, Mass.: Cambridge Univ. Press, 1993.

Romero, W., and W. L. Rose, eds. *A Black Woman's Civil War Memoirs*. New York: Wiener, 1988.

Sears, Cyrus. *The Battle of Milliken's Bend and Some Reflections Concerning the "Colored Troops," The Debt We Owe Them, and How We Paid It*. Columbus, Ohio: F. J. Heer, 1909.

Shannon, Fred A., ed. *The Civil War Letters of Sergeant Onley Andrus*. Urbana: Univ. of Illinois Press, 1947.

Shaw, Robert G. *RGS*. Cambridge: Harvard Univ. Press, 1864.

Smith, Lyman A. *A Tribute to a Beloved Son and Brother*. N.p.: privately published, 1864.

Stevens, William B. *History of the Fifteenth Regiment of Infantry Massachusetts Volunteer Militia in the Late War of the Rebellion*. Boston: Stillings Press, 1886.

Summers, O. "The Negro Soldiers in the Army of the Cumberland." In George W. Heer, *Episodes of the Civil War*. San Francisco: Bancroft, 1890.

Supervisory Committee for Recruiting Colored Regiments. *Free Military School for Applicants for Commands of Colored Troops*. Philadelphia: Supervisory Committee, 1863.

———. *Free Military School for Applicants for Commands of Colored Troops*. Philadelphia: Supervisory Committee, 1864.

Swint, Henry L. *Dear Ones at Home: Letters from Contraband Camps*. Nashville, Tenn.: Vanderbilt Univ. Press, 1966.

Tarbox, Increase N. *Missionary Patriots: Memoirs of James H. Schneider and Edward M. Schneider*. Boston: Massachusetts Sabbath School Society, 1867.

Taylor, Susie K. *Reminiscences of My Life in Camp with the 33d United States Colored Troops Late 1st S.C. Volunteers*. Boston: privately published, 1902.

Ullmann, Daniel. *Address by Daniel Ullmann, LL.D., before the Soldiers and Sailors' Union of the State of New York, on the Organization of Colored Troops and the Regeneration of the South, delivered at Albany, February 5, 1868*. Washington, D.C.: Great Republic Office, 1868.

U.S. Military School for Officers. *U.S. Military School for Officers Prospectus*. Philadelphia: U.S. Military School for Officers, 1865.

Van Alstyne, Lawrence. *Diary of an Enlisted Man*. New Haven, Conn.: Tuttle, Morehouse, and Taylor, 1910.

Vanderslice, Catherine H., ed. *The Civil War Letters of George Washington Beidelman*. New York: Vantage Press, 1978.

Weaver, C. P., ed. *Thank God My Regiment an African One: The Civil War Diary of Colonel Nathan W. Daniels*. Baton Rouge: Louisiana State Univ. Press, 1998.

Weber, John B. *Autobiography of John B. Weber*. Buffulo, N.Y.: J. W. Clement, 1924.

Wilder, Burt G. *The Fifty-Fifth Massachusetts Volunteer Infantry Colored, June, 1863–September 1865*. Brookline, Mass.: Riverside Press, 1919.

Williams, George W. *A History of the Negro Race in America from 1699–1880*. 2 vols. New York: G. P. Putnam, 1883.

———. *A History of the Negro Troops in the War of Rebellion, 1861–1865*. New York: Harper and Brothers, 1888.

Wilson, Joseph T. *The Black Phalanx: A History of the Negro Soldiers of the United States in the Wars of 1775–1812 and 1861–1865*. Hartford, Conn.: American, 1890.

Woodbury, Augustus. *Major General Ambrose E. Burnside and the Ninth Army Corps*. Providence, R.I.: S. S. Rider and Brother, 1867.

Yacovone, Donald, ed. *A Voice of Thunder: The Civil War Letters of George E. Stephens*. Urbana: Univ. of Illinois Press, 1997.

SECONDARY SOURCES

BOOKS

Alotta, Robert I. *Civil War Justice: Union Army Executions under Lincoln*. Shippensburg, Pa.: White Mane, 1989.

Angell, Stephen W. *Bishop Henry McNeil Turner and African-American Religion in the South*. Knoxville: Univ. of Tennessee Press, 1992.

Aptheker, Herbert. *The Negro in the Civil War*. New York: International Publishers, 1938.

Armstrong, Warren B. *For Courageous Fighting and Confident Dying: Union Chaplains in the Civil War*. Lawrence: Univ. Press of Kansas, 1998.

Bailey, P. *Leisure and Class in Victorian England: Rational Recreation and the Contest for Control, 1830–1885*. London: Routledge and Kegan Paul, 1978.

Belz, Herman. *Emancipation and Equal Rights: Politics and Constitutionalism in the Civil War Era*. New York: W. W. Norton, 1978.

Benson, B., and L. Kirstein. *Lay This Laurel: An Album on the Saint-Gaudens Memorial on Boston Common Honoring Black and White Men Together Who Served the Union Cause with Robert Gould Shaw and Died with Him July 18, 1863*. New York: Eakins Press, 1973.

Berlin, Ira. *Slaves without Masters: The Free Negro in the Antebellum South*. New York: Random House, 1974.

Berlin Ira, Barbara J. Fields, Steven F. Miller, Joseph P. Reidy, and Leslie S. Rowland. *Slaves No More: Three Essays on Emancipation and the Civil War*. New York: Cambridge Univ. Press, 1992.

Berry, Mary F. *Military Necessity and Civil Rights Policy: Black Citizenship and the Constitution 1861–1868*. Port Washington, N.Y.: Kennikat Press, 1977.

Blassingame, John W. *The Slave Community: Plantation Life in the Antebellum South*. New York: Oxford Univ. Press, 1979.

———. *Black New Orleans, 1860–1880*. Chicago: Univ. of Chicago Press, 1973.

Blatt, Martin H., Thomas J. Brown, and Donald Yacovone, eds. *Hope & Glory: Essays on the Legacy of the Fifty-Fourth Massachusetts Regiment*. Amherst: Univ. of Massachusetts Press, 2001.

Blight, David W., and Brooks D. Simpson, eds. *Union and Emancipation: Essays on Politics and Race in the Civil War Era*. Kent, Ohio: Kent State Univ. Press, 1997.

Boatner, Mark M. *The Civil War Dictionary*. New York: David McKay, 1959.

Boles, John B. *Religion in Antebellum Kentucky*. Lexington: Univ. Press of Kentucky, 1976.

———. *Black Southerners, 1619–1869*. Lexington: Univ. Press of Kentucky, 1984.

———, ed. *Masters and Slaves in the House of the Lord: Race and Religion in the American South, 1740–1870*. Lexington: Univ. Press of Kentucky, 1988.

Bowen, James L. *Massachusetts in the War, 1861–1865*. Springfield, Mass.: Clark W. Bryan, 1889.

Brewer, James H. *The Confederate Negro: Virginia's Craftsmen and Military Laborers, 1861–1865*. Durham, N.C.: Duke Univ. Press, 1969.

Brownmiller, S. *Against Our Will: Men, Women, and Rape*. Harmondsworth, U.K.: Pelican Books, 1986.

Burchard, Peter. *One Gallant Rush: Robert Gould Shaw and His Brave Black Regiment*. New York: St. Martin's Press, 1965.

———. *"We'll stand by the Union": Robert Gould Shaw and the Black 54th Massachusetts Regiment*. New York: Facts on File, 1993.

Burton, William I. *Melting Pot Soldiers: The Union's Ethnic Regiments*. New York: Fordham Univ. Press, 1998.

Butchart, Ronald E. *Northern Schools, Southern Blacks and Reconstruction: Freedmen's Education in the South, 1865–1870*. Westport, Conn.: Greenwood Press, 1981.

Castel, Albert. *A Frontier State at War: Kansas, 1861–1865*. Ithaca, N.Y: American Historical Association, 1958.

Cavanaugh, Michael A., and William Marvel. *The Petersburg Campaign: The Battle of the Crater, "the Horrid Pit," June 25–August 6, 1864*. Virginia Civil War Battles and Leaders Series. Lynchburg, Va.: H. E. Howard, 1989.

Cornelius, Janet D. *"When I Can Read My Title Clear": Literacy, Slavery, and Religion in the Antebellum South*. Columbia: Univ. of South Carolina Press, 1991.

Cornish, Dudley T. *The Sable Arm: Negro Troops in the Union Army, 1861–1865*. New York: W. W. Norton, 1956.

Cott, N. F. *The Bonds of Womanhood: "Woman's Sphere" in New England, 1780–1835*. New Haven, Conn.: Yale Univ. Press, 1977.

Cox, La Wanda. *Lincoln and Black Freedom: A Study in Presidential Leadership*. Columbia: Univ. of South Carolina Press, 1981.

Crawford, Samuel F. *Kansas in the Sixties*. Chicago: A. C. McClury, 1911.

Creel, M. W. *"A Peculiar People": Slave Religion and Community—Culture among the Gullahs*. New York: New York Univ. Press, 1988.

Cunningham, Edward. *The Port Hudson Campaign, 1862–1863*. Baton Rouge: Louisiana State Univ. Press, 1963.

Curry, Leonard P. *The Free Black in Urban America, 1800–1850: The Shadow of the Dream*. Chicago: Univ. of Chicago Press, 1981.

Daniels, Jonathan. *Prince of Carpetbaggers*. Philadelphia: J. B. Lippincott, 1958.

David, P. A., et al. *Reckoning with Slavery: A Critical Study in the Quantitative History of American Negro Slavery*. New York: Oxford Univ. Press, 1976.

Davis, George B. *A Treatise on the Military Law of the United States together with Practice and Procedure of Courts-Martial and other Military Tribunals*. New York: Wiley, 1898.

Dillon, Merton L. *The Abolitionists: The Growth of a Dissenting Minority*. DeKalb: Northern Illinois Univ. Press, 1974.

Durden, Robert F. *The Grey and the Black: The Confederate Debate on Emancipation*. Baton Rouge: Louisiana State Univ. Press, 1972.

Dyer, Frederick H. *A Compendium for the War of Rebellion Compiled and Arranged from Official Records of the Federal and Confederate Armies, Reports of the Adjutant Generals of the Several States, the Army Registers, and other Reliable Documents and Sources*. Des Moines, Iowa: 1908; reprint Dayton, Ohio: National Historical Society, in cooperation with Press of Morningside Bookshop, 1979.

Edelstein, Tilden G. *Strange Enthusiasm: A Life of Thomas Wentworth Higginson*. New York: Atheneum, 1970.

Elkin, Stanley M. *Slavery: A Problem in American Institutional and Intellectual Life*. 2d ed. Chicago: Chicago Univ. Press, 1968.

Epstein, B. L. *The Politics of Domesticity: Women, Evangelism, and Temperance in Nineteenth-Century America*. Middletown, Conn.: Wesleyan Univ. Press, 1981.

Epstein, Dena J. *Sinful Tunes and Spirituals: Black Folk Music to the Civil War*. Urbana: Univ. of Illinois Press, 1977.

Escott, Paul D. *Slavery Remembered: A Record of Twentieth-Century Slave Narratives*. Chapel Hill: Univ. of North Carolina Press, 1979.

Fellman, M. *Inside War: The Guerilla Conflict in Missouri during the American Civil War*. New York: Oxford Univ. Press, 1989.

Fogel, R. W., and S. L. Engerman. *Time on the Cross: The Economics of American Negro Slavery*. Boston: Little, Brown, 1974.

Foner, Eric. *Free Soil, Free Labor, Free Men: The Ideology of the Republican Party before the Civil War*. New York: Oxford Univ. Press, 1970.

———. *Politics and Ideology in the Age of the Civil War*, Oxford: Oxford Univ. Press, 1980,

Fox, Stephen, R. *The Guardian of Boston: William Munroe Trotter*. Studies in American Negro Life. New York: Atheneum, 1970.

Fox-Genovese, E. *Within the Plantation Household: Black and White Women of the Old South*. Chapel Hill: Univ. of North Carolina Press, 1988.

Frazier, E. Franklin. *Negro Family in the United States*. Chicago: Chicago Univ. Press, 1939.

Fredrickson, George M. *The Arrogance of Race: Historical Perspectives on Slavery, Racism, and Social Inequality*. Middletown, Conn.: Wesleyan Univ. Press, 1988.

———. *The Inner Civil War: Northern Intellectuals and the Crisis of the Union*. New York: Harper and Row, 1968.

———. *The Black Image in the White Mind: The Debate over Afro-American Character and Destiny, 1817–1919*. New York: Harper and Row, 1971.

Fry, Gladys Marie. *Night Riders in Black Folk History.* Knoxville: Univ. of Tennessee Press, 1975.

Genovese, Eugene D. *Roll, Jordan, Roll: The World the Slaves Made.* New York: Random House, 1972.

———. *The World the Slaveholders Made: Two Essays in Interpretation.* New York: Pantheon Books, 1969.

Gerteis, Louis S. *From Contraband to Freedmen: Federal Policy toward Southern Blacks, 1861–1865.* Westport, Conn.: Greenwood Press, 1973.

Glatthaar, Joseph T. *Forged in Battle: The Civil War Alliance of Black Soldiers and White Officers.* New York: Macmillan, 1990.

Gosett, Thomas F. *Race: The History of an Idea in America.* Dallas, Tex.: Southern Methodist Univ. Press, 1963.

Greenslet, Ferris. *The Lowells and their Seven Worlds.* London: Ernest Benn, 1947.

Grossberg, M. *Governing the Hearth: Law and the Family in Nineteenth-Century America.* Chapel Hill: Univ. of North Carolina Press, 1985.

Gutman, Herbert G. *The Black Family in Slavery and Freedom, 1750–1925.* New York: Random House, 1976.

Gutman, Herbert G., ed. *Slavery and the Numbers Game: A Critique of Time on the Cross.* Urbana: Univ. of Illinois Press, 1975.

Hareven, T. K., ed. *Anonymous Americans: Explorations in Nineteenth-Century Social History.* Englewood Cliffs, N. J.: Prentice-Hall, 1971.

———. *Family Time and Industrial Time: The Relationship between the Family and Work in a New England Industrial Community.* Cambridge: Cambridge Univ. Press, 1982.

Hargrove, Hondon B. *Black Union Soldiers in the Civil War.* Jefferson, N.C.: McFarland, 1988.

Harrington, Fred H. *Fighting Politician: Major General N. P. Banks.* Philadelphia: Univ. of Pennsylvania Press, 1948.

Heaps, Willard A., and Porter W. Heaps. *The Singing Sixties: The Spirit of Civil War Days Drawn from the Music of the Times.* Norman: Univ. of Oklahoma Press, 1960.

Hollandsworth, James G. *The Louisiana Native Guards: The Black Military Experience during the Civil War.* Baton Rouge: Louisiana State Univ. Press, 1995.

Houghton, Walter E. *The Victorian Frame of Mind.* New Haven, Conn.: Yale Univ. Press, 1957.

Irwin, Richard B. *History of the Nineteenth Army Corps.* New York: G. P. Putnam, 1893.

Jackson, Irene V., ed. *More than Dancing: Essays on Afro-American Music and Musicians.* Westport, Conn.: Greenwood Press, 1985.

Jimerson, Randall J. *The Private Civil War: Popular Thought during the Sectional Conflict.* Baton Rouge: Louisiana State Univ. Press, 1988.

Jones, Jacqueline. *Labor of Love, Labor of Sorrow: Black Women, Work, and the Family from Slavery to the Present.* New York: Basic Books, 1985.

———. *Soldiers of Light and Love: Northern Teachers and Georgia Blacks 1865–1873.* Chapel Hill: Univ. of North Carolina Press, 1980.

Jones, LeRoi. *Blues People: Negro Music in White America.* New York: William Morrow, 1963.

Jordan, Ervin L. *Black Confederates and Afro-Yankees in Civil War Virginia.* Charlottesville: Univ. Press of Virginia, 1995.

Joyner, Charles. *Down by the Riverside: A South Carolina Slave Community.* Urbana: Univ. of Illinois Press, 1984.

Kasson, J. K. *Civilizing the Machine and Republican Values in America, 1776–1900.* New York: Grossman, 1976.

Keegan, John. *The Face of Battle.* London: Jonathan Cape, 1976.

Kern, S. *The Culture of Time and Space, 1880–1918.* Cambridge, Mass.: Harvard Univ. Press, 1983.

Kirkland, Edward Chase. *Charles Francis Adams Jr., 1835–1915: The Patrician at Bay.* Cambridge, Mass.: Harvard Univ. Press, 1965.

Kolchin, Peter. *American Slavery 1619–1877.* New York: Hill and Wang, 1993.

———. *Unfree Labor: American Slavery and Russian Serfdom.* Cambridge, Mass.: Belknap Press, 1987.

Landes, D. S. *Revolution in Time: Clocks and the Making of the Modern World.* Cambridge, Mass.: Belknap Press, 1983.

Lathrop, George P. *History of the Union League of Philadelphia, from Its Origin and Foundation to the Year 1882.* Philadelphia: J. B. Lippincott, 1884.

Lauer, R. H. *Temporal Man: The Meaning and Uses of Social Time.* New York: Praeger Press, 1981.

Levine, Lawrence W. *Black Culture and Black Consciousness: Afro-American Folk Thought from Slavery to Freedom.* New York: Oxford Univ. Press, 1977.

———. *The Unpredictable Past: Explorations in American Cultural History.* New York: Oxford Univ. Press, 1993.

Litwack, Leon F. *North of Slavery: The Negro in the Free States, 1790–1860.* Chicago: Univ. of Chicago Press, 1965.

———. *Been in the Storm so Long: The Aftermath of Slavery.* New York: Random House, 1980.

Lord, Francis A., and Arthur Wise. *Bands and Drummer Boys of the Civil War.* Da Capo Press. New York: 1979.

Lowry, Thomas. *The Story the Soldiers Wouldn't Tell: Sex in the Civil War.* Mechanicsburg, Pa.: Stackpole Books, 1994.

Luck, Wilbert H. *Journey to Honey Hill: The 55th Massachusetts Regiment (Colored) Journey South to Fight the Civil War That Toppled the Institution of Slavery.* Washington, D.C.: Wiluk Press, 1977.

Macey, S. L. *Clocks and the Cosmos: Time in Western Life and Thought.* Hamden, Conn.: Archon Books, 1980.

Malone, Ann Patton. *Sweet Chariot: Slave Family and Household Structure in Nineteenth-Century Louisiana.* Chapel Hill: Univ. of North Carolina Press, 1992.

Marshall, S. L. A. *Men against Fire: The Problem of Battle Command in Future War.* New York: William Morrow, 1947.

McPherson, James M. *Abraham Lincoln and the Second American Revolution.* New York: Oxford Univ. Press, 1991.

———. *Battle Cry of Freedom: The Civil War Era.* New York: Oxford Univ Press, 1988.

———. *For Cause and Comrades: Why Men Fought in the Civil War.* New York: Oxford Univ. Press, 1997.

———. *Ordeal by Fire: The Civil War and Reconstruction.* New York: Knopf, 1982.

———. *The Struggle for Equality: Abolitionists and the Negro in the Civil War and Reconstruction.* Princeton, N.J.: Princeton Univ. Press, 1964.

McRae, Norman. *Negroes in Michigan during the Civil War.* [Lansing]: Michigan Civil War Centennial Observance Commission, 1966.

Mays, J. H. *Black Americans and Their Contributions toward Union Victory in the American Civil War, 1861–1865.* Lanham, Md.: Univ. Press of America, 1984.

Messner, William F. *Freedmen and the Ideology of Free Labor: Louisiana, 1862–1865.* Lafayette: Univ. of Southwestern Louisiana, 1978.

Meyer, Howard N. *The Colonel of the Black Regiment: The Life of Thomas Wentworth Higginson.* New York: W. W. Norton, 1967.

Miller, Edward A., Jr. *The Black Civil War Soldiers of Illinois: The Story of the Twenty-ninth U.S. Colored Infantry.* Columbia: Univ. of South Carolina Press, 1998.

Mitchell, Reid. *Civil War Soldiers: Their Expectations and their Experiences.* New York: Viking, 1988.

———. *The Vacant Chair: The Northern Soldier Leaves Home.* New York: Oxford Univ. Press, 1993.

Montgomery, David. *Beyond Equality: Labor and the Radical Republicans, 1862–1872.* New York: Knopf, 1967.

Moore, C. W. *Timing a Century: The History of the Waltham Watch Company.* Cambridge, Mass.: Harvard Univ. Press, 1945.

Morris, Robert C. *Reading, 'Riting and Reconstruction: The Education of Freedmen in the South, 1861–1870.* Chicago: Univ. of Chicago Press, 1981.

Mullen, Robert W. *Blacks in America's Wars: The Shift in Attitudes from the Revolutionary War to Vietnam.* New York: Monad Press, 1973.

Mumford, L. *Technics and Civilization.* New York: 1934.

Munden, Kenneth, and Henry P. Beers. *Guide to Federal Archives Relating to the Civil War.* Washington, D.C.: National Archives, National Archives and Records Service, General Services Administration, 1962.

Olson, Kenneth E. *Music and Musket Bands and Bandsmen of the American Civil War.* Westport, Conn.: Greenwood Press, 1981.

O'Malley, M. *Keeping Watch: A History of American Time.* Harmondsworth, U.K.: Penguin, 1991.

Owens, Leslie H. *This Species of Property: Slave Life and Culture in the Old South.* New York: Oxford Univ. Press, 1976.

Pease, Jane H., and William H. Pease. *Bound with Them in Chains: A Biographical History of the Anti-Slavery Movement.* Westport, Conn.: Greenwood Press, 1972.

Phillips, Ulrich B. *American Negro Slavery.* New York: D. Appleton, 1918.

Potter, David M. *The South and the Sectional Conflict.* Baton Rouge: Louisiana State Univ. Press, 1968.

Powell, Lawrence N. *New Masters: Northern Planters during the Civil War and Reconstruction.* New Haven, Conn.: Yale Univ. Press, 1980.

Prude, J. "The Social System of Early New England Textile Mills: A Case Study, 1812–40." In H. G. Gutman, D. H. Bell, *The New England Working Class and the New Labor History.* Urbana: Univ. of Illinois Press, 1986.

Quarles, Benjamin. *Black Abolitionists.* New York: Oxford Univ. Press, 1969.

———. *The Negro in the Civil War.* Boston: Little, Brown, 1953.

Raboteau, Albert J. *Slave Religion: The "Invisible Institution" in the Antebellum South.* New York: Oxford Univ. Press, 1978.

Rawick, George P. *The American Slave: A Composite Autobiography*, ser. 1, no. 1, *From Sundown to Sunup: The Making of the Black Community*. Westport, Conn.: Greenwood, 1972.

Redkey, Edwin S. *Black Exodus: Black Nationalism and Back-to-Africa Movements, 1890–1910*. New Haven: Yale Univ. Press, 1969.

Rifkin, J. *Time Wars: The Primary Conflict in Human History*. New York: Henry Holt, 1987.

Ripley, C. Peter. *Slaves and Freedmen in Civil War Louisiana*. Baton Rouge: Louisiana State Univ. Press, 1976.

Robertson, James I. *Soldiers Blue & Gray*. New York: Warner Books, 1991.

Romero, P. W., and W. L. Rose, eds. *A Black Woman's Civil War Memoirs*. New York: Wiener, 1988.

Rose, Willie L. *Rehearsal for Reconstruction: The Port Royal Experiment*. New York: Bobbs Merrill, 1964.

Ross, Joseph B. *Tabular Analysis of the Records of the U.S. Colored Troops and Their Predecessor Units in the National Archives of the United States*. Washington, D.C.: National Archives and Records Service, 1973.

Rugoff, Milton. *The Beechers: An American Family in the Nineteenth Century*. New York: Harper and Row, 1981.

Schultz, Stanley K. *The Culture Factory: Boston Public Schools, 1789–1860*. New York: Oxford Univ. Press, 1973.

Sefton, James E. *The United States Army and Reconstruction, 1865–1877*. Baton Rouge: Louisiana State Univ. Press, 1967.

Shannon, Fred A. *The Organization and Administration of the Union Army*. 2 vols. Cleveland: Arthur H. Clark, 1928.

Singletary, Otis A. *Negro Militia and Reconstruction*. Austin: Univ. of Texas Press, 1957.

Sobel, M. *Trabelin' On: The Slave Journey to an Afro-Baptist Faith*. Westport, Conn.: Greenwood Press, 1979.

Southern, Eileen. *The Music of Black Americans: A History*. 2d ed. New York: Norton, 1983.

Stampp, Kenneth M. *The Peculiar Institution: Slavery in the Antebellum South*. New York: Random House, 1956.

Stanton, William. *The Leopard's Spots: Scientific Attitudes towards Race in America, 1815–59*. Chicago: Univ. of Chicago Press, 1960.

Starobin, Robert S. *Industrial Slavery in the Old South*. New York: Oxford Univ. Press, 1970.

Stearns, Frank P. *The Life and Public Service of George Luther Stearns*. Philadelphia: Lippincott, 1907.

Steiner, Paul E. *Medical History of a Civil War Regiment: Disease in the Sixty-fifth United States Colored Infantry*. Clayton, Mo.: Institute of Civil War Studies, 1977.

Stephenson, Brenda E. *Life in Black and White: Family and Community in the Slave South*. New York: Oxford Univ. Press, 1996.

Stern, Philip V. D., ed. *Soldiers' Life in the Union and Confederate Armies*. Bloomington: Indiana Univ. Press, 1961.

Stouffer, Samuel A., et al. *Studies in Psychology in World War II: The American Soldier*. 2 vols. Princeton, N.J.: Princeton Univ. Press, 1949.

Straley, George H. *Inferno at Petersburg.* Philadelphia. New York: Chilton, 1961.

Swint, Henry L. *The Northern Teacher in the South, 1862–1870.* Nashville, Tenn.: Vanderbilt Univ. Press, 1941.

Taylor, Frank H. *Philadelphia in the Civil War, 1861–1865.* Philadelphia: City of Philadelphia, 1913.

Trefousse, Hans L. *Ben Butler: The South Called Him BEAST!* New York: Twayne, 1957.

———. *Benjamin Franklin Wade: Radical Republican from Ohio.* New York: Twayne, 1963.

Trudeau, Noah A. *Like Men of War: Black Troops in the Civil War 1862–1865.* Boston: Little, Brown and Company, 1998.

Turner, Victor, *From Ritual to Theatre: The Human Seriousness of Play.* New York: PAJ, 1982.

[Union League of Philadelphia]. *Chronicle of the Union Legion of Philadelphia 1862 to 1902.* Philadelphia: Union League of Philadelphia, 1902.

Vaughn, William P. *Schools for All: The Blacks and Public Education in the South, 1865–1877.* Lexington: Univ. Press of Kentucky, 1974.

Voegeli, V. Jacque. *Free But Not Equal: The Midwest and the Negro during the Civil War.* Chicago: Univ. of Chicago Press, 1967.

Wagandt, Charles Lewis. *The Mighty Revolution: Negro Emancipation in Maryland, 1862–1864.* Baltimore: Johns Hopkins Univ. Press, 1964.

Wallace, Andrew. *Gen. August V. Kautz and the Southwestern Frontier.* Tucson, Ariz.: privately published, 1967.

Walters, Ronald G. *The Antislavery Appeal: American Abolitionism after 1830.* Baltimore: Johns Hopkins Univ. Press, 1976.

Walvin, J. *Leisure and Society: 1830–1950.* London: Longman, 1978.

Ward, G. C., R. Burns, and K. Burns. *The Civil War: An Illustrated History.* New York: Knopf, 1990.

Warner, Ezra J. *Generals in Blue: Lives of the Union Commanders.* Baton Rouge: Louisiana State Univ. Press, 1964.

Washington, Versalle F. *Eagles on Their Buttons: A Black Regiment in the Civil War.* Columbia: Univ. of Missouri Press, 1999.

Webber, Thomas L. *Deep Like the Rivers: Education in the Slave Quarter Community, 1831–1865.* New York: W. W. Norton, 1978.

Westwood, Howard C. *Black Troops, White Commanders, and Freedmen during the Civil War.* Carbondale: Southern Illinois Univ. Press, 1992.

Wharton, Vernon L. *The Negro in Mississippi, 1865–1880.* Chapel Hill: Univ. of North Carolina Press, 1947.

White, Deborah Gray. *Ar'n't I a Woman? Female Slaves in the Plantation South.* New York: W. W. Norton, 1985.

Whiteman, Maxwell. *Gentlemen in Crisis.* Philadelphia: The League, 1975.

Whitrow, G. T. *Time in History: The Evolution of Our General Awareness of Time and Temporal Perspectives.* Oxford: Oxford Univ. Press, 1968.

Wiley, Bell I. *The Common Soldier of the Civil War.* Gettysburg, Pa.: Historical Times, 1973.

———. *The Life of Billy Yank: The Common Soldier of the Union.* Baton Rouge: Louisiana State Univ. Press, 1978.

———. *Southern Negroes 1861–1865.* New Haven, Conn.: Yale Univ. Press, 1938.

Williamson, Joel. *After Slavery: The Negro in South Carolina during Reconstruction, 1861–1877.* Chapel Hill: Univ. of North Carolina Press, 1965.

Wood, Forrest G. *Black Scare: The Racist Response to Emancipation and Reconstruction.* Berkeley: Univ. of California Press, 1970.

Wood, Gordon S. *The Radicalism of the American Revolution.* New York: Knopf, 1992.

Woodward, C. Vann. *American Counterpoint: Slavery and Racism in the North South Dialogue.* Boston: Little, Brown, 1971.

Yellin, Jean F. *Women and Sisters: The Antislavery Feminists in American Culture.* New Haven, Conn.: Yale Univ. Press, 1989.

Yellin, Jean F., and J. C. Van Horne, eds. *The Abolitionist Sisterhood Women's Political Culture in Antebellum America.* Ithaca, N.Y.: Cornell Univ. Press, 1994.

Zerubavel, E. *Hidden Rhythms: Schedules and Calendars in Social Life.* Chicago: Univ. of Chicago Press, 1981.

ARTICLES

Abbott, Richard H. "Massachusetts and the Recruitment of Southern Negroes, 1863–1865." *Civil War History* 14 (September 1968): 197–210.

Abrams, Ray. "The Copperhead Newspapers and the Negro." *Journal of Negro History* 20 (October 1935): 131–52.

Aptheker, Herbert. "Negro Casualties in the Civil War." *Journal of Negro History* 32 (1947): 10–80.

Armstrong, Warren B. "Union Chaplains and the Education of Freedmen." *Journal of Negro History* 52 (April 1967): 104–15.

Bailey, K. K. "Protestantism and Afro-Americans in the Old South." *Journal of Southern History* 41 (November 1975): 451–72.

Belz, Herman. "Law, Politics, and Race in the Struggle for Equal Pay during the Civil War." *Civil War History* 22 (September 1976): 197–213.

Berlin, Ira. "The Structure of the Free Negro Caste in the Antebellum United States." *Journal of Social History* 9 (Spring 1976): 297–318.

Berlin, Ira, Francine C. Cary, Steven F. Miller, and Leslie S. Rowland. "Black Family and Freedom: Black Families in the American Civil War." *History Today* 37 (January 1987): 8–15.

Berlin, Ira, Steven F. Miller, and Leslie S. Rowland. "Missing: A Freedman Seeks His Family." *American Visions* 3 (February 1988): 8–9.

———. "Afro-American Families in the Transition from Slavery to Freedom." *Radical History Review*, no. 42 (1988): 89–121.

Berry, Mary F. "Negro Troops in Blue and Gray: The Louisiana Native Guards, 1861–1863." *Louisiana History* 8 (Spring 1967): 165–97.

Binder, Frederick M. "Pennsylvania Negro Regiments in the Civil War." *Journal of Negro History* 37 (October 1952): 383–417.

Blassingame, John W. "Negro Chaplains in the Civil War." *Negro History Bulletin* 27 (October 1963): 23–24.

———. "The Recruitment of Negro Troops in Maryland." *Maryland Historical Magazine* 58 (March 1963): 20–29.

———. "The Recruitment of Negro Troops in Missouri during the Civil War." *Missouri Historical Review* 58 (1964): 326–38.

———. "The Recruitment of Colored Troops in Kentucky, Maryland, and Missouri, 1863–1865." *Historian* 29 (August 1967): 533–45.

———. "The Selection of Officers and Non-Commissioned Officers of Negro Troops in the Union Army, 1863–1865." *Negro History Bulletin* 30 (January 1967): 8–11.

———. "The Union Army as an Educational Institution for Negroes, 1862–1865." *Journal of Negro Education* 34 (Spring 1965): 152–59.

Cain, Marvin R. "A 'Face of Battle' Needed: An Assessment of Motives and Men in Civil War Historiography." *Civil War History* 28 (March 1982): 5–27.

Castel, Albert. "Civil War Kansas and the Negro." *Journal of Negro History* 51 (April 1966): 125–38.

———. "The Fort Pillow Massacre: A Fresh Examination of the Evidence." *Civil War History* 4 (March 1958): 37–50.

———. "Fort Pillow: Victory or Massacre?" *American History Illustrated* 9 (April 1974): 4–10, 46–48.

———. "Kansas Jayhawking Raids into the Civil War." *Kansas Historical Quarterly* 20 (1953): 417–29.

Catton, Bruce. "Billy Yank and the Army of the Potomac." *Military Affairs* 18 (1954): 169–76.

———. "Union Discipline and Leadership in the Civil War." *Marine Corps Gazette* 40 (1956): 18–25.

Chambers, Karen C. "'The Alphabet Is an Abolitionist': Literacy and African Americans in the Emancipation Era." *Massachusetts Review* 32, no. 4 (1991–92): 545–80.

Cimprich, John, and Robert C. Mainfort Jr. "Fort Pillow Revisited: New Evidence about an Old Controversy." *Civil War History* 28 (December 1982): 293–386.

Cornish, Dudley T. "Kansas Negro Regiments in the Civil War." *Kansas Historical Quarterly* 20 (1953): 417–29.

———. "The Union Army as a School for Negroes." *Journal of Negro History* 37 (October 1952): 368–82.

Cowdrey, Albert E. "Slave into Soldier: The Enlistment by the North of Runaway Slaves." *History Today* 20 (October 1970): 704–15.

Donald, David. "The Confederate as a Fighting Man." *Journal of Southern History* 25 (May 1959): 178–93.

Dunning, Tom P. "Convict Leisure and Recreation: The North American Experience in Van Diemen's Land, 1840–1847." *Sporting Traditions* 9, no. 2 (May 1993): 3–15.

Dyer, Brainerd. "The Treatment of Colored Union Troops by the Confederates, 1861–1865." *Journal of Negro History* 20 (July 1935): 273–86.

Everett, Donald E. "Demands of the New Orleans Free Colored Population for Political Equality, 1862–1865." *Louisiana Historical Quarterly* 38 (April 1955): 43–64.

———. "Ben Butler and the Louisiana Native Guards 1861–1862." *Journal of Southern History* 24 (May 1958): 202–17.

Fox, William F. "The Chances of Being Hit in Battle: A Study of Regimental Losses in the Civil War." *Century Magazine* 15 (April 1930): 198–259.

Frankel, N. "The Southern Side of 'Glory': Mississippi African-American Women during the Civil War." *Minerva: Quarterly Report on Women and the Military* 8, no. 3 (1990): 28–36.

Genovese, Eugene D. "Black Plantation Preachers in the Slave South." *Louisiana Studies* (Fall 1972): 188–214.

Gorn, Elliot, J. "Black Spirits: The Ghostlore of Afro-American Slaves." *American Quarterly* 46 (Fall 1984): 549–65.

Hall, J. D. "'The Mind That Burns in Each Body': Women, Rape, and Racial Violence." *Southern Exposure* 12, no. 6 (1984): 61–71.

Haller, John S. "Civil War Anthropometry: The Making of a Racial Ideology." *Civil War History* 16 (December 1970): 309–24.

Harrington, Fred H. "The Fort Jackson Mutiny." *Journal of Negro History* 27 (October 1942): 420–31.

Heller, Charles E. "Between Two Fires: The 54th Massachusetts." *Civil War Times Illustrated* 11 (1972): 32–41.

———. "George Luther Stearns." *Civil War Times Illustrated* 13 (1974), 20–28.

Hicken, Victor. "The Record of Illinois Negro Soldiers in the Civil War." *Journal of the Illinois State Historical Society* 56 (1963): 529–51.

Jordan, J. L. "Was There a Massacre at Fort Pillow?" *Tennessee Historical Quarterly* 6 (June 1974): 99–133.

Joshi, Manoji K., and Joseph P. Reidy. "'To Come Forward and Aid in Putting Down this Unholy Rebellion': The Officers of Louisiana's Free Black Native Guard during the Civil War Era." *Southern Studies* 21 (Fall 1982): 326–42.

Kolchin, Peter. "Re-evaluating the Antebellum Slave Community: A Comparative Perspective." *Journal of American History* 70 (December 1983): 579–601.

Levstik, Frank R. "The Fifth Regiment, United States Colored Troops, 1863–1865." *Northwest Ohio Quarterly* 42 (1970): 86–98.

MacLeod, B. A. "Quills, Fifes, and Flutes before the Civil War." *Southern Folklore Quarterly* 42, nos. 2–3 (1978): 201–8.

MacMaster, Richard K. "The Colonel Died with His Men: Led by Shaw, Negro Troops Proved Courageous and Reliable under Fire." *New York State and the Civil War* (September–October 1962): 26–35.

Martin, Richard A. "The *New York Times* Views Civil War Jacksonville." *Florida Historical Quarterly* 53 (1975): 409–27.

Maslowski, Pete. "A Study of Morale in Civil War Soldiers." *Military Affairs* 34 (1970) 121–26.

McLaughry, John. "John Welcott Phelps: The Civil War General Who Became a Forgotten Presidential Candidate in 1880." *Vermont History* 38 (1970): 263–90.

McMurray, Richard. "The President's Tenth and the Battle of Olustee." *Civil War Times Illustrated* 16 (1978): 12–24.

Messner, William F. "Black Education in Louisiana, 1863–1865." *Civil War History* 22 (Mar. 1976): 41–59.

Miller, Edward A., Jr. "Garland H. White, Black Army Chaplain." *Civil War History* 43 (1997): 201–18.

Mohr, Clarence L. "Before Sherman: Georgia Blacks and the Union War Effort, 1861–1864." *Journal of Southern History* 45 (August 1979): 331–52.

Murray, Donald M., and Robert M. Rodney. "Colonel Julian E. Bryant: Champion of the Negro Soldier." *Illinois State Historical Society Journal* 56 (1964): 257–81.

Pease, William H., and Jane H. Pease. "Anti-slavery Ambivalence: Immediatism, Expediency, Race." *American Quarterly* 17 (1965): 682–95.

Powell, Lawrence N. "The American Land Company and Agency: John A. Andrew and the Northernization of the South." *Civil War History* 21 (December 1975): 293–308.

Rampp, Lary C. "Negro Troops Activity in Indian Territory, 1863–1865." *Chronicles of Oklahoma* 34 (1969): 531–59.

Reddick, L. D. "The Negro Policy of the United States Army, 1775–1945." *Journal of Negro History* 34 (1949): 9–29.

Redkey, Edwin S. "Black Chaplains in the Union Army." *Civil War History* 33 (1987): 331–50.

Richards, Ira D. "The Battle of Poison Spring." *Arkansas Historical Quarterly* 18 (Winter 1959): 336–49.

Reid, R. M. "Black Experience in the Union Army: The Other Civil War." *Canadian Review of American Studies* 21, no. 2 (1990): 145–55.

Ripley, C. Peter. "The Black Family in Transition: Louisiana, 1860–1865." *Journal of Southern History* 41 (August 1975): 369–80.

Robbins, Gerald. "The Recruiting and Arming of Negroes in the South Carolina Islands, 1862–1865." *Negro History Bulletin* 28 (1965): 150–51, 163–67.

Roediger, David R. "And Die in Dixie: Funerals, Death and Heaven in the Slave Community, 1700–1865." *Massachusetts Review* 22 (Spring 1981): 163–83.

Ross, Steven J. "Freed Soil, Freed Labor, Freed Men: John Eaton and the Davis Bend Experiment." *Journal of Southern History* 44 (May 1978): 213–22.

Saum, Lewis D. "Death in the Popular Mind of Pre–Civil War America." *American Quarterly* 26 (1974): 477–95.

Seraile, William. "The Struggle to Raise Black Regiments in New York State, 1861–1864." *New York Historical Society Quarterly* 63 (July 1974): 215–33.

Shannon, Fred A. "The Federal Government and the Negro Soldier, 1861–1865." *Journal of Negro History* 11 (1926): 563–88.

Small, Sandra E. "The Yankee Schoolmarm in the Freedmen's Schools: An Analysis of Attitudes." *Journal of Southern History* 45 (August 1979): 359–400.

Smith, John D. "The Recruitment of Negro Soldiers in Kentucky, 1863–1865." *Kentucky Historical Society Register* 27 (1974): 364–90.

Sommers, Richard J. "The Dutch Gap Affair: Military Atrocities and Rights of Negro Soldiers." *Civil War History* 31 (Mar. 1975): 51–64.

Starkey, K. "Time and Work Organisation: A Theoretical and Empirical Analysis." In M. Young, T. Schuller, eds., *The Rhythms of Society.* London: Routledge, 1988.

Stephenson, Nathaniel W. "The Question of Arming the Slaves." *American Historical Review* 18 (January 1913): 295–308.

Stuckey, S. "Through the Prism of Folklore: The Black Ethos in Slavery." *Massachusetts Review* 9 (Summer 1968): 417–37.

Suderow, Bryce A. "The Battle of the Crater: The Civil War's Worst Massacre." *Civil War History* 43 (September 1997): 219–24.

Swart, Stanley L. "The Military Examination Board in the Civil War." *Civil War History* 16 (September 1970): 227–45.

Thompson, E. P. "Time, Work-Discipline, and Industrial Capitalism." *Past and Present* 38 (December 1967): 56–97.

Thrift, N. "Owners' Time: The Making of Capitalist Time Consciousness, 1300–1800." In A. Pred, ed., *Space and Time in Geography: Essays Dedicated to Torsten Hagerstrand*, Lund Studies in Geography, ser. B, Human Geography no. 48, Royal University of Lund. Lund: C. W. K. Gleerup, 1981, 57–76.

Toppin, Edgar A. "Humbly They Served: The Black Brigade in the Defence of Cincinnati." *Journal of Negro History* 48 (April 1963): 75–97.

Wagandt, Charles L. "The Army versus Maryland Slavery, 1862–1864." *Civil War History* 10 (June 1964): 141–48.

Watriss, W. "Celebrate Freedom: Juneteenth." *Southern Exposure* 5, no. 1 (1977): 80–87.

Wert, Jeffrey D. "Camp William Penn and the Black Soldier." *Pennsylvania History* 46 (October 1977): 335–46.

Wesley, Charles H. "The Employment of Negroes as Soldiers in the Confederate Army." *Journal of Negro History* 4 (1919): 239–53.

Westwood, Howard C. "Captive Black Union Soldiers in Charleston: What to Do?" *Civil War History* 28 (March 1982): 28–44.

White, John. "Veiled Testimony: Negro Spirituals and the Slave Experience." *Journal of American Studies* 17 (August 1983): 251–63.

Wilson, Keith. "Black Bands and Black Culture: A Study of Black Military Bands in the Union Army during the Civil War." *Australasian Journal of American Studies* 8, no. 1 (July 1990): 31–37.

———. "Thomas Webster and the 'Free Military School for Applicants for Commands of Colored Troops.'" *Civil War History* 29 (June 1983): 101–22.

———. "Education as a Vehicle of Racial Control: Major General N. P. Banks in Louisiana, 1863–64." *Journal of Negro Education* 50 (Spring 1981): 156–70.

Zerubavel, E. "The French Republican Calendar: A Case Study in the Sociology of Time." *American Sociological Review* 42 (1977): 868–77.

DISSERTATIONS

Bahney, Robert S. "Generals and Negroes: Education of Negroes by the Union Army, 1861–1865." Ph.D. diss., University of Michigan, 1965.

Fields, Barbara J. "The Maryland Way: From Slavery to Freedom." Ph.D. diss., Yale University, 1978.

Lovett, Bobby L. "The Negro in Tennessee, 1861–1866: A Socio-Military History of the Civil War Era." Ph.D. diss., University of Arkansas, 1978.

Messner, William F. "The Federal Army and Blacks in the Gulf Department 1862–1865." Ph.D. diss., University of Wisconsin, 1972.

Rotundo, Edward A. "Manhood in America: The Northern Middle Class 1770–1920." Ph.D. diss., Brandeis University, 1982.

Schneider, Robert. "Samuel Chapman Armstrong and the Founding of the Hampton Institute." Senior Honors thesis, Williams College, 1973.

Seraile, William. "New York's Black Regiments during the Civil War." Ph.D. diss., City University of New York, 1977.

Van De Mark, J. "James Montgomery." B.A. thesis, Washburn College, 1906, typescript.

Whitted, B. L. "The History of the Eighty U.S.C.T." M.A. thesis, Howard University, 1960.

Wiggins, W. H. "Free at Last! A Study of Afro-American Emancipation Day Celebrations." Ph.D. diss., Indiana University, 1974.

Wilson, Keith P. "'Manhood Education': An Analysis of the Efforts Made by Northern White Army Officers to Educate Black Union Army Soldiers during the Civil War and an Assessment of the Response of the Black Soldiers." Ph.D. diss., La Trobe University, 1986.

Index

Abolitionism, 74–75; leadership of, 113, 261n.37; as motivation of black enlisted men, 13; in soldier-students' education, 94, 96

Abolitionist societies, helping soldiers' families, 176–77

Abolitionists, 173, 192, 285n.21; black troops appealing to, 35, 48–49, 51; and education of troops, 89, 106; as officers of black troops, 18–19, 27, 29–30, 34, 40–41, 45–46, 85, 119–20, 177; songs of, 150–53; support for black troops, 1–3, 18–21, 43–44, 63, 89, 110

Adams, Charles Francis, Jr., 26, 170, 248nn.27, 28

Addeman, Joshua M., 64, 98

Africa, legacy of, 160, 162–63, 170, 174

Alexander, James, 26, 66, 248n.28

"All Hail" (song), 166

Alvord, J. W., 87

American Freedmen's Inquiry Commission, 23–24, 59

American Missionary Association, 101

Anderson, Robert, 21

Anderson, Samuel, 102

Andrew, Christopher, 62–63

Andrew, John A., 2; black soldiers appealing to, 31, 34–35, 72, 177–78; and chaplains, 111, 123; and unequal pay, 46–47, 54, 178–79

Andrews, G. L., 253n.21

Andus, Lymas, 104

Armstrong, Samuel C., 37, 85, 86, 87; on burials, 136–37; paternalistic racism of, 59–60; on soldiers' music, 154, 157

Army, Union, 25, 66, 136, 245n.21; benefits of service to black troops, 30–32, 37, 61, 128, 211; black soldiers' expectations of, 28–29, 33; black soldiers' performance in, 4, 36–37, 44, 113–16, 118, 150–51, 164; burials in, 136–37; chronicles of black service,

241–42; communities within, 7–15, 110; criticism of white soldiers in, 22, 27; demobilization of black troops from, 211–12; education through, 91, 193, 263n.8; effects of black service on racism, 4, 36–37; enlisted men vs. officers in, 8–10; grievances about, 28, 40–43, 47–51; ideals of black soldiers in, 22, 27; influences on effectiveness of, 84–85, 196; and music, 147–48, 154, 156–58, 162–65, 174; religion helping men in, 143–44; and soldiers' families, 181, 183–85; support for blacks in, 2–3; training in, 32–33, 87, 247n.3; uses of black troops in, 11–12, 38–39, 43–44; war news of, 71, 78–79, 113, 209. See also Discipline, military

Army Life in a Black Regiment (Higginson), 162

Asher, Jeremiah, 112, 124

Babb, Eli, 30

Bailey, Lucy, 179

Baldey, George, 43

Banks, Nathaniel P., 38–39, 84, 94, 206, 253n.21; free labor system of, 189–90, 286n.34, 287n.39

Barnard, O. W., 3–4

Barnes, George, 94, 106

Barnes, Samuel, 186

Bartholomew, Orion A., 125

Bates, Edward, 57

Battle, 41; inadequate arms and training for, 62–63; use of black troops in, 12, 34, 38–39, 41; value of success in, 4, 113–14, 194

Beecher, James C., 29, 41, 46, 63, 68, 70, 89; limiting liquor sales, 64, 258n.12; and soldiers' religion, 130, 133

Benedict, Augustus W., 205–6

Bergen, V., 62

Berlin, Ira, 104

Birney, William, 44, 63, 109

Self-image, 14, 20–23, 79–80, 129–30. *See also* Pride

Self-reliance: as goal of family settlement schemes, 187–92; as goal of military, 26, 60, 69, 85, 87; in quest for education, 83, 95, 101, 106

7th Louisiana Volunteers, African Descent, 188

7th U.S. Colored Heavy Artillery, 147

76th U.S. Colored Infantry, 206–7

Sexual immorality, 183–84, 193, 208; chaplains struggling against, 132–33, 142, 195–97; and marriages, 197, 199–200; prostitutes, 63, 198; women accused of, 194–95, 197

Sexuality, in camps, 69–70

Shaw, George, 103

Shaw, Robert Gould, 3, 27, 61, 64–65, 65, 123, 194, 253n.24; honored, 212, 213

Shurtleff, Giles, 59–60, 166

Sieges, resulting in excessive fatigue duty, 43–44

Signature: importance of, 83, 97–98; and literacy levels, 104

6th U.S. Colored Infantry, 112

Slavery, 57, 150.; black families in, 182–83, 283n.2, 285n.21; black troops trying to defend rights not to be treated as, 30–32; echoed in inequalities in work assignments, 39–41; effects on personalities of blacks, 19, 59–60, 90–91, 130, 132; effects on religion, 246n.28, 275n.13; efforts to overcome legacy of, 130–32, 170, 193–94, 247n.3; influence on expectations of black soldiers, 26, 27–28, 131; legacy of, 8, 78–79, 115–16, 127, 162–63, 203, 207–8; legacy of, and soldiers' education, 90, 94, 97, 99, 103; legacy of, in religion, 130–31, 274n.8; military communities compared to, 7–8, 276n.25; and music, 152, 155–56, 156; officers' perceptions of, 68, 89–91; religion in, 155, 273n.3; soldiers' belief in supernatural as legacy of, 137, 139–40; soldiers' families in, 71–72, 175–76, 181; and theological meaning of Civil War, 144. *See also* Plantations

Slaves, 180, 188; clothing and appearance of, 61–62; communities of, 268n.51, 287n.43; education of, 83–84, 262n.3, 266n.33; liberation of, 115, 209, 291n.85; marriage and intimate affairs of, 195, 197–98, 289n.64; morality of, 199; music of, 281n.50, 282n.71. *See also* Plantations

Slaves, ex-, 131, 209, 289n.61; chaplains' duty toward, 119–20; and education, 70, 77, 95, 101, 103–4, 269n.47; literacy rates of, 83–84; and music, 159–63, 171; and Northern blacks, 95, 140, 164–65, 269n.47; as preachers, 140–41, 143–44; protesting pay inequities, 51–53; religion of, 126–30, 133–35, 277n.37; resettlement schemes for, 188, 190–93; as soldiers, 2, 62

Smalley, Palemon, 175

Smith, Jerry, 175

Smith, John M., 290n.70

Smith, Morgan, 132

Socia, Joseph, 93–94

Social cohesion: and divisiveness, 52–53, 140; effects of pay inequities on, 51–52, 52–53; in military camp communities, 7–15; between officers and men, 29–30, 168; through education, 106–8; through music, 154, 160–61, 164–65; through newspaper reading, 75; through religion, 128, 141, 145; through sharing extra food, 64; through storytellers, 72–73

"Song of the First Arkansas," 152–53

"Song of the Negro Boatman," 151, 279n.8

South, 192, 211. *See also* Confederacy; changing relations in, 118–19, 273n.41; churches in, 129, 273n.41; fear of encroachment of Confederacy, 180–81; Northern blacks as missionaries to, 246n.28, 274nn.6, 8; postwar, 87, 95, 104; use of black military bands in, 170–71

Stanton, Edwin, 2, 207; appeals and protests to, 31, 42, 177–79, 181–82, 251n.12

Stearns, George L., 191–92

Storrett, N. B., 144

Storytellers, 60, 72–73, 78, 81

Sturgis, James, 54

Supernatural, 137–40, 276n.27

Sutherland, George, 148, 160–62

Sutlers, 63–64, 70

Sutton, Robert, 6

Swails, Stephen, 47–48, 48

Swamp Angel (camp newspaper), 77–80, 262n.51

Sweeney, John, 101

Sydel, Theodore, 33

Taylor, Charles W., 179

Taylor, Chauncey, 199–200

Taylor, Maria, 94

Taylor, Susie K., 29, 101, 183

Campfires of Freedom

was designed and composed by Christine Brooks

in 10/13.5 Cycles Roman with display type in Shelley Allegro Script;

printed on 50# Supple Opaque stock

by Thomson-Shore, Inc., of Dexter, Michigan;

and published by

THE KENT STATE UNIVERSITY PRESS

Kent, Ohio 44242